Kafka, Angry Poet

THE FRENCH LIST

Kafka, Angry Poet

PASCALE CASANOVA

Translated by Chris Turner

LONDON NEW YORK CALCUTTA

Seagull Books, 2015

First published in French as *Kafka en colère*
by Pascale Casanova © Éditions du Seuil, 2011

English translation © Chris Turner, 2015

ISBN 978 0 8574 2 162 3

British Library Cataloguing-in-Publication Data
A catalogue record for this book is available from the British Library

Typeset in Scala and PT Sans by Seagull Books, Calcutta, India
Printed and bound by Maple Press, York, Pennsylvania, USA

For D., because.

CONTENTS

Acknowledgements

I would like to thank Dominique Eddé, Xavier Galmiche, Éric Hazan, Hugues Jallon, Laurent Jeanpierre, Carole Matheron, Jean-Pierre Morel, Xavier Person, Franck Poupeau and Gerald Stieg for generously reading this text and for all their suggestions which in a sense 'gave me permission' to strike out on the paths of Kafka criticism and also enabled me to avoid many pitfalls. If there are errors, they are, of course, my own. I also thank Sarah Frioux-Salgas for opening the doors of the library of the Musée du Quai Branly to me, together with Bernard Hoepffner, Alban Lefranc and Denise Virieux.

> And as in that game in which the Japanese amuse themselves by
> filling a porcelain bowl with water and steeping in it little pieces
> of paper until then indistinct, which, the moment they are
> immersed in it, stretch and shape themselves, colour and differ-
> entiate, become flowers, houses, human figures, firm and recog-
> nizable, so now all the flowers in our garden and in M. Swann's
> park, and the water-lilies on the Vivonne, and the good people of
> the village and their little dwellings and the church and all of
> Combray and its surroundings, all of this which is assuming form
> and substance, emerged, town and gardens alike, from my cup
> of tea.

> Marcel Proust, *The Way by Swann's*

Franz Kafka is a cult figure the world over. He is read, commented
upon and quoted in every language. *The Trial* and *The Castle* are
among the most widely distributed, widely admired novels in the
world.[1] And for more than 60 years we have seen a kind of fetishiza-
tion of his writings: readers identify passionately with the writer of
the diary; the tiniest quotation, wrenched out of context and set up
as the standard of a wisdom which is mysterious but all the more
'profound' for that, is positively venerated.[2] The cult of Kafka is
encouraged by the critics, who find in him the most perfect embodiment of literature with a capital L: obscurity, secrecy, singularity
and apparent artistic autonomy. For a very long time now, Kafka
himself has not been described in the ordinary terms of biography.
Most notably, Max Brod, in a portrait of the author that has been
highly influential because it claimed the status of first-hand testimony, made him out to be a saint and a sage, a paragon of goodness
and patience, whose kindness and equanimity were matched only
by his calm, aloof indulgence.[3] 'The category of sacredness (and not
really that of literature) is the only right one within which Kafka's

life and work can be viewed.'[4] It is on this belief in Kafka's timeless wisdom that many of the psychological or sociological portraits are constructed, which forget his polemical violence, his harsh assessments of many of his contemporaries, his irony, his laughter and his aesthetic loathings—in short, the peremptory character of his likes and dislikes, which sits uncomfortably with his supposed saintliness.

Kafka has also been turned into a prophet. When rediscovered after the Second World War, he was initially lauded for having (allegedly) foretold the horrors of Nazism (despite his death in 1924). Acquiring on the way one of the most ancient, archaic roles assigned to the poet, that of *vates* or soothsayer, he thus attained a virtually divinatory status, to the point where he became a kind of almost preternatural genius predicting horror. This reading, which rides roughshod over all historical reality, chooses to overlook the real conditions of the writing of the texts and presupposes a meaning inferred from what happened *after*, while showing no interest in what was happening *during*, the writing of the texts, was for a very long time one of the main obstacles to a proper historicization of Kafka's texts. Since he was supposed to have predicted the future, there was no longer any need to concern oneself with his history. Kafka was, as it were, twice submerged: once by the outbreak of war, in which the material, physical and political world of the Jews of Prague was put to the sword; and a second time by the application of an interpretive grid that arose out of categories of thinking produced *after* the war which prevent us from understanding what was going on *before* it occurred.

Kafka is also one of the writers most commented upon in the whole world. By dint of their dual universal and enigmatic character, his writings have become an enormous battlefield. In parallel with the prophetic *doxa*—and not in contradiction with it, since the various interpretations seem to accumulate rather than cancel out—critics have been constantly at one another's throats over the meaning of his narratives. It would seem that the absence of a genuine history of Kafka's literary project has made it possible (and still does) for each intellectual 'corporation' to appropriate the texts and to propose, without any historical sanction, an interpretation dictated solely by the logic of the debates internal to each interpreter's field of origin, be it philosophical, literary, metaphysical, psychoanalytic, religious or sociological. In the course of criticizing the 'deep' interpretations of Kafka in circulation, Hannah Arendt slips in a remark to the effect that interpretations of his work tell us more about the reader than the author.[5] Marthe Robert, summing up the critical reception of Kafka in France, was able to write, for example, in 1984:

> Since Kafka retained no trace of his origins and nothing of any earthly affiliations whatever, he quite naturally came to be granted a sort of right of extraterritoriality, thanks to which his person and his work—in exchange, admittedly, for their real existence—were assigned a perfection and a purity that can only belong to abstract things. This right of extraterritoriality was, ultimately, a celestial privilege: coming from nowhere and belonging to everyone Kafka quite naturally seemed to have fallen from the Heavens—even to those writers least inclined to take Heaven as a reference.[6]

His is one of the rare global bodies of literary work that still gives rise, even today, to such uninterrupted interpretative passion. Each year, after a massive trawl through the endless bibliography of Kafka commentary, exhausted researchers propose new hypotheses which, most often, contradict one another. Each year, Kafka fever produces at least one innovative book which states a new truth about the Prague writer and for a time redefines the type of legitimate research that will be discussed within the little world of interpreters about the enigma he represents. This battlefield is itself, of course, an international arena. The battles are fought out mainly in three languages: English, German and French. This is why the tiniest piece of writing on Kafka excludes naivety or, in other words, the illusion of solitude. To venture to interpret Kafka—that is to say, to propose a new interpretation—presupposes a familiarity (albeit in some cases only partial) with the compact international field of Kafka interpretation and the various different options available within that field at the point when one is seeking entry. Since I began working on this book, at least five important works have been published, modifying critical certainties or providing essential historical details on areas relating to the writer's life and career, about which we had previously been very much in ignorance.

Today, following Michael Löwy's very fine summary of the situation,[7] we can classify writing on the Prague author into six major strands: (1) internalist literary readings that deliberately ignore the 'context'; (2) biographical, psychological or psycho-analytic readings; (3) metaphysical or religious readings; (4) readings that foreground his Jewish identity; (5) historical and sociopolitical readings; (6) postmodern readings (for which the meaning of Kafka's writings is undecidable). Though each of these lines of enquiry develops almost independently of the others and, hence, produces its own advances, we may say that we have in the last few years seen history make a strong comeback. The recent critical editions of Kafka's texts in German have substantially changed the relationship to the text itself. We now have available two critical (and competing) editions in German: the Fischer edition by Jürgen Born, Gerhard Neumann, Malcolm Pasley and Jost Shillemeit, which began to appear in 1982; and the Reuss and Staengle edition currently being published by Stroemfeld/Roter Stern which began in 1995.[8] In the Fischer edition, each type of text—published stories, novels, unpublished narrative fictions, personal diaries—is presented in two parts: one volume with the text alone and no editorial notes, and another containing the critical apparatus. In this way, Kafka's authorial use of notebooks, in which his personal diary, aphorisms and narrative fictions are closely intermingled, is restored, giving a much more accurate view of his work.[9] Reuss and Staengle have made quite different editorial choices. Taking account of the unfinished nature of many pieces, they have challenged the idea of a definitive text. At the same time, unlike the Fischer edition, they assert the fluid, changing, incomplete and, at times, even incoherent character of the writing. They therefore offer a facsimile text that enables both the writing and the re-writing to be read—deletions, ambiguities and incomplete corrections are all accorded equal right to significance.[10] As a result, problems relating to the choice of variants, which give rise to innumerable disputes among specialists, become obsolete.

This return to the materiality and historicity of the text has undeniably made for a renewed awareness among researchers of the decidedly 'earthly' character, to use Robert's term, of Kafka's life and the material dimension of his career. Among Francophones, these new editions have also contributed to de-naturalizing the French translation. They have reminded readers that the original text was neither by Alexandre Vialatte nor Marthe Robert, and that the assumptions on which the edition of Kafka's complete works in French rests—including the invention of a volume of 'narrative fragments' made up of texts taken arbitrarily from the diaries that makes no distinction between the unpublished 'sketches' and the texts published during Kafka's lifetime—arose out of a more-than-questionable a priori conception of the relations between a writer's life and work. They have also made possible a new French translation of the stories and novels which is much more faithful to the original texts.[11]

Moreover, new historical research, often drawing on advances made possible by the critical editions of the texts, has made enormous strides in advancing the knowledge of Kafka's intellectual, political and aesthetic universe. After Klaus Wagenbach, Marthe Robert, Ritchie Robertson and Hartmut Binder, who all produced pioneering historicizing works, Mark Anderson focuses on the description of *fin de siècle* aestheticism in the Habsburg Empire in his book *Kafka's Clothes* (1992), a milestone of scholarship.[12] He produced an unexpected portrait of the young Kafka as a Prague dandy, thus providing evidence that the historical exploration of Kafka's aesthetic and political world could prove very fertile and open up unprecedented new angles on his work. Then came, to name but a few, the works of Sander L. Gilman (1995), who sees Kafka as (consciously or otherwise) re-enacting in his texts most of the anti-Semitic clichés forming at the time; of Scott Spector (2000), who reconstructs the literary and political discussions at Prague at the turn of the twentieth century; of Michael Löwy (2004) who asserts Kafka's closeness to the anarchists and the libertarian socialism of Bohemia; of Iris Bruce (2007) who studies Prague Zionism and its specificities; and of Bernd Neumann (2007) who, subscribing to the methods of New Historicism, concludes that Kafka had assimilationist convictions.[13] The collective work edited by Bettina von Jagow and Oliver Jahraus, the *Kafka Handbuch*, updates Hartmut Binder's project of 1979 and sums up all the historical, biographical, theoretical and other advances.[14] This international discussion 'opens the way', so to speak, for a historical re-examination of Kafka's writings.

It is at this point in the debate that I too shall attempt to intrude into this game and, despite the objections just raised and the obstacles just described, propose my own hypothesis for deciphering Kafka's texts. I should note that I confine myself to decoding a number of fictional texts (though I claim no explanatory monopoly on these), taking the gamble that, even with such an exceptional case, it was possible—nay, necessary—to start out from as great a distance as possible (from the political and literary field of Prague) to get back to the extreme singularity of the narrative fictions themselves.

Even today, biography remains one of the only forms of history permitted in literary studies.[15] It is conceived as the narration of a psychological singularity, reduced most often merely to the events of sentimental, family or sexual life. And that psychology is immediately applied to the texts, the aim being to find in the work the psychological characteristics that have been identified in the life. At this point, the literary work is regarded as the obvious product of a peculiar inner life which is supposedly narrated, expressed or poured out 'authentically' in one form or another and immediately transposed into the texts. It is seen as a kind of outlet for a life's discontents and psychological difficulties. The necessary match between 'a life and a work' presents the one as the formal translation of the other, a translation consequently conceived as confession or, better, since the advent of psychoanalysis, as a receptacle for unconscious desires and/or unformulated fantasies. We know almost everything about Kafka's life today, though some chapters remain contested, particularly his relationship with politics (I shall turn to this question later in this volume). This is precisely where the problem lies—in the fact that we often think we have done with the writer's life when we have exhausted (if such a thing is possible) the series of events which, in their succession, make it up and have then tracked down and interpreted the series of questions, problems, inner dilemmas and neurotic traits that enable us to deliver a 'psychology' of the writer.[16] Moreover, that life is regarded as the only possible source for understanding or deciphering an author's work.

Now, it seems to me, it is possible to work on developing another kind of history by using the instrument of the literary field or space— a history that reconstructs all the components of a universe of thought, of positions adopted and of literary and political productions; a history of the relations maintained by coexisting and contemporary works within a given space, an archaeology of commitments, ruptures, friendships, likes and dislikes; a reconstruction that is written not on the basis of an individual (as traditional literary history has it) but a collective entity to which the writer belongs whether or not he likes it, and whether or not he is aware of it. It is about renewing and extending the notion of 'biography' by reconstructing the intellectual world to which the creative artist in question belongs. This kind of history ultimately enables us to situate a writer within this collective entity and understand a literary project in terms of its own guiding principle—the individual *oeuvre* is then viewed on the basis that it is one of the components of an ensemble without which it would not exist.

Parenthetically, I would like to reassert here my desire to operate as a literary critic. It seems to me that, at the intersection of history, sociology (as developed by Pierre Bourdieu) and textual criticism, literary criticism should tend to become a fully fledged social science, not dependent on any other discipline. The essential condition for such a project to succeed appears to me to be a reassertion of a specificity and autonomy for criticism. I have, in fact, allowed myself this incursion into this hyper-specialized, highly contested field, which is situated in a (apparently) restricted space and relates to a very singular individual, only, paradoxically, so as to pursue my investigation of the workings of world literature.[17] At the outset, I wanted to know if it was possible to show—in respect of a (highly) singular case—the advantages of observing literary phenomena from the international vantage point.

It seems to me, first, that in order to work out Kafka's paradoxical position in this international space, it is not possible to confine ourselves to what was happening in the Prague literary space at the turn of the century. We have to take account of the different spaces in which texts and ideas circulated (most notably, the whole of the Habsburg space, the configuration of the German cultural area, the transnational space of Jewish political and nationalist discussion). We have also to bring in the structure of the global literary space. We shall, in fact, see that Kafka embodies within his own person the great structural divide in the world republic of letters. By his— dominated—position in a powerful literary space, by his simultaneous membership of two literary spaces which are very wide apart in the global structure, he epitomizes the division that sets the old, powerful spaces producing an autonomous literature (which is reflexive and preoccupied with aesthetic concerns) against the recent ones that are lacking in capital and are united around a national (political) definition of their specificity. And it is the wrench consequent on these two ordinarily antagonistic definitions of self, this split and this constitutive instability, that explain Kafka's inseparably literary and combative drive. The study of his work is also, then, the opportunity for me to bring to bear on a particular case the notion of world literary space conceived as a critical instrument.

Lastly, the reconstruction of this lost intellectual universe requires reflection on the categories of thought to be deployed in this type of critical historical enterprise. The major bias to which every reader of literary texts is prone, particularly the reader of private diaries, is the illusion of immediate understanding. What Robert Darnton calls the 'false sense of familiarity with the past'.[18] When reading, the historian often believes that, in order to understand a text far removed in time, it is sufficient simply to explicate what is set forth in it. In reality, the apparent 'solid facts' and, most importantly, the categories of thought mobilized to describe them are as often as not 'screen-thoughts', post hoc reconstructions which contribute—through the illusion of obviousness, transparency and shared thinking—to mask the real meaning of a text with which the reader believes, in all good faith, he can identify. Through diaries, which give an impression of very great transparency, we identify immediately with the writers. They seem close to us, accessible, crystal clear. They comply with our expectations and assumptions as twenty-first-century Western readers. In particular, they seem in tune with our own categories of understanding and knowledge of the world. Yet, literary (or artistic, cultural or philosophical) history is not written (or not *only* written) with what is stated, with the objective traces that come down to us from the creative artists we study. It is also written, paradoxically, through silences, things left unsaid and blanks—in a word, through what is, precisely, not said, cannot be said and is therefore not explicitly formulated in any way. And this is so because the world in which writers move is precisely what is not commented on, never expressed, what is self-evident to such an extent that it is never in question. Now, a great many analyses of Kafka's *oeuvre* are based exclusively on what he 'said' and make no reference whatsoever to what he 'did not say'.

Let us take as an example this formula, as lapidary as it is disappointing, which appears in Kafka's diary in the early part of 1911: 'Früher Vortrag Loos und Kraus [Before that, lecture by Loos and Kraus].'[19] No comment is appended, no critical analysis, no evaluative remark. But we certainly cannot deduce from this, as the positivist historian or the biographer in search of facts and tangible, measurable evidence might ask us to do, that Kafka was uninterested in the Viennese critical intellectual—or even interested to only a limited extent. At first reading, these few words tell us nothing—nothing we know, nothing we can pin down, nothing interesting—except that Kafka attended some lectures here and there, but that he was much more interested in what he was writing about a few lines before, namely, the theosophy of Dr Rudolf Steiner, to which he devotes a dozen or so lines of commentary. Yet, if we are prepared to pay attention and try to restore all that is presupposed and implied in it, the sentence contains almost the totality of the (intellectual, literary, aesthetic, political and linguistic) world to which Kafka belongs. This factual line itself encapsulates, in its very terseness, the whole of the intellectual universe in which Kafka lives. It bespeaks, in its very laconicism, the trans-national character of the cultural and intellectual life of the Austro-Hungarian Empire in the years preceding the war. It tells us also what the diary is, tells us what is said in it and what is not said for the simple reason that it is self-evident. We may attempt to bring out from these few words—which resemble nothing so much as Proust's little Japanese piece of paper before it is dipped in the water—the veritable universe contained within them in dehydrated or freeze-dried form.

Charles Taylor elaborates on the idea that, in order to understand an action—and literary texts can be regarded as a certain kind of action that is visible and decipherable only in a specific space—we have to call on the notion of a shared, unformulated, 'background knowledge' which includes implicit meanings. He writes: 'Understanding is always against a background of what is taken for granted [. . .] Someone who lacks this background can always come along and so the plainest things can be misunderstood, particularly if we let our imagination roam and imagine people who have never even heard of arrows.'[20] The philosopher considers the example of an outsider who 'might misunderstand what to us are perfectly clear and simple directions'—namely, the fact of following arrows in order to follow a route. 'We can,' Taylor continues, 'imagine a scenario: there are no arrows in the outsider's culture.' He does not, therefore, understand that 'you follow arrows towards the point.'[21] If we tried to help this stranger find his way, the only way of getting around the tacit assumption contained in the very definition of 'shared background knowledge'—which, if it is to act on a community, must necessarily remain unformulated—is precisely to articulate it. 'When the misunderstanding stems from a difference of background,' Taylor adds, 'what needs to be said to clear it up articulates a bit of the explainer's background which may never have been articulated before.'[22]

The literary critic is very often in the position of this outsider— she does not really know how to find her way around the distant world of the writer she is studying (a world all the more distant for her belief that she is close to it). It seems, therefore, that a large part of the interpretative work in literary studies is precisely of this order—we have to formulate, in order to understand and convey it, the 'background knowledge' characteristic of the social world of the writer whose actions—that is to say, whose texts—we are trying to understand, to remove the ambiguities and, most importantly, to put an end to the illusion that this shared background (the product of a lost state of the literary field, an earlier stage in the political and aesthetic relations of force) is immediately understandable.

This 'embodied knowledge' is very changeable. It depends at every point on the relations of force internal and external to the literary field; it is the product of a specific history that has to be reconstructed at every moment; and it is made up of elements that have disappeared by the time reading takes place and which, consequently, the historian cannot restore spontaneously. Against this background which is unformulated and gives, as it were, a foundation to the tacit agreement undergirding the social world, Taylor ranges the field of 'representations', which for their part are conscious and explicitly formulated. But, he emphasizes that 'rather than representations being the primary locus of understanding, they are similarly islands in the sea of our unformulated practical grasp on the world.'[23] What Taylor calls intellectualism, and what might also be termed the philosophy of consciousness, leaves us only a choice 'of an understanding which consists of representations or of no understanding at all'; in other words, a choice between an understanding of things formulated and made explicit—the product of the clear representations of a consciousness transparent to itself—and the impossibility of understanding anything whatsoever. But, adds Taylor, 'embodied understanding provides us with the third alternative we need to make sense of ourselves.'[24]

In this volume I have tried, in large measure, to make explicit and formulate the 'background knowledge' of the members of the group of Jewish intellectuals in Prague born between 1875 and 1890—a group to which Kafka belongs. The distance between them and us has become so great, the unexamined presuppositions, ways of thinking and classifying and the oppositions in terms of which they attempt to describe, apprehend and understand the world have become so opaque and distant to us that, in confronting them, we are almost in the situation of Taylor's outsider who has never seen an arrow and is therefore incapable of finding his way around. Almost every 'common' (in every sense) notion current in early-twentieth-century Prague needs to be deciphered and formulated precisely today in order to avoid misunderstanding notions with which we believe we are familiar but which are often far removed from our 'common sense' understanding of them. One of my main tasks in this work, for example, has been to reconstruct the connotations and more banal meaning in *fin de siècle* Prague of pairs of ordinary words such as Eastern and Western which, despite their apparent familiarity, refer not only to geography but also to social divides, prejudices, political utopias and a representation of the world that have all now completely disappeared. Very often, the mere evocation of what is of the order of the unformulated within the literary or intellectual field opens up possibilities the historian must take into account if he wants to understand everything that ensues from that unformulated element.

This is why I want to stress at the beginning that, in order to give myself a chance of seeing—that is to say, of restoring—Kafka's viewpoint and, hence, grasp why and how he writes what he writes, I have aimed to carry out what Bourdieu calls a 'double historicization'.[25] This involves, first, the study of Kafka's precise position in his universe; and second, as far as is possible, of course, taking into consideration and reconstructing not only what he knows—which means, what we know that he knows while knowing that we forcibly exclude what we do not know that he knows—but also what he does not know that he knows—in other words, what we know that he does not know that he knows.

This knowledge which is unrecognized as such may belong to several fields: it may either be about the world around him (both aesthetic and political) which, being the very air he breathes, is never articulated or taken as his subject (this being part, in other words, of what he knows that he knows but does not think to express); or about the structure and form of the national and global space itself which, being a second unexamined presupposition or a second tacit, unknown knowledge is hardly ever described or hardly ever formulated (it being possible to define this as what he does not know that he knows). A part of the task of researching into Kafka has consisted in attempting to understand and articulate a tiny part of this embodied, unformulated knowledge which we need to make explicit in order to understand what Kafka does, starting out from what *he* knows but *we* have forgotten. I shall, therefore, have to attempt (within the limits of what we know) to open out for the reader what Kafka knows and does not say because he does not know that he knows it and, at the same time, what it is difficult for us to know that he knows since he does not say it.

Lastly, I have tried to distance myself, both in theory and practice, from the illusory belief that one can gain access to Kafka's secret, private life by trying to find it in his diary or correspondence. His 'private' writings are deceptive, yielding up only a misleading surface. Kafka does not disclose any 'truth' or, at any rate, any 'profundity' in them that might give access to his fiction, nor does he offer any key to help unlock the secret of his work. His work is not a secret—it is solely the trace of the forms of *prises de position* on all the subjects that were dear to his heart. In other words, it is in the fictional texts that we should look for the answer to the questions we ask ourselves about Kafka's real convictions. These texts will enable us to grasp, in a way that involves denial, dissembling, mild distortion, warping and irony, where, at what point in the discussion—that is to say, at what position in the literary field—Kafka really situates himself. The novels, short stories and narrative fragments are, as it were, cryptic messages intended for certain persons. But they are so well encrypted that they have, in eluding their initial addressees, become universalized—that is to say, lost—at the point where the work met with global acclaim.

This volume is made up of two relatively distinct parts. The first, comprising Chapters 1 and 2, offers a historicization of Kafka's position at Prague and within the Jewish political movements. The second, comprising Chapters 3 and 4, is given over to the close reading and interpretation of Kafka's stories and novels. I am, of course, aware that the decipherment of the texts of a world writer can present itself only as a hypothesis which has to stand up against all those that have already been proposed. Here, then, is the hypothesis I advance.

NOTES

1 [Franz Kafka, *The Trial* (Mike Mitchell trans.) (Oxford: Oxford University Press, 2009); originally written in 1914–15 and published in 1925 as *Der Prozess* (Berlin: Die Schmiede); Kafka, *The Castle* (Willa and Edwin Muir trans) (London: Vintage Books, 2005); originally written in 1922 and published in 1926 as *Das Schloss* (Leipzig: Kurt Wolff). All quotes in this volume are from these two translations unless otherwise mentioned.]

2 The theatrical production *Kafka-Fragmente*, directed by Antoine Gindt, with music by György Kurtàg, 'based on texts by Franz Kafka (diary and correspondence)', which was presented at the Théàtre de Gennevilliers in January–February 2010, is a striking example of this kind of fetishism to which Kafka's texts give rise. The sentences pronounced entirely without context and the juxtaposed narrative extracts form a kind of mysterious statement whose meaning is presumed to be all the more profound for being uncertain. The production has only to bear Kafka's name for the effect of profundity and faith in it to operate at full bore.

3 Max Brod, *Franz Kafka: A Biography* (G. Humphreys Roberts and Richard Winston trans) (Cambridge, MA: De Capo Press, 1995). On this alleged saintliness of Kafka, see Milan Kundera, *Testaments*

Betrayed (Linda Asher trans.) (London: Faber & Faber, 1995), pp. 37–46.

4   Brod, *Franz Kafka*, p. 49.

5   'His [The reader of the 1920s'] interpretation of Kafka revealed more about himself than about Kafka.' Hannah Arendt, 'Franz Kafka, Appreciated Anew' (Martin Klebes trans.) in Susannah Young-ah Gottlieb (ed.), *Hannah Arendt: Reflections on Literature and Culture* (Stanford: Stanford University Press, 2007), pp. 94–109; here, p. 98.

6   Marthe Robert, 'Kafka en France' in Yasha David and Jean-Pierre Morel (eds), *Le Siècle de Kafka: N mcová, Avenarius, Masaryk, Kubin, Gordin . . .* (Paris: Centre Georges Pompidou, 1984), pp. 15–20; here, p. 16.

7   Michael Löwy, *Franz Kafka, rêveur insoumis* (Paris: Stock, 2004), p. 10.

8   Jürgen Born, Gerhard Neumann, Malcolm Pasley and Jost Shillemeit (eds), *Franz Kafka: Kritische Ausgabe. Gesammelte Werke in der Fassung der Handschrift in 12 Bänden* (Frankfurt: Fischer); and Roland Reuss and Peter Staengle (eds), *Franz Kafka: Historisch-kritische Ausgabe sämtlicher Handschriften, Drucke und Typoskripte* (Basel and Frankfurt: Stroemfeld/Roter Stern).

9   In the more recent Fischer edition, the new version of the octavo notebooks in particular differs radically from Brod's, in chronology as well as in structure and content.

10 Their edition presents a scanned facsimile of each page of manuscript, accompanied by a typographic transcription, a CD and an introductory booklet including various documents that assist in the understanding of the genesis of the various texts.

11 Gérard Rudent and Brigitte Vergne-Cain (eds), *Franz Kafka: Récits, romans, journaux* (François Matthieu, Axel Nesme, Marthe Robert, Gérard Rudent and Brigitte Vergne-Cain trans) (Paris: Le Livre de Poche, 2000).

12 Klaus Wagenbach, *Franz Kafka: Biographie seiner Jugend* (Berlin: Verlag Klaus Wagenbach, 2006); for Marthe Robert, see especially *As Lonely As Franz Kafka* (Ralph Manheim trans.) (New York and London: Harcourt, Brace, Jovanovich, 1982); Ritchie Robertson, *Kafka: Judaism,*

Politics and Literature (Oxford: Clarendon Press, 1985); Hartmut Binder (ed.), *Kafka-Handbuch in zwei Bänden* (Stuttgart: Alfred Kröner, 1979); Mark Anderson, *Kafka's Clothes: Ornament and Aestheticism in the Habsburg* Fin de Siècle (Oxford and New York: Oxford University Press, 1992).

13 Sander L. Gilman, *Franz Kafka: The Jewish Patient* (New York and London: Routledge, 1995); Scott Spector, *Prague Territories: National Conflict and Cultural Innovation in Franz Kafka's Fin de Siècle* (Berkeley, Los Angeles and London: University of California Press, 2000); Löwy, *Franz Kafka, rêveur insoumis*; Iris Bruce, *Kafka and Cultural Zionism: Dates in Palestine* (Madison: The University of Wisconsin Press, 2007); and Bernd Neumann, *Franz Kafka: Aporien der Assimilation; Eine Rekonstruktion seines Romanwerks* (Munich: Wilhelm Fink, 2007).

14 Bettina von Jagow and Oliver Jahraus (eds), *Kafka Handbuch: Leben-Werk-Wirkung* (Göttingen: Vanderhoeck & Ruprecht, 2008).

15 The last two—monumental—biographies of Kafka to be published are Reiner Stach, *Kafka: Die Jahre der Entscheidungen* (Frankfurt: Fischer, 2002); and Peter-André Alt, *Franz Kafka: Der ewige Sohn* (Munich: C. H. Beck, 2008).

16 Bernard Lahire argues that he has founded a sociology of literature and a 'theory of literary creation' on what he calls a 'sociological biography' of Kafka and reintroduces the assumptions of biographical criticism, namely, that the literary work is nothing but a mere transposition, through various metaphors of varying degrees of literary elaboration, of his psychological difficulties, his relations with his father, his sense of guilt, his relations with women, etc. This is, in reality, one of the variants of the theory of literary art as a 'reflection' of reality. See Bernard Lahire, *Franz Kafka: Éléments pour une théorie de la création littéraire* (Paris: La Découverte, 2010).

17 Cf. Pascale Casanova, *The World Republic of Letters* (M. B. DeBevoise trans.) (Cambridge and London: Harvard University Press, 2004).

18 Robert Darnton, *The Great Cat Massacre and Other Episodes in French Cultural History* (New York: Vintage Books, 1985), p. 12.

19 Franz Kafka, '26 March 1911' in Max Brod (ed.), *The Diaries of Franz Kafka 1910–1923* (Joseph Kresh and Martin Greenberg trans)

(Harmondsworth: Penguin Books, 1972), p. 45; this work is hereafter referred to as Kafka, *Diaries*.

20 Charles Taylor, 'To Follow a Rule . . .' in Craig Calhoun, Edward LiPuma and Moishe Postone (eds), *Bourdieu: Critical Perspectives* (Cambridge: Polity Press, 1993), pp. 45–60; here, p. 47.

21 Ibid., p. 45.

22 Ibid., p. 47.

23 Ibid., p. 50.

24 Ibid., p. 53.

25 See Pierre Bourdieu, *The Rules of Art: Genesis and Structure of the Literary Field* (Susan Emanuel trans.) (Stanford: Stanford University Press, 1992), pp. 309–12.

Kafka's anger is everywhere. How, then, can anyone choose to repeat, again and again, that one of his most famous short stories, 'A Hunger Artist', is an (ultimately rather banal) allegory of the artist doomed to failure and oblivion?[1] An insipid moralism bolstered by eternal but vapid truths about the destiny of the artist and—which is not contradictory—a biographical confession, seem to me as far as can possibly be from Kafka's aesthetic convictions and conceptions.[2] It seems to me that this cruel story is much rather a statement of the infinite paradoxes and subtle perversities of domination—upon which he tirelessly vented his anger—when it operates without any apparent violence.

Who is the hunger artist? A man obsessed by the desire to prove to the rest of the world his conformity with what he claims to be and do, and his scrupulous respect for the most drastic conditions he imposes on himself to achieve the title of record-breaker. The hunger artist exists—for himself and for others—only through this absurd performance which keeps him constantly at death's door. He could cheat; he could eat and drink from time to time, as some of his 'watchers' urge him to do. But it is a matter of honour for him to show his absolute respect for the rules of the most radical fasting—he is not so much showing his suffering body as the pointlessness and unfairness of the suspicions that might hover about him. He remains, however, incapable of proving to everyone that he has fully kept to his fast and—despite his success and absolute conformity with the rules—he is overwhelmed by a sense of failure. Like Josef K., the artist has so well understood the burden of suspicion upon him or, to put it another way, has so well incorporated into himself the fact of being dominated that he will spend his life trying (in vain) to prove that he is indeed what he claims to be—despite the fact that no one requires him to justify himself. Or, more than this, that he is the first in the field of self-effacement. With the dissatisfaction that his genuine worth is not recognized 'always rank[ling]', he imposes sufferings on himself beyond what anyone asks of him and tries to push back the limits of what is ordinarily bearable—showing his bones again and again, his ribs that stick out, his bony arms; obliging his audience to accord unhesitating recognition to the irreproachable quality of his fasting; forcing the onlookers to concede the exceptional character of his action. The hunger artist is so dependent on the opinions of others that he is slowly destroying himself in order to escape this kind of constitutive distrust and, above all, to be recognized as an extraordinary human being. He blackmails himself with his own death, as it were, so as to be able to be acknowledged as 'the record hunger artist of all time'.[3] In other words, in order to achieve his ends, the hunger artist adopts a paradoxical strategy —his modesty and weakness become formidable weapons in his fight for recognition. He exhibits his fragility, then, as though it were his only strength or, rather, as if to force the onlookers, in spite of their disgust and their prejudices, to recognize him for what he is and grant him fully what he asks— acknowledgement of his quite extraordinary strength. This is the power of weakness, the strength of fragility. But there is a price to pay for the use of these inverted weapons—the artist himself becomes both the site of, and the stakes in, the battle. This form of hunger art makes him a 'suffering martyr'.[4] But why does the hunger artist, unlike all the others, use these dangerous weapons? It would seem that in this tale Kafka is dissecting the most refined, unremarked, paradoxical, self-imposed forms of suffering of a dominated human being who himself becomes the site of the violence inflicted on him by the social world. Misrecognizing the violence the world metes out to him, the artist turns that violence against himself, believing himself to be the cause of it. In other words, this anatomy lesson is a dissection of the most internalized forms of the soft violence exerted on all dominated individuals.

However, no one will really grant him the recognition he asks. Indeed, he is himself persuaded that he will not achieve it, insofar as he has internalized the invisible violence to which he is subject. He embodies at one and the same time the impossibility of achieving the fullness of his art and of receiving total recognition. The description of the distaste of the women who had come up to accompany the artist from his cage at the end of his fast—'one of the ladies [. . .] first stretched her neck as far as she could to keep her face at least free from contact with the artist'[5]—underscores both the pathos of this inverted greatness and the constitutive failure of this act which will never entirely be recognized for what it is, either by the public or the artist himself. He is therefore condemned constantly to push back the limits of fasting. He acts almost like Josef K. in *The Trial*, who, being subject to a suspicion he can neither overcome nor allay, anticipates—and facilitates—his own death sentence. He transforms his own body into a battlefield.

There is then, logically, nothing to halt the artist in his descent into invisibility and death. Taken on by a circus, he becomes a secondary attraction for the audience who come to see the animals in the menagerie.

Then one day, completely forgotten at the back of his cage 'with dirty straw inside it',[6] he is found dying, still pursuing his fast and his dream of recognition. It is at this point that he tries to explain the paradoxes of his behaviour. Against all expectations, he states that, despite his longing for it, he does not deserve admiration for his fasting. Why? ' "Because I have to fast, I can't help it," said the hunger artist.'[7] In other words, a force was compelling him to inflict this ordeal on himself. Or, to put it another way, the social world's hold over him, the importance accorded to public opinion, has such a devastating, powerful effect on him that it is something he cannot escape. He adds: 'I couldn't find the food I liked. If I had found it, believe me, I should have made no fuss and stuffed myself like you or anyone else.'[8] He is saying, then, that his fasting was a sham, since it was not the product of a will but the result of an invisible constraint. If he could have, he would, of course, have eaten like everyone else. But he could not. He could not act differently. All the contempt felt for this discredited little bag of bones is summed up in the words of the overseer, intent upon emptying the cage as quickly as possible after the artist's death: 'Well, clear this out now!' ['Nun macht aber Ordnung!']⁹

The entirely unexpected conclusion of this unbearable fable, a conclusion wholly at odds with the rest of the narrative, is an (very rare) almost explicit invitation to hear Kafka's point of view. Breaking off his story suddenly, cutting short the account of the last humiliations inflicted on the artist's body, he introduces a panther into the last paragraph—and into the cage. And we very quickly see that this 'wild creature' is the absolute antithesis of the hunger artist. It embodies life itself, self-assuredness, the calm, unquestioning, remorseless, guiltless assertion of force. '[H]is noble body, furnished almost to the bursting point with all that it needed, seemed to carry freedom around with it too.'¹⁰ But the very unusual definition Kafka gives of this total independence (which even makes light of the cage) provides us with quite a transparent clue to his point of view: '[S]omewhere in his jaws [. . . freedom] seemed to lurk; and the joy of life streamed with such ardent passion from his throat.'¹¹ Perhaps the freedom of the writer Kafka is asserted in his literature, conceived as a sharpened set of teeth [Gebiss] and a weapon in his relentless battle against the world, because that literature is one of the ways to tell the truth—even by the roundabout paths of fiction. Literature is an 'axe', a sharp weapon whose role it will be to help readers to make their way towards emancipation. And his work can be understood as the relentless denunciation of the least remarked forms of authority, obedience and the infinite cruelties of domination.

NOTES

1 Franz Kafka, 'A Hunger Artist' in *The Complete Short Stories of Franz Kafka* (Nahum N. Glatzer ed., Willa and Edwin Muir trans) (London: Vintage Books, 2005), pp. 268–77 [originally published in 1922 as 'Ein Hungerkünstler' in *Die neue Rundschau*].

2 'Kafka has rarely drawn such a cruel self-portrait,'—Claude David, 'Notice' in Claude David (ed.), *Franz Kafka: Oeuvres complètes*, VOL. 2 (Jean-Pierre Danès, Claude David, Marthe Robert, Alexandre Vialatte trans) (Paris: Gallimard, 1980), p. 1196.

3   Kafka, 'A Hunger Artist' in *The Complete Short Stories*, p. 271.

4   Ibid.

5   Ibid., pp. 271–2.

6   Ibid., p. 276.

7   Ibid., p. 277.

8   Ibid.

9   Ibid.; Franz Kafka, 'Ein Hungerkünstler' in Hans-Gerd Koch (ed.), *Franz Kafka: Gesammelte Werke in zwölf Bänden, Volume 1: Ein Landarzt; und andere Drucke zu Lebzeiten* (Frankfurt: Fischer Taschenbuch, 2008), pp. 261–73; here, p. 273.

10 Kafka, 'A Hunger Artist' in *The Complete Short Stories*, p. 277.

11 Ibid. [The term translated here as jaws is *Gebiss* which refers more properly to the animal's teeth. Trans.]

I've noticed a really silly thing. That words don't exist, absolutely
not, they're . . . a word on its own . . . it . . . it doesn't really mean
anything [. . .] it needs pals, neighbours, a little group, more than
a little group even, it also needs a little context. A lot of fleshing
out's needed around the little word. So, it—it on its own—can't
do anything, and in a little group, a little set of them, they can produce a meaning.

Christophe Tarkos (1963–2004), *Pâte-Mot, discussion.*

The Prague space we are going to describe here is highly complex.
At the point that concerns us—between 1890 and 1920—it was the
site of profound political and social transformations, and the political,
economic and linguistic relations of force were subject to large-scale
gradual but irreversible change. Each of the contending camps, each
of the positions was constantly evolving. And rather than freeze
them at a given moment, I propose to describe them in terms of a
dynamic. The social group Kafka belonged to, which will be at the
centre of this work, was the group of Prague Jews.

Moreover, I do not think we should restrict ourselves to a description of the situation and the political relations of force in Prague
alone. These are, admittedly, essential, but to analyse them exclusively
would be to perpetuate the notion that literary and political phenomena are closed affairs and nationally or regionally self-contained.
Prague was, in reality, at the intersection of several spaces which
partially overlapped, were interlinked and did not depend on national
boundaries or even on linguistic or cultural areas. Every Prague Jewish intellectual was situated in a number of spaces that were distinct
but interconnected: the transnational space of emergent Zionism
(especially in Western Europe); the German-language intellectual
area, which had its capital at Berlin; the transnational space of
Bundism and Jewish socialism (in Eastern Europe), etc. One of the

major paradoxes of this particular universe, as is evident—and this partly related to the specific nature of the Jewish world—was that, though focused exclusively on the national question, it was nonetheless highly internationalized.

It is obviously not my ambition to describe all these universes in detail here. A lifetime would not be long enough. I would simply like to suggest that they formed—in their partial overlapping, interweaving and opposition—the real intellectual and political space in which these writers operated, the cultural air they breathed, the true territory of the struggles they conducted, often without even realizing it. I am aware that I shall necessarily disappoint or annoy the specialists in the various fields to which I am going to refer. However, it is precisely by bringing together elements and fields that are often separated by the specialization of knowledge and disciplines that it seems to me possible to reconstruct a logic of the thinking, problems and questions that arose in that universe.

PRAGUE, AUSTRIAN CITY

Over the long history of the interpretation of Kafka's work, the only way the writer has been historicized has been by making him exclusively a man of Prague and by transforming Prague into an island—thus making it possible to keep faith with the ordinary representations of literary greatness, associated with the idea of solitude and isolation. The so-called 'three ghettos' interpretative grid, first proposed by Pavel Eisner in the 1930s[1] and developed from the 1950s onwards,[2] became for many years one of the most widely shared assumptions of Kafka studies. According to this hypothesis, the German writers of Prague were confined within three ghettos that were, in a sense, interlocking: a German ghetto, since they lived in a city where Czechs were in the majority, while being cut off from Germany and Austria; a social ghetto, since they all belonged to the upper or middle bourgeoisie and the German proletariat was practically absent from Prague; and, lastly, a national ghetto, because they were, in very large majority, Jewish. Concentration on these three 'ghettos' made Prague the only historical 'context'—a kind of separate cultural space that could have been isolated on the map and studied for its own sake. Though it is still invoked at times, this thesis is very widely questioned today.[3] Having said this, given the transformation of the status of Prague over this same period and its transition from a city of middling importance within the Habsburg Empire to the capital of the Czech nation after 1918—the year of the proclamation of Czechoslovakia's independence—it is possible to slide the cursor to one side or the other to 'Germanize' or 'Czechize' the city, depending on whether one is aiming to present Kafka's work as part of the body of literature in German or seeking to integrate it into the history of Czech literature.[4]

For my part, I propose to put Prague back, initially, into the political and intellectual space of the Austrian empire and show that Kafka, before being a Germanized Jew from Prague, is primarily an Austrian intellectual. This assertion, which may seem mundane, is, in fact, far from being accepted as obvious among Kafka-studies 'contextualists'. Ernst Fischer was the first to show the importance of Kafka's Austrian identity through the representation of the empire's bureaucracy in the texts.[5] Then, Richard T. Gray, among others, strove to reinsert his *oeuvre* into the Austrian cultural space by way of his cultural heritage.[6]

As a German-speaking Austrian, Kafka is heir, first of all, to the spatial structure of the empire. The network of Austrian cities was not a simple horizontal system of exchange and communication. It was, in fact, highly hierarchical. In that set of cities, Prague may be regarded—at least between 1880 and 1918—as a provincial city, a 'provincial satellite' of Vienna,[7] of middling importance at the political level. It was only the third-largest city of the empire in number of inhabitants—on the eve of the First World War, Vienna had a population of more than 2 million, Budapest was approaching a million and Prague had 600,000.[8] Bohemia was, admittedly, booming economically, and even becoming the richest region of the empire.[9] The population of Prague grew by 70 per cent between 1870 and 1910.[10] Industry, which had up to that point been wholly in the hands of the Germans, gradually became Czechized and the

Czech bourgeoisie was progressing markedly.[11] However, the relative prestige and influence of Prague barely changed during the period. In his study of higher education in Vienna at the end of the nineteenth century, Viktor Karády provides an objective index of the non-centrality of Prague (or the centrality of Vienna) in the Austrian Empire when he shows that in 1880–81 there were twice as many students at the University of Vienna (4,600) as at the University of Prague (2,057) and that the disproportion was almost the same for the academic year 1912–13, during which Vienna received some 9,000 students while Prague received only 6,500.[12] Lastly, before 1918 Prague was not able to play any role—'even a minor one'—in the field of international relations.[13] In other words, it was never anything other than a regional metropolis.

So far as Vienna is concerned, we cannot deduce from this structure and from its centrality in the political and intellectual life of the empire that it may be regarded as a great capital at the European or even regional level. Seen from beyond Austria's borders, Vienna is hardly more than a secondary capital, a metropolis 'on the road to provincialization', to use Michael Pollak's expression.[14] At that point, the political, economic and intellectual capital of the Germanic area, particularly from 1910 onwards, was indisputably Berlin.[15] This was treated as more or less self-evident by contemporaries. In his memoirs, Stefan Zweig writes: '[W]ithout the ceaseless stimulating interest of the Jewish bourgeoisie, Vienna, thanks to the indolence of the court, the aristocracy, and the Christian millionaires [. . .] would have remained behind Berlin in the realm of art as Austria remained behind the German Reich in political matters.'[16] Berlin controlled both economic capital and symbolic prestige.

At the exact intersection of the economic and symbolic domains, the field of publishing provides an objective index of the position of Vienna in the German-speaking space. The virtual absence of large, prestigious national publishers (apart from a number of bookseller-publishers) in the Austrian capital is, in fact, a precise measure of the dominated character of Vienna. For this reason, a very large part of Austrian German-language literary, theatrical and poetic production was published in Germany—first at Leipzig[17] and Jena, then at Berlin.[18] But we have to take into account how the domination of the German-language cultural space was structured—and, hence, the dependence of Vienna—to understand fully the structural incapacity of Austrian publishers to compete at the symbolic level with the powerful, prestigious publishers of Berlin and Leipzig.

From this dominated character of Viennese literary production we can logically deduce that Prague, a provincial city of the empire, was itself dominated by Vienna or, rather, that it was doubly dependent, both in political and literary terms: first on Vienna, then on Berlin. In a letter to Felice, Kafka underscored this phenomenon from the standpoint of theatrical creation and production, stating it as something more or less obvious, given the hierarchy between the cities. We know that while he was living and working in Prague, Felice was living in Berlin. He wrote to her on 24 October 1912: 'You talk about your visits to the theatre and this interests me very much, firstly because there in Berlin you are at the hub of all theatrical events, secondly because your choice of theatres is very good.'[19] On 4 February 1913 he wrote to her again: 'I realize that everything in Berlin is bound to be noisier and gayer than here (yet even our noise and gaiety are more than I can cope with).'[20]

From this twofold domination we can, admittedly, deduce some shared features but also some differences between the Vienna and Prague spaces. And the major difference between the two relates to the intense politicization of the latter. This increasing importance accorded to the political question, mainly in the form of nationalist demands, is itself a measure of Prague's degree of dependence.[21]

A Divided Political Metropolis

At the turn of the twentieth century, in Prague, one could observe almost all the political conflicts that were then playing out in the Habsburg Empire but in a more acute form than elsewhere. Perhaps because everything was taking place in a relatively limited territory, the city was a kind of laboratory in which Austrian tensions and struggles presented themselves in concentrated form.

Daily life, in practically all fields, was carried on in an atmosphere of antagonism, violence, division into entrenched and hostile camps, and nationalist campaigning. In the very first pages of his autobiography, which actually bears the title *Streitbares Leben* [A Pugnacious Life], Brod points out: 'Old Austrian Prague was a city in which not only were individuals at odds with one another but the three nations fought among themselves: the Czechs as majority, the Germans as minority and the Jews as a minority within that minority.'[22]

Within the empire, Czech nationalism was the most powerful and most radical of the nationalist movements and it was the first to threaten the empire's stability and integrity. From the second half of the nineteenth century onwards, no other provincial capital of the empire saw such violent clashes.[23] After the failure of their federal demands, the Czech nationalists had become radicalized and, despite the establishment of a military government in the 1870s and the declaration of martial law, which was imposed several times in the wake of riots, relations hardened considerably between Germans and Czechs. The Czech nationalist parties began increasingly openly to challenge the monopoly of power that had been held by the Germans up to that point.

Gradually, then, political, economic, social and cultural life assumed a marked bipartite character. Germans and Czechs founded a dual network of professional associations and, little by little, established deep divisions, both symbolic and physical, that became written into the city of Prague itself. The new bridges were given the names of Czech artists, and monuments were raised to the heroes of national history. In 1893, the Czechs won a measure which meant that the nameplates of streets would now be bilingual—as they had previously been in all parts of the city—only in the districts where a majority of Germans lived. In other words, they were written only in Czech everywhere else.[24] The Czech bureaucrats were supported in their campaign over this by the authorities of the empire.

The education system itself split into two after the 1860s and two parallel systems of schooling were established, though Czechs could still attend German schools and vice versa. In 1882, the University of

Prague, prestigious for being the oldest in the empire, was also split into two with the agreement of the Germans who, fearful of being overwhelmed by the Czech section, wished to preserve a university that was properly, exclusively Germanic. The division of higher education at Prague into two distinct units, which clearly caused intense professional and political rivalry between the two institutions,[25] contributed greatly to strengthening Czech national positions. And even if it was recognized that qualifications delivered by the Germanophone university had greater value on the imperial market and opened up access to higher, better-remunerated positions, many Czech students chose the Czech university out of patriotism and a refusal to pursue a career on the Austrian market.[26] The social and geographical divisions of Prague became increasingly rigid. 'The German university and the Czech university [. . .] were as far apart from each other as if one were at the North pole and the other at the South,' relates Egon Erwin Kisch. 'Each of the hundred or so university chairs had its counterpart in the other linguistic sphere, but there were no shared buildings, clinics [. . .] libraries or morgues.'[27] From 1890 onwards and up to the war, it was taken for granted that there was no exchange between Germans and Czechs, either social or cultural.[28] 'Even concerts were either German or Czech; similarly divided were the swimming pools, parks, stadia and most restaurants, cafes and shops,' stresses Kisch.[29] This bipartite division naturally led to the appearance, in all fields, of constant rivalries and competition. After the Czechs had succeeded in founding a Czech national theatre, the Národní Divadlo, in 1868 (it was inaugurated in 1881), the two communities each developed their own acting companies and theatrical institutions. In addition to the Deutsches Landestheater—and to assert their preeminence—the Germans built the Neues Deutsches Theater in 1888. For many years (1888–1910) its director was the famous Angelo Neumann, who, by his highly prestigious programming—particularly in the lyrical field—'raised' the Prague stage to the level of its competitors in the Germanic area.[30]

From the 1880s and 1890s onwards, this division, far from re-establishing equality between the two groups, was, in reality, the mark of a progressive turnabout in the relation of forces in favour of the Czechs and the sign of a transformation of Prague. Having been up to that point a German city, where Czech had for decades merely been the language of the popular classes,[31] gradually in both its symbols of power and its economic reality it became a Czech city.

That said, despite the 'voluntary segregation'[32] and increasing Czechization, the structure of exchanges and of the social hierarchy lived on in the city: Czechs continued to occupy junior positions— particularly as domestic servants in German bourgeois households and as clerks in companies run by Germans.[33] And it is striking to see that, even among the writers who professed an interest in—and accorded genuine legitimacy to—the nationalist demands of the Czechs, opposing the perpetuation of German domination, literary representations continued to display a virtually consubstantial belief in their social inequality. In his *Two Stories of Prague* (1899), René Rilke speaks, for example, of the Czechs as a people 'still utterly childlike' and writes: 'And then they learn hate so early. The Germans are everywhere, and one has to hate the Germans.'[34] Similarly, in *Ein tschechisches Dienstmädchen* (1909; A Czech Servant Girl), Brod tells the story of a Viennese bourgeois who falls in love with a young Czech woman who happens to be—as the obvious fact of Prague's social hierarchies might suggest—a domestic servant. In the novel, everything on the masculine—that is to say, German—side belongs to the field of culture, the refinement of aestheticism and psychological strife, whereas on the feminine—Czech—side, the vocabulary of 'nature' dominates, and with it spontaneity and the 'primitive', an adjective used several times to qualify that nature.[35]

On the other side, as proof that political conflicts were refracted very faithfully and powerfully into the literary space, the publication of *The Golem* by Gustav Meyrink in 1915 (which met with immense success) was poorly received in Czech literary circles, where it seemed to have renewed and reproduced the clichés—and hence the unspoken assumptions—of social division and hierarchy.[36] After the translation of *Golem* into Czech in 1917, Arne Novák, a Czech literary critic, wrote, for example:

This is a matter of a systematic and pre-meditated attack by German writers, who are imposing a fully refined concep-tion of the world of our Prague: they look at life here through a dualistic curtain. Two races live on the Moldau, of differing languages, customs, and blood: one born to spiritual and physical pleasure, noble manners and enterprise [. . .] and the second servile and uneducated, cowering at the wall and waiting there for alms or a slap in the face.[37]

The nationalist campaign mainly found expression in the struggle over language. Hungarian historian István Bibó (1911–79) has shown that campaigning over language is one of the characteristic forms of the nationalisms of Central and Eastern Europe generally, on account of the importance accorded to the theories—originating with Herder (I shall come back to this point)—contending that 'the birth of a nation comes about from the union of people speaking a single lan-guage and resolved to form a state.'[38] This explains why Czech nation-alists largely assessed the political situation in terms of linguistic relations of force.[39] It was out of this language issue, and out of what became, in a sense, a language war, that most Czech demands arose and were expressed and, in turn, the defensive reactions of the Germans developed. To begin with, the 1871 law on the protection of nationalities gave the Czech language equal legal standing with German.[40] Then, from 1880 onwards, the Czechs gained a firmer foothold for their language, first in the civil service, then in the school and university systems. The Germans, seeing a challenge mounted to all their former positions of power, suddenly felt severely threat-ened. Since conflicts between Czechs and Germans over the com-pulsory use (or not) of one or other of the two languages in territories demarcated in the law were becoming increasingly frequent and since negotiations begun in 1890 to find a compromise for Bohemia had failed, in 1897 the Badeni government issued language decrees (*Sprachverordnungen*)—which unhappily acquired notoriety as a result of the very serious riots they provoked.[41] These made bilingualism obligatory for all civil servants in Bohemia. In other words, they extended bilingualism in the civil service to the German-speaking districts. The Germans felt that these measures favoured the Czechs, since they alone were in very large majority bilingual. Most importantly, the measures ended the predominance (not to say the monopoly) of German in the territories where Germans were in the majority. They protested and the strife prompted by the Badeni Crisis was extremely violent. The Germans of Bohemia fought Badeni's language regulations; there were, in turn, savage anti-German riots in late 1897, involving large numbers of Czechs. For a whole week, buildings and businesses identified as German in the city were attacked or looted. Once again it was martial law that restored peace in Prague.[42] Up until the 1914 war, the numerous clashes often turned into genuine street fights between Czech and German students and secondary or even primary schoolchildren: one of Kafka's friends, Oskar Baum, lost his sight in such fighting.

Despite the Czechs' struggles to have their language recognized and achieve legal equality between the two tongues, German retained an unquestionable prestige at the symbolic level, to such an extent that many Czechs continued to send their children to German schools. Prominent social figures, whether Czech, German or Jewish, wanted to be able to show that they were good German speakers. In 1900, German was still the language of power and prestige. It was, in other words, the language through which the Czech and Jewish lower-middle classes could hope to ascend socially. Kafka's father, for example, who came from a little village in Southern Bohemia and from a very poor family, spoke Czech, but he had learnt rudimentary German in his village school and, being determined to succeed and integrate into the German minority, chose the 'noblest' schooling for his son (who entered university in 1901)—that is to say, the German system.

I shall not here follow the hypothesis formulated by, among others, Wagenbach that Prague's German speakers had their own linguistic specificity and insecurity, related to their isolation in a Slavonic environment. I prefer to stress that languages, which had become a political issue of the first importance, were at the heart of struggles and preoccupations.

However, Czech nationalist campaigning, which attempted to create a state of rivalry between the two languages—there was an effort among Czech intellectuals, at least from the 1820s onwards, to restore a 'purity' to the national vocabulary (in other words, to root out the many German words or words of Germanic origin)— contributed to modifying the attitudes of both groups towards their own language.[43] The Germans—in particular, the most nationalistic among them—began to practise a sort of hyper-correctness, the better to combat the aggressive 'purism' of the Czechs, and all the forms of linguistic 'compromise' that had appeared over the years in which Czechs, Germans and Jews had lived side by side were now rejected: the various different dialects and accents were rejected in the name of their supposed linguistic 'impurity', deemed unworthy of the aspiration to nationhood.

Rilke, also born in Prague 12 years before Kafka, felt his language to be a mark of infamy or provincialism, which doubtless amounted to the same for him. He wrote, for example, to August Sauer:

> The baneful contact between linguistic bodies [*Sprachkörpern* . . .] has led in our countries to the inevitable wearing down of the extremities of the two languages. It follows that anyone who grew up in Prague, who was nourished from the first with such rotten refuse of language, will not later be able to avoid developing a distaste for, or even shame towards, everything he was taught during his tenderest childhood.[44]

This strange expression 'linguistic bodies', associated with that of 'rotten refuse' and 'distaste', shows the extent to which the ideology and representation of linguistic 'purity' were dominant at the time.[45]

THE TRANSFORMATIONS OF THE JEWISH GROUP

German-speakers (Germans and Jews) gradually came to be in the minority, while continuing to occupy the highest positions. Kisch describes them as follows: 'These 25,000 Germans [in the broad sense], 5 per cent only of the population of Prague, possessed two magnificent theatres, an enormous concert hall, two universities, five grammar schools and four higher technical schools [*Oberre-alschulen*], two daily newspapers printed morning and evening,[46] large clubs and a lively social life.'[47] Between 1880 and 1900, they had fallen from 15.5 to 7.5 per cent of the population of Prague.[48] In 1900, out of 450,000 inhabitants only 34,000 spoke German.[49]

The statistical studies of Ján Havránek have demonstrated that the Czech and German-speaking groups were very different in their social composition: between 1890 and 1920, blue-collar workers and lower-grade clerical workers were mainly Czechs (only 1 per cent of workers, apprentices and day-labourers in industry spoke German) while German-speakers were over-represented in commerce and education.[50] In short, at the turn of the twentieth century, Prague had few German-speaking blue-collar workers and, as Havránek notes, there were more typographers among them than stonemasons. Moreover, until the 1914 war, Prague received very few Jewish immigrants from Eastern Europe.[51] In other words, one met few poor Jews from village backgrounds there.

The German-speakers were, in their great majority, merchants (like the fathers of Feliz Weltsch and Franz Kafka),[52] industrialists (like the father of Franz Werfel),[53] lawyers (like the father of Willy Haas), doctors, clerical workers, journalists, teachers, etc.

This minority, forming less than 10 per cent of the population, was divided between the liberal Jews and Germans on the one hand, who remained faithful to the empire and its policies, and, on the other, the violently anti-liberal German nationalists who, under the increasing influence of Georg von Schönerer,[54] were growing radically and openly pan-Germanist and anti-Semitic. German liberals faced very strong challenge and criticism within the German minority from these virulent nationalists (though there were fewer of them at Prague than at Vienna).[55] Divisions within the German-language population simply grew wider in the first decade of the twentieth century, with positions become increasingly clear-cut and exclusive between the liberals and the pan-German nationalists. These latter gained adherents after every Czech nationalist uprising.

However, the Jews effected a twofold secession which, more than the political division within the German group, threatened the survival of this declining population. They opted either for Zionism or for assimilation into the Czech majority.

In 1893, the year Kafka entered the German grammar school—the *Staatsgymnasium*, a classical grammar school from which the monarchy recruited its lawyers, doctors and civil servants—the Jews were not only Germanized but also largely identified with German culture and, in most cases, they subscribed to the values of the Austro-Hungarian monarchy to which they owed their emancipation.[56] They were, in other words, allies of the German liberals. Unlike the Jews of Eastern Europe, they had been freed from almost all controls between 1848 and 1867 and were not in any way bound by ghetto laws which had, in any case, disappeared in the late eighteenth century. They practised a formal Judaism with simplified ritual prescriptions.[57] This identification on the part of Prague's Jews with the values of German culture—and also with the ambitions of the German-speaking commercial and entrepreneurial bourgeoisie[58]—was reinforced by the fact that the Prague German community, though it attempted to establish social criteria of selection, did not put up ethnic or religious barriers. This policy on the part of the Prague liberals is explained by the fact that, in this context of the demographic and economic decline of Prague's German-speaking population, they had a vital need of Jews to swell their ranks.[59] Thus, for example, in the 1860s and 1870s, Jews who wanted to join the German professional associations were co-opted on the same basis as Germans—they had to speak German, support the German Liberal Party of Austria and belong to the petty or middle bourgeoisie.[60] Brod, speaking of the philosopher Fritz Mauthner (1849–1923)—that is to say, referring, through him, to the Jewish intellectuals of his parents' generation—gave this perfect definition of the liberal Jews: '[H]e belonged to that precise generation of Jews who regarded themselves unreservedly as Germans and who were fanatical adherents of a pugnacious Germanism.'[61] Brod himself, at least until 1910–11, had remained virtually an ideal typical representative of these liberal Jews who were sympathetic to the interests of the empire, depoliticized, aesthetic in inclination, Germanized, unalloyed admirers of Germanic cultural values and, in their own eyes, 'as German as anyone else'.

The assimilated Jews divided into two groups: the Germanized groups who were the more numerous until the turn of the century, and the Czechized Jews.[62] Although those who had been settled in Prague for several generations were traditionally German-speaking and liberal, the most recent immigrants, in pursuit of social and economic success, were bilingual and assimilated rather quickly into the Czech population.[63] Hillel J. Kieval shows that in the last quarter of the nineteenth century the social group of Prague Jews changed a great deal in composition: although present in greater numbers in the rural areas and the small towns of Bohemia than in Prague itself, larger and larger numbers of Jews, particularly among the least favoured strata of the population, assimilated into the Czech majority. After 1848, but especially from the 1870s onwards, several cultural and political associations led by Czechized Jews strove to promote the idea of assimilation into the Czech language and people.[64] As a result, a growing number, particularly among those who lived in the outlying districts of Prague, declared their allegiance to the majority group. This is why, though 75 per cent of Jews still claimed to be German-speaking in 1890, the percentage had fallen to 45 by 1900,[65] the others claiming to be Czech-speaking, a group which continued to increase until the war.[66]

However, by dint of the concomitant rise of the most radical nationalisms—German (in its Schönererian form) and Czech (with the radicalization of the Young Czech Party in the 1890s)—anti-Semitism quickly became established in public and political discourse. The Jews were rejected and insulted by both camps. Theodor Herzl, the founder of Zionism, wrote: 'What had they done, the little Jews of Prague? At Prague they were criticized for not being Czechs, at Saaz and Eger for not being German [. . .] What attitude could they adopt? Those who wanted to be German were attacked by the Czechs and, at the same time, by the Germans.'[67]

They were suspect, then, to both the camps: rejected by the Czechs on the one hand as Germans and as Jews and accused by the nationalists of belonging to the dominant group, they were, on the other hand, suspected by the Germans as Jews and tacitly required to provide 'proof' of their allegiance to the German camp. In his memoirs, Haas recalls the cries of the Czech rioters: 'Germans! Jews! [. . .] Germans and Jews: they were nearly identical at that time for Czech Prague. And both, Germans and Jews, were equally hated.'[68] In other words, they were what might be called the dominated section of the dominant group. Their stigmatization continued in subtler but equally powerful forms—they were never, for example, appointed to the empire's highest functions.[69]

There was, moreover, a great deal of anti-Semitic violence. Riots and disturbances grew more numerous and, during them, the ultra-nationalist Young Czech Party sparked a reign of terror on the streets, molesting Jewish shopkeepers, looting their shops, profaning and burning synagogues.[70] The Jews were regularly accused of 'ritual murder', a collective fantasy which received a lot of noisy press coverage and led to trials that attracted enormous attention. During Kafka's childhood and adolescence, there was a string of sensational trials: that of Tisza Eszlár in Hungary in 1882–83, of Leopold Hilsner in Bohemia from 1899 onwards and, later, of Mendel Beilis in 1911 in Ukraine.[71] The Hilsner Affair unleashed an extremely violent wave of anti-Semitism throughout the country and carried on until 1916,[72] giving rise to countless press articles and, among other things, the publication of postcards depicting the murderer and his victim. This collective madness was even featured in a large number of dioramas and pantoscopes throughout Bohemia.[73] The particularly terrible feature of the affair was that the innocent Hilsner was twice found guilty at two successive trials. After the first, he was condemned to death. Then, in 1900, following the pattern of the Dreyfus Affair, several lawyers and intellectuals—including Tomáš Masaryk, the future president of Czechoslovakia—defended him at a second trial. Hilsner was, however, found guilty once again and sentenced, this time, to life imprisonment. He was finally pardoned in 1918 by the last Habsburg emperor.

Assimilation/Disassimilation

As a result of these multiple tensions and the conflicts and stances taken within each of the competing camps, the Austrian Jewish world, which had until then defined itself mainly in relation to the liberal Germans, underwent very great upheavals and splits at the end of the century. The appearance of Zionism, in particular, was experienced as a genuine revolution. Once the need for the establishment of a state and, consequently, for a Jewish nationalism had been proclaimed (first in 1896 with the publication of Herzl's *Jewish State*,[74] then with the founding of the Zionist movement in 1897), within a few years Zionism became a force throughout the entire Jewish world—including for those who rejected it. This political upheaval marked the beginning of a new era, introducing divisions where for many years there had been relative unanimity. Because Zionism, in a sense, gave the Jews 'permission' to defend a national idea—a position from which they had previously been excluded—because it 'normalized' them in terms of the categories of political thought of the day, their range of political options expanded considerably. From 1900 onwards, the decision to assimilate was contested by those who adopted the new path available to them. They were now no longer forced to assimilate. They had the possibility of disassimilating.

Zionism was the name they gave to this break. Enumerating the various possible positions available to the Prague Jews at the point of his own 'conversion' to Zionism, Brod describes the configuration as follows:

> Among the Jews, there were some who felt themselves members of the German people and who were able to adduce the weightiest arguments for this. Then there were others who, advancing very similar arguments, contended that they were part of the Czech nation. And finally there were Jews who simply and unaffectedly declared themselves to be Jews [sich . . . zum Judentum bekannten].[75]

'The Zionists were the malcontents at the time,' he adds. 'They were the "angry young men" of the day.'[76]

The Zionist option was, then, the option of national protest and separation. In other words, it was a political choice of anti-German, anti-liberal and anti-consensual commitment. It was a sort of declaration of war and an assertion of a rift within the German camp. We hardly need say that, in these conditions, it was mainly an option favoured by young people and intellectuals and for that reason remained very much a minority choice. Until around 1910, Bar Kochba, the influential Zionist student association (founded in 1899), which, as we shall see, attracted young German-speaking Jewish Prague intellectuals in the first two decades of the twentieth century, could claim no more than 150 to 200 members. 'These "Jewish Jews" were initially,' stresses Brod, 'a tiny minority. A joke went around that if the ceiling collapsed in a certain cafe, then that would be the end of Zionism in Prague, so few in number were the faithful in those early days.'[77]

To gain a better understanding of the state of mind of these angry young men, the issues they were struggling over and the reasons for their ire, I propose to make a comparison with another figure who lived at the same time in the Germanic area: Gershom Scholem. He has provided testimony and analyses of these years which are very precious in that they enable us to reconstruct the ways of the period and reconstitute the world view of a young German-speaking Jew before the First World War. To make a reasoned comparison between Scholem's world and that of Kafka and his friends, we have to bear in mind that they are slightly offset from each other in both space and time. Scholem was born in Berlin in 1897. He was, therefore, a little younger than the group of writers and intellectuals who gathered around Brod in Prague *circa* 1905.[78] However, all were German-speaking Jews, active from 1906 onwards[79] (Scholem says he joined the Zionist movement in 1911),[80] living in two of the metropolises of the German cultural area. They belonged to the same intellectual milieu, were steeped in the same political atmosphere, read the same publications, discussed the same problems with the same intellectual tools and were all close in those years—apart from Kafka, as we shall see—to Cultural Zionism.

Scholem came from a Berlin Jewish family and describes it as belonging to the 'Jewish petty bourgeoisie, which was then on the rise'.[81] They had been assimilated into the German bourgeois milieu for several generations and had espoused Germanic cultural values.[82] They owned two print shops.[83] 'The transition in our family from Orthodoxy at the beginning of the nineteenth century to almost total assimilation at the beginning of the twentieth was a matter of three generations—from my grandfather, through my father, to my own generation,' he observes in *On Jews and Judaism in Crisis*.[84] While still very young, he committed himself to the Zionist movement and to the study of Hebrew and the Talmud, seeking, as he put it, 'a path towards the essence of Judaism and its historical development'.[85] In short, despite some marked differences from the world of Prague, Scholem depicts a world and a range of assumptions very similar to those of the members of the Prague Circle.

By his own admission, the political and intellectual logic governing the action and commitment of those young people is almost impossible to reconstruct today, simply because of the break represented by the Second World War and the total disappearance of that world. To explain it from the inside, Scholem recounts not only his education but also the political atmosphere permeating the Jewish intellectual circles of Berlin in those years, the range of debates and ideas in circulation and, most importantly, the convictions that made up the contemporary zeitgeist.[86] He recalls, also, at length, the conceptual universe of his parents who for him represent the ideal type of the assimilated Jews with whom he broke as a very young man.

According to Scholem, the range of diverse political opinions available to the Jews from 1900 onwards could sometimes be met with in the same family group:

> One could rub shoulders in the same family with Jews who now felt their Germanic sensibilities were entirely legitimate and who, consequently, inclined towards nationalism, others who had socialist and later communist sympathies, and yet others who were Zionists, while the majority of people were concerned above all with their peace and quiet and wanted

to stay out of these controversies. I experienced all this within my own family.[87]

Scholem tells, in fact, how his father was a fervent assimilationist, a member of the Centralverein deutscher Staatsbürger jüdischen Glaubens (Central Association of German Citizens of Jewish Faith), which was, in his words, 'radically anti-Zionist';[88] one of his brothers, a socialist, joined the SPD [Social Democratic Party]; another was a militant assimilationist and became a member of the German People's Party;[89] one of his uncles was a Zionist,[90] as he was himself, being active in the cause of Cultural Zionism. It goes without saying that all these irreconcilable allegiances produced very great tensions, and also some irrevocable splits.[91]

Contrary to the spontaneous notion we might have today of the appearance of the Zionist movement, anti-Semitism was neither the primary enemy nor the element around which the commitment of these intellectuals coalesced.[92] Scholem even states: 'I can't say that I suffered from anti-Semitism as a boy. I had virtually no encounters with anti-Semitism, and those I did have did not leave a deep mark on me, although at that time—thirty years after its beginning —the anti-Semitic movement in Germany had already gathered real strength.'[93] In fact, Prague Zionism was structured initially around the opposition to assimilated Jews.

The journal *Selbstwehr* (that bore the subtitle *Unabhängige jüdische Wochenschrift*—Independent Jewish Weekly), founded in 1907 in Prague by Zionists and intended, as its name indicates, as a 'self-defence' organ for the Jews of Prague, was to become the most widely distributed nationalist publication in the whole of Bohemia. It made no secret of its categorical rejection of those it called the 'German Jews'—that is, those Jews who chose to assimilate into German culture. In the first issue, for example, the editors of *Selbstwehr* made a 'declaration of war' but it was directed explicitly against the assimilated Jewish bourgeoisie who would hear nothing of a 'Jewish' nation[94] and who, in their concern to blend in with the German population, were trying to dispel all memory of their Jewishness. Of course, *Selbstwehr* also condemned the anti-Semitic leaflets that circulated in Prague, published scandalized commentaries on the various accusations of ritual murder that continued to be levelled at Jews, alerted its readers to whatever new slanders were directed against them, campaigned for a specifically Jewish school system and announced the events and public meetings that punctuated the life of the (non-assimilated) community of Prague.[95] But the rallying point for these young people was, much rather, the question of assimilation, seen as a dissolution of Jewish identity into the German nation, the betrayal of a belonging, a submission to the dominant Germanic order and, moreover, a process doomed to failure on account of anti-Semitism. The editors pointed to assimilation as a social evil which they intended to combat—and also as a fiction and a fable which only the most credulous and naive of Jews could still believe in and accept, given their increasing stigmatization in political and social life.[96] It is in this same spirit that Brod sketches the portrait of a Prague assimilationist met at a public meeting of the Zionist party which he chaired during the war:

> [I remember] the white-bearded university professor who, in a public meeting of the 'Jewish Party' declared himself a national German [nationaler Deutscher], a fierce assimilationist in the old—one might almost say 'patriarchal'—style. And when someone shouted out, 'You are still a Jew,' the man (who was, incidentally, most kind-hearted and a not insignificant scholar) proudly declared: 'I have withdrawn from Judaism.' At which a heckler shouted, 'But Jewishness hasn't withdrawn from you, Professor!'[97]

In criticism of the religious definition to which, in their eyes, the assimilationists reduced their Judaism and also of the fact that they were sick with self-hatred,[98] the Zionists called them 'Germans of Mosaic persuasion'.[99] Czech-assimilationist Jews were also targeted by Selbstwehr but less repeatedly and insistently.[100]

The battle against assimilation was not a theme specific to the Prague Zionists. Among politicized Jews, the general tone towards assimilated groups was extremely violent, in a way that may seem shocking today. That theme was omnipresent in those years, both in West and East, among the most politicized strata and in Jewish intellectual circles. It was almost unanimously supported (even if the situation was not described identically by the various individuals involved) and it was at the heart of debates and campaigns among both the nationalists and the socialists. The Bundists spoke of the Germanized Jewish bourgeoisie in very vehement terms. Historian Simon Dubnow, among others, was very attentive to this question.[101] The fifth 'letter', entitled 'On National Education', in his book *Nationalism and History*, which contained pieces written and published between 1897 and 1907, dealt with it at great length. Speaking of assimilation as a 'malady', a 'course of deterioration' and the 'tragic national dualism of the Jewish youth of our time',[102] Dubnow raised the case of German Jewish writer Ludwig Jacobowski (1868–1900) and reconsidered the question of his suicide at the age of 32:

> Jacobowski became known in German literature only after his death [. . .] He published a novel, *Werther the Jew* (*Werther der Jude*),[103] and a collection of a few poems expressing the anguish of a crushed and tormented soul [. . .] The hero of the novel *Werther the Jew* is presented as the product of the psychological tension besetting the assimilated German Jew under the impact of antisemitic expression.
>
> The hero of the novel, the son of a Jewish merchant, who was educated at home as a 'German of the Mosaic faith,' who went to a German school and attended the university, is painfully vacillating all his life between two national feelings, the German and the Jewish [. . .] The tragedy of Werther the Jew consists in the fact that he is an undesirable stepson in an alien family, while he should be, by his nature, the favorite son of the very family which he left in mourning.[104]

Dubnow provides an excellent description of the representations of assimilation among the politicized Jews of the time. The refusal to assimilate also underlay Scholem's political commitment and his desire to study Hebrew and the Talmud. Moreover, he discloses the centrality of this problem and the major division it engendered among German-speaking Jews themselves, the recurring nature of these debates and, as a result, the violence of the stances taken towards it. Scholem argues:

> We [the committed Jews] were all driven by the following deep conviction: the massive majority of the Jews around us were living in a vacuum and also—and this was more serious and for us more unbearable—in a state of wilful self-delusion, taking their desires for realities and getting carried away by an illusory Judaeo-German harmony that had no basis in fact [. . .] The more seductive the dream, the more nightmarish it was to wake from it.[105]

As a result, says Scholem, when a Zionist went so far as to 'challenge the Germanness of German Jews—which many people of my generation certainly did between 1910 and 1920—it wasn't regarded as a purely theoretical contribution to a discussion but as a personal provocation, a destructive attack on something inviolable.'[106]

Assimilation was also a social reality.[107] The German-speaking population of Prague in 1900 is estimated at 33,776 inhabitants, of which, writes Jean-Pierre Danès, around 40 per cent were Jewish.[108] Within this group (and there was no fundamental difference between the Prague and Berlin groups), Scholem estimates that around 20 per cent were orthodox Jews, 'that is to say, people who conformed more or less to the rules of the Jewish tradition in their way of life'.[109] The other 80 per cent had, in his view, 'almost totally eliminated that tradition from their personal lives'.[110] Among them, Scholem distinguished two main subgroups. First, there were the Jews who were totally 'Germanized'. For that group, he writes, 'Jewishness was no longer a problem. Those people regarded themselves entirely as Germans and had nothing to do with their Jewish heritage, no longer feeling any obligation towards it. From their standpoint, there was no longer any basis for any of the problems that set Jews and Germans against each other.'[111] Then there was a larger second group: the Jewish petty and middle bourgeoisie, who were most often involved in commerce. Overall, says Scholem, 'these people had lost all their religious ties, but they had not entirely abandoned the practices and customs connected with them.'[112]

At Prague, the 'internal' rhetoric of denunciation within the Jewish community was taken almost word for word from Czech nationalism, which defined itself as a movement of renewal, youth and vitality against a German model denounced as decadent and corrupt—for the young militant Jews, it was a matter of defining themselves as a nationality like the others; of defining and claiming, against the passivity of assimilation, a combative position for Jews.

Assimilation was all the more intolerable in the eyes of politicized Jews because it was conceived as a disappearance, a self-dissolution. When he broaches this question in his autobiography in relation to the German Jews who had to make this choice in the years between 1890 and 1920, Scholem uses the verb *verschwinden*—disappear. 'The hope for social emancipation (which was supposed to follow the political emancipation completed in 1867–70)' was, he writes, 'in part also the outright hope for full integration and absorption in the German people'. The phrase translated here as 'absorption in the German people' is in the German, 'verschwinden im deutschen Volk'—implying *disappearance* within the German people.

Fathers and Sons

One form of the rejection of assimilation expressed itself in a revolt against fathers. Carl E. Schorske observes that, in Arthur Schnitzler's 1908 novel *Der Weg ins Freie*,[113] whatever the differences among the characters, 'the youthful characters have all espoused outlooks that set them off from their fathers.'[114] The gulf that opened up between Jewish fathers and sons in the years 1900–14 was the great historical, social and political break within German-speaking artistic milieus (in Germany and in the Austrian Empire). This split, accompanied at times by very great animosity, is, in many respects, the pendant and mirror image of the crisis that Schorske describes the preceding generation at Vienna undergoing.[115] As is well known, the American historian developed the famous argument that, in the years 1890–1900, the basis for the Jung-Wien movement of aestheticist artists lay in the rejection of their fathers' liberal values.[116] He describes the aestheticism and *Gefühlskultur* (culture of feeling) of that generation as an evasion and a way of denying the political and social violence that characterized turn-of-the-century Vienna which had seen the failure of liberalism and the rise of populist and anti-Semitic movements.

At Prague, around 1910–20 (that is to say, some 20 years later), the fathers and sons of the petty and middle bourgeoisie were also in open conflict.[117] But this conflict took symmetrically opposite forms. The same rejection of liberalism was seen, but, where those at Prague were concerned, it was not a question of rejecting any reference to political action, as though it bore the stamp of illusion and disenchantment, but of pitting the belief in the political rupture Zionism represented for them against the half-heartedness and continuity of liberalism. In other words, though the conflict was repeating itself, different things were at stake than for the previous generation. The politicized writers of Prague violently challenged the natural assumptions and certainties of their fathers, their patriotic adherence to the cause of Austria—in other words, their liberalism and also their mercantilism. There was a thoroughgoing revolt of the sons against the way of life and convictions of their fathers. Everywhere, a great many young Germanized Jews questioned their fathers' decision to assimilate into German society and values and to 'disappear' as Jews.

This disruption very often caused unbridgeable rifts which led the sons to make definitive choices that prevented them from ever reverting to the feelings, convictions and assumptions on which the lives of their parents had been based. The insurmountable character of their dissension, with no way out or back from it, doubtless explains the violence of their relations.[118] There has been much study of the omnipresence of father–son conflict in the case of the Expressionist movement. This was such an influential theme that contemporaries themselves highlighted it and, on occasion, satirized it, as Karl Kraus did in his 'operetta'.[119] But it was also met with—far beyond Expressionist circles—throughout the Jewish bourgeoisie. And it was Zionism that was, very often, the form of the sons' revolt and self-assertion. 'Zionism was a revolt against the life-style of the run-of-the-mill bourgeoisie, to which my family belonged,' states

Scholem.[120] In other words, the emergence and subsequent intensification of Zionist convictions and commitment among the sons aggravated all forms of conflict.[121]

Scholem has contributed to wresting this problem from the sphere of individual psychology alone. He has shown that this antagonism was the product of a vast structure and of more general relations of force. It reproduced itself, therefore, on a very large scale, for a whole generation: namely, that of the sons born between 1880 and 1900. Scholem tells how he constituted and asserted himself against his father, a convinced assimilationist who could not bear the younger man's challenges to his ideas or commitment to Zionism. The break between them was very violent: he was turned out of his father's house and left penniless in 1917.[122] Scholem later encountered an antagonism of the same kind between Martin Buber and his father, who, he reports, asked him one day, 'to write a bit less about quirky Jewish matters'.[123] We know that Werfel and Haas also both broke with their respective fathers;[124] and Kafka's 'Letter to His Father' is notorious.[125] 'To sum up,' writes Scholem, 'our parents thought they knew what they wanted but they were more greatly mistaken about themselves than about their environment, about which many of them had few illusions.'[126]

EASTERN FASCINATIONS

Prague had a special place within the space of Jewish nationalist political discussion—it became one of the sites of opposition to, and dissidence from, Zionist orthodoxy. Before the war, Prague Zionism was associated with Bar Kochba, the only Jewish student organization in Prague, which became openly Zionist as early as 1899.[127] Though only a small minority of Jewish students in Prague were members of the organization at the turn of the century (others preferring to join the German liberal organization Lese- und Redehalle der deutschen Studenten), it may be regarded as the centre of Bohemian Zionism in this period.

Very early on, at the instigation of Hugo Bergmann, one of Kafka's fellow students, who was also one of the first in Prague to join the Zionist movement (in 1901), the Prague version of the Jewish nationalist movement came to be opposed to Viennese Zionism. In order to distinguish between the two, the Prague movement is often spoken of as a 'cultural' or 'spiritual' Zionism, by contrast with the 'political' Zionism of Theodor Herzl and Max Nordau.[128] This *Kulturzionismus*, influenced by Ahad Ha'am and Martin Buber, was at odds on almost every point with Political Zionism.[129] As early as 1903, Bergmann announced that the members of his group had no intention of following Herzl's policies so far as the non-engagement of Zionists in the internal affairs of Austria was concerned. By contrast, he stressed the importance of *Gegenwartsarbeit* (present-work), that is to say, a determination to work for the improvement of the cultural, economic, social and political condition of the Jews of the diaspora in the here-and-now and not wait for what was then a hypothetical way out through emigration to Palestine.[130] That programme had been rejected by the leaders of the movement.

In the Austrian context, this meant that the Praguers were opposed to the Zionist rejection of everything relating to the diaspora, that they favoured recognition of a Jewish nationality in the secondary schools and the universities and a rapprochement between Eastern and Western Jews, etc.

Moreover, the Kulturzionisten argued for Jewish emancipation as inner liberation and not just political engagement. The spiritual question was regarded by Buber and Bergmann as a kind of preliminary to the territorial question and seen as an absolute precondition for a rebirth of modern Judaism. 'Everything in me was ploughed up and turned on its head,' reports Brod, writing of the moment at which he became engaged in Zionism. 'Everything had to be directed towards a goal, towards a total existence that was new in every respect.'[131] The spirituality to which this dissident tendency appealed was highly tinged with religiosity. The work of Bergmann attests to this: it represents the working out of a philosophy sharply characterized by religious practice and faith.[132] 'In his personal life,' argues Brod, '[Bergmann] strove in exemplary fashion after the internalization of his religious attitude to all the problems of daily life.'[133] Not only political choices but also intellectual commitments, cultural convictions and ethical and aesthetic choices were subordinated to the allegiance to this Prague Zionism and it reinforced the overlap between the literary and political fields in the German-speaking Prague of those years.[134]

Martin Buber and Hasidism

As one of the last European nationalist movements to enter the fray, Zionism, like the others, developed cultural, linguistic and literary demands. We know that, from the late eighteenth century onwards, in order to contest French domination, Herder proposed the idea that ancientness (as a measure of power) should not be the only way to evaluate national capital but that another measure of cultural and literary greatness, genius and power should be accepted in Europe—that of the 'people' (in the sense of 'nation', embodied in the peasantry).[135] For a people to exist in all its potency, wrote Herder, it had to be able to display its genius first in the form of a language, but then also in folk tales, songs, legends, proverbs and epics—the supposed literary emanations and objectivizations of the peculiar spirit of that people. This is why, throughout the continent, but particularly in Central and Eastern Europe, there were countless instances of the accumulation of literary resources along these lines.

In the case of Jewish nationalism, the pursuit of this 'popular' literary capital proved particularly difficult. First, because of dispersion and literary and linguistic division. Second, because the Jewish 'people' in the Herderian sense (a peasantry) was virtually non-existent. It was at this point that the Western intellectuals (re)discovered the existence of the *Ostjuden*. These latter came to be taken to represent an ideal typical form of the 'people', offering Western Jews a living storehouse and repertoire of Jewish cultural traditions. These communities, grouped in shtetls (*shtetlekh*) virtually cut off from the outside world and living in great poverty, had in fact preserved Judaism's religious rituals.

Buber (1878–1965) exerted great influence on the entire group of Cultural Zionists. In the first place, he played a unifying role through his work as editor of the journal *Der Jude* (The Jew) which was founded in 1916 and ran until 1928.[136] This came very quickly to be regarded as the main platform for Jewish intellectuals engaged in the national emancipation movement and enabled a great many intellectuals, theorists and authors to find an outlet for their writings. Scholem, Brod, Bergmann and Kafka himself all published in this journal with varying degrees of regularity. Even among Buber's opponents it was regarded as one of the most prestigious in that world.[137] Indeed, Scholem writes explicitly that he regarded *Der Jude*—the title of which, he writes, is still hugely provocative—as '[s]urely the best Jewish journal in the German language that ever existed'.[138] In 1902, Buber also created the Jüdischer Verlag (Jewish Press) with Berthold Feiwel and Ephraim Moses Lilien, which rapidly became a hub and meeting place for Jewish intellectuals of East and West.

The publication of *The Tales of Rabbi Nachman* and *The Legend of the Baal-Shem*, two collections of Hasidic stories rewritten and 'adapted' by Buber, was of considerable importance for Jewish intellectuals throughout the German-speaking space.[139] Almost the entire literary, philosophical and intellectual world in the wider sense set about reading them. Georg Simmel discovered for the first time an affinity with the Jewish people; both Gustav Landauer and György Lukács were avid readers of Buber's texts, as were Rilke, Hugo von Hofmannsthal and Arnold Zweig, among others.[140] Scholem stresses in his article—though it is highly critical of the Buberian interpretation of Hasidism—the very strong impression the philosopher made on his first Jewish readers in the first decade of the twentieth century and the enormous influence his writings exerted not only on Jewish nationalists but also on the wider Jewish public.[141] He recalls also how epigones and disciples of the man they called 'the great master' increased in number from that point onwards and that his style was widely imitated in a great number of publications.

In reality, Buber was removing a last obstacle which would, in Zionist terms, enable the Jewish people to be 'normalized',[142] insofar as he was attempting to wrest the main forms of Jewish popular culture from the religious life that virtually monopolized them. The philosopher-storyteller's contention was that he was delivering non-religious tales and legends that possessed all the recognized features of the 'creative genius' of the people (at the cost, admittedly, of a number of 'interpretations' and compromises with the historical reality of the tales, as Scholem would point out). In other words, Buber pulled off a remarkable coup in showing that there existed in the shtetls of the Pale of Settlement forms of popular piety not reducible to mere religious formalism, that creativity was possible there and that he was drawing on that properly Jewish culture and religiosity and refusing to give in to the demands of official piety. In so doing, he enabled Germanized Jews to identify with his approach and enthuse over the rediscovery of what, at that moment, enabled Zionist Jews to proclaim themselves (and see themselves as) a people 'like any other'. That Arnold Zweig was able to declare in 1914 that 'there was no longer any need for Jews to feel a sense of shame or inadequacy, for in Buber's legends they could find their own version of the Brothers Grimm and the Greek myths,'[143] is the clear sign that the Cultural Zionists had enabled the Jews to enter the great inter-national literary competition and vie with the other contestants.

Moreover, in 1909–10, he gave three lectures to the Bar Kochba association at Prague which were subsequently to become famous.[144] Brod attended these and admits that, despite his initial opposition to Zionism, he was converted by listening to Buber.[145] With the Hasidic tales he published a little earlier, these three Prague lectures form the core of his reputation within the Zionist movement in this period. He had embarked on a rediscovery of Hasidism, a mystical-pietistic movement founded in Poland in the mid-eighteenth century by Yisroel ben Eliezer (1700–60), known by the name of Baal Shem Tov (Master of the Good Name).[146] In substance, the Hasidim stressed the primacy of piety and trust in God and in his representative the *zadik*, to whom supernatural powers were ascribed, against the rigid religious and legal authority of the rabbis within Jewish communities, which placed emphasis on observance of the commandments and prohibitions of the Torah.[147] This religious practice met with enormous success among all social strata of Eastern Jewry, though it gave rise, at the same time, to some very deep rifts. In the latter half of the nineteenth century, there were two opposing camps in the Jewish villages: on the one hand, the adherents of Hasidism and, on the other, the orthodox who continued to respect the rabbinical order. The Hasidim were still numerous and Hasidic practices still relatively alive in the shtetls at the point when Western Jews rediscovered their existence with some amazement at the end of the nineteenth century.

For Buber and his disciples, Germanized Jews who had attended German universities, the rediscovery of Hasidism was a way of reaching back to an 'authentic' Judaism that could not be said to be synonymous with religious obscurantism, rabbinical conservatism or strict observance of restrictive laws. For them the movement paradoxically represented the possibility of a reappropriation of Judaism by rejecting its most conservative version and at the same time appealing to a creative, 'popular' version (in Herder's sense).[148] Hasidism (in the simplified, idealized version presented by Buber) seemed to them one of the subversive forces that had appeared within the Jewish world and shown an ability to undermine the foundations of religious authority.

The Ostjudenfrage

The Buberian stance was just one of the possible responses to the 'rediscovery' of the Jews of Eastern Europe. A great many intellectuals and political groups also joined in an internal struggle to advance their own conception of the Jews as a people and provide rival representations of this new Eastern Jewish population.

Let us observe, first, the overall situation of European Jewry and the changes taking place within that population in the last years of the nineteenth century. As is generally accepted, the specific feature of the Jewish people, when seen through the nation-based view of the world that became dominant in the nineteenth century, lies in the fact that it was a people without territory and without a state. At that point the Jewish world was fragmented geographically, linguistically and socially. Two main groups coexisted in that world: impoverished, subordinated communities in the East; and progressively emancipated, assimilated and stigmatized individuals in the West.

Around 1900, half the world's Jewish population—around 5 million people—lived under the control and subjugation of the Russian Empire. They were kept down mainly by being maintained within the Pale of Settlement (a territory in which they were forced to reside and which it was difficult to leave), comprising Lithuania, Belorussia, Poland, Ukraine and Bessarabia. Apart from the obligation to reside in certain places, their lives were governed by almost 150 restrictive or prohibitive laws: occupational limitations; a *numerus clausus* system in the universities; the dissolution of community organizations; diverse forms of censorship; regular expulsions; and, especially after 1881, brutal pogroms which were tolerated by the central government.[149] Moreover, their economic situation was bad and went on deteriorating after 1880. Very few of them were permitted to till the earth and there were too many artisans among them, condemning a large number to unemployment. The majority of men who lived within the Pale were without stable employment; they wandered from village to village surviving as best they could. These were the famous *Luftmenschen* described by Nordau, people who 'live[d] on air', wretched survivors bereft of any future. 'The majority of Russian Jews lived in conditions even worse than the poorest of Russian peasants and workers.'[150] After the interlude of Alexander II's reign (1855–81), who in his relative liberalism abolished the most restrictive laws, the accession of Alexander III (1881–94) worsened their situation and intensified their misery.

In Western Europe, particularly in Germany and Austria-Hungary, Jewish living conditions were very different. They began to assimilate as early as the first decades of the nineteenth century. They left their villages in large numbers, rapidly became urbanized and entered the education systems.[151] Between 1815 and 1848, despite the many restrictions still imposed on them, they managed to enter a large number of the professions from which they had previously been banned (bookselling, publishing, journalism, politics),[152] thus contributing to the emergence of a substantial Jewish bourgeoisie. In Germany and Austria-Hungary (as well as in Italy and Scandinavia) they were granted full equality in civil rights between 1850 and 1860 and rapidly achieved such a presence in the secondary-school system and the universities that, within a few years, they were, proportionately, better represented there than in the population as a whole.[153] This mass influx enabled them, from the first decade of the twentieth century onwards, to enter the professions. As a result, their social structure was much more diversified than in the previous century.[154]

The two groups—the Eastern and Western Jews—remained cut off from each other and, apart from a few who crossed over from the one group to the other at the turn of the century (more from the Eastern to the Western group than vice versa), they lived completely separate lives, ignoring each others' real conditions of existence. In his fine book on Western representations of Eastern Jews at the turn of the twentieth century, Steven E. Aschheim shows that the very idea of the existence and difference of the Eastern Jew was created in Western Europe in the first half of the nineteenth century and that, at least until the 1880s, that idea and the various representations attaching to it had remained largely negative and even repellent: East European Jews 'were held to be dirty, loud and coarse. They were regarded as immoral, culturally backward creatures,' vegetating in anachronistic ghettos.[155] According to the American historian, this image was formulated and propagated to enable those who had been assimilated to distinguish themselves from the groups that had stayed in Russia and Poland and had not been emancipated; in a way, it also enabled them to reference what it was they wished to turn their backs on once and for all. Assimilation had occurred— and had thus been tacitly conceived—not as a reciprocal act but, much rather, as a definitive break with traditional forms of life. The ghetto was identified with a social pathology, thus implying the need to undergo a sort of 'cure' through conversion to German culture and the German way of life. The external signs of Jewishness (such as the wearing of the caftan) were, therefore, turned into objects of shame. This is what explains both the constitution of the stereotype and the rejection of the Ostjuden which can be observed throughout the nineteenth century. The mere sight of these Jews wearing the caftan was a source of shame for their Western families.[156] The return of Jirí Langer (1894–1943), a friend and cousin of Brod who had left Prague to go and live among Hasidim, is described by his brother in the following terms:

Father told me with a note of horror in his voice that Jiri had returned. I understood what had filled him with dread as soon as I saw my brother. He stood behind me in a frayed, black overcoat, clipped like a caftan, reaching from his chin to the ground. On his head he wore a broad round hat of black velvet, thrust back towards his neck. He stood there in a stooping posture; his whole face and chin were covered with a red beard; and side whiskers in front of his ears hung in ringlets down to his shoulders. All that remained to be seen of his face was some white, unhealthy skin and eyes which at moments appeared tired and at others feverish. My brother had not come back from Belz, to home and civilization; he had brought Belz with him.[157]

Zionism produced important changes in these representations. It enforced a revision of the assumptions that had previously guided people's convictions. The central proposition of the movement— that the Jews, despite their differences, formed a single nation— would by itself wholly transform the relations between East and West. In other words, the national movement promised to transform the Eastern Jew, who had until then been the object of the liberals' ambiguous and disdainful philanthropy, into a national partner possessing equal rights.[158] It effected a 'glorification' of the Eastern Jews for their alleged perpetuation of an authentic Judaism which they could be said to embody.[159] However, Aschheim argues that this position remained purely theoretical. As products of the educated strata of the Germanized bourgeoisie, the Zionist leaders in fact remained persuaded of the superiority of the German model. Since Zionism was based on the rejection of the *Galout* (diaspora), the Eastern Jews seemed to personify all the anomalies of diaspora life and therefore lend support to the central idea that it was necessary to emigrate to Palestine to give the Jewish people a 'normality' it could so far be said to be lacking.[160] The Zionists' negative perception of the East Europeans' way of life and their rejection of the ghetto remained very close in reality to the liberals' conceptions.

The fact remains, however, that during 1900–20, among the politicized Jews of Western Europe, there was a very great infatuation with the Jewish populations of the East. Scholem attests to this when he writes of Berlin around 1915:

> I was particularly interested in the members from Eastern Europe, and this interest was shared by others. The more we encountered the not at all infrequent rejection of Eastern European Jewry in our own families, a rejection that sometimes assumed flagrant forms, the more strongly we were attracted to this very kind of Jewishness. I am not exaggerating when I say that in those years, particularly during the war and shortly thereafter, there was something like a cult of Eastern Jews among the Zionists. All of us had read Martin Buber's first two volumes about Hasidism, *The Tales of Rabbi Nachman* and *The Legend of the Baal Shem*, which had appeared a few years earlier and had made Buber very famous. In every Jew we encountered from Russia, Poland or Galicia we saw something like a reincarnation of the Baal Shem Tov or at any rate of an undisguised Jewishness that fascinated us.[161]

This fascination was also a rejection and a reversal of the accepted collective view prevailing up to that point among Western European Jews, which implied a distancing from this group or even a denial of its existence. And then their passionate interest in the groups of Eastern Jews who had taken refuge during the war in the great metropolises of the empire—wretched, famished people dressed in threadbare caftans—was a new source of dissension between fathers and sons. Or rather, as Scholem suggests, the interest shown by the sons was in inverse proportion to the ostentatious aversion of their fathers for the same population. This quasi-ethnological interest was evidence for the fathers, who were intent upon shaking off the memory of their origins, of their sons' folly and irresponsibility. For the sons, it was proof of the betrayal of Judaism by their fathers. This is very much attested, of course, by the words exchanged by Kafka and his father on the subject. When his son formed a deep friendship with Yitzchak Löwy, a Polish Jewish actor temporarily resident in Prague who lived in extreme poverty and whom he invited several times to dinner in the winter of 1911–12, Hermann Kafka was open in his hostility. As Franz Kafka writes: 'Without knowing him you compared him, in a dreadful way that I have now forgotten, to vermin and as was so often the case with people I was fond of you were automatically ready with the proverb of the dog and its fleas.'[162]

Thanks in part to the spur given by Buber, the East European Jews came gradually to represent a sort of model for these young people who had been through the German or Austrian school system and had recently turned to questioning their own identity. They became for them a living repository of traditions and age-old Jewish ways of life that they themselves had forgotten, an object of fascination, yet, at the same time, of distrust. Bergmann was one of the first to be enthused by the question of East European Jewry. As early as 1903, he set out on a trip to Galicia on the eastern frontier of the Austro-Hungarian Empire: 'It has long been my passionate wish one day to see Jews with caftans, side locks, and real, right Jewish blood,' he wrote in the diary he kept during his wanderings.[163] This fascination affected many members of the Prague Circle, whether or not they were Zionists, although in different ways and at different times for each of them—Franz Werfel, Paul Kornfeld, Rudolf Fuchs, Otto Pick and, outside the Circle but very close to it, Egon Erwin Kisch and Franz Kafka—showing that this question was at the heart of all their debates.

These intellectuals, fascinated as they were by the Jewish East and the culture of the shtetl, had in many cases an abstract, idealized vision of those things.[164] They did, however, have some opportunities to come into contact with them—mainly during the war—either when, as soldiers, they entered the Jewish villages of Galicia or when, as residents of the empire's cities, they saw large numbers of refugees fleeing the combat zones.[165]

At the end of September 1914 there were only 200 refugees in Prague, half of them Jews. By November, however, they began to flood into the city as a result of the expulsion of Jewish populations by the Russians between August 1914 and the spring of 1915. 'Entire families were to be seen on the roads with interminable rows of carts,' writes Henri Minczeles, 'children dying in doorways, hospitals swamped, a cruel soldiery.'[166] In the early days of 1915, the number of refugees in Prague was put at around 10,000. By April there were 13,000 (more than 30,000, in fact, if those who had settled on the outskirts are included). At the beginning of October 1915, Russia's advance was halted and its army forced to retreat. A significant number of refugees therefore returned whence they had come. In early November 1915, when Galicia was retaken, we find in Kafka's diary a brief, emotional evocation of the departure of the families of Jewish refugees from Prague to return home:

The recent departure of the Jews from the railway station. The two men carrying a sack. The father loading his possessions on his many children, the smallest one as well, in order to mount the platform more quickly. The strong, healthy, young, but already shapeless woman sitting on a trunk holding a suckling infant, surrounded by acquaintances in lively conversation.[167]

At the end of the war, while the great majority of refugees had returned to Galicia, there were still more than 5,000 who had decided to stay in Prague.[168] As in the other great cities of the empire and Germany, several Jewish voluntary organizations came to their aid to give them food, clothing and shelter. Kafka, along with Brod, took part in this charitable work when the influx of refugees occurred in November 1914. In the early months of 1915, schools were organized for more than 2,500 children, set up hastily and staffed by, among others, the Zionist militants. During 1916 and 1917, Brod taught lessons on world literature there.[169] Through Felice, Kafka kept in contact with the Jüdisches Volksheim (Jewish Community Centre) which was founded at Berlin in May 1916 by Siegfried Lehmann with the support of Gustav Landauer. I shall return to this in detail.[170]

THE LITERARY SPACE

Incorporated, Unformulated Knowledge: The Folkist System of Thought

Before describing the literary space in detail, I would like to turn back to one of the fields of incorporated knowledge which informed the world we are speaking of. I am not claiming in the slightest to provide a 'history of ideas' of the period. I am attempting, rather, to describe the 'background knowledge', as Charles Taylor calls it,[171] that underlies the convictions, reasonings, logics and, most importantly, sheer self-evidence of ways of thinking. Many convictions, unformulated because everyone took them for granted, have become so alien to us that we no are longer able to understand what is at stake in them. More than this, because of our knowledge of the events that followed in the historical chronology, we commit anachronisms by attributing to Praguers, for example, categories of thought which are our own and are so because historical events have occurred to modify assumptions, to change the nature of the discussion and overturn presuppositions, etc. Yet, it is on the basis of these different configurations shared by all the protagonists in a single space that stances, oppositions, rapprochements, etc., are structured—in other words, that an intellectual and literary field is constituted.

The 'separate [system] of coherences', as Michel Foucault puts it,[172] on which turn-of-the-century intellectuals at Prague drew—without even realizing it—to shape an 'order of things', has become entirely alien to us or, in any event, very distant. We have forgotten the logic that governed the assembly of the various elements of that system. It seems to me, for example, that it has to be possible to rethink and re-elaborate the entire discussion around the notions of *Volk, Volkstum, Volkskunst*, etc.—central notions of this Austrian *epistémê* that concerns us here—if we are not to fall into various chronological biases and traps.

Since the Herderian revolution, belief in the existence of necessary bonds between nation, language and people had been reinforced, thematized, theorized and widely disseminated in the German linguistic and cultural area. This belief enabled an intrinsic link to form between national[ist] and linguistic demands. The logic of this thinking puts the *Volk* at the centre of reasoning—its definition, its reality and, above all, its claim to legitimacy. Folkist thought rested on a three-pronged construction with three terms interlinked in complex configurations: nation (*Volk*, people), language (literature, culture) and territory (country, fatherland). These three inseparable, key notions, a kind of basic outline of the Herderian model, formed the background to all theoretical or aesthetic debates. The elements of this 'system' of folkist thought were linked together by two main types of connection:

1 There was a necessary dependence between the nation and the set of people speaking the same language (who thereby became the 'people' in the sense of 'nation'—hence, the importance of linguistic nationalism).

2 There was another form of dependence, also necessary, between the writers and the 'people', whose responsibility it was to be the bearers, guides and supporters of what the writers wrote. This belief assumed that the writer (bard, poet, spokesman, etc.) had no autonomous existence, that he did not draw on his own authority to produce pure, abstract, aesthetic forms which were beautiful in and for themselves (the strict definition of autonomy) but that he was the emanation of a people who explained, justified and produced his existence. The writer reciprocated by transforming his literary production and was then defined as 'popular'.

This conception, crucial for understanding all the national movements throughout Central and Eastern Europe in the latter half of the nineteenth century, was formed in opposition to aestheticism and to any conception of autonomous art—regarded then as intellectualist, abstract, cold and unjustifiable. It also provided a new way of accumulating specific capital, accessible to the most recent nations or to those groups claiming both a political and a literary existence.[173] This is precisely what explains its omnipresence in a wide range of diverse circles within the Germanic area. According to this conception, literature had some value or interest only if it was written by and for the people (if it was *volkstümlich*).

This is how, since Herder, 'popular' forms, including stories from what is called 'folklore', folk tales, legends, proverbs and songs—in short, all those forms linked to the existence of a people or the claim that a people exists—came to be regarded as noble. This is why writers, rather than producing aesthetic forms underwritten by themselves alone, became spokespersons for the people, in the service of the people, justified and legitimated in their existence by the people of which they were emanations. Literary production itself acquired a totally different definition when it became 'popular': it was supposed to be addressed to the people; it showed what the people was like; in short, it made the people the be-all and end-all of literary production.[174] This very powerful and widespread ideology, which was highly convincing to all the protagonists involved, and essential for understanding most aesthetic issues (though 'aesthetics' was actually disavowed by it), permeated almost the entirety of the literary space. It was present in all the debates as an indisputably self-evident fact and was found within all groups, even those who opposed it and had to defend themselves against it. It established itself in many different forms at every stage; it contradictorily served the interests of the many different camps in play and was, above all, omnipresent as a category of thought, even when those concerned were involved in combatting it.

Obviously, however, it did not exist everywhere to the same degree, in the same form, with the same persuasive force, to the same end or to serve the same interests. All the various degrees, choices, nuances and combinations that might be derived from these basic data were present in what was going on at Prague (and beyond, of course). This is why it would be wrong to confuse the racial and racist ideology of the nationalist Germans, adherents of the most radical *völkisch* ideology, and the convictions of the Czech nationalists, for example, who argued for the celebration of poetry as an embodiment of the life and existence of a people. At Prague, folkist ideology could be found within the three coexisting spaces: among the Germans, though as a minority presence; among the Czechs; and among the Jews. Where the latter were concerned, it was particularly noticeable in the thinking of Buber.[175]

I believe that we may, in fact, treat this literary or literary-political representation as a collective fact (which has a great many consequences at the level of aesthetics, form, genre, etc.). In other words, it was a type of multiple, variable, omnipresent thought, changeable in its form and expression, undergoing important variations between one author and another, subject to diverse and, at times, contradictory, formulations, appropriable—and, indeed, appropriated—by actors who had nothing in common or who might even occupy opposing positions within the space, and dependent on antagonistic political beliefs or convictions, etc.

I stress this point because it seems to me that this configuration of ideas is too often treated as a dangerous, suspect, ambiguous 'ideology' and as a form of 'political thought' which we should not so much attempt to understand—in its logic and the issues involved—as merely condemn. I intend to confine myself here to what was unfolding in the German cultural space between 1890 and Kafka's death in 1924. But, when it comes to setting out these matters, the very great difficulty lies in the subsequent history of these notions. Many are the historians and social anthropologists who have demonstrated the direct genealogical connection between the major notions of *Volkskunde* (as it developed through the nineteenth century) and Nazi ideological configurations.[176] It seems to me, however, that it would be glaringly anachronistic to present the writers and intellectuals of the Viennese and Prague spaces at the turn of the century as systematically 'suspect' from the outset, as soon as they used this type of vocabulary or displayed political convictions associated with the 'people'. We cannot attempt to understand forms of thought and politico-literary convictions by applying to them categories and judgements that are the product of events which took place only subsequently.[177]

It seems to me, on the contrary, that the historian's work is not only to try to understand before condemning but also to treat this 'system of thought' not as an articulated, deductive set of ideas but as a form of belief with respect to very diverse objects, as a type of arbitrary connection between conceptions and objects we have forgotten or, rather, can no longer understand without undertaking archaeological work. The adoption of this folk-centrism among the writers of the empire who identified with one of the 'national' causes had many consequences. It was not a matter of mere vocabulary or a declaration of belonging to a people; Herderian thought was, as we have said, a novel logic of artistic thinking and production. It changed the categories by which literature had up to that point been evaluated and, consequently, gave rise to a genuine revolution in literary hierarchies, convictions and values. Term for term, it stood out against the aesthetic values and beliefs—that is to say, to some extent, the autonomous values and beliefs—which had dominated the literary space of German culture.

This is why I propose to transform to some extent the vocabulary associated with these groups and forms of thinking and reserve the term *völkisch* for the most radical groups, movements and manifestos which articulated a race-based thinking. By contrast, where the other movements, writings, debates, commitments and questioning around the notion of the people are concerned—and the literature from which that notion might be said to emanate—and in order to try to neutralize the anachronistic, a posteriori reading prompted, as it seems to me, by the term *völkisch*, I shall use neologisms here such as 'folk-centrism', 'folkism' or 'Herderian thought'.

Three Competing Spaces

Because of its direct dependence on Vienna, many of the characteristics of the Austrian capital apply with even greater force to Prague, even though they are seldom mentioned or highlighted. The intellectuals of Prague inherited the conflicts, struggles and issues which were those of the intellectual world of the Habsburg Empire in that period. Moreover, because it was highly dependent on the political structures, literary Prague, like political Prague, was very much a dominated place. One of the objective signs of the persistent peripheral character of Prague was the high number of German-language intellectuals and writers who left the city quite early on to pursue their careers elsewhere in the German-speaking area. Among these were Rilke (the first in 1896), Werfel, who left Prague in 1912 to become a reader with the publisher Kurt Wolff in Leipzig,[178] Ernst Weiss and Willy Haas.[179] Exile, as I have tried to show elsewhere, is one of the major characteristics of dominated spaces,[180] a consequence of the absence of publishing structures and also of effective mechanisms of literary consecration. For a writer, it is practically impossible to obtain national recognition (to say nothing of the international level) from a provincial position.

However, this hierarchy imposed by the political structure of the empire in no way made the Prague literary space, in either its German or Czech parts, a submissive environment, restricted to fearfully and timidly aping the Viennese. There are many indications that the artists of Prague, probably on account of just this domination, constituted themselves in opposition to, and in rivalry with, their Viennese counterparts. These competitive relations confirm the structure of the relations of force within this space. The Prague Expressionist movement was presented by its members, for example, as one of the great features of the city, 'elevating' it (that is to say, raising 'its' writers) to the level of Vienna. In his preface to one of the first anthologies of Germanophone Prague literature published in 1919, Oskar Werner writes: 'Over the last twenty years, Prague has assumed an increasingly significant place among the cities in which German literature is produced. The discussion now is of the relations between Berlin, Munich and Prague, while the city of Vienna stands apart, ignored and without influence.'[181]

This strategy on the part of the Praguers of 'standing apart' from Vienna may explain why, far from aspiring to recognition from Viennese sources of literary consecration—whose weakness we have already seen—Praguers turned immediately towards Berlin or Leipzig: for them the aim was to beat the Viennese at their own game and assert their equality. This twofold domination, characteristic of many polycentric areas, enabled writers to opt for one domination against another, to escape political domination by deliberately opting for another cultural capital and playing the one off against the other.[182] We shall see that the Czech part of the literary field will apply exactly the same strategy on another terrain and will turn towards Paris.

Moreover, outside the empire, Prague belonged to a network of German cities within which there circulated newspapers, literary and political magazines, literary criticism, plays, films, books, political discussions and polemics, actors, political personalities, lecturers, etc. The majority of debates and innovations, aesthetic or political, were the products of a clearly transnational space which was itself hierarchical, with Berlin occupying the topmost place.[183] Thus, when Edward Timms, the biographer of Karl Kraus, analyses the range of the readership of Kraus' *Die Fackel* and its sphere of influence, he shows that in the 1910s, quite apart from the city of Vienna, that journal was read simultaneously in Berlin, Munich, Innsbruck and also Prague.[184] It was internationalized from the outset.

In artistic and literary terms, Prague was, then, both a provincial city and an international capital open to a very wide space. The literary, political or critical journals, such as *Die Aktion, Der Brenner, Die Fackel, Der Kunstwart, Das Literarische Echo, Die Neue Rundschau, Der Sturm, Die weissen Blätter* and *Der Jude* came in from all the metropoles of the German area and were both an integral part of the discussions and stances of the various groups and individuals, and potential places where anyone might be published.[185] Similarly, Brod was in contact with publishers in various German metropolitan centres: first, between 1906 and 1912, with Axel Juncker in Berlin, then with the avant-garde publishers Ernst Rowohlt and Kurt Wolff in Leipzig.[186]

The Prague literary space was made up of three sub-universes: the German, the Czech and the Jewish. Though apparently close, they were in fact far removed from one another. Having neither the same volume of literary capital nor the same relative seniority, they each occupied different positions in the global literary space. To decipher both the structure of this threefold space and what was at stake within each of the sub-universes between which these writers operated and moved (in every direction), it is necessary, I believe, to examine the structure of the international literary space. This is, in fact, organized around the opposition between old literary spaces endowed with national resources of their own and more recent spaces (relatively) poorly endowed with capital and largely dependent on national-political authorities and struggles. At Prague, the German sub-universe was characterized by all the usual features of the 'richest' fields (a high degree of autonomy, prestige, relative seniority, resources of its own, international recognition, ex-translations,[187] etc.); the Czech space was, by contrast, dependent on nationalist demands and its products were, for the most part, subject to the same pressure (though Czech writers had been claiming autonomy since the late nineteenth century). Among other problems, the resources were (relatively) scarce and only just being inventoried, the writers had little or no international recognition and the work of producing in-translations—aimed at augmenting the volume of national literary capital—was one of their main tasks.

Then, with the appearance of the Zionist movement, came a split in the German space and specificity was claimed for the literary and artistic production of Jewish writers. The birth of a new—Jewish —literary space was then to be seen. This new emergent, transnational space drew part of the German-language space within the ambit of political struggle.

The Czech Space

From the beginning of the nineteenth century, Joseph II's reforms and, most importantly, the influence of the Enlightenment had enabled Czech intellectuals to instigate resistance to Germanization and German cultural omnipotence and the first elements of an independent national literature to emerge. Of all the literary subspaces existing side by side in Prague, the Czech sub-universe was no doubt the most highly folk-centric, the most deeply marked and structured by Herderian thought. The short chapter in Herder's *Outlines of a Philosophy of the History of Man* (1784–85) devoted to the Slavs played a central role in its development. In that chapter Herder described the history of the Slavic peoples as a history of peaceful groups of traders who were constant victims of Teutonic 'oppression'.[188] This is why, from the century's beginning, the campaign for Czech nationhood was based on Herder's writings and philosophy of history. The Slovak poet Ján Kollár (1793–1852) studied at Jena with the German philosopher himself. At the heart of his only work *Slávy dcera* (1824; 'The Daughter of Sláva'),[189] a vast sonnet cycle conceived on the pattern of German Romanticism, he addressed himself to Herder: 'You were the first to defend and praise the Slavs, that people whose destiny has not been easy.'[190] Above all, in his *Outlines of a Philosophy*, the German thinker called on the Slavs to rise up against the Germans:

> Ye deeply bowed, but once so industrious and happy peoples, you will at last awake refreshed from your long listless slumber and, having shaken off the chains of slavery, will enjoy again the possession of your fair lands from the Adriatic to the Carpathian Mountains, from the Don to the Moldau, and celebrate on them your ancient festivals in peace together with the prosperity of your industry and trade.[191]

Such are the terms and prophetic tone of this text which must, I believe, be kept in mind if we are fully to grasp the actual emancipatory role this form of thought played for the people of the region. This brief chapter closed with a call to assemble the ethnological capital of the Slavs that might enable them to free themselves from German domination.

As in other nascent literary spaces, the initial accumulation of literary capital began, then, with the assembling of linguistic resources: a grammar and a Czech–German dictionary (by Josef Jungmann).[192] Work was then done to celebrate the literary past while ennobling translations were also undertaken. Lastly, František Palacký commenced publication of his monumental *Dějiny národu českého v Čechách a na Moravě* (A History of the Czech Nation in Bohemia and Moravia) in 1848. All the succeeding generations of writers throughout the nineteenth century were almost exclusively concerned with playing their part in the elaboration of their national literature. The object of their struggles was not so much their claim to literary specificity (as something self-evident, this was not in question) as the provenance of the models to which they appealed. After a first period of exclusive dependence on German literary tools and models (encouraged, obviously, by political domination and, most particularly, by bilingualism), the Czechs sought to liberate themselves from the sway of those models. Thus, throughout the century, though particularly from the 1850s onwards, there was a struggle between two major tendencies. The first of these, following the strict Herderian course, sought to develop forms and texts by drawing on popular traditions and, generally, on Slavic *Volkskunde* which was elaborated in parallel with the effort of literary construction and accumulation. The writers who chose this path often turned also towards Russian ethnologico-literary capital which was itself being constituted at this time.[193]

The other literary trend was the so-called 'cosmopolitan' one and it sought out other models and other support in Europe. English Romanticism, particularly the writings of Byron—a kind of 'offset' Romanticism that enabled writers to subscribe to Romanticism's ideas without being accused of subordinating themselves to a German aesthetic—played an important role. At the turn of the century, as national demands were becoming more radical, the opening towards European literature on the part of the cosmopolitans became more explicit. In fact, employing a specific strategy whose effectiveness I have demonstrated in many other contexts elsewhere,[194] some spaces that were heavily dominated politically made a rapprochement with one or more spaces that were neutral politically and, specifically, powerful. The interest of Czech artists and writers in the European avant-gardes may be analysed along these lines—they were in contact with the Italian Futurists, the Russian Constructivists, the Scandinavian dramatists and French Cubism.[195] It is initially in the area of painting and, more widely, in the artistic world that this active 'influence' can best be seen. Mainly because of the absence of linguistic issues, painters were more open to European artistic creation. Cubism arrived in Prague through the efforts of the art critic and collector Vincenc Kramár who, very early on, purchased works by Georges Braque and Pablo Picasso, and African art. In the years up to 1914, Cubism became a modernizing watchword that permeated the literary, musical, artistic and theatrical spaces and, by dint of this tropism, the Czech artistic space turned in very large measure towards Paris and the French avant-garde.

This dependency continued after the war, that is to say, after Czechoslovakia gained independence. From 1918 onwards, the collective discovery of Guillaume Apollinaire through his short story 'Le passant de Prague' ('The Wandering Jew')[196] and, above all, the 1909 poem 'Zone'[197] stunned the literary world. Karel Čapek, one of the great figures of the Czech literary milieu, discovered the poem, translated it and published it in a magazine in February 1919 in a version illustrated with woodcuts made by his brother Josef. It was an enormous success, achieving literary cult status.[198] The great theorist of Prague Poetism Karel Teige would call Apollinaire 'the symbol of the "new spirit" for whose victory we still struggle in his shadow. For us Apollinaire is the axis of all modern poetry, his work the milestone from which we date the new era of modern creation.'[199]

Tell Guillaume Apollinaire
That in the agates of Saint Vitus
You saw a spider's web
It covers our little eternity
Over which his breath passed at century's dawning.

This is what Vitězslav Nezval wrote to Philippe Soupault in 1927 in a dialogue published in the Czech magazine ReD.[200] 'Little eternity' is a magnificent metaphor for this decisive affirmation of a literary existence that had previously been overshadowed or denied and which proclaims its eternal character only in the unpretentious modality of the 'little'.

The German Space and the Birth of the Jewish Space

At the dominant pole of the Germanophone literary space were to be found the official poets of Germanic academicism, who referred to themselves as the established representatives of German culture. These writers had a natural home in an association named Concordia, founded in 1871. Hugo Salus (1866–1929) and Friedrich Adler (1857–1938)—whom Max Brod dubbed the 'popes of literature'—were its driving figures. Before the immense success of Werfel and the bolt from the blue of his *Weltfreund* [The Philanthropist] in 1912,[201] they were the most highly reputed poets on the Prague literary scene. In aesthetic terms, their work ranged from neo-classicism to neo-Romanticism.[202] Of Salus and Adler, Kafka's friend Emil Utitz wrote: 'Both acknowledged Jews, they nevertheless felt themselves to be the authentic representatives of all Germans in Bohemia, as well as further afield. Those Germans wanted little to do with Prague in any case, and least of all with its Jews. But Salus and Adler were liberals of the old stamp.'[203]

Brod even calls Salus 'extremely assimilationist' and says that he later broke with him for that reason.[204] However, in his formative years he venerated him as a master and dubbed him the prince of Prague poets;[205] he set three of his poems to music, including 'Stilles Glück' [Quiet Happiness], just as Arnold Schönberg had produced a setting of his 'Einfältiges Lied' [Simple Song] some years earlier in 1901. Kafka was not attracted to him at any point. Each year in Germany, Salus brought out a volume of neo-Romantic verse in a melancholy vein. 'Hugo Salus' prestige,' writes Brod, 'was at its zenith [. . .] Rarely had anyone been more popular than he in German Prague.'[206] Adler, nine years older than Salus, was his implacable rival. To make fun of them, Brod and his fellows referred to their group as the 'Discordia'.

The perpetuation of neo-Romantic poetics through the publication of timeless, elegant, outdated verses, genuflecting to the cult of beauty and the contemplation of a world at peace, and the refusal to see the political violence of Prague abut into the 'pure' world of poetry provide one of the clues that might enable us to situate German-speaking Prague in the Germanic area on the one hand, and in global literary space on the other. Despite the apparent serenity of these poets hymning a peaceable eternity, it seems to be the case that, from 1905/1910 onwards, they were now mimicking an autonomy that no longer genuinely reflected their position: they were situated in a declining space. From the 1890s onwards, these poets could be seen as being forced to submit to the modality of the 'as if', which is a very strong marker of the decline from their previous position. Danès writes: 'In the same way as the Germans strove to live an isolated life in Prague, to act as if the Czechs did not exist and Prague was still a German city, Salus and his colleagues wrote as if they were living in Germany and were not surrounded by an alien people that had developed its own culture.'[207]

To this small group of writers we may add other positions that are relatively close within the same space but much more aggressive —the positions of the German nationalists. Let us mention, among these, August Sauer, who played a central role in the dissemination of German poetry and culture at Prague. He was the editor of *Deutsche Arbeit*, founded in 1901, an important journal for the nationalist faction. Conceived as an instrument of struggle against Czechization, the magazine claimed to afford insight into the 'cultural achievements of the Germans in Bohemia'.[208] Rilke's first poems appeared there, as later did the earliest writings of Brod. Sauer was a professor of German literature, one of the most influential and renowned teachers at Charles University in Prague. He dominated German literary criticism and history there and became rector of the university in 1907. His journal and the scholarly societies that gravitated around the university milieu came to cultivate an increasingly aggressive nationalism.[209] They laid claim to, and used, literature as a weapon in the struggle for the preservation of the status quo—that is to say, for perpetuating the self-evidence of the supposed intrinsic 'superiority' of German cultural forms.[210]

Despite, as Brod attests, their deep respect for this type of poetry, the groups of German-speaking poets and writers of the following generations formed themselves *in opposition* to these poets. In this tiny milieu, it is difficult to trace precise boundaries between the various circles and schools that formed. The little groupings were porous; the places they met were interchangeable or coincided; many members of different groups knew one another and the publications in which they appeared sometimes brought them together artificially.[211] Brod speaks of two 'half-generations'. First, the so-called Jung-Prag group (which Brod also calls the 'middle generation')[212] in which we can include Paul Leppin (1878–1945), Viktor Hadwiger, Oskar Wiener, Gustav Meyrink (1868–1932) and René Rilke before he left Prague.[213] 'Late Romantics, surrendering,' in Brod's words, 'to the charm of the

alchemists' Prague', they practised a *fin de siècle* decadence that was a
mixture of 'modernism and superannuated pathos'.[214] Brod was close
to this movement in his youth and tells in his memoirs how, at the
point when he met Kafka, he venerated that particular aesthetic: 'I
was enthusiastic about Meyrink [. . .] at this time, in a proper "storm
and stress" mood, I welcomed everything that was out-of-the-way,
unbridled, shameless, cynical, extreme, over-caustic [. . .] I quoted
him "purple passages" by heart. One from Meyrink's "Purple Death"
compared butterflies to great opened-out books of magic.'[215]

Then, from 1904 onwards, there appeared the group (made up
of younger poets than those mentioned above) known as the Prague
Circle, the main members of which were Willy Haas, Franz Werfel
(1890–1945), Max Brod, Paul Kornfeld (1889–1941),[216] the brothers
Hans and Franz Janowitz, Norbert Eisler, Oskar Baum, Rudolf Fuchs,
Otto Pick, Felix Weltsch, Ernst Polak, Johannes Urzidil and Ludwig
Winder.[217] Leopold Kreitner, who was born in 1892 and met Kafka
briefly, broke this circle of writers down into two further groups: 'At
this time, there were in fact two groups of young German writers in
Prague. On the one hand, there was the group represented by Max
Brod and his circle of friends, who were born around 1880 and, on
the other, that of Franz Werfel and his associates: Willy Haas, Paul
Kornfeld, Franz Janowitz and Otto Pick.'[218] It is this second group
that would come to be termed Expressionist.[219]

The—uncertain, fluctuating—aesthetic of this particular group
(or of these groups in general) was less central than the personality
of Brod who brought young poets together around him and (classi-
cally) built himself an identity in opposition to the preceding generation. Brod asserts:

> I was no neo-Romantic. I strove for that simple, quiet
> goodness, without pathos [*unpathetischen*] which I did not
> find in any of the Prague poets of the generation that had
> preceded me—not even in Leppin [. . .] Against the neo-
> Romantics and their effusive [*überschwenglichen*] prose, my
> friends and I ranged clarity of language and the simple,
> inexhaustibly deep matters of life and thought.[220]

Brod encouraged his friends to publish, struck up and maintained relations with publishers in the Germanic area and was a kind of one-man driving force, instigator or even literary entrepreneur. Without him, very few magazines or collective publications would have come into being in Prague. He was the intermediary through whom many young authors began to be published and known and to exist on the German literary scene.

At least during the years 1904–09, the Prague Circle had, then, an aesthetic, apolitical attitude not at all unlike that described by Schorske so far as the Jung-Wien group is concerned. It did, indeed, reduplicate, at a remove of some 15 years, a certain number of the characteristics attributed by the American historian to the 1890s group of Viennese writers. They were sons of the upper or middle bourgeoisie, in many cases Jewish; they were raised in the religion of art, theatre and literature and were apolitical and aesthetic; they met in cafes and were supported quite early on by publishers.[221] Brod may be regarded, *mutatis mutandis*, as a structural equivalent at Prague of Hermann Bahr in Vienna—both (at one generation's remove) played the same role as distributor or intercessor with publishers, literary critic, publicist, mediator and theorist for young unknown authors.[222]

Everything changed with the sudden emergence of Zionism. Some of the members of the Prague Circle (Weltsch, Baum and Brod) shifted between 1904 and 1909–10 from an aestheticism tinged with criticism of German liberalism to a commitment to Zionism—that is, to a nationalism—and, hence, a gradual transformation of their literary and existential conceptions.[223] Of his university years, Brod writes:

Initially, I went calmly with the general flow towards assimilation, which was in keeping with my entirely German upbringing. It was only much later, when I had already taken my doctorate, that [. . .] I discovered the blessings of an honest, affectionate distance (*ehrlichen Distanz-Liebe*) between Germans and Jews, the doctrines of Hugo Bergmann and Buber, Zionism and the Jewish Bar Kochba student association.[224]

These intellectuals, who were raised in the values of Germanism on the one hand, and to treat aesthetic categories as unproblematically autonomous on the other (being convinced, for example, that the poetry of Goethe or the music of Wagner were, all political considerations apart, the most important things in the world), were suddenly confronted, through Zionism, with national, ethnic and political questions for which their training had not (or had not greatly) prepared them.

It was as though, from 1909 onwards, two conceptions of literature clashed in the German-speaking camp: on the one side, an aesthetic conception, which, as in Jung-Wien or the Prague Circle, saw the writer as working on new forms, new themes, celebrating the cult of beauty in art and asserting a break between the artistic realm and the political domain,[225] and, on the other, a Herderian, folkist conception for which the only legitimate literature was that which arose from the—or from a—people. Felix Weltsch, the cousin of Robert, sums up Brod's personal itinerary magnificently when he writes: 'A highly sophisticated and versatile Jewish intellectual, he moved from an almost exclusive and deliberate preoccupation with aesthetic aspects to complete identification with the Jewish people.'[226]

These two virtually irreconcilable conceptions, which structured the whole of the literary field very deeply and intensely, were at odds with each other—at times within the same individual. In other words, this small portion of German literary space, long dominant and continuing to function on an acceptance of relative autonomy as the norm, had, from the beginning of the twentieth century onwards, only apparent dominance. From the standpoint of the symbolic struggle, the turn of the century saw a real reversal of the relation of forces, leading to a challenge to what had, until that point, been wholly beyond question: the monopoly and potency of the German cultural space. And it is in the split between the two German-speaking sub-fields that the Germano-Jewish cultural and literary debate is to be understood.

The particular case of Brod is characteristic of the itinerary of that generation of intellectuals and may perhaps help us to understand this paradoxical political-intellectual logic. His copious *oeuvre*—82 volumes published in his lifetime, not counting opera libretti and musical compositions—ranged across works on the philosophy of perception (including *Anschauung und Begriff* [Intuition and Concept], written in collaboration with Felix Weltsch in 1913), religious philosophy (his *Heidentum, Christentum, Judentum* [Paganism, Christianity, Judaism] of 1921), essay collections, plays, poetry and, of course, novels.[227] Some of his works met with great critical and popular success on publication.[228] The analysts of Brod's works have shown that it was his ambition not so much to write novels that were innovative in form or content as to develop and disseminate a philosophy of life (*his* philosophy) and explore metaphysical arguments and themes.[229] The very title of one of his texts on Kafka—*Franz Kafkas Glauben und Lehre* (1948; Franz Kafka's Faith and Teaching)[230]—attests to his conception of literature as having to provide, through a declared, articulate doctrine or world view, teaching of a philosophical (or religious) order.[231] Similarly, one of his first successful novels, *Schloß Nornepygge* (1908; Nornepygge Castle), was a vehicle for his philosophy of the age—indifferentism[232]—personified by a young aesthetic aristocrat who commits suicide precisely as a result of the dilemma of aestheticism he faces. The novel he published in 1916, *Tycho Brahe's Path to God* (*Tycho Brahes Weg zu Gott*) is, in similar vein, an illustration of the notion developed by Buber of 'realization' (*Verwirklichung*).[233] And it is this, too, which explains why his books make no narrative innovations, why they have omniscient narrators who often express themselves in the first person and relate the action as the events unfold.[234] In other words, Brod wrote his whole life long ignoring—at least in practice—all the major formal and narrative innovations that profoundly changed novel-writing over the course of the century. He also wrote many biographies or autobiographical works that were in no way innovative with regard to the tradition of these genres. In this sense, his work is more that of a moralist (*Ethiker*) than a novelist.[235]

His first great successes enabled him very early on to become the spokesperson for the group of writers of his generation at Prague and also to be regarded as one of the representatives of the Expressionist movement.[236]

However, from 1909 onwards, after hearing the lectures on Judaism Buber gave in Prague, Brod came to accept the arguments for Zionism. This was a very radical change in his life. Writing of his entry into the movement, Brod tells how, Hugo Bergmann and Oskar Epstein, my two new mentors, were very severe [. . .] Both made a sharp distinction between a purely formal nationalism that contented itself with propaganda and associative life [*Vereinsleben*] and an essential nationalism which sought to shape a new spiritual human being [*einen neuen Menschen des Geistes*] and embraced the whole being of the individual, including his most private relations, his sexuality and his psychical dispositions.[237]

As a consequence, he found himself in a highly contradictory position. On the one hand, he was still able to conceive of the literary art only as an autonomous activity, whereas he was called upon, in the name of Zionism and his loyalty to his Judaism, to break with the aesthetic (and hence supposedly German) forms of literature. Thus, for example, throughout his autobiographical text, despite his commitment to Zionism, Brod refers to some of his literary writings as 'pure art'—an expression which is for him strictly synonymous with 'uncommitted' art.

Once the Zionists asserted—and campaigned for—a discontinuity between German and Jewish spaces, the differentiation of the two bodies of literary production came on to the agenda, largely in order that Jewish authors could accumulate capital without it immediately being appropriated or embezzled by German sources of literary consecration. This is why one of the major questions raised in these debates was that of the specificity of Jewish artistic production. In the present state of the discussion (and of their linguistic competences), it was impossible for these writers to adopt another writing language than German; and this problem, linked obviously to the configuration of folkist thought, became a central one. With the Herderian scheme of thinking implying that the only way for a people to accede to a legitimate existence was to be able to exhibit the three founding elements of the theory, language was the most problematical element for them. We know that in the East battle raged between the advocates of Yiddish and the supporters of Hebrew.[238] However, in the West, the major issue in this generation revolved around being able to legitimize and rationalize the use of the German language, the only literary idiom available and the mother tongue of the Germanized Jewish writers.[239] Some, such as Julius Bab, writing in *Selbstwehr* in October 1911, asserted that a 'Jewish race' existed within the German people and that it could and should affirm its specificity within the German language.[240] Such people defined the Jews as a *Stamm* or tribe of the German people like the Swabians, Bavarians or Saxons.[241] Then an article signed by Moritz Goldstein, in *Der Kunstwart* of March 1912, triggered a massive polemic, argued that the artistic and intellectual milieus had a large number of Jews. 'We Jews,' he asserted, 'administer the intellectual property of a people that denies our entitlement and capacity to do so.'[242] He was arguing that there was a disavowal, both among Germans and Jews, of this undeniable cultural activity of the Jews and that the latter were kept in a subordinate position by the Germans. On this basis, Goldstein contended that there was a radical difference between the two groups and hence rejected the idea that an alliance was possible between Germanness and Jewishness. He proposed that Jews should wrest themselves from 'the unrequited love that binds them to Germany, and [. . .] drive out the beloved from their hearts rather than pine endlessly for her'.[243]

There is every reason to believe that this debate was so animated and passionate only because this was a crucial and burning question for people deeply attached to the German language and German literary traditions. For the most part, they had identified deeply, since earliest childhood, with Germanic culture, as is shown in the portrait Schorske draws of the young Herzl, who 'personified the assimilationist ideal'. A Jewish liberal like his parents, Herzl was hyper-identified with Germanic values and literature[244] and a great admirer of the German aristocracy.[245] In his autobiography, Brod goes back over this crucial point:

> For me personally, as a result of the inner revolution I was then undergoing [. . .] I came to define my relations with

the German ethnic group as a cultural attachment (*Kulturverbundenheit*), for I had been raised most intimately and decidedly in the German culture; this no longer meant, however, that I might hope to merge with the German people and become as one with it.[246]

If we do not take account of this simultaneous dual membership (experienced as a painful inner conflict) of two literary spaces not endowed with the same degree of literary independence and generating contradictory imperatives, then we are condemned, as critics, to opt for just one of the two parties in presence and cleave to that camp.[247] Yet, only the constitutive gap between the two, the multiple, insoluble contradictions engendered by their links with two partially opposed worlds, the aesthetic German and the politicized Jew, can enable us to understand the work and action of these intellectuals. Each one, as their various positions developed, moved closer to, or further from, these two inescapable poles, and it was around them that the discussions, debates and the evaluations of each person's work revolved. In terms of strategy, their collective situation was as follows: if we accept that 'Germanness' on the one hand and 'Jewishness' on the other were the two poles around which German Jewish intellectuals defined and positioned themselves, then they were closer to or further from each of those poles in the manner of a cursor moving along a line stretched between two points. Those who asserted a radical difference between Germans and Jews—that is to say, that the one was irreducibly alien to the other—proclaimed, in the absence of any alternative, that they used the German language in a way that was, to say the least, defiant. By contrast, those who expressed great nostalgia for German culture and values strove to find a 'middle way' so as not to break with a culture they still admired. As we shall see, Brod and Kafka stood at opposite ends of this fictional line.

Brod has clearly expressed how, for his generation, this was not a mere abstract, dispassionate salon debate but involved a heart-rending, painful experience for those had just committed themselves to Zionism. He writes in his autobiography of the divorce from German culture that was asked of him:

A painful parting which thoroughly upset me. Especially when a discussion in *Der Kunstwart* had clarified my mind. There could be friendship with the German people, gratitude for the spiritual values created by the German genius [. . .] I loved Germanism and the German character while, at the same time, being aware of a certain distance separating me from it [. . .] My criticism had to be of a more restrained, more serious kind. This difficult attitude, which I maintained coherently so far as I was able, brought me a great many enmities, in both the German and Jewish camps.[248]

Being required to make choices engaging the whole of their intellectual and literary lives and to make a profession of faith, they had to break with the forms of greatness with which they had previously felt able to identify as fervent Germans, raised to worship the 'German spirit'. They were suddenly called upon to cut themselves off from all this as Jews and experienced the break not as a mere formality but, rather, as a 'painful parting'. What was involved was an irrevocable separation, setting them at an infinite distance from a language and a culture of which they had, until that point, considered themselves the legitimate 'owners'. And it was precisely because of this inner wrench that Brod, unlike the most radical of the politically committed Jews, took a stand on a midway position which some years later, at the risk of shocking the most committed Zionists, he would term *Distanz-Liebe* (literally, 'distance love').[249]

NOTES

1   Pavel Eisner, 'Erotische Symbiose', *Prager Presse* (23 March 1930). Cited in Bernard Michel, *Prague, Belle Époque* (Paris: Aubier, 2008), p. 26.

2   Pavel Eisner, *Franz Kafka and Prague* (Lowry Nelson and Rene Wellek trans) (New York: Arts, 1950).

3   For a critique of the idea of the insularity of Prague, see Hartmut Binder, 'Entlarvung einer Chimäre: die deutsche Sprachinsel Prag' in Maurice Godé, Jacques Le Rider and Françoise Mayer (eds), *Allemands, Juifs et Tchèques à Prague—Deutsche, Juden und Tschechen in*

Prag, 1890–1924, Actes du colloque international de Montpellier, 8–10 décembre 1994 (Montpellier: Bibliothèque d'études germaniques et centre-européennes, 1996), pp. 183–209. See also Richard T. Gray, *Constructive Destruction: Kafka's Aphorisms; Literary Tradition and Literary Transformation* (Tübingen: Max Niemeyer, 1987), pp. 121–4.

4 See, for example, Michel, *Prague, Belle Époque*.

5 See Ernst Fischer, *Von Grillparzer zu Kafka* (Vienna: Die Buchgemeinde, 1962), pp. 289–94.

6 See Gray, *Constructive Destruction*, pp. 121–5.

7 Spector, *Prague Territories*, p. 7.

8 See Michel, *Prague, Belle Époque*, p. 18.

9 Ibid., p. 55.

10 Xavier Galmiche, 'Multiculturalité et uniculturalisme: Le paradoxe de Prague' in Delphine Bechtel (ed.), *Les Villes multiculturelles en Europe centrale* (Paris: Belin, 2008), pp. 41–63; here, p. 47.

11 Michel, *Prague, Belle Époque*, pp. 56–62.

12 Viktor Karády, 'De la métropole académique à l'université de province. Note sur la place de Vienne dans le marché international des études supérieures (1880–1938)', *Revue germanique internationale* 1 (1994): 221–42; here, pp. 223–4.

13 Michel, *Prague, Belle Époque*, pp. 79–80.

14 Michael Pollak, *Vienne 1900: Une identité blessée* (Paris: Gallimard 'Folio', 1992[1984]), p. 9.

15 Christophe Charle, 'Les théâtres et leurs publics: Paris, Berlin et Vienne, 1860–1914' in Christophe Charle and Daniel Roche (eds), *Capitales culturelles, capitales symboliques: Paris et les expériences européennes* (Paris: Publications de la Sorbonne, 2002), pp. 403–20; here, pp. 417–18. See also Lionel Richard, *D'une apocalypse à l'autre: Sur l'Allemagne et ses production intellectuelles de Guillaume II aux années 20* (Paris: UGE, collection 10/18, 1976).

16 Cited in Pollak, *Vienne 1900*, p. 41.

17 See Frédéric Barbier, 'Construction d'une capitale: Leipzig et la librairie allemande, 1750–1914' in Charle and Roche, *Capitales culturelles, capitales symboliques*, pp. 335–57.

18 See Murray G. Hall, 'L'édition littéraire à Vienne entre 1900 et 1914' in François Latraverse and Walter Moser (eds), *Vienne au tournant du*

siècle (Paris: Albin Michel, 1988), pp. 359–72; here, p. 359; Pollak, *Vienne 1900*, p. 68; Jacques Le Rider, 'Prague à l'époque de Kafka' in Jacques Le Rider and Fridrun Rinner (eds), *Les Littératures de langue allemande en Europe centrale des Lumières à nos jours* (Paris: PUF, 1998), pp. 93–114; here, p. 107. Without a publisher and without circuits of distribution—that is to say, without the internal organization of a national circulation of literature—but, most importantly, equipped with too little prestige to be able to establish a writer's reputation on their own, the agencies whereby reputations could be made (publishers, but also critics) were themselves dependent on the German centres, and there is much testimony to the effect that it was almost impossible for Austrian writers to publish their books in Austria (see Hall, 'L'édition littéraire à Vienne entre 1900 et 1914', p. 360). However, this can only be a partial explanation of the phenomenon.

19 Franz Kafka, '24 October 1912' in *Letters to Felice* (Erich Heller and Jürgen Born eds, James Stern and Elisabeth Duckworth trans) (New York: Schocken Books, 1988), p. 11.

20 Kafka, '4 February 1913' in *Letters to Felice*, p. 182.

21 See Pascale Casanova, 'La guerre de l'ancienneté' in Pascale Casanova (ed.), *Des littératures combatives: L'internationale des nationailismes littéraires* (Paris: Raisons d'agir, 2011), pp. 11–31.

22 Max Brod, *Streitbares Leben: Autobiographie 1884–1968* (Frankfurt: Insel Verlag, 1979), p. 9.

23 See William M. Johnston, *The Austrian Mind* (Berkeley, Los Angeles and London: University of California Press, 1983), p. 269; see also Gary B. Cohen, *The Politics of Ethnic Survival, 1861–1914* (Princeton: Princeton University Press, 1981), pp. 233–73.

24 See Jean-Pierre Danès, 'Situation de la littérature allemande à l'époque de Kafka' in *Prague, Kafka, Chweïk: études* (Versailles: Marie-Dosée Danès, 1989), pp. 39–62; here, p. 48; see also Hillel J. Kieval, *The Making of Czech Jewry: National Conflict and Jewish Society, 1870–1918* (Oxford and New York: Oxford University Press, 1988), pp. 14–15.

25 Jiří Pešek, 'Les étudiants des pays tchèques entre Prague et Vienne: comparaison du rôle des trois universités en 1884' in Godé, Le Rider and Mayer, *Allemands, Juifs et Tchèques à Prague*, pp. 101–13; here, pp. 102–03.

26 Ibid., pp. 104–05.

27 Egon Erwin Kisch, *Gesammelte Werke in Einzelausgaben*, Vol. 7: *Marktplatz des Sensationen* (Berlin and Weimar: Aufbau, 1974), p. 82.

28 Cohen, *The Politics of Ethnic Survival*, p. 123.

29 Kisch, *Marktplatz des Sensationen*, p. 86. For his part, Galmiche speaks of a 'progressive nationalization of spaces' in 'Multiculturalité et uniculturalisme: Le paradoxe de Prague', p. 49.

30 Spector, *Prague Territories*, p. 15.

31 'Czech was spoken, but for a few exceptions, mainly among the poorest strata of the population' (Brod, *Streitbares Leben*, p. 122).

32 Hans Kohn, *Living in a World Revolution: My Encounters with History* (New York: Simon and Schuster, 1970), pp. 9–10. Kohn (1891–1971) was a disciple of Martin Buber and a great propagator of his ideas.

33 On the inequality of development between the Czech group and the Germans, see Binder, *Kafka-Handbuch*, VOL. I, pp. 59–73.

34 René [Rainer Maria] Rilke, *Two Stories of Prague* (Angela Esterhammer trans.) (Hanover: University Press of New England, 1994), p. 16 and p. 21 [originally published in 1899 as *Zwei Prager Geschichten* (Stuttgart: Verlag von Adolf Bonz & Co)].

35 [*Ein tschechisches Dienstmädchen* was published by Axel Juncker in Berlin.] See Maurice Godé, 'Un "petit roman" qui a fait du bruit: Une servante tchèque de Max Brod' (1909) in Godé, Le Rider and Mayer, *Allemands, Juifs et Tchèques à Prague*, pp. 225–40.

36 [Gustav Meyrink, *The Golem* (Mike Mitchell trans.) (Cambridgeshire: Dedalus European Classics, 2011); originally published by Kurt Wolff, Leipzig.]

37 Arne Novák, 'Prazsky román?', *Venkov* 12(86) (April 1917). Cited in Spector, *Prague Territories*, p. 177.

38 István Bibó, *Misère des petits États d'Europe de l'Est* (G. Kassai trans.) (Paris: Albin Michel, 1993), p. 137.

39 Spector even asserts that the language question occupied the entire political arena (*Prague Territories*, pp. 68–92).

40 Le Rider, 'Prague à l'époque de Kafka' in Le Rider and Rinner, *Les Littératures de langue*, p. 93.

41 Johnston, *The Austrian Mind*, pp. 94–5. See also Kieval, *The Making of Czech Jewry*, pp. 72–4.

42 See Christoph Stölzl, *Kafkas böses Böhmen: Zur Sozialgeschichte eines Prager Juden* (Munich: Text + Kritik, 1975), pp. 61–3.

43 Eric Hobsbawm, *Nations and Nationalism since 1780: Programme, Myth and Reality* (Cambridge: Cambridge University Press, 1992), pp. 55–6.

44 Cited in Wagenbach, *Franz Kafka*, p. 85. [I have stayed close to the French translation of this text used by Casanova. Trans.]

45 This shame associated with his provincial origins is doubtless one of the reasons for the insatiable efforts throughout his life on the part of Rilke, the son of an Austrian civil servant, to create for himself other, nobler national and family origins and his oft-restated certainty that he descended from a very old Carinthian noble family.

46 The *Bohemia* and the *Prager Tagblatt* and, after the war, the *Prager Presse* (see Danès, 'Situation de la littérature' in *Prague, Kafka, Chweïk*, p. 52).

47 Kisch, *Marktplatz des Sensationen*, p. 85. Cited in Wagenbach, *Franz Kafka*, p. 71.

48 Johnston, *The Austrian Mind*. See the figures given by Danès, who adjusts these slightly upwards ('Situation de la littérature' in *Prague, Kafka, Chweïk*, pp. 45–6). According to Cohen, German-speakers represented 13.7 per cent of the population in 1860, 7 per cent in 1910 and 4.6 per cent in 1921 (*The Politics of Ethnic Survival*, p. 57).

49 Wagenbach, *Franz Kafka*, p. 71.

50 By contrast, in 1900 we find 78 per cent of workers and 8 per cent of clerical workers among the Czechs. To take another indicator of social difference, in 1900 there were domestic servants in 64.2 per cent of German households whereas, at the same period, only 20 per cent of Czech households reported domestic staff in their service, only 2.5 per cent of them having two or more such personnel, as against 17 per cent of German households. (Ján Havránek, 'Structure sociale des Allemands, des Tchèques, des chrétiens et des Juifs à Prague, à la lumière des statistiques des années 1890–1930' [A. Madelain trans.] in Godé, Le Rider and Mayer, *Allemands, Juifs et Tchèques à Prague*, pp. 71–81; here, pp. 71–8.

51 Le Rider, 'Prague à l'époque de Kafka' in Le Rider and Rinner, *Les Littératures de langue*, p. 98.

52 Felix Weltsch was the scion of a great family of textile merchants who were virtually assimilated into the aristocracy. Michel notes that Kafka did not suggest using the familiar 'du'-form with him until 1912, so great was the social distance between them (*Prague, Belle Époque*, p. 44, p. 67).

53 Franz Werfel was doubtless one of the richest of this group of intellectuals, His father, a millionnaire, had a glove factory at Prague with subsidiaries throughout Europe (ibid., p. 66).

54 In the early 1880s in Vienna, Georg von Schönerer (1842–1921) was the leader of the German ultra-nationalist movement, a movement that made anti-Semitism one of the dominant themes of Austrian politics and discourse at the turn of the century. See Carl E. Schorske, 'Politics in a New Key: An Austrian Trio' in *Fin-de-siècle Vienna: Politics and Culture* (New York: Vintage Books, 1981), pp. 116–80. See also Johnston, *The Austrian Mind*, pp. 61–3.

55 See Binder, *Kafka-Handbuch*, VOL. I, pp. 70–3. See also Michel, *Prague, Belle Époque*, pp. 35–8.

56 See Viktor Karády, 'Les juifs et les États-nations dans l'Europe contemporaine (XVIIIe–XIXe siècle), *Actes de la recherche en sciences sociales* 118 (June 1997): 28–54.

57 I use here the typology proposed by Albert Memmi who distinguishes between 'Jewishness', 'Jewry' and 'Judaism'. Jewishness is the fact and the manner of being Jewish; Jewry is the entire group of Jewish persons; Judaism is the set of Jewish doctrines and institutions. See Memmi, *Portrait d'un juif* (Paris: Gallimard, 1962), p. 28.

58 Cohen, *The Politics of Ethnic Survival*, p. 77.

59 On this point, see Gaëlle Vassogne, 'Max Brod et Prague: Identité et médiation' (doctoral thesis, University of Paris-III-Sorbonne nouvelle, 2004), p. 25.

60 Ibid., pp. 76–7.

61 Max Brod, *Der Prager Kreis* (Frankfurt: Suhrkamp, 1993), p. 40.

62 On the assimilation of the Jews into the Czech group, see Kieval, *The Making of Czech Jewry*, especially pp. 64–92.

63 Ibid., p. 17.

64 Cf. Helena Krejková, 'L'assimilation tchéco-juive' in Godé, Le Rider and Mayer, *Allemands, Juifs et Tchèques à Prague*, pp. 323–30. Michel

points out that the Czech-Jewish National Union (Národní Jednota Českožidovská) which was formed in 1893 called for the abolition of German-language Jewish schools, for Jewish children to attend Czech schools and for the introduction of the Czech language into the Jewish liturgy (Michel, *Prague Belle Époque*, p. 43).

65 Danès, 'Situation de la littérature' in *Prague, Kafka, Chweïk*, pp. 46–7.

66 See Kieval, *The Making of Czech Jewry*, pp. 45–57.

67 Theodor Herzl, *Die entschwundenen Zeiten* (Vienna, 1897). Cited in Wagenbach, *Franz Kafka*, p. 75.

68 Willy Haas, *Die Literarische Welt* (Munich: Paul List, 1958), p. 10. Cited in Cohen, *The Politics of Ethnic Survival*, p. 175.

69 The senior reaches of the public services, particularly the army and the diplomatic corps, remained closed to the Jewish bourgeoisie. See Pollak, *Vienne 1900*, p. 54. See also Binder, *Kafka-Handbuch*, VOL. I, p. 63.

70 Kieval, *The Making of Czech Jewry*, p. 66.

71 On these trials and their impact on Kafka, see Bruce, *Kafka and Cultural Zionism*, pp. 18–20.

72 Leopold Hilsner, a Jewish cobbler in a little provincial town, was accused of murdering a seamstress at Polna in south-eastern Bohemia. See Claude David, *Franz Kafka* (Paris: Fayard, 1989), pp. 15–16.

73 See Stölzl, *Kafkas böses Böhmen*, p. 112.

74 [Theodor Herzl, *The Jewish State* (Sylvie d'Avigdor trans.) (New York: Dover, 1988); originally published as *Der Judenstaat* (Leipzig and Vienna: M. Breitenstein).] The French translation was entitled *L'État des Juifs*. On this translation, see Alain Dieckhoff, *L'Invention d'une nation: Israël et la modernité politique* (Paris: Gallimard, 1993), pp. 58–9.

75 Brod, *Streitbares Leben*, p. 50.

76 Ibid., p. 227.

77 Ibid., p. 50.

78 Max Brod was born in 1884 and Kafka in 1883.

79 The publication date of Brod's first book, *Tod den Toten* (Stuttgart: Juncker, 1906).

80 Gershom Scholem, 'With Gershom Scholem: An Interview' in *On Jews and Judaism in Crisis: Selected Essays* (Werner Dannhauser ed. and trans.) (New York: Schocken Books, 1976), pp. 1–48; here, p. 1.

81 Gershom Scholem, *Walter Benjamin: The Story of a Friendship* (Harry Zohn trans.) (Philadelphia: The Jewish Publication Society of America, 1981), p. 10.

82 Gershom Scholem, *From Berlin to Jerusalem: Memories of My Youth* (Harry Zohn trans.) (Philadelphia: Paul Dry Books, 2012), p. 3.

83 Scholem, 'With Gershom Scholem: An Interview' in *On Jews and Judaism*, p. 5.

84 Ibid., p. 1.

85 Ibid.

86 Another witness to, and analyst of, the particularly complex, tense situation in which the German-speaking Jews of Austria found themselves in those years was the Viennese novelist and playwright Arthur Schnitzler. His 1908 novel *Der Weg ins Freie* (Berlin: Fischer), available as *The Road to the Open* (Horace Samuel trans.) (Evanston: Northwestern University Press, 1991[1913]), may in fact be regarded as a kind of testimony to the times, enumerating the possible options. In it he describes the situation of the Viennese Jews as a series of positions adopted that can only be understood in relation to one another. Moreover, Scholem remembers the book being read in this way at the time of its publication. It was, he writes, 'probably the first novel by an important prose writer in which the crisis of German-speaking Jewry in its Viennese manifestation was described and presented for general discussion with astonishing objectivity and incisiveness' (Scholem, *From Berlin to Jerusalem*, p. 45).

87 Gershom Scholem, 'A propos de la psychologie sociale des juifs d'Allemagne entre 1900 et 1930' in *De la Création du Monde jusqu' à Varsovie* (Maurice-Ruben Hayoun trans.) (Paris: Le Cerf, 1990), pp. 223–44; here, p. 237.

88 Scholem, *From Berlin to Jerusalem*, p. 40.

89 Ibid., p. 42.

90 Ibid., p. 21.

91 We should note here, among the liberal Jews, the difference between those who lived in Prague and the Berliners or, more broadly,

between the Austrian and the German Jews. The latter were German nationalists while the former were not attached to any precise national identity. On the contrary, they took the view that this supranational attitude could protect them from anti-Semitism and nationalist excesses. This non-national identity enabled them, as it were, to stand out against the nationalism of the 'German nationals'. It is, indeed, for this reason that it has been said that the Jews were the only true Austrians. See Marsha L. Rozenblit, 'The Jews of Austria and Germany: A Comparative Perspective' in Robert S. Wistrich (ed.), *Austrians and Jews in the Twentieth Century: From Franz Kafka to Waldheim* (New York: St Martin's Press, 1992), pp. 1–18. See also Edward Timms, *Karl Kraus: Apocalyptic Satirist; The Post-War Crisis and the Rise of the Swastika* (New Haven and London: Yale University Press, 2005), pp. 33–8; Dieckhoff, *L'Invention d'une nation*, p. 59; Viktor Karády, 'Les Juifs, l'État et la société dans la monarchie bicéphale' in Miklós Molnár and André Reszler (eds), *Le Génie de l' Autriche-Hongrie* (Paris: PUF, 1989), pp. 83–98.

92 See Spector, 'New Orientations: Judaism, Desire and the Gaze Eastward' in *Prague Territories*, pp. 160–94.

93 Scholem, 'With Gershom Scholem: An Interview' in *On Jews and Judaism*, p. 7.

94 Gershom Scholem, *Fidélité et Utopie* (Marguerite Delmotte and Bernard Dupuy trans) (Paris: Calmann-Lévy, 1978), p. 161.

95 See Bruce, *Kafka and Cultural Zionism*, pp. 57–61.

96 Ibid., p. 163.

97 Brod, *Streitbares Leben*, p. 233.

98 On this point, see Bruce, *Kafka and Cultural Zionism*, pp. 29–33.

99 Spector, *Prague Territories*, p. 163.

100 Ibid., p. 164.

101 The arguments of Simon Dubnow had a considerable influence of the tenor of the debates among the various groups. He was regarded as the greatest historian of the age and was one of the first Jewish intellectuals who, rejecting the spiritualist, theological conception of history, introduced a positivistic, scientific approach to the history of the Jews, claiming intellectual kinship with August Comte, John Stuart Mill or Hippolyte Taine. His *Nationalism and History: Essays on*

Old and New Judaism, published in Russian from 1897 onwards and, in the case of the first two, in German in 1907, played a very great role among the Jewish intellectuals of Eastern Europe. He created the ephemeral Jewish People's Party, the *Volkspartei* in 1906, a party that gained the allegiance of many non-Marxist intellectuals (including S. An-sky, who was both a writer and an ethnologist). The main strength of the so-called Folkists lay at Warsaw and Vilnius.

102 Simon Dubnow, 'On National Education' in *Nationalism and History: Essays on Old and New Judaism* (Philadelphia, PA: The Jewish Publication Society of America 1958), pp. 143–54; here, p. 149, p. 152.

103 The very title of Jacobowski's book [*Werther der Jude* (Berlin-Wien: E. Pierson's, 1905)] sums up all the contradictions besetting these intellectuals born into assimilated or assimilating families and brought up to respect German cultural values.

104 Ibid., pp. 146–9.

105 Scholem, 'A propos de la psychologie' in *De la Création*, p. 238.

106 Ibid., p. 236.

107 Ibid., pp. 223–43.

108 Danès, 'Situation de la littérature' in *Prague, Kafka, Chweïk*, p. 45.

109 Scholem, 'A propos de la psychologie' in *De la Création*, p. 224.

110 Ibid., p. 225.

111 Ibid., p. 227.

112 Ibid., p. 229.

113 See note 122.

114 Carl E. Schorske, 'Generational Tension and Cultural Change: Reflections on the Case of Vienna' in *Thinking with History: Explorations in the Passage to Modernism* (Princeton University Press, 1998), pp. 141–56; here, p. 147.

115 See Schorske, 'Politics and the Psyche: Schnitzler and Hofmannsthal' and 'Gustav Klimt: Painting and the Crisis of the Liberal Ego' in *Fin-de-siècle Vienna*, pp. 3–23 and pp. 208–78.

116 Ibid., p. 7.

117 Though this is doubtless true also in other centres of the Germanic area.

118 See Spector, *Prague Territories*, p. 103.

119 See Chapter 3, pp. 191–3.

120 Scholem, 'With Gershom Scholem: An Interview' in *On Jews and Judaism*, p. 2.

121 Spector stresses the fact that this so-called generational conflict was not reducible to family conflicts and the family sphere. In his view, it has to be regarded as a conflict between the liberal fathers and 'post-liberal' sons (*Prague Territories*, pp. 104–08). See also Hans Dieter Zimmermann, 'Kafkas Prag und die kleine Literaturen' in von Jagow and Jahrhaus, *Kafka Handbuch: Leben-Werk-Wirkung*, pp. 165–80; p. 168.

122 Scholem, *From Berlin to Jerusalem*, pp. 83–4.

123 Scholem, 'A propos de la psychologie' in *De la Création*, p. 243.

124 See Michel, *Prague, Belle Époque*, p. 113.

125 Franz Kafka, 'Letter to His Father' in *Dearest Father: Stories and Other Writings* (Ernst Kaiser and Eithne Wilkins trans) (New York: Schocken Books, 1954), pp. 138–97.

126 Scholem, 'A propos de la psychologie' in *De la Création*, p. 243.

127 Kieval, *The Making of Czech Jewry*, pp. 93–123.

128 Cf. Pamela Vermes, *Martin Buber* (London: Halban, 1988), p. 6; Théodore Dreyfus, *Martin Buber* (Paris: Le Cerf, 1981), p. 23.

129 Ahad Ha'am was the pseudonym of Asher Ginsberg (1856–1927). A Hebrew-speaking Russian essayist and leader of the Hibbat Zion movement, he enjoyed great fame in these years, and was regarded as the spokesman for Cultural Zionism. On this point, see Scholem, *From Berlin to Jerusalem*, pp. 36–59. The ideas of Ahad Ha'am had currency in Prague circles thanks to Nathan Birnbaum, Bertold Feiwel, Martin Buber and Hugo Bergmann. Cf. Kieval, *The Making of Czech Jewry*, p. 101.

130 Bruce, *Kafka and Cultural Zionism*, pp. 21–2.

131 Brod, *Streitbares Leben*, pp. 54–5.

132 Ibid., pp. 228–31.

133 Ibid., p. 239.

134 Spector, *Prague Territories*, p. 140. See also Kieval, *The Making of Czech Jewry*, pp. 116–19.

135 See Casanova, 'La guerre de l'ancienneté' in Casanova, *Des littératures combatives*, pp. 11–31. Being reserved for the most ancient nations,

until Herder, the accumulation of specific resources was achieved only on the basis of ancientness. The accumulation of capital on the basis of the notion of the 'people' enabled the youngest, most recent entities to build up resources that would have been regarded as inaccessible before Herder's innovation.

136 Dreyfus, *Martin Buber*, p. 29.

137 Brod published 13 articles in *Der Jude* during the first five years of its publication (see Vassogne, *Max Brod et Prague*, p. 199).

138 Scholem, *From Berlin to Jerusalem*, p. 72.

139 [Martin Buber, *The Tales of Rabbi Nachman* (Maurice Friedman trans.) (New York: Humanity Books, 2011; originally published in 1906 as *Die Geschichten des Rabbi Nachman* (Frankfurt: Rütten und Loenin); Martin Buber, *The Legend of the Baal-Shem* (Maurice Friedman trans.) (Princeton: Princeton University Press, 1995); originally published in 1908 as *Die Legende des Baalschem* (Frankfurt: Rütten und Loenin).]

140 Cf. Steven E. Aschheim, 'Chapter 6: From Rationalism to Myth: Martin Buber and the Reception of Hasidism' in *Brothers and Strangers: The East European Jew in German and German Jewish Consciousness 1800–1923* (Madison: University of Wisconsin Press, 1982), pp. 121–38.

141 Gershom Scholem, *The Messianic Idea in Judaism and Other Ideas on Jewish Sprituality* (Michael A. Meyer and Hillel Halkin trans) (New York: Schocken Books, 1971), pp. 228–31.

142 Aschheim, 'Chapter 5: Identity and Culture: The Ostjude as Counter-Myth' in *Brothers and Strangers*, pp. 100–20; here, pp. 108–09.

143 Cf. Arnold Zweig, 'Uber jüdische Legenden', *Mitteilungen des Verbandes der jüdischen Jugendvereine Deutschlands* (1914), pp. 16–17. Cited in Aschheim, 'Chapter 6: From Rationalism to Myth' in *Brothers and Strangers*, p. 128.

144 Buber was first invited in January 1909. Then, given the unexpected success of this first appearance, he was reinvited by the Zionists of Prague on two occasions—in April and December 1910. He published these lectures in 1911 as *Drei Reden über das Judentum* (Frankfurt: Rütten and Loenin, 1911).

145 The first lecture, on 'Judaism and the Jews' was immensely successful with the public. Cf. Binder, *Kafka-Handbuch*, VOL. I, pp.

373–4. In the announcement in *Selbstwehr* for the second lecture, to be delivered in April 1910, Buber was described as the 'new Theodor Herzl' (Bruce, *Kafka and Cultural Zionism*, p. 27).

146 Legend has it that he was a charismatic character possessing magical powers who was very popular among the Jewish populations of Eastern Europe. Cf. Martin Buber, *Tales of the Hasidim: The Early Masters* (Olga Marx trans.) (London: Thames and Hudson, 1956).

147 Walter Laqueur, *A History of Zionism* (New York: Schocken Books, 2003), p. 62.

148 On this point, see Michael Löwy, *Rédemption et Utopie* (Paris: PUF, 1988), p. 67.

149 Dieckhoff, *L'Invention d'une nation*, p. 71.

150 Laqueur, *A History of Zionism*, p. 57.

151 Ibid, p. 8.

152 Ibid, p. 11.

153 In the last decade of the nineteenth century, figures show that 10 per cent of German students and 23 per cent of Viennese students were Jewish, whereas Jews represented only 1 per cent of the overall population, according to Ismar Elbogen and Eleonore Sterling, *Die Geschichte der Juden in Deutschland* (Frankfurt: Athenäum, 1988), p. 251.

154 Cf. Laqueur, *A History of Zionism*, pp. 26–7.

155 Aschheim, 'Chapter 1: German Jewry and the Making of the Ostjude 1800–1880' in *Brothers and Strangers*, pp. 3–31; here, p. 3.

156 Ibid., pp. 6–14.

157 The life story of Jiří Langer was related by his brother Frantisek Langer in his foreword to Jiří's collection of Hasidic tales, published in Czech in 1937 (cited in Aschheim, 'Chapter 5: Identity and Culture' in *Brothers and Strangers*, pp. 112–13).

158 Ibid., pp. 80–3.

159 Ibid., pp. 83–6.

160 Ibid, pp. 87–90.

161 Scholem, *From Berlin to Jerusalem*, pp. 43–4.

162 Kafka, 'Letter to His Father' in *Dearest Father*, pp. 146–7.

163 Hugo Bergmann, *Tagebücher und Briefe*, pp. 9–10.

164 Cf. Aschheim, 'Chapter 6: From Rationalism to Myth' in *Brothers and Strangers*.

165 Cf. Delphine Bechtel, *La Renaissance culturelle juive: Europe centrale et orientale, 1897–1930: langue, littérature et construction nationale* (Paris: Belin, 2002), pp. 160–3.

166 Henri Minczeles, *Histoire générale du Bund: Un mouvement révolutionnaire juif* (Paris: Austral, 1995), p. 294.

167 Kafka, '5 November 1915', *Diaries*, p. 351.

168 Jirí Kudela, 'Die Emigration galizischer und osteuropäischer Juden nach Böhmen und Prag zwischen 1914–1916/17' in M. P. Beukers and J. J. Cahen (eds), *The Problem of Jewish Immigration and Jewish Identity* (Amsterdam: University Library of Amsterdam, 'Studia Rosenthaliana', 1989), pp. 119–34.

169 Cf. Bruce, *Kafka and Cultural Zionism*, p. 118. See also Max Brod, 'Brief an eine Schülerin nach Galizien', *Der Jude* 2 (May 1916), p. 124. Cited in Spector, *Prague Territories*, p. 187.

170 See, in particular, Niels Bokhove, '"The Entrance to the More Important": Kafka's Personal Zionism' in Mark H. Gelber (ed.), *Kafka, Zionism and Beyond* (Tübingen: Max Niemeyer, 2004), pp. 23–58; see especially pp. 35–46. On this community centre, see the testimony of Scholem in *From Berlin to Jerusalem*, pp. 60–82.

171 Taylor, 'To Follow a Rule . . .' in Calhoun, LiPuma and Postone, *Bourdieu*, p. 47.

172 Michel Foucault, *The Order of Things: An Archaeology of the Human Sciences* (Alan Sheridan trans.) (London: Tavistock Publications, 1986), p. *xxi*.

173 Cf. Casanova, 'La guerre de l'ancienneté' in Casanova, *Des littératures combatives*, pp. 13–21.

174 On this, cf. Casanova, *The World Republic of Letters*, pp. 75–81.

175 See, for example, this extract from Buber's *Der Jude und sein Judentum*: 'It is upon these three elements that constitute his experience—fatherland, language and customs [*Heimat, Sprache und Sitte*]—that is constructed the individual's sense of belonging to a community which is more than the primary, given community that is, the family and the chosen community made up of friends. He feels he belongs to those who share these constant elements with him on which experience is

based, and he feels this entity, at this stage, to be his people' (cited in Vassogne, *Max Brod et Prague*, p. 138). The importance of folkist ideology in the thinking of Buber himself and among the Buberians has been studied, in particular, by George L. Mosse, 'The Influence of the *Völkisch* Idea on German Jewry' in *Germans and Jews: The Right, the Left and the Search for a 'Third Force' in Pre-Nazi Germany* (New York: Howard Fertig, 1970), pp. 77–115. See also Abraham Shapira, 'Buber's Attachment to Herder and German 'völkism'', *Studies in Zionism* 14(1) (1993): 1–30.

176 'If there is a science in which National Socialism must be understood not as intruding from outside [nicht als *Einbruch von aussen*], but as an inner consequence, then that science is Volkskunde.' Hermann Bausinger, *Volkskunde: von der Altertumsforschung zur Kulturanalyse* (Tübingen: Tübinger Vereinigung für Volkskunde, 1987), p. 63.

177 It was not until 1937 that Max Hildebert Boehm imposed the four notions of *Blut, Boden, Volkstum und Volksordnung* [blood, soil, national essence, popular order]. Ibid., p. 107.

178 Cf. Le Rider, 'Prague à l'époque de Kafka' in Le Rider and Rinner, *Les Littératures de langue*, p. 107.

179 Richard, *D'une apocalypse à l'autre*, p. 66.

180 Cf. Casanova, *The Word Republic of Letters*, pp. 205–09.

181 Oskar Wiener, *Deutsche Dichter aus Prag: Ein Sammelbuch* (Vienna and Leipzig: Strache, 1919), pp. 6–7. Cited in Vassogne, *Max Brod et Prague*, p. 52.

182 Cf. Casanova, *The World Republic of Letters*, pp. 116–19.

183 Cf. Richard, *D'une apocalypse à l'autre*, pp. 16–64.

184 Timms, *Karl Kraus*, pp. 199–201.

185 Cf. Richard, *D'une apocalypse à l'autre*, pp. 39–50.

186 Joachim Unseld, *Franz Kafka: Ein Schriftstellerleben; Die Geschichte seiner Veröffentlichungen* (Frankfurt: Fischer Taschenbuch, 1984), pp. 39–49.

187 'Ex-translations' and 'in-translations' are neologisms I used in *The World Republic of Letters* (see pp. 133–7 and pp. 235–8).

188 Johann Gottfried Herder, *Outlines of a Philosophy of the History of Man* (T. O. Churchill trans.) (London: J. Johnson, 1808).

189 [Available in English as Ján Kollár, 'The Daughter of Slava' in Paul Selver (ed. and trans.), *An Anthology of Czechoslovak Literature* (London: Paul Kegan, Trench, Trubner and Co., 1929), pp. 42–6.]

190 Karol Rosenbaum, 'Herder und die slowakische nationale Wiedergeburt' in Gerhard Ziegengeist, Helmut Grasshof, Ulf Lehmann, (eds), *Zur Herder-Rezeption in Ost- und Südeuropa* (Berlin: Akademie-Verlag, 1978), pp. 92–106; here, p. 102.

191 Cited in Frederick M. Barnard, *Herder on Nationality, Humanity and History* (Montreal: McGill-Queen's University Press, 2003), p. 14.

192 The dictionary was published in five volumes between 1834 and 1839. Cf. Hana Voisine-Jechova, *Histoire de la littérature tchèque* (Paris: Fayard, 2001), especially pp. 259–323.

193 The Czechs saw the Russians as a very closely related people, all the more so as Russia was, at that time, the only Slavic country to enjoy political independence (ibid., pp. 285–6). The famous *Czech National Songs* (1822–27) of František Čelakovský (1799–1852), followed by his *Echoes of Russian Songs* (1829) and *Echoes of Czech Songs* (1839), are evidence of this.

194 Casanova, *The World Republic of Letters*, pp. 122–5.

195 Cf. Patrizia Runfola, *Prague au temps de Kafka* (Paris: La Différence, 2002), pp. 249–65.

196 Guillaume Apollinaire, 'The Wandering Jew' (1902) in *The Wandering Jew: And Other Stories* (Rémy Inglis Hall trans.) (London: Rupert Hart-Davis, 1967), pp. 3–16; originally published as 'Le passant de Prague' (1902) in *L'Hérésiarque et Cie* (Paris: Stock, Delamain et Boutelleau, 1910).

197 'Zone' was placed first in Apollinaire's 1913 anthology *Alcools: Poèmes (1898–1913)* (Paris: Mercure de France).

198 Angelo Maria Ripellino, *Magic Prague* (David Newton Marinelli trans.) (London: Picador, 1995), pp. 254–63.

199 Karel Teige, 'Guillaume Apollinaire a jeho doba' in *Svet stavby a básne: studie z dvacátých let* (Prague: Ceskoslovenský spisovatel, 1966), pp. 371–404; Angelo Maria Ripellino, *Magic Prague*, p. 261.

200 See Runfola, *Prague au temps de Kafka*, p. 265.

201 [Franz Werfel, *Der Weltfreund* (Berlin: Axel Juncker, 1911)]. Danès, 'Situation de la littérature' in *Prague, Kafka, Chweïk*, p. 55.

202 Spector, *Prague Territories*, p. 14.

203 Emil Utitz, *Egon Erwin Kisch: Der klassische Journalist* (Berlin, 1956), p. 31. Cited in Spector, *Prague Territories*, p. 39.

204 Brod, *Streitbares Leben*, p. 164.

205 Danès, 'Situation de la littérature' in *Prague, Kafka, Chweïk*, p. 55.

206 Brod, *Streitbares Leben*, p. 142.

207 Danès, 'Situation de la littérature' in *Prague, Kafka, Chweïk*.

208 Wagenbach, *Franz Kafka*, p. 100. Godé adds that 'for this population on the defensive', the magazine had 'crucial importance as a mirror to its identity' ('Un "petit roman" qui a fait du bruit' in Godé, Le Rider and Mayer, *Allemands, Juifs et Tchèques à Prague*, pp. 225–40).

209 Cf. Danès, 'Situation de la littérature' in *Prague, Kafka, Chweïk*, p. 50.

210 Cf. Gilbert Ravy, 'Les années de jeunesse à Prague de Fritz Mauthner' in Godé, Le Rider and Mayer, *Allemands, Juifs et Tchèques à Prague*, pp. 439–49; here, pp. 442–3. See also Spector, *Prague Territories*, p. 39.

211 On all these groups and circles, see Hartmut Binder (ed.), *Prager Profile: Vergessene Autoren im Schatten Kafkas* (Berlin: Mann, 1991), p. 164ff.

212 Brod, *Streitbares Leben*, p. 149. See also Runfola, *Prague au temps de Kafka*, pp. 87ff.

213 Ibid., p. 10. Painter, engraver and writer Alfred Kubin (1877–1959) also moved in circles close to this small core of writers. Rilke was not to change his first name until 1897.

214 Wagenbach, *Franz Kafka*. The words of Brod are cited in *Streitbares Leben*, p. 10.

215 Brod, *Franz Kafka*, p. 44. Meyrink's original is cited in Wagenbach, *Franz Kafka*, p. 82: 'Schillernde, handgrosse Falter, seltsam gezeichnet, sassen mit offenen Flügeln wie aufgeschlagene Zauberbücher auf stillen Blumen.' This group created the mythology of a dark, malefic Prague with tortuous little alleys inhabited by ghostlike figures. This literary mythology enjoyed great popularity throughout the German area. See also Brod, *Streitbares Leben*, p. 161.

216 Cf. Runfola, *Prague au temps de Kafka*, pp. 83–102.

217 Ibid. See also Le Rider, 'Prague à l'époque de Kafka' in Le Rider and Rinner, *Les Littératures de langue*, pp. 110–11.

218 See Michel, *Prague, Belle Époque*, p. 150; and Spector, *Prague Territories*, pp. 93–134.

219 Cf. Binder, *Kafka-Handbuch*, VOL. I, pp. 93–4. Michel confirms this (*Prague, Belle Époque*, p. 154).

220 Brod, *Streitbares Leben*, pp. 148–9.

221 The members of the Prague Circle were often called the 'Arconauts' because they gathered at the Arco Café in Prague.

222 See Jean Launay, 'Introduction' in *Ce monsieur de Linz qui inventa Vienne* (Paris: Anatolia/Éditions du Rocher, 2006), pp. 7–17. On Brod's activity as a literary 'entrepreneur' at Prague, see Vassogne, *Max Brod et Prague*, pp. 388–424.

223 I use the term 'aestheticism' in its widest sense here—as a conception of the literary art as 'art for art's sake,' rather than 'social' or 'committed' art—not in the restricted sense of the historical period with which it is often associated, a period in which the term aestheticism often appeared virtually synonymous with the European movement known as *fin de siècle*, Decadentism, *l'art pour l'art*, *Jugendstil*, etc. On the transition of these Jews to Zionism, see Kieval, *The Making of Czech Jewry*, pp. 138–9.

224 Brod, *Streitbares Leben*, p. 153.

225 Schorske gives several parallel definitions of Viennese aestheticism: it is a 'devotion to art'; a conviction that art is an 'essence' and 'a source of value'; 'the affirmation of art and the life of the senses' (*Fin-de-siècle Vienna*, pp. 9–10).

226 Robert Weltsch, *Max Brod and His Age* (New York: Leo Baeck Institute, Leo Baeck Memorial Lecture 13, 1970), p. 5. Cited in Spector, *Prague Territories*, p. 60.

227 [Max Brod and Felix Weltsch, *Anschauung und Begriff: Grundzüge Eines Systems Der Begriffsbildung* (Leipzig: Kurt Wolff, 1913); Max Brod, *Heidentum, Christentum, Judentum: ein Bekenntnisbuch* (Leipzig: Kurt Wolff, 1922).]

228 Evelyn Tornton Beck has provided a translation (from Yiddish to English) of an article published by Löwy in 1924 and written to honour Brod on his fiftieth birthday, which was supposed to eulogize both Brod and Kafka, who had died 10 years earlier, by relating

memories of winter 1911/12. However, no doubt flattered by the honour paid to him on this occasion, Löwy entirely forgot to name Kafka and ascribed to Brod conversations, gifts and invitations clearly attributable to Kafka. This silence around Kafka provides a clear measure of the social importance, real influence and great renown of Brod at the time. Kafka, for his part, was practically unknown and, by this point, long dead (Yitzchak Löwy, 'Tsvey Prager Dikhter' [Two Prague Writers], *Literarisher Bleter* 34 (1934), pp. 557–8. Cited and translated in Evelyn Tornton Beck, *Kafka and the Yiddish Theater: Its Impact on His Work* (Madison, Milwaukee and London: The University of Wisconsin Press, 1971), pp. 220–3.

229 Cf. Vassogne, *Max Brod et Prague.*

230 [Max Brod, *Franz Kafkas Glauben und Lehre* (Winterthur: Mondial, 1948).]

231 Cf. Ritchie Robertson, 'The Creative Dialogue between Brod and Kafka' in Gelber, *Kafka, Zionism and Beyond*, pp. 283–96; here, p. 289.

232 Ibid., p. 285; Max Brod, *Schloß Nornepygge: Der Roman Des Indifferenten* (Berlin: Axel Juncker, 1908).

233 [Max Brod, *Tycho Brahe's Path to God* (Felix Warren Crosse trans.) (Evanston: Northwestern University Press, 2007).]

234 Ibid.

235 Margarita Pazi, 'Max Brod—von *Schloß Nornepygge* zu *Galilei in Gefangenschaft*' in Günter Grimm and Hans-Peter Bayerdörfer (eds), *Zeichen Hiobs: Jüdische Schriftsteller und Deutsche Literatur im 20; Jahrhundert* (Königstein: Athenäum, 1985), pp. 193–212.

236 Vassogne, *Max Brod et Prague*, pp. 85ff.

237 Brod, *Streitbares Leben*, p. 54.

238 See Chapter 2, pp. 126–8.

239 Cf. Andreas Kilcher, 'Sprachendiskurse im jüdischen Prag um 1900' in Marek Nekula, Ingrid Fleischmann, Albrecht Greule (eds), *Franz Kafka im sprachnationalen Kontext seiner Zeit: Sprache und nationale Identität in öffentlichen Institutionen der böhmischen Länder* (Cologne, Weimar and Vienna: Böhlau, 2007), pp. 61–86.

240 Cf. Bechtel, *La Renaissance culturelle juive*, pp. 145–6.

241 *Stamm*, a key concept of *Volkskunde*, is one of the 'four capital *Ss*' that are supposed to define the *Volk*, alongside *Sprache* (language), *Sitte* (custom) and *Siedelung* (settlement). The *Stamm* is one of the units making up the nation. The German tribes (the Swabians, the Bavarians, the Palatines, etc.) form an autonomous part of the nation. The tribe is a sort of community of communities and, as an homogeneous ensemble, it is situated half way between community and nation. Cf. Bausinger, *Volkskunde*, pp. 98–9.

242 Moritz Goldstein, *Begriff und Programm einer jüdischen National-literatur* (Berlin: Jüdischer Verlag, 1912). Cited in Bechtel, *La Renaissance culturelle juive*, pp. 146–7.

243 Ibid., p. 147. See also Sander L. Gilman, *Jewish Self-Hatred, Antisemitism and the Hidden Language of the Jews* (Baltimore and London: The Johns Hopkins University Press, 1986), especially 'Chapter 5: The Science of Race', pp. 209–308; here, pp. 224–5.

244 See Schorske, 'Politics in a New Key' in *Fin-de-siècle Vienna*, pp. 146–75.

245 Enzo Traverso, 'Une utopie ambiguë: notes sur l'histoire du sionisme' in *Pour une critique de la barbarie moderne: Écrits sur l'histoire des Juifs et de l'antisémitisme* (Lausanne: Page Deux, 1996), pp. 117–21.

246 Brod, *Streitbares Leben*, p. 52.

247 Bergmann also sought ways of communicating or mediating between traditional Jewish culture and German culture. Cf. Bechtel, *La Renaissance culturelle juive*, pp. 96–8 and p. 119.

248 Brod, *Streitbares Leben*, p. 52.

249 On the notion of *Distanzliebe*, see Vassogne, *Max Brod et Prague*, pp. 359–64. This notion was greatly criticized by Bergmann himself; cf. letter from Bergmann to Brod of 1934 cited in Vassogne, *Max Brod et Prague*, p. 362.

On the other hand, what good does it do me to learn about your visits to the theatre if I don't know everything that happened before and after, if I don't know what you wore, which day of the week it was, what the weather was like, whether you dined before or after, where you sat, in what kind of mood you were and why, and so on, as far as thought can reach.

Franz Kafka, 24 October 1912, *Letter to Felice.*

If I have spent so long on the complex configuration of the Germano-phone political universe and literary space of Prague, I have done so only to show how Kafka fits into it. He was unquestionably located within the two-tiered German-language space, which means that he was in no way, as a persistent literary mythology has it, an 'outsider' or situated in an extra-territoriality that placed him from the outset beyond reach of all historical determination.[1]

Let us begin with his political stance. Given the configuration of this over-politicized landscape, it is practically impossible to argue that Kafka was locked away in his ivory tower and exclusively preoccupied with psychological troubles, Oedipal conflicts and instances of private guilt. We could go back over each of the traits characterizing the group of young Prague Zionists, as described in the first chapter, to show that he shared most of the concerns and convictions of the Jewish intellectuals of his generation in Prague. By this I mean the centrality of the investigation into Jewish identity, the need to create a specific nationalism, the rejection of assimilationism and Germanism, the conviction that the writer's role is 'national' or 'popular', the rejection of the German language as 'foreign', etc.

Within this riven, hyper-politicized space, Kafka obviously did not escape the divide constitutive of his milieu. He too belonged simultaneously to two spaces that were very far apart in the global field and hence operated in distinct ways. Yet, the whole difficulty in situating him precisely derives from the fact that he was both dependent on that universe, sharing its assumptions and categories of thought—that he was, in short, a fully fledged protagonist within it—while being entirely marginal in his convictions, occupying a dissident, divergent position, being very solitary, difficult to fathom and, in a sense, out on a limb. Or, in any event, very far removed from the assumptions of the intellectual and political *doxa* of the Prague of his day.

GENESIS OF A POLITICAL HABITUS

'I could not but side with the staff'

To situate Kafka in the most precise possible way in relation to the transformations of the space we have just outlined, I think we must locate his personal trajectory or, in other words, take stock of the changes and developments in the stances he adopted over time. Unlike the families of Scholem and Brod, Kafka's was only relatively recently assimilated, since his father Hermann (1852–1931) came from a little village in Bohemia where he was a simple pedlar. He moved to Prague in 1881. There he grew rich in the wholesale and retail trade. Kafka, born in 1883, belonged, therefore, to a petty-bourgeois trading family and was, himself, a first-generation intellectual, unlike Brod, Scholem or the members of the Prague Circle, for example. Having said that, Hermann Kafka's lifestyle approximated to that of the middle class to which he aspired—he occupied a flat in a good neighbourhood, his daughters were raised by a governess and he had three domestic servants.[2] Kafka belonged indisputably to the turn-of-the-century group of Prague Jewish intellectuals, though he occupied an inferior social position to many of them. Logically, as one of them, and as a product of the Austrian education system, he had, like all his fellows, incorporated and internalized the questions, issues and categories of thought specific to that universe. The young Kafka, like the young Brod, was perfectly assimilated into German society. Both had been raised to respect the values and achievements—especially, literary achievements—of German culture.[3] Kafka particularly admired Goethe and, among the Austrians, Hofmannsthal. One of the indicators of this unproblematic identification and respect was his five-year-long subscription, between 1899 and 1904 (that is between the ages of 17 and 22), to *Der Kunstwart*, an artistic and literary journal that claimed to defend the 'purity of German style'. It was the organ of a staunch Germanism and proclaimed the need to advocate authenticity, the presence of the people, archaism and the national 'character'. It was very fashionable at the time and published, among others, Arno Holz, Stefan George and Hugo von Hofmannsthal. Edited by Ferdinand Avenarius (1856–1923), a nephew of Richard Wagner and an influential critic, its focus was almost exclusively on German art. On the advice of his friend Oskar Pollak (1883–1915), Kafka also read *Die neue Rundschau* which had a mainly liberal-German readership. In this same period (summer 1902), Kafka also attended the courses of the German nationalist Sauer in the history of German literature (*Germanistik* and the history of art) mentioned in the previous chapter. According to Robert, up to the point of writing 'The Judgment' ['Das Urteil', 1912] Kafka remained under the influence of that literary aestheticism.[4] We can thus see how, for him as for many others, culture was the main mode of identification with Germanism. More exactly, for some years he very happily combined a hesitant political disposition (where the political values of the empire and the assumptions of Austrian liberalism were concerned) with an unquestioning attitude to his membership of the German social group.

However, cracks appeared quite early on in his battery of assumptions and from a very early age it seems Kafka refused to reproduce his father's convictions. It was no doubt in his refusal to submit to his father's will that his first rebellion against the social order was expressed. Admittedly, he belonged to a generation of Jewish sons who were in revolt against their fathers and the conflict that set Franz against Hermann Kafka was by no means an isolated clash: as has been said, this production-line of despairing sons produced some very major rebellions against paternal authority. However, within a generation of young men deeply at odds with their fathers—I am referring to their refusal to reproduce the ways of life but also, more profoundly, the convictions and even the world views of their fathers—Kafka was no doubt one of those whose rebellion was deepest and most lasting, as is attested, in its violence, by the 'Letter to His Father'. Analysing that letter, Michael Löwy clearly shows that the 'authoritarian character' of Hermann Kafka and the domination he exerted over the whole family were at the heart of Kafka's worldview. The 'clash with paternal authority' represented a central dimension of his identity.[5] The 'Letter to His Father' is entirely a description of what he termed, in that very strong expression, paternal 'tyranny' (*Tyrannei*): 'For me you took on the enigmatic quality that all tyrants [*Tyrannen*] have whose rights are based on their person and not on reason.'[6] His revolt against paternal power is analysable in terms of an initial rebellion, a disposition acquired during childhood, amounting thereby to a habitus which enabled him in a second phase to develop a sort of coherent, logical system of thought. As though rebelliousness against an absolute, arbitrary power had assumed the form of a durable structure of his personality and had been the starting point for a long thought process which, on the basis of his personal situation, strove to decipher that situation as emblematic of a broader social functioning, as pointing to a collective, political configuration. Refusing to submit to the paternal order, Kafka encompassed in a single gesture not only what belonged to the family and individual sphere but everything that was its direct consequence at the collective level. Based on this rejection of paternal authority, he declared, in fact, at a very early stage, that he necessarily 'side[d] with the staff'.

Referring to the way Hermann Kafka (mis)treated the employees in his shop, Kafka writes:

> Or your constant mode of referring to an assistant with t.b. lungs: 'Sooner he dies the better, the mangy dog.' You called the employees 'paid enemies,' and that was what they were too, but even before they became such you seemed to me to be their 'paying enemy.' [. . .] I]t made the business insufferable to me, reminding me far too much of my relations with you: quite apart from your proprietary interest and apart from your mania for domination even as a businessman, you were so greatly superior to all those who ever

came to learn the business from you that nothing they ever did could satisfy you, and you must, as I assumed, in the same way be forever dissatisfied with me too. That was why I could not but side with the staff.[7]

This assertion is interpreted by Rose-Marie Ferenczi as a 'profession of faith', 'as the statement of the fundamental principle or the central—fixed, unwavering—point of his thinking'.[8] With these words, Kafka asserts his decision to side with the 'humiliated', as Elias Canetti has it.[9] Standing, from earliest childhood, *with* his father's employees *against* his father, rebelling against the arbitrariness and brutality of his paternal power, Kafka refuses to recognize his authority. And a few lines further on, as though to clarify the content of this declaration, he adds: 'This relationship that I came to have towards my fellow men extended beyond the limits of the business and on into the future (something similar, but not so dangerous and deep-going as in my case is for instance Ottla's taste for associating with poor people, sitting together with the maids, which annoys you so much, and the like).'[10]

It is as though, in this passage, he himself were providing the explanation for the origin of his adult commitment to 'socialist' struggles, his interest in everything to do with the popular classes and the question of their emancipation.[11] Or, to put it another way, if the revolt against the arbitrariness of paternal power was so foundational for Kafka, we may conclude that the connection between this sustained impulse of rebelliousness and his declaration about siding with the staff bore for him the name 'socialism'. To the matter of Kafka's refusal to submit to paternal authority, we may add the testimony of Max Pulver (1889–1952), a Swiss writer who lived in Munich between 1914 and 1924. He briefly met Kafka in that city, to which the Czech had come to give a reading in the winter of 1917. Pulver writes:

Franz Kafka was a rumour [*ein Gerücht*]. The rumour of a sufferer who tormented himself, a masochist who took hatred of his father to such a pitch that he was destroying himself. The rumour of a suicide who was acting, as it were, in the name of a punitive justice. His father, all fathers, the world of the fathers [*Vaterwelt*], the authorities were all brought into the charge sheet he levelled against the world—that was the legend told of him [. . .] This rumour around him had a great part to play in the fascination he exerted; there was a strange prestige in his defiance, in his desire not to reveal himself in his entirety, in his contempt for authority: the prestige of intransigence and its seductive power [*werbende Kraft*].[12]

As Wagenbach has established, Kafka expressed strong socialist convictions at a very early age, convictions he displayed by, among other things, wearing a red carnation.[13] Bergmann, who was a fellow pupil of his at the time, gives two or three other clues to the habitus of the young Kafka. In 1900, at the time of the Boer War,[14] he remembers 'very clearly the enthusiasm with which Franz talked of the Boers fighting for their freedom, and the passion with which he spoke out against the English'.[15] The impassioned tone and the commitment of Kafka, who was only 17 at this point, provide some very precious indications, it seems to me, of his political drive which bears all the marks of a passionate rage. Bergmann points out another fact that will turn out to be crucial for understanding the writer's itinerary: his atheism (which was far from being a mere passing phase). Bergmann writes:

> At that time Franz went through an atheistic or pantheistic period and really tried to lure me away from my Jewish faith. He was a very good dialectician. This was in the spring before Pesach and Seder Evening, which I loved very much on account of my parents. The wish burnt in my heart that I may at least hold out until Seder Evening! And I managed to. On this occasion Franz's dialectical skill did not defeat me.[16]

These early commitments to socialism have been treated by many biographers and Kafka specialists as fits of youthful anger that passed rapidly. Michael Löwy, however, pursues this question thoroughly and very convincingly explains that Kafka's socialist convictions cannot be regarded as a young man's passing fad. Through readings of the author and through his well-attested interest in the activities of a Czech anarchist group, Löwy shows that Kafka remained faithful to this initial commitment at least until 1912.[17] Moreover, the claim to 'side with the staff' is one of the signs that his interest in the fate of the popular classes was not a product of mere juvenile ardour: the 'Letter to His Father' was written in 1919, when Kafka was more than 35 years old.

This said, it is very difficult to reconstitute today the precise content of this word 'socialism' for the Prague author and to say what kind of political ideas and hopes were close to his heart. Despite his extensive reading in the field, to which both his diaries and his library attest,[18] he makes no very precise assertions and his political orientation remains very vague over a long period.[19] A kind of general stance seems to guide all his choices and political inclinations. The hypothesis developed by Löwy—picking up on evidence reported by Brod[20] and Wagenbach[21]—of a Kafka who was an anarchist sympa- thizer and attended meetings of Czech anarchists with great interest seems wholly convincing to me,[22] provided we make clear that he seemed generally to keep his distance and did not display anything comparable, in respect of anarchism, to the great enthusiasm he felt for Yiddish theatre in the winter of 1911–12. We must, above all, make clear, as Löwy does, without actually explaining it, that Kafka stopped attending the meetings of this group from 1912 onwards.

The World of Labour

When it comes to defining his political choices more closely, we have other clues at our disposal. The first of these arises out of the pursuit of his occupation. It is too simple to imagine Kafka as a lit- erary dreamer, far removed from social and political realities and driven by 'romantic' conceptions of the people.[23] It seems likely, from the reality of his daily work and the content of the writings associated with that activity, that he had, on the contrary, a very real- istic view of the concrete violence and injustice of the social world. His so-called 'Office Writings' [*Amtliche Schriften*'][24] are highly reveal- ing of the lucidity and pragmatism of his view of the daily realities of Czech working-class life, a view far removed from the ordinary idealism and idealization of the intellectuals, often cut off from the world of labour. He was employed from October 1907 to mid-July 1908 at Assicurazioni Generali. However, his job turned out in very short order to be unbearably tedious. To escape from that post as quickly as he could, he attended 'evening classes, a "course in workers' insurance"'.[25] He was subsequently employed by the Workers' Accident Insurance Institute for the Kingdom of Bohemia (Arbeiter-Unfall-Versicherungs-Anstalt für das Königreich Böhmen), where he rose rapidly through the ranks. He was recruited as an auxiliary in July 1908, became a clerk in 1910, vice secretary in 1913, secretary in 1920 and secretary in chief in 1922.[26]

The system of industrial-accident insurance had been set up in Austria in 1899. Under pressure from the labour movement, first Germany, then Austria, had passed relatively innovative social legislation. The aim was to define the state's responsibilities to the individual worker. In 1887, the law made industrial-accident insurance mandatory. It was to be paid for entirely through wage contributions. Two years later, sickness insurance was added. The system was managed by six regional directorates, and the Prague branch, responsible for the Kingdom of Bohemia, was by far the largest in the Austrian Empire. The institute that employed Kafka was, however, constantly in deficit. Though every firm was obliged to contribute, the insurance premiums were calculated solely on the basis of the number of employees in each firm without regard to risk factors. This explains why employers cheated by declaring a very small number of employees.

The institute was reorganized in 1908, the year Kafka joined. A decree of 1909 equipped it to seek out and, subsequently, prosecute the companies not contributing in proportion to their actual numbers of employees. This is why 1910 was the first year the institute was able to present a positive balance sheet.[27] Kafka's work consisted in classifying companies into different 'risk categories', drafting legal submissions against fraudulent firms, codifying accident cases, etc. For example, he drew up annual reports for the insurance institute and wrote newspaper articles commissioned by the institute's management. We may deduce from these occupational tasks that he came into contact with some very precise cases of company fraud (infringing the mandatory contributions principle) and had detailed knowledge of the situation of workers in various sectors of activity. 'The fate of the workers in these circumstances became especially clear to Kafka through processing accident compensations and in his work promoting accident prevention, another duty assigned to him. (The compensation payments averaged 1,000 crowns, about a year's wages.)'[28] Wagenbach cites, for example, a memo Kafka had drafted in which he recommended the use of cylindrical spindles on circular saws revolving at 3,800–4,000 rpm in order to avoid accidents, which, in very many cases, meant horrendous mutilations 'when the blade is completely unprotected'. Kafka writes:

> The hand of even the most cautious operator was bound to be drawn into the cutter space if it slipped, particularly when, as often happened, the timber was hurled back (by the cutter block) while the operator was pressing the article to be planed against the table with one hand and feeding it to the cutter spindle with the other.[29]

At the end of his career, Kafka was still handling the cases of workers injured or crippled by dangerous or inadequate machinery.[30] Moreover, Gustav Janouch cites a number of anecdotes relating to Kafka's interest in unjustly treated victims of occupational accidents. Janouch's father, who worked with Kafka, recounts how:

> Not so long ago an old labourer whose leg had been smashed by a crane on a building site [. . .] was to receive only a paltry pension from us. He brought an action against us which was not in the proper legal form. The old man would certainly have lost his case, if at the last moment a well-known Prague lawyer had not visited him and—without being paid a penny by the old man—had not expertly redrafted the labourer's case, so that he helped the poor devil to win it. The lawyer, as I learned later, had been instructed, briefed and paid by Kafka, so that, as the legal representative of the Accident Insurance Institution, he might honourably lose the case against the old labourer.[31]

This anecdote is characteristic of the way a fact that is probably historically accurate and has clear political connotations is neutralized in Janouch's album of memories by a more or less moralizing, implicitly religious commentary that dilutes it into 'fine feelings'. Despite his conviction that Kafka harboured religious inclinations, Brod himself also stresses this aspect of his friend's personality: 'His social conscience was greatly stirred when he saw workers crippled through neglect of safety precautions. "How modest these men are," he once said to me, opening his eyes wide. "They come to us and beg. Instead of storming the institute and smashing it to little pieces, they come and beg." '[32]

Claude David provides two examples of 'Office Writings' that seem to me highly revealing of Kafka's relationship with the activities that arose from his occupational functions. The first of these, entitled 'The Scope of Compulsory Insurance for the Building Trades' was included in the institute's *Annual Report for the Year 1907* (drafted and published in 1908).[33] In it, Kafka discusses the meaning of an article of the 1887 law on 'workmen's accident insurance' which was susceptible of contradictory interpretations, thus preventing the smooth functioning of insurance. That article had been modified by a decision of the Administrative Court in 1906. This is why Kafka was attempting, in the highly euphemistic terms of legal vocabulary, to contest the employers' view that they were entitled to insure their employees only very partially, drawing on interpretations of the law that were in his view quite false. In fact, the entire very long and highly detailed text revolves around the defence of the 'idea of insurance' itself. Kafka tries to demonstrate that the point was not to restrict the workers' right to insurance, as the construction company owners sought to do, but to extend it to everyone, not merely those working on the building sites but also those 'whose sole job is merely the execution of occasional repairs in construction'[34]—in other words, everyone connected in any way at all with construction work. The precision of the argumentation is impressive and Kafka uses all the resources of legal logic. Having said this, we may also note that he does not confine himself to abstract rhetoric. He refers in highly concrete fashion to the various trades associated with construction work which were entitled to insurance and, in each case, represented a special case. Speaking clearly of a 'complete turning point in jurisprudence' and, most importantly, of 'remarkable progress', he names, among others, 'watchmen, messengers and transport workers', stonemasons, well-diggers and metalworking companies, locksmiths, carpenters, plumbers, glaziers, varnishers, painters and joiners.[35] 'No one can assert, for example, that the workshop work of carpenters, the preparation of roof frames or workshop work near forge fires are not extremely dangerous in nature,' he states in support of his argument.[36] We have confirmation that the document is an instrument in the struggle against the powerful construction-company owners, as well as a defence of the institute, from the fact that, at the end of his article, Kafka makes reference to the 'propaganda' and 'open hostility' of the entrepreneurs opposed to workers' insurance. Speaking of the 'intensity of the agitation for eliminating workshop insurance',[37] Kafka's argument waxes increasingly condemnatory as he goes on. Of course, he confines himself in appearance to respect for the law, to the intentions of the legislative body and the interests of the institute. However, summing up the general sense of his explanations, he imparts a tone of conviction to his text that cannot merely be attributed to the requirements of the institute. He is, in reality, pleading the case for 'the broadest possible generalization of insurance' that would 'grant the benefit of insurance to as many segments of the working population as possible'.[38] It becomes clear at this point that, far from being the absurd faceless bureaucrat's job described by Brod, Kafka's work was actually for him a way of fuelling his anger and political convictions through indirect channels and, most importantly, a very discreet but very clear way of fighting for a social cause he believed in. In so doing, he entirely and unreservedly espoused the cause of the institute.

Another indication of his socialist convictions was the way he persistently recommended the German socialist and feminist Lily Braun's *Memoiren einer Sozialistin* (Memoirs of a Socialist) to people in his close circle.[39] He sent the two volumes to Felice in 1915, gave a copy to Brod, recommended the book to his sister Ottla in 1920 and also to Minze Eisner at the end of the same year.[40] In 1916, when she made the decision to work at the Jewish Community Centre in Berlin, he suggested once again to Felice that she read the book. From these repeated gifts and his persistence (between May and June 1920, he asked Ottla on three occasions whether she had obtained the volumes), we may deduce that he attached particular importance to the work and thought reading it could contribute to converting his friends to political positions close to his own. He wrote to Felice in September 1916, at the point when he became excited about her new job at the cultural centre which would afford her contact with young Jews from Eastern Europe:

> In any case, for the kind of work to be done there at first, even a faint breath of the spirit pervading the *Memoirs*— which I sent you some time ago and which I warmly recommend to you once again and for ever—would be sufficient [. . .] I recently gave the *Memoirs* to Max and I shall shortly be giving them to Ottla. I am giving them to all and sundry. They are, so far as I know, the encouragement that is closest to us in time and the most concrete as well as the liveliest.[41]

And in a letter to Eisner in late 1920, he wrote:

> When you have some time for reading, borrow a copy of Lily Braun's *Memoirs of a Socialist*—you can find it in any lending library. It consists of two very thick volumes but you will race right through, one cannot help it. When she was your age, I believe, she too was entirely on her own and suffered a great deal from the morality of her class (such a morality is at any rate a tissue of falsehood, but beyond it conscience obscurely begins). She struggled through like a conquering angel.[42]

Lily Braun (1865–1916) was a German socialist activist and SPD member who campaigned for feminism within the German Marxist movement. That commitment enabled her to adopt a critical position within her party and assert twofold political priorities. In effect, she proclaimed the inseparable character of two struggles: the class struggle and women's struggle. Most importantly, she wrote in an unvarnished way of the difficulties she had in gaining acceptance within her own party. It seems likely that Kafka was fascinated by a stance of this kind, as Lily Braun never ceased asserting her freedom of thought and criticism, while remaining a member of a great revolutionary movement.

Furthermore, she saw the link between the Black liberation movement in the US, the women's movement within socialism and the first stirrings of the movement for Jewish national emancipation.[43] I am not in any way suggesting that this interest may have made Kafka a precursor of feminism but, rather, as we shall see, that he became someone whose political thinking proceeded by way of comparisons, homologies or parallels.[44] This said, Braun's book also does not provide any content for Kafka's spontaneous, non-doctrinal socialism. It is, however, certain that, taking the consequences of his initial revolt against the gratuitousness and violence of his father's tyranny to their logical conclusions, he widened his range of concerns and thereby came to question the whole of the social world. At the same time, his political thinking was built on the interdependence of the various forms of domination weighing on him and all the members of his generation (the domination of women by men, of Blacks by Whites, of workers by employers, of the colonized by colonizers, etc.).

Being 'Against'

We might also attempt to define Kafka's position from a negative angle—in other words, by the choices he did not make. We know, for example, that he kept his distance from the commonest form of politicization among his friends: the reassertion of Jewish identity through a commitment to Zionism. He never joined that movement and stayed away from the events that might have brought him closer to it. Scholars diverge on whether he maintained ambivalent relations with Zionism, deliberately turned his back on it or signed up to it in the last seven or eight years of his life. Many have concluded, on the basis of the lessons in Hebrew which he took in Berlin from 1917 onwards, that he was a late recruit to it.[45] However, learning that language was not necessarily evidence of a political choice. We know that in Eastern Europe, for example, Dubnow campaigned for trilingualism. That is to say, he accepted the use and legitimacy of two Jewish languages, Hebrew and Yiddish, without excluding the language of the country in which Jews were living (Russian in his case, German or French, etc., in others). And, as Gelber reminds us, we do not find a clear affirmation of enthusiasm for the Zionist ideal in any of Kafka's autobiographical writings.[46] In other words, though he was an assimilated German Jew who, like all the intellectuals who constituted his circle and whom he frequented daily, had passed through the Austrian education system, he did not join the Zionist movement which many of them regarded at the time as their natural home or as a form of necessary emancipation. And he did not do so even in the dissident form of Cultural Zionism that was prevalent in Prague.

Let us say, rather, that his intransigence and rebellion against the (paternal) order of the world were such that the ordinary response of all his friends to their fathers' imposed assimilation—namely, collective commitment to Zionism—did not satisfy him.[47] Moreover, he defined himself as a non-Zionist. In a letter to Grete Bloch of 1914 in which—being in a hurry to tell the truth about himself so that she might act as an 'advocate' for him with Felice—he drew a convincing kind of self-portrait:

Now please disregard the recognizable characteristics that distinguish me as an individual, and take the whole as a typical case. Owing to circumstances, as well as to his own temperament, a completely anti-social man in an indifferent state of health hard to determine at the moment, excluded from every great soul-sustaining community on account of his non-Zionist (I admire Zionism and am nauseated by it), non-practising Judaism; the most precious part of his nature continually and most agonizingly upset by the enforced labour of his office—a man of this kind, certainly under the deepest inner compulsion, decides to get married—to undertake, in other words, the most social of acts. For a man of this kind, that strikes me as no mean venture.[48]

So, in a matter of the greatest importance to him, Kafka presented himself as a non-Zionist, non-practising Jew. At the conclusion of a study extremely valuable for its attention to detail, Bruce, who has closely studied Kafka's complex, critical relations with Prague Zionism, asserts that Kafka subscribed to some of the political choices of the Zionists (the fight against assimilationism, for example) but never wanted to commit himself to it as he would have disapproved of its dogmatism.[49] In her view, there is neither ambiguity here towards a—not fully accepted—Jewish identity, nor irresponsible, infantile incoherence, but a determined choice.

Furthermore, during the years of Kafka's youth, to call oneself a 'socialist' was a tacit way of not defining oneself as a Zionist. In the first years of the century in Western Europe, the Zionist option was, in fact, incompatible with a socialist commitment. Bergmann, a fellow student of Kafka's and a convinced Zionist from 1898–99 onwards, attests to this when, in writing of his youth, he recalls:

> As a reaction (*Gegenreaktion*) [to German nationalism], around 1899, came socialism and Zionism. Franz wore [. . .] the red carnation of the socialists, I became a Zionist [. . .] The subsequent fusion (*Verschmelzung*) of the two ideals in a 'socialist Zionism' was as yet unknown. When the Prague Zionists held their first official meeting on 24 April 1899 [. . .] it was Jewish socialists who broke it up.[50]

Scholem confirms this fact, reporting that, when very young, he fought violently with his brother because they had not made the same choice in politics. His brother, who was initially a Zionist, joined the (socialist) Sozialdemokratische Arbeiterjugend, 'saying that he had found a broader, more comprehensive sphere of activity [. . .] He and I came to blows because he tried to force me to listen to socialist speeches of his own devising, which he delivered to an imaginary audience.'[51]

It might be objected, of course, that Kafka could have subscribed (even in theory) to one of the socialist variants that appeared a little later, during the first decade of the new century, within Zionism itself. In 1909–10, at the point when Brod converted to Jewish nationalism, Zionism and socialism were no longer two antagonistic options and Brod himself enthusiastically voiced non-Marxist 'socialist' convictions.[52] Yet Kafka did not commit himself to this socialist Zionism either.

It is very difficult, then, to give a content to what I propose for the moment to call his combative drive. Almost all recent historical research shows a Kafka preoccupied with the social and political world around him. The hypotheses are, however, many and varied. As I have already said, Löwy ranges him among the anarchists and libertarian socialists. He excludes from the outset Kafka's relationship with Judaism being imbued with a political or critical dimension. He sees his position as lying in a 'nostalgia for the traditional community [. . .] as well as (more ambiguously) the romantic, Cultural Zionism of his Prague friends'.[53] Moreover, as a result of historical research largely carried out by Americans, cracks have begun to emerge in the last 20 years in the received image of a Kafka entrenched in his own psychological fortress. This has given rise to a wide range of legitimate discussions, though these have taken place largely beyond the borders of France. Robertson describes Kafka as indifferent for many years to Zionism but allowing himself to be convinced by the national movement after 1916, thanks to a return to Judaism that came about through Yiddish theatre and Hasidism.[54] Gilman portrays a Kafka yielding to the prejudices of the day—that is to say, reproducing in his writings the anti-Semitic clichés proclaiming the 'weakness' of the Jews. According to Gilman, Kafka's literary ambition was to be recognized wholly as a German author and to suppress any trace of his Jewishness.[55] And then there are those—many, indeed—who analyse the absence of the word Jew from his fictional texts as proof of a fundamental ambiguity or a kind of 'guilty indifference' on Kafka's part towards his Jewish identity. This ambiguity hypothesis often encourages us to see Kafka as a dreamy, irrational writer or even an irresponsible one where the most essential questions are concerned. At the end of a well-documented study, Niels Bokhove, for example, concludes that

Kafka merely ' "feigned" being a Zionist' out of a kind of social conformism. 'Basically, Kafka was egoistic and unpolitical [. . .] And, in this sense, he was also superficial, which was an aspect of his mimetic external social behaviour.'[56] From this angle, the reason most often mentioned for his refusal to become a Zionist is his constitutive loneliness, his inability to commit himself, his indifference to politics, his withdrawal into writing and into his inner world—in short, we have here a Kafka wholly devoted to his task as a writer, rejecting any form of engagement with the world. At the other extreme of the interpretative spectrum, Bernd Neumann, drawing on the methods of New Historicism, produces a portrait of Kafka as an assimilationist author. In his view, Kafka's novels tell of a desire for assimilation (into Kakania, into the values of the empire), an attempt that allegedly fails because of the gradual entrenchment of anti-Semitic political forces at Prague.[57]

However, in this international discussion, it is as though the range of choices—political, social, identitary and philosophical— which presented themselves to Kafka were reduced to four options: indifference (towards the political question and, more broadly, towards Jewishness); commitment to a libertarian socialism in isolation from the debates at Prague (which is another form of indifference); an ambiguity verging on self-hatred (assimilationist conformism is one possible version of this) or adherence (albeit qualified) to the arguments of Zionism. The thesis of an indifference to politics is the most widely shared and disseminated—in France, at any rate. It conforms to the most widespread of literary ideologies, which states that there must be a watertight separation between literature and politics. Such a divide is even required if international consecration is to be effective—a writer is not regarded as great unless he has broken with every form of political belief.

However, this conviction, which also assumes Kafka's neutrality towards, or lack of interest in, his Jewishness, is barely credible given the state of the field I have just described. The 'Jewish' question was omnipresent in publications, literary works, the press and lectures, etc. And it seems really difficult, if only because of the high degree of politicization of the literary field in which these intellectuals operated, to separate Judaism from politics. For Brod's and Kafka's generation, to speak of Judaism, emancipation and the refusal to assimilate was to speak of politics, not of mere 'spirituality'.

But neither does distancing oneself from Zionism, as Kafka did, provide evidence of a lack of interest in the politicization of the Jewish question. For the politicized Jews of the time, Zionism was just one possibility among others. In 1911–12, the range of political options open to a young Western Jew interested in the destiny of the Jewish people and in his own identity was much wider and more diverse than has been portrayed by Kafka criticism since the 1950s. We have, in particular, to include in it the socialist movements that appeared in Eastern Europe, the existence of which Kafka discovered thanks to the actor Yitzchak Löwy who had come to Prague to present some of the plays in the Yiddish theatrical repertoire.

In order to reconstitute the range of Kafka's choices and inclinations and of his anger, it seems to me we have to favour not just the zoom lens—putting Praguers alone under the microscope, as it were—but also to employ the panoramic option and the wide lens, to restore in their full (theoretical and geographical) scope the debates around Jewish nationalism. In short, to reconcile Kafka's acceptance of the need for an emancipatory struggle on the part of Jews with his reticence to fall in with Zionist slogans, we may hypothesize that he opted for another alternative that had remained unknown to him until 1911—namely, Yiddishism. The existence of that movement opens up an enormous range of new possibilities for him, both on the strictly political level and in the literary and aesthetic sphere.

In short, it seems to me that a plausible description of his impossible situation—which implied a constant disequilibrium, with prodigious contortions to recover his balance, refocus and reinvent himself—would be to say that he was in a position of double refusal: he wished neither to be as submissive as the assimilated Jews, nor to fall in with Zionist directives or perspectives. And it is within this 'neither/nor' that we can attempt to understand and describe his untenable, enigmatic position. Similarly, Kafka's main modality of belonging to the Prague space at the turn of the century might be said to be that of opposition but an opposition paradoxical in its nature. Kafka did not position himself 'alongside', as the critics have long decreed. He positioned himself essentially 'against'. His choices (which are also spontaneous inclinations, convictions and preferences —that is to say, un-thought-out and untheorized) were made in large measure in opposition to what was being written, produced and thought at Prague at the same moment: against the assertions and tales of Buber, against the return to religious practices, against the terms in which educational theories were being debated, against the customary condescension of Western Jews for Easterners, etc. Where every major political stance taken by the Prague Zionists is concerned, it would appear that Kafka adopted what we might term 'a logic of radicalization' or, in other words, moved to outdo them.

A radical in the political sense is someone who is not satisfied with the existing positions and convictions—including those which claim to be the most radical, as Cultural Zionism did—and is driven by a twofold impulse: criticizing the dominant political positions and laying claim to difficult positions that are presented as 'absolute', uncompromising, 'pure', etc. Hence, to show that Kafka is a radical writer, there are at least three preconditions. We must show: first, his dependency on the field in which he is socialized; second, his angry or critical impulse against the dominant stances within that field, whether literary or political; third, his resolve to hold the most extreme positions on the most topical subjects. I employ the term radicalism here without any precise political connotation. I mean to indicate by it only that, with each of the existing—and widely recognized and debated—options, Kafka sought to outbid them, and that it was most often the most widely shared presuppositions that were his targets. Within the Prague space Kafka was, admittedly, close to the Zionists. He adopted many of their postures and convictions but he constructed himself in opposition to what seemed to him the dominant postures. I shall demonstrate how, adopting highly critical attitudes in the political space, he also, understandably, engaged in highly marginal behaviour very far removed from the dominant positions within the strictly literary field.

Suddenly, during the winter of 1911, Kafka discovered Yiddish theatre and that discovery brought about a profound change in his life. This crucial moment is often interpreted as a melancholy return to a lost Judaism, a nostalgic interest in a Hasidism which, as we have said, then held in its thrall the group of writers and intellectuals who were Kafka's friends. Michael Löwy even speaks of a 'nostalgia for the past, represented in his eyes by the Yiddish culture of the Jewish communities of Eastern Europe'.[58] Even for those scholars who conclude that he was uninterested in Zionism, Kafka's sudden passion for Eastern Judaism is most often regarded as a regression. For example, Bokhove's article, referred to above, hypothesizes an interest in Hasidism on Kafka's part.[59] He sees this not as the sign of a politics but as evidence of a kind of infantile nostalgia for retreat into a small village community: 'Kafka in fact became the little East European Jewish boy he wanted to be.'[60]

I disagree strongly with this position. It seems to me, on the contrary, that to understand what is at stake in the profound change that occurred in Kafka's life from late 1911 onwards, we have to take account of the fact that what he discovered was not the mystical, religious domain of Hasidism but the political, cultural and literary world of the Jewish East. Through Yitzchak Löwy, who lifted him out of the closed, provincial, little world of Prague's quarrels, Kafka suddenly came into contact with the immensity of the Jewish political struggles which then had the whole of Eastern Europe in ferment. And he found in them the beginnings of an answer to his aesthetic and political questions. If he had up to that point harboured vague socialist or anarchist sentiments without any genuine commitment, the discovery of Jewish socialism suddenly opened up an immense range of possibilities and political issues that fired his enthusiasm.

In these years of great politicization of German-speaking Jews, the reference to the Jewish East, far from being that kind of backward-looking, 'romantic' nostalgia often described in writing on Kafka, was a genuine entry point into a space of struggle with complex issues at stake, a highly differentiated political scene offering clear-cut options. And his socialism, which was until late 1911 merely an instinctive, visceral drive—a romantic impulse, perhaps, as Michael Löwy has it—found something concrete with which to engage. By the same token, Kafka's enthusiasm over his discovery of Yiddish theatre is a precise measure both of his strictly political passion, of his certainty of having at last found a realistic option, a course of action and a programme. The Yiddishist-Bundist arguments seemed so close to his own convictions that they enabled him, even with his distance from these matters, to persevere down the socialist road while reconnecting with the specificity of the problems and questions associated with Jewishness.

This is why the hypothesis of a Kafka who subscribes (in principle) to the arguments and general stances of socialism does not seem entirely convincing unless accompanied by its Jewish dimension. Although he understood quite quickly that his identification with this model and these principles could only be theoretical and distant, the sum of overall Bundist stances and the choices of the Yiddishist intellectuals who were often very close to the Bund would in future form a kind of base upon which to establish his own marginality. His choices cannot be said to be merely the product of a 'politics'; they are to be seen as inseparably literary *and* political: all the evidence is that his presence at anarchist meetings in Prague stopped totally after 1912—that is to say, precisely at the point when Löwy's acting troupe arrived in Prague.[61] Most biographers draw the conclusion that he gradually lost interest and ceased involvement in political matters, a distancing corroborated by the immersion in his own writing which occurred at precisely that moment. Heinz Politzer describes the year 1912 as the *Durchbruch* (breakthrough). That year, Kafka wrote 'The Judgment' and *The Metamorphosis*; began *Amerika: The Man Who Disappeared* which he completed over the next two years; and then wrote *The Trial* and 'In the Penal Colony'.[62] This means he set to work just after his discovery of Yiddish theatre. It seems to me, therefore, that we actually have to see a direct link between the two events. Was it not his encounter with Jewish actors that made possible—and transformed—his literary work?[63]

THE DISCOVERY OF *YIDDISHKEIT*

The Café Savoy

It is the case, then, that Kafka met a troupe of Polish Jewish actors led by Yitzchak Löwy. They were called the Jüdische Gesellschaft aus Lemberg (Jewish Company from Lemberg).[64] They stayed at Prague from 24 September 1911 to 21 January 1912 and during those four months presented a number of plays from the Yiddish repertoire in a rather run-down Prague cafe, 'the tiny, not very inviting Café Savoy,' as Brod puts it, he being the first to show interest in the troupe.[65] From the first days he saw them and despite their state of material impoverishment, Kafka was passionate about the Jewish Company. He was suddenly gripped by an exceptional fervour, attended performances almost every evening, sometimes saw the same play several times and befriended certain members of the group.[66] He fell in love with one of the actresses, Mrs Tschissik, and admired another—Mrs Klug—with a passion. Of the latter he wrote on 1 November 1911: 'I beamed when she sang, I laughed and looked at her all the time while she was on the stage, I sang the tunes with her, later the words.'[67] He came very quickly to describe himself as consumed with passion for this group of people, who became the object of his exclusive attention. 'Some songs, [. . .] some of this woman's acting (who, on the stage, because she is a Jew, draws us listeners to her because we are Jews, without any longing for or curiosity about Christians) made my cheeks tremble,' he noted after the very first performance he attended on 5 October 1911.[68] 'At times,' he wrote on 10 October, 'we did not interfere in the plot only because we were too moved, not because we were mere spectators.'[69] His admiration for Löwy was such that he confessed on 14 October: 'At the end of the performance we still wait for the actor Löwy, whom I would admire in the dust.'[70] On 22 October, he tried to give an objective account of his feelings: 'The sympathy we have for these actors who are so good, who earn nothing and who do not get nearly enough gratitude and fame is really only sympathy for the sad fate of many noble strivings, above all of our own.'[71] Much later, at the time of his conversations with Janouch (between 1920 and 1922), he again expressed his attachment to the Jewish actors: 'And I should like to run to those poor Jews of the Ghetto, kiss the hem of their coats, and say not a word. I should be completely happy if only they would endure my presence in silence.'[72]

In its most extreme manifestations, Kafka's sudden devotion to this poverty-stricken theatre company at first assumed forms very close to the cult of East European Jewry and general atmosphere of fascination with the East that prevailed in Jewish intellectual circles at the time. But Kafka rapidly became a friend of Löwy's, invited him to his home and spent almost all his free time with him during these four months. A year later, when the troupe were staying in Berlin, Kafka encouraged Felice to attend one of their performances. In an effort to encourage her, he wrote—thereby giving an idea of the personality of the actor—'Löwy is, moreover, a perpetual enthusiast, an "ardent Jew" as they say in the East.'[73] Brod adds: '[H]e treated the actor Löwy as a friend, often took him back home with him—to the intense annoyance of his father, who never could get on with any of Franz's friends.'[74] Kafka helped Löwy to organize some poetry recitals (including the one he introduced with his 'Introductory Talk on the Yiddish Language' on 18 February 1912) to enable him to earn a little money and offered his assistance in putting a tour together.[75]

Subsequently, his meeting with the actor lent a quite different slant to his passion for Yiddish theatre—after a few weeks, he turned from an appreciation of that theatre as something mystical to the discovery of a cultural and political universe totally new to him. '[H]e [. . .] made this passionate person tell him all about his life, his surroundings and his development,' relates Brod. He also took on board everything Löwy told him about 'the customs and spiritual crises of the Polish-Russian Jews',[76] set about reading specialist works of scholarship with a sort of intense desire, particularly Heinrich Graetz's *History of the Jews* and, in French, Méir Pinès's *Histoire de la littérature judéo-allemande* [1911, 'History of German-Jewish Literature'], which had just been published in Paris.[77] 'I [. . .] read, and indeed greedily, Pinès's *Histoire de la littérature judéo-allemande*, 500 pages, with such thoroughness, haste and joy as I have never yet shown in the case of similar books.'[78] Gradually, from the tenor of these notes, the content of the reported discussions that he had with Löwy and what he retained of the Yiddish plays he had seen, an attitude emerges that is increasingly distant from the idealized vision of East European Jews commonly found in his milieu. While he was close to the Cultural Zionists, who in these very years invented novel forms of dissidence and critique within Zionism itself, and while his closest friends (including Brod) allowed themselves to be carried away by a mysticism glorifying Eastern Judaism, Kafka kept his distance from the most widespread forms of that veneration. Thanks to the explanations and the tools for understanding supplied by Löwy, Kafka did not see the Yiddish theatre as the expression of an 'essence of Judaism' or the representation of an 'authentic' Judaism. He observed it, rather, as an art that could be said to possess all the attributes recognized by the Herderian theory of an authentically popular, national (*volkstümlich*) art: a specific language spoken by the people, Yiddish; a literature written in that language which asserted its genuinely popular character; and a theatre which he had difficulty grasping in all its aspects because of his ignorance of the language, but which suddenly opened up unsuspected political and aesthetic horizons. The reader of Kafka's diaries very quickly understands that it was insofar as they were Jewish artists presenting a specifically Jewish art that Kafka literally fell in love with the Jewish Company of Lemberg.

In order to fully grasp what was implied for Kafka by this kind of political and social 'revelation', and to have an idea of the content of the almost daily conversations he had with Löwy over these four months, we must first examine the personality and position of that actor. Kafka, who neither read nor spoke Yiddish, actually knew the literary, theatrical and political production in that language only through what was said—or read—to him by Löwy. It was only from Löwy's standpoint, then, that in the winter of 1911–12 Kafka discovered the Yiddishist politico-literary movement, the scope of the linguistic (or linguistic-political) debates in the Eastern Jewish world and the development of a Jewish literature in Yiddish. And the clues

Kafka gives about Löwy's personality, career and choices suggest he was not a neutral informant.

The Viewpoint of Yitzchak Löwy

When, in October 1917 (more than five years after they first met), Kafka returned to his memories of Yitzchak Löwy, he traced a portrait of an adolescent raised in a highly religious family, who, concealing the fact from his parents and against the prohibitions of religious law, had discovered Polish theatre, opera and subsequently theatre in Yiddish (which was his mother tongue).[79] Löwy himself recounts his discovery of Jewish theatre as a genuine revelation:

> That completely transformed me [. . .] On the whole, I liked it better than the opera, the dramatic theatre, and the operetta all rolled into one. For first it was, after all, Yiddish; true, it was German-Yiddish, but still Yiddish, a better and more beautiful Yiddish; and secondly here was everything all at once: drama, tragedy, singing, comedy, dancing, all of them together—life! All that night I could not sleep for excitement, my heart telling me that I too must some day serve in the temple of Jewish art, that I must become a Jewish actor.[80]

His father condemned his escapades on grounds of religious orthodoxy:

> Father did not sit down again; he kept on walking up and down the room; with his hand on his little black beard he talked, not to me, but only to Mother. 'You must be told. He becomes worse every day. Yesterday he was seen in the Jewish theatre'. Mother clasped her hands in horror. Father, quite pale, continued to pace up and down the room. My heart tightened. I sat there like a condemned prisoner, I could not bear to see the sorrow felt by my loyal, devout parents.[81]

The revival of Yiddish popular theatre was inseparable at this time from a political context and struggle: if only by the secular artistic practices it presupposed, it represented a rebellion against religious traditions and prohibitions. In other words, Löwy was himself a man of the Enlightenment who had broken with the religious practices of his parents, favoured the secularization of Jewish culture and campaigned for a Jewish art capable of rivalling the Russian or the German.

We may deduce from this that he had a detailed knowledge of the debates out of which the Yiddishist movement originated, that he read the Jewish press and the Yiddish writers who had emigrated to the US, and kept abreast of the political and literary controversies. Consequently, he could not but have informed Kafka, over several months, of this massive movement and also of the political, national, linguistic and aesthetic issues that were being fought over at this time not in Prague, a Western provincial capital, but in Warsaw, Vilnius and New York. At a stroke, through this actor playing in one of the most run-down *cafés chantants* in Prague, Kafka gained an insight into the vast world of political and literary debates and struggles of Eastern Europe. The Jewish Company of Lemberg revealed to him the emergence not of a Jewish literary 'modernity' but of a new national literature which, through the accompanying forms of political struggle, was seeking to challenge traditional Jewish practices. I am not saying that Löwy was a political activist who was trying to convert Kafka, nor that Kafka became in these few months an established supporter of the Bund or member of the Volkspartei.[82] However, the actor was certainly committed to these struggles.

Kafka notes, for example, on 7 January 1912, that Löwy read him a letter he sent to Hersh David Nomberg (1876–1927). The fact that Löwy was in correspondence with Nomberg is proof that he was closely involved in the Yiddishist movement. Alongside Yitzkhok Leybush Peretz and Sholem Ash, Nomberg had been one of the driving forces behind the famous Czernowitz Conference on Yiddish (held at present-day Chernivtsi in Bukovina). Organized in September 1908, it brought together Jewish intellectuals, writers and political leaders on the theme of the Jewish national language.[83] Nomberg was a very popular writer, who was close in his political and linguistic positions to Peretz. In 1905 he had published a novella entitled *Fligelman* which created a great stir in the Jewish world.[84] Similarly, the texts Löwy chose for the evening of readings of Yiddish poetry were very much linked to what at this same time Kafka in his diaries calls the 'national struggle'.[85] As a historian seeking to re-evaluate Yiddish literature and confer legitimacy—i.e. literary modernity—on it, Régine Robin takes the view that the authors for the evening 'were not well chosen'. In her view, 'none of the three can represent great Yiddish poetry in 1912.'[86] Yet, all judgements of literary value aside, the choice of these three poets is renewed confirmation of the meaning Löwy attributed to the development and dissemination of Yiddish literature. For him—and for all the intellectuals involved in the development of a new Jewish literature—poetry was inseparable from political and national commitment. Readings of Rosenfeld, David Frischmann and Samuel Frug (1859–1916) were on the programme for that evening. The latter, initially a Russian-language poet, had converted to Yiddish after the pogroms of 1881 and strove to produce a poetry that was national in character. Löwy recited his 'great national poem' 'Zamd un Schtern', which all Yiddish-speaking Jews knew by heart at the time:[87]

> I read these words so sacred, so dear
> I seem to hear a voice: I swear to you
> My people, you will be like the stars in the sky,
> That everyone tramples [. . .]
> We've been scattered, dispersed, mocked and shamed,
> But where are the stars, those bright, brilliant lights—
> The stars, the stars oh, where are they God?[88]

The political nature of Löwy's choices is even clearer if we compare them with a poetry reading he gave some time before, on 17 October 1911. On 20 October Kafka recalls the programme of that evening: 'Löwy read humorous sketches by Sholem Aleichem, then a story by Peretz, the *Lichtverkäuferin* by Rosenfeld, a poem by Bialik' and he adds in brackets: '(the one instance where the poet stooped from Hebrew to Yiddish, himself translating his original Hebrew poem into Yiddish, in order to popularize this poem which, by making capital out of the Kishinev pogrom, sought to further the Jewish cause)'.[89] All three were great figures of Yiddish literature and, in the case of Peretz and Rosenfeld, writers committed to movements close to Bundism. As for Bialik, he was a Hebrew-language author, but Löwy chose the Yiddish version of one of the most famous poems in the whole of the Eastern Jewish world, 'Be-'ir ha-haregah' ('In the City of Slaughter'), which was regarded at the time as a kind of collective voicing of protest against the Kishinev massacres. Kafka's comments on the translation of this poem underline its political dimension. By reading all the great Yiddish authors of the moment to him, Löwy was also initiating Kafka into the controversies internal to the political movements, and the great split that ranged the partisans of Hebrew against the advocates of Yiddish.

What were these movements? Because of the social and geographical division within the Jewish world at the time, pitting those who lived in Eastern Europe against those who lived in the West, the intellectuals and theorists of Jewish nationalism proposed, in a nutshell, two types of response that would come to underlie the great dichotomy within Jewish political struggles in the late nineteenth century. That is to say, they proposed two versions of Jewish nationalism. In 1897, two antagonistic political movements appeared simultaneously: Bundism and Zionism. The two presented highly differentiated options, bodies of doctrine and convictions and these structured the Jewish political field between the latter years of the nineteenth century and the 1920s. The Bund, founded at Vilnius, was the Jewish workers' movement (The Union of Jewish Workers of Russia, Poland and Lithuania), uniting all the Jewish socialist organizations. Drawing on the doctrines of the Austro-Marxist thinkers, the Bundist theorist Vladimir Medem appealed to the principles of diasporic nationalism and national-cultural autonomy.[90] This movement for the secularization of Judaism developed thanks to the dissemination and normalization of the demotic language of the Jews: Yiddish. Yiddish (also known as 'jargon'), which was spoken by the Jewish workers resident in Russia, became the secular language of the Bund and the tool for disseminating its theories.[91] A whole array of socialist and revolutionary movements and organizations gravitated around this party (autonomists, Sejmists, Folkists, etc.),[92] debating and wrangling over questions relating to the contradictions inherent in communist internationalism, nationalism and Judaism. Rather than established bodies of doctrine in struggle, there was a *continuum* of complex, interlinked stances.[93] The emergence of these multiple parties contributed to the publication of manifestos, the appearance of newspapers and magazines—in short, the consolidation and unification of this emergent political space. The Bund became one of the most influential political parties in the pre-war Eastern Jewish world. By 1905 it had more than 30,000 members and the provinces where it was most powerful (in the Pale of Settlement, of course), saw the most—and the most determined—strikes, at Lodz, Riga, Vilnius and Bialystok.[94] It provided a home for a 'workshop proletariat' responsive to its—both social and national—appeal. It was after the war (and the Russian Revolution) that the Bund lost ground to Zionism because it lost its support-base among what were now 'Sovietized' populations.

Whereas the Bundist intelligentsia had a preference for the life and emancipation of Jewish diaspora communities, the theorists of Zionism—of whatever stamp, Left, Centre or Right, secular or religious —rejected diaspora life and worked for the construction of an independent Jewish society in Palestine.[95] They were hostile both to the traditional way of life and to all those attempting to build a Jewish culture within the diaspora. Hence they were opposed to the development of a Yiddish popular culture. For them, that language embodied Jewish 'archaism' and constituted an obstacle to the Jews entering modernity. It was a non-noble idiom, presented as the product of linguistic hybridity and countless borrowings, a despised jargon because, far from giving the Jews a language of their own, it was seen as the very symbol of their oppression as a people, the 'mark of the humiliation of the diaspora'.[96] Since it was seen as a mingling of the languages of all the countries in which the Jews had settled, Yiddish was proof for them, in their Herderian nationalist logic, of the constitutive inferiority to which the diaspora might be said to have consigned them by removing all their distinctive features and cultural identity. Hence Zionist logic called for Hebrew to be favoured over Yiddish. In an almost term-for-term opposition to the Bund, which was socialist, autonomist, diasporist and Yiddishist,[97] the Zionists were optionally socialist, nationalist, in favour of the settlement of Jews in Palestine and pro-Hebrew.

The social origins of the political and intellectual leaders of the two parties were very different. The Easterners were products of the popular classes or the Jewish petty bourgeoisie, for whom access to the universities was difficult. The Zionist leaders, for their part, were largely products of the assimilated Jewish upper-middle class and had been educated in the universities of Germany and Austria. Thus the main criticism levelled at the Zionists by the Bundist leaders was that they knew nothing of the concerns and real life of the poor Jews of Eastern Europe. There was another major difference between the two parties: the Bundists were militantly anticlerical and opposed the perpetuation of religious practices—and hence beliefs—among the people. Zionism, by contrast, wished to promote the unity of the Jewish community and, as a result, did not denounce any traditional or religious practice.[98] By the same logic, it refused to defend one social class—the working class—above any other. The core of the political conflict between the two close rivals was the place to be accorded to nationalism as compared with socialism. It revolved around whether the class struggle was to be given priority over the national struggle and whether class solidarity was needed (or not), as compared with national solidarity.[99]

The linguistic divisions could also be deduced, in part, from the social rift between Western and Eastern Jews. The Zionists accepted only Hebrew as the symbol of the Jewish national spirit. Within the Zionist camp, only the socialist Zionists were happy to use Yiddish for propaganda purposes. The Eastern socialist organizations, for their part, refused to accept Hebrew as the Jewish national language because they said they wanted to stay close to the reality of the people: the immense majority of the Jews of Eastern Europe and, to a lesser degree, of Central Europe—and North America—spoke Yiddish.

There were four great dialects of Yiddish at the beginning of the century, divided along regional lines, and the language was spoken by 10 to 11 million people worldwide before 1939, from Strasbourg to Moscow and from New York to Tel Aviv.[100] It has been estimated that, of 10.5 million Jews in 1900, around 9 million were Yiddish-speaking.[101] The Yiddishist activists and socialist organizations rejected the idea that the Hebrew which was spoken (and, particularly, written) by intellectuals and 'aesthetes' should or could be imposed on all Jews. For example, they openly criticized the fact that Herzl spoke only German.[102] Those advocating the recognition of Yiddish generally took the view that there was a close relationship between Yiddish and the ways of life, customs and social practices of the Jewish world, which they encapsulated in the term *Yiddishkeit*, meaning by that both Judaism and Jewishness.[103]

The idea of a secular expression of culture, a novel one within the highly religious world of the shtetl, made its appearance with the struggle of these intellectuals.[104] To explain this progressive movement of cultural secularization, Rachel Ertl distinguishes between the Western Haskalah (the Enlightenment movement within the Jewish world) and the Eastern Haskalah: in Western Europe, she says, the Enlightenment involved a confessionalization of the Jewish religion, shorn of its national features, and a linguistic and cultural assimilation; in the East, by contrast, the Enlightenment movement came much later and had secularization as its goal.[105] Arising from within the Jewish world, this did not seek either to abandon Jewish culture or to dissolve it into the dominant one. On the contrary, it produced a culture that was both new and marked by specific traditions—the culture termed *Yiddishkeit*.

Modern Yiddish literature was born, paradoxically, out of the Western Haskalah which, despite its aversion for the language—seen as the symbol of obscurantism—used Yiddish in Eastern Europe to disseminate its ideas. This is summed up in the highly illuminating notes Kafka hastily made as he was reading Pinès's book:

> Adherents [of the Haskalah movement . . .] are opposed to the popular Yiddish, tend towards Hebrew and the European sciences. Before the pogroms of 1881 it was not nationalist, later strongly Zionist [. . .] To spread its ideas the Haskalah

must use Yiddish and, much as it hates the latter, lays the foundation of its literature.[106]

The Enlightenment writers could not in fact spread their ideas through the use of Hebrew, which was the preserve of an elite, nor by speaking the major European languages (Russian or Polish), which were little used by the popular classes.[107] Given the contempt in which the language was held, the first writers to adopt Yiddish published under noms de plume and continued to use two (or even three) languages: they wrote in Hebrew for an educated audience and in Yiddish for the people.[108]

This modern literature in Yiddish, which first developed 'by default', was carried on, as it were, at the point when national movements emerged, by all those who were to pronounce themselves 'Yiddishists', to strive to reverse the negative image of Yiddish and to work from the late nineteenth century onwards for the full literary and political recognition of the language. At that point, a literature in Yiddish emerged and gradually asserted itself, coming to play a major role: 'End of Haskalah 1881,' notes Kafka in his diary. 'New nationalism and democracy. Flourishing of Yiddish literature.'[109] The great figures among the Yiddish writers of 1860–80 were Yakov Abramovich (1835–1917), who wrote under the name of Mendele Mocher Sforim, Solomon Rabinovich (1859–1916), far better known by his pseudonym Sholem Aleichem, who was born in Ukraine and is renowned for countless humorous stories, and the Pole Yitzhok Leybush Peretz (1852–1915), the greatest and most celebrated of the three, who was an immense innovator, active in all literary genres, and became the guiding light of Yiddish letters.[110] The Haskalah movement also enabled literature and journalism in Hebrew to flourish: Abraham Mapu was the author of the first modern Hebrew novel, *Ahavat Zion* (1853) [The Love of Zion].[111]

At the point when Kafka discovered it, Yiddish literature was seeking to make progress among the European literary movements and undergoing renewal through the fragmentation of its territorial base. From the beginning of the century, the Yiddish literary world was divided between three main centres: the US (and Britain), Poland and Russia.

In 1881, large-scale pogroms in Russia prompted the departure of great numbers of Jews. That migration increased further in the 1890s. In 1903 and 1905, particularly bloody massacres at Kishinev caused another major outflow.[112] From that moment on, the US became the principal destination for Jewish emigrants from Eastern Europe.[113] Renée Poznanski notes more precisely that the annual average of Jewish people from Central Europe emigrating to America was 16,000 in 1881–89, 31,000 in 1890–98, in excess of 34,000 between 1899 and 1902 and as high as 96,000 between 1903 and 1907. According to some estimates, Jewish emigration to the US represented between 75 and 80 per cent of total Jewish emigration in the period 1881–1914.[114] During these years, approximately 2 million Jews—that is to say, in the course of around 33 years, something like a third of the Jewish population—left Eastern Europe, Russia, Poland and Rumania for the US.[115] This migration speeded up in the first years of the twentieth century, since the figures indicate that, after 1901, 1.6 million people made the journey. Of these, 84 per cent settled in the US and 6 per cent in Canada. The social—and hence linguistic—geography of that world changed substantially. The immigrants settled mainly in New York which, over the course of a few years, became the biggest Jewish city in the world.[116] This wave of migration was so strong that Dubnow called it the 'second in importance' since 1492, the year of 'the expulsion of the Jews from Spain'.[117] Moreover, on several occasions, in his correspondence or diaries, Kafka associated the Eastern refugees quite unambiguously with the exodus to America. In the beautiful letter to Milena of 7 September 1920, Kafka writes:

> If I'd been given the choice last night (it was 8 p.m. when I looked from the street into the banqueting room of the Jewish Town Hall, where far more than 100 Russian Jewish émigrés —they're waiting here for their American visas—are housed, the room is packed full as during a public meeting [. . .]), then I'd have chosen to be a small Eastern Jewish boy in the

corner of the room, without a trace of worry, the father in the centre discussing with other men, the mother [. . .] rummaging in the travelling bundles [. . .]—and in a few weeks one will be in America.[118]

For all these rootless immigrants, who had been wrenched brutally from their places of birth and subjected to the exploitation of the sweatshops, Yiddish was the affective, cultural connection with their community.[119] It also became the vehicle for the expression of a Jewish immigrant political culture characterized by a high degree of radicalism. As early as the 1880s, territorialist or anarchist socialist theories had spread widely in Yiddish-speaking working-class circles in New York.[120] Moreover, the Bund built a network of active sympathizers in the US. From 1904–05 onwards, after the failure of the first Russian Revolution, numerous political activists went into exile in New York.[121] The biggest Yiddish daily newspaper in the world, *Forverts* (The Jewish Daily Forward), which was also the most popular daily in the Lower East Side, the home of Jewish socialism in its American version, was founded in New York in 1897.[122]

Immigration to the US had so transformed the geography and numerical distribution of the Jewish population that it had become an important political theme in Europe, an object of discussion and dissension. Since they were calling for a Jewish national state to be founded in Palestine and for Jews to move to that country, the Zionists were (at least in theory) opposed to emigration to the US. Conversely, the territorialists and autonomists (Bundists or Sejmists) regarded emigration to—and settlement in—America as a necessary evil, a product of the persecution to which Jews were subjected in Russia and Poland and a phenomenon continuous with the diasporic history of the Jews that would merely displace the 'centre' of Jewish life. Thus, in his introduction to the German translation of his first two 'letters on Judaism',[123] the historian Dubnow proclaims:

In the last twenty years, Russia has sent close to a million Jews to North America alone. This important flow of emigration indicates to us the direction in which the Russian Jewish centre is moving. And there can be no doubt that the enormous reserve of national resources concealed within Russian Judaism will find external conditions more favourable for its development in the land of liberty [America] than in the land of slavery and arbitrary rule [Russia].[124]

In parallel with this working-class immigration, a specific poetry developed. The Yiddish publications produced in London and New York saw the first attempts at a proletarian poetry in that language. It was, largely, into the American side of Jewish socialism—and also the accompanying Yiddish literature and drama—that Löwy initiated Kafka in the last months of 1911.

The quarrel within Löwy's acting troupe, which Kafka reported in his diary on 23 October 1911, provides very clear evidence of this. The dispute pitted Löwy against one of his actors over two proletarian poets who had emigrated to the US. It reveals a great deal of the avant-garde references that formed the cultural baggage of the members of the Lemberg company and also of the stances adopted by these actors, since one announced that 'Edelstatt [was] the greatest Jewish writer' and the other that that honour belonged to Rosenfeld.[125] Now, notes Kafka, David Edelstatt (also spelt Edelstadt) was the editor of a Jewish socialist newspaper in London.[126] He was also close to the anarchist movements and one of the most tragic figures of early Yiddish poetry in the US, dying at 25 from tuberculosis, and a rare example of a genuine worker-poet. The other, Morris Rosenfeld (1862–1923), was one of the founders of the Jewish proletarian poetry known as the 'sweatshop school'. Rosenfeld's career, very similar to that of Edelstatt, was the stuff of legend at the time. An immigrant to the US, employed for 10 years in the sweatshops of New York, he evoked in his poems the tragic lives and exhausting labour of the immigrants in dramatic or lyrical tones. This saw him greatly venerated in the workshops and labour-union meeting halls of New York. 'Né [sic] 1851. Rosenfeld: The poor Yiddish public took up a collection to assure him of a livelihood,' writes Kafka in his diary.[127] His poems, often set to music, were known to readers of Yiddish the world over. And if Löwy was able to assert in the course of the quarrel that, 'the world knows Rosenfeld,'[128] it was because he had acquired a certain notoriety in 1898 with the translation into English of his collection *Lider Bukh* as *Songs of the Ghetto*.[129] Pinès devotes a long chapter to Rosenfeld.[130] He confirms that he was famous, adding that it was 'a popularity unique in the history of a [. . .] little-known literature'.[131] Pinès provides a long quotation in Yiddish from Rosenfeld's poem 'Di svet shap' (German: 'Der Sweat Shop'), followed by a translation:

I work and work and work with no accounting,
it produces and produces and produces without end:
Why? And for whom? I do not know, I do not ask,
how would a machine know how to think?[132]

And Pinès adds: 'In the literature inspired by modern working life, one would seldom find anything as grandiose and, at the same time, as tragic as this poem entitled "The Sweat Shop", in which the poet shows us the agony of his soul, his slow, painful transformation into a machine, but a machine made of flesh and sinew.'[133] This is why, seen from Prague, the reason for the quarrel is of less significance than the repeated assertion by these two actors of their passionate interest in Yiddish proletarian poetry, which presupposed a deep knowledge of these poetico-political movements connected with Jewish immigration to New York. As artists within, and activists for, Yiddish culture, they were linked to the Jewish labour movements and their aesthetic choices themselves bore the clear stamp of a 'socialist' or near-socialist conception of literary production.

The other striking feature of Yiddish writing in the New World was the development of a popular theatre. It was precisely this 'Americanized' theatre that Kafka discovered at the Café Savoy. That theatre, devised, disseminated and developed for a mass audience and for commerical ends, was not a thing of great literary refinement. In the chapter of his *Histoire de la littérature judéo-allemande* on Yiddish theatre, Pinès speaks generally of a production 'of no great literary value'.[134] The often shabby character of this drama was stressed by Löwy himself, who one day read Kafka a letter from a young Warsaw Jew who was explaining that 'he prefer[red] to go to the "Nowosti", the Polish operetta theatre, rather than to the Jewish one, for the miserable equipment, the indecencies, the "mouldy" couplets, etc., [were] unbearable.'[135] Although it first emerged in Eastern Europe, Yiddish drama was very quickly exported to the US and a great many of the successful actors and authors emigrated to play to the massive immigrant audiences. 'Yiddish performances were forbidden in Russia 1883. They began in London and New York 1884,' observes Kafka.[136]

The chief landmarks in the very short history of this modern Yiddish theatre are provided by a few great names. Abraham Goldfaden (1840–1908) is regarded as its founder. A kind of Jewish Molière, he led a troupe of actors, wrote the plays, composed the music, painted the sets and in the 1880s became the most popular Yiddish dramaturge in Eastern Europe.[137] He emigrated to New York in 1884, writing countless melodramas and operettas there.[138] Then, in the 1890s, Morris Horowitz (1844–1910) and Joseph Lateiner (1853–1935) became the two great rivals within popular 'American Judaeo-German theatre'.[139] They produced over 200 plays—melodramas, musical comedies, 'historical' operas, farces and comedies—for a preponderantly working-class audience.[140] Lastly, Jacob Gordin (1853–1909) is regarded as the reforming figure of this commercial drama. The theatre was, for him, a place for reflection and the teaching of morality. The author of more than a hundred plays inspired by Western models, he arrived in the US in 1891 and was to remain, for 20 years, one of the central figures of New York Yiddish theatre. Kafka quotes him at length.[141] Several of his plays became classics of the repertoire and, in the early 1900s he was a kind of 'East Side culture hero'.[142] His anticlericalism, familiarity with European drama and rejection of folk themes made him a famous figure in politicized Jewish workers' circles. At Prague, Löwy's troupe presented plays by Goldfaden. Kafka saw at least two of these, including *Sulamith*, a sort of operetta, famous in particular for its popular songs.[143] They also staged plays by Gordin (including *Der vilde Mensh* [The Wild Man] and *Got, Mensh un Tayvl* [God, Man and Devil], one of his most famous plays, inspired by Goethe's *Faust*).[144] Lastly, the actors performed works by Joseph Lateiner, Abraham Scharkansky and Sigmund Feinmann,[145] which Kafka, like Pinès, often found quite poor.[146]

Kafka's Notes

Apart from Löwy's views on Yiddish literary production, Kafka drew on a second source for information on developments in Yiddish literature—the book by Pinès. Presenting itself as the first 'attempt at popularization [of Yiddish literature] in Europe',[147] it was the declared aim of Pinès's work to 'improve the familiarity with appreciation of a literature that was born *intra muros*, in poverty and darkness, but aspired to the light and deserved to have its place in the sun [. . .] Born out of struggle, Judaeo-German literature has remained in large part a combative literature,'[148] he wrote in his 'Introduction'.[149] The work, written and published in French in 1911, has often been very harshly treated by critics because it has been taken to represent an anti-Haskalah (anti-Enlightenment) perspective. Moreover, it is sometimes contended that it is error-strewn and provides poor-quality information or retails clichés on Yiddish literature from a standpoint favourable to Hasidism—in other words, that it takes a view unfavourable to Yiddishism.[150] The inference is drawn from this critical verdict that Kafka had an unrealistic, idealistic view of the shtetls and that, hence, his penchant for Hasidism conceived as nostalgia for a lost Judaism is 'proved'.

Yet Bruce has, in fact, demonstrated that the book is a serious historical work, written and published in accordance with the academic norms prevailing in France in the early twentieth century. Pinès's thesis is followed by a 63-page bibliography containing more than a thousand titles and it has a great many footnotes to works in Yiddish, German, French and English.[151] Furthermore, far from taking a sentimental and nostalgic Western viewpoint on Hasidic practices, Pinès's work actually provides a realistic perspective on the Jewish communities of Eastern Europe, a vision highly critical of Hasidism, and develops a standpoint staunchly favourable to the secularization of popular practices. His thesis is, admittedly, not greatly original and there are many factual errors (particularly in the chapter on the history of the language: Pinès, as he admits himself, was no linguist) and, as Delphine Bechtel points out, it repeats several misconceptions about Yiddish that were widely believed in Western Europe, but it articulates a number of the features that were characteristic of Yiddish literary production itself (giving the most famous names, the themes, the main features and contents), translates long extracts, summarizes a large number of texts and, as it seems to me, achieves its stated goal, which is not to address groups of specialist scholars but to 'popularize' this literature and 'make it known' to a non-specialist public. Pinès may not be close to the Yiddishist literary circles of Czernowitz and we find many prejudices and clichés regarding the life of diaspora Jews in his writings—for example, that their language is 'always subject to foreign influences'—but, generally speaking, he describes a literature which is indissociably popular and national, written simultaneously against religious conservatism and anti-Semitic stigmatization.

In the chapter on Peretz, to whom Pinès seems genuinely devoted, the commentary on the Hasidic movement is quite long.[152] He emphasizes the writer's great interest in this pietistic movement while clearly stressing that his work is not an apologia for Hasidism and that Peretz himself is a rationalist and not in any sense a believer:

It would [. . .] be an error to believe that Peretz was seeking in these short stories to write an apologia for Hasidism or preach adoration of the *tzadikkim* and faith in their miracles. Peretz is ultimately a sceptical thinker and it was in his very scepticism that he found the force of detachment and serenity required to admire a faith and a devotion the he himself could not share.[153]

Thus, though Kafka's attitude was, at least initially, very greatly influenced by Pinès's explanations and value-judgements where Hasidism was concerned, that influence did not run in the direction normally attributed to it. And in Kafka's interested, respectful but, at the same time, distant attitude to these practices, we seem to rediscover Peretz's (quasi-political) interest in Hasidism, as explained and interpreted by Pinès.[154]

As he read the work, which had just been published in Paris, Kafka, as we have said, took countless, detailed notes in his diaries. All the features he found worthy of recording or copying form an impressive convergent bundle of significations. Kafka comments on the existence of popular songs within Jewish village communities, notes the opposition of the Haskalah to popular Yiddish and the reticent use of the language among writers. He cites the names of Eliakum Zunser (1836–1913), Jewish poet and bard, whose songs were very famous in the Yiddish world, and of Eisik Meir Dick (1808–94) and Shomer as representatives of the 'popular novel'.[155] Shomer was the pen name of Nahum Meyer Shaikevich (1849–1905), the author of countless cheap novels, episodic tales of out-landish adventure and barely credible love stories: 'Shomer's novels, which you bought from the local pedlar,' writes Robin, 'moved women and servants—in short, the people—to tears.'[156]

Kafka writes next of the famous Mendele Mocher Sforim, choosing to mention from among his novels one about a sort of archetypal 'man of the people', *Fishke the Lame*.[157] He notes the ballads of Frug, which were famous in the shtetls, especially 'Dem Shames Tokhter' (The Daughter of the Shammes), which he summarizes at length.[158] He recalls Rosenfeld's name once again and lingers over Sholem Aleichem to mention his—also very well known—tragicomic character Menachem Mendel and his fictional home town Kasrilevke. He twice cites Peretz's name and comments on '[t]he figure of the *batlan*, frequent in the ghettos, lazy and grown clever through idling'.[159] He also refers to Baal Shem, the founder of Hasidism ('the Torah for all'), then chooses to mention the two great creators of modern Yiddish theatre, both of them emigrants to the US: Goldfaden, the founder, and Gordin, the reformer, noting that '[t]he Yiddish theatre has an audience of hundreds of thousands.'[160]

The only connecting thread in all these scattered notes is, clearly, a definition of Yiddish literature as emanation of the people (the common people, the 'popular classes'), whether presented as arising from the people (songs, poems, ballads) or written for them (novel and drama). This all seemed consistent with the representation conveyed to Kafka by Löwy of a literature that brought the people onto the stage as a community through the creation of characters who themselves personified the people (Fishke the Lame, Menachem Mendel, the *batlan*), texts that evoked Hasidism as a 'democratized' religious practice and the appearance of a theatre that was so popular it drew in the crowds.

In other words, what Kafka chose to focus on in the development of Yiddish literature was its most communal, collective side only. He highlighted everything that corroborated the ideal representation of a 'genuine' popular literature in the sense Herder gave to the term— that is to say, a literature that could be said to emanate from the Jewish people and to legitimate its claim to existence and national recognition.

This is why one cannot share Robin's surprise—that Kafka fails to mention what she calls 'Yiddish literature's first steps toward modernity' or that he 'overlooks Yiddish modernity'.[161] Being convinced over several months that he had at last made a breakthrough in his literary and political questing, he was suddenly fired with great enthusiasm. The 'national' and, above all, popular character of this Yiddish literature was what primarily interested him, even before any formal, literary concerns. It was the discovery of a literary expression in its simplicity, 'collective enunciation',[162] linearity and naivety that thrilled him, much more than what the least market-dependent writers regarded as worthwhile aesthetic innovations. It was not the aesthetic modernity of that literature, in the sense in which we understand it, that attracted him but much rather its very heteronomy, its lack of literary 'finish', which made it for Kafka a kind of 'virgin territory'. In this regard we may take the view that Yiddish literature was, for him, a variety of literature 'unsullied' by aestheticism of any kind, free of any assimilatory 'lies' or deception. In total contrast to the 'Gypsy literature' he would write of much later—by which he meant German-language Jewish literature—which had 'stolen the German child out of its cradle and in great haste put it through some kind of training',[163] Yiddish literature appeared to Kafka in all its 'innocence'—that is to say, with its particular genres and in all its popular 'truthfulness'.

Apart from the theatre, Kafka was also interested in the proletarian poetry produced in New York, about which Löwy had spoken to him. In that area too, one should not be surprised—as Robin is again—that Kafka names only the most 'primitive' representatives of that poetry which came out of New York Jewish immigrant worker circles. This naive proletarian lyricism was entirely in keeping with his definition of a literature written by and for the people. The enchantment he felt when he discovered the Yiddish literary movements had to do precisely with the fact that they provided a twofold definition of the people which was at the heart of the political and literary debates of the time: the people as nation (with its tradition, rites and language); and the people as working class (even better illustrated by the Jewish immigrant sub-proletariat in the US than by the small craft producers of the shtetls). Why, asks Robin, did Kafka not cite the first 'modernist' opponents of Rosenfeld and Edelstatt, the Yunge movement, created in New York as early as 1907–08? As soon as one attempts to explain his choices, the reason becomes clear: despite their status as workers, the Yunge poets were the first to claim aesthetic autonomy for poetry. These 'proletarian aesthetes'[164] translated European contemporary poetry—Heine, Rilke, Verlaine (whose *Romances sans paroles* had been translated and published in Moscow in 1894), Baudelaire, Rimbaud, Hofmannsthal, etc.—into Yiddish or read it in (Russian or German) translation and refused to support nationalist ideals. They were, all of them, also manual workers, cobblers, housepainters or wallpaper hangers, but they refused to be answerable to the Yiddish press which, in its affiliation to the political parties, imposed aesthetic and political norms on them. Standing out against the requirement for easy readability and the demand that they produce political slogans, which reduced them, as they put it, to a mere 'rhyme department of the Jewish labour movement',[165] they claimed their autonomy through the creation of an independent literary magazine. Löwy, who was also largely self-taught, knew nothing of European cultural movements and had a poor command of German, could not understand what was at stake in this paradoxical new 'art for art's sake' movement that had arisen from the poverty-stricken New York immigrant world. Moreover, he no doubt also rejected it, being unable to conceive of art as anything other than a practice in the service of a political cause. He could not, therefore, communicate such a call for artistic autonomy to Kafka, who was himself bedazzled at that date by the 'national struggle' he found at work in the Yiddish texts he was discovering and not at all minded to question the political role of poetry, as is attested by his text of 25 December on the 'literature of small peoples'.[166]

The notes made in his diary between October 1911 and January 1912 are, therefore, a precise indication of Kafka's very lively interest in popular literary manifestations: in Pinès's literary history, he was looking for confirmation of the irrefutable existence of a genuine Jewish culture that came out of the people itself and was not merely religious. In his conversations with Janouch he stressed this same point. It was insofar as it was popular that Yiddish literature interested him: 'Peretz, Ash and all the other writers of the Jewish East never give us anything, in fact, but popular stories. They are right in this, for Judaism is not just a matter of faith, it is above all a matter of social practice: that of a community determined by its faith.'[167]

AN EASTERNIZED WESTERNER

Misunderstandings

The Yiddishist positions of the actors in the Polish troupe enabled Kafka to reactivate his socialist convictions and apply them to a national struggle which, for the first time in his existence, he was able to fight in the first person and actively—in contrast to his, no doubt lively, but passive interest in the Czech anarchist movements. In other words, the battle for Yiddish was a sort of concretization, or application to himself and what he now perceived as 'his' people, of the socialist theories to which he had subscribed for a long time, as Wagenbach, Robert and Michael Löwy have established.

Moreover, from 1912 onwards, Kafka adopted the standpoint and posture towards Western Jews that the 'enlightened' intellectuals of the East took towards the Eastern Jewish people: he did not attempt simply to take over their political positions—that is, their choice of socialism and Yiddishism—but to reproduce in his own location, that is to say, amid a community of assimilated, intellectual

Jews, the ethnological posture of the Eastern intellectuals, their humour and their reflexivity. And he sought to draw out all the consequences from this reversed situation.

Hence the gigantic misunderstanding that developed between Brod and Kafka. Hence Kafka's increasingly evident marginality. It was precisely at the moment when this *Yiddishkeit* was developing in Eastern Europe, at the high point of the movement of popular emancipation and education within Jewry, during this 'period of intense transformation of [Eastern] Jewish life',[168] at a moment when Yiddish literature was developing and the traditional structures of the Jewish world were being massively contested, that the Germanized Western Jews discovered the Eastern Jewish world and were filled with wonder. At the turn of the century, they first glimpsed—then, as I have said, contemplated with fascination—this world which seemed to them frozen and immobilized in time and which they saw as a reservoir of rites, traditions and ancestral customs they had now forgotten as a result of the assimilation imposed by their fathers. In other words, it was exactly during the period in which the Jewish townships were experiencing the greatest upheavals (urbanization, secularization, the emergence of social and political struggles) that the assimilated Jewish bourgeoisie believed it was getting back, through accounts of life in the shtetls and Hasidic rituals and tales—and all with a kind of rather naive wonderment—to the undiluted past of its forefathers or, in other words, to its own lost Judaism. And this is why there was total misunderstanding between the two groups: while the Western Jewish intellectuals were working to re-appropriate their identity, rediscovering forgotten religious rituals and marvelling at the richness of the Hasidic legends, the Eastern Jewish intellectuals were working to pull these pauperized populations out of the ghetto, to secularize Jewish culture, to invent forms of the novel, poetry and drama that would enable them to accede to literary modernity, to lay claim to a popular language and literature—in short, to 'modernize' their culture without denying their Jewishness.

In the memoirs of his stay in Prague which he published in 1934 (more than 22 years after the events), Yitzchak Löwy reports a conversation with Max Brod that clearly conveys the total misunderstanding that had arisen between Brod, for whom the Lemberg theatre troupe represented the embodiment of a religious 'exoticism', and Kafka, who better understood the intentions of the dramaturges and the social and political reality of these Eastern Jews. In the article in which he speaks of his encounter with Brod, Löwy recalls precisely the reasons for these dissensions: 'I remember my agitation when, in one of his conversations with me, Max Brod spoke of the beauty of the fur hat and silken, long coat, truly Rembrandt-like. I answered him heatedly. "The fanatic Eastern Jewry can impress you, modern cultivated Jews, but we are happy that we pulled ourselves out and freed ourselves from that world." '[169] Similarly, the German Jews, who did not know the religious rituals well, had the impression that they recognized extracts from the religious repertoire or from synagogue worship in the non-religious melodies of these operettas and plays.[170] This was precisely how Brod saw matters, believing himself to be in the presence of 'the essence of Judaism':

> I, for example, was a frequent member of the audience at the performances in the Café Savoy, and learned a lot there towards appreciating Jewish folklore [. . .] I zealously championed the thesis that however near to unconscious humour and trash they might come, from the performances of these actors more could be learned about the essence of Judaism than from the philosophic deductions of Jews of the West, who were, it is true, striving to get to the people, but who were at heart already estranged from them.[171]

Brod was convinced that he was in the presence here not of one of the first attempts of a secularized Jewish dramatic art mounting a profound challenge to the immobilism of religious rituals (which was what this Yiddish theatre was in reality and what the troupe led by Löwy were trying to promote) but, directly or in unmediated fashion, of the Jewish tradition itself, the purest essence of the tradition. In a laudatory article he published in the *Prager Tagblatt*, Brod stresses this point, comparing the Yiddish theatre with Greek classical drama, 'where religious ceremonies appear on the stage with the same naïveté as here'.[172]

At this same point in time, Kafka, informed by Löwy, had understood the reality of this theatre and of the movements stirring within Eastern Jewry. Even though the two friends attended the same performances of the acting troupe together and showed great enthusiasm (though much more moderate on the part of Brod, who did not become a friend of Löwy's), Brod and Kafka were not looking for, and did not see, the same thing. At exactly the same time, they discovered and were fascinated by direct evidence of the existence, practices and language of a real Jewish people—or, in other words, one that was not assimilated. However, within this entity named the 'Jewish people', Brod stressed the word Jewish while for Kafka the emphasis was on the word people. Brod saw in it a changeless essence freighted with religiosity while Kafka glimpsed the first signs of the 'battle' of a people on the way to cultural and political emancipation.

Kafka's attitude towards 'miracle-working' rabbis seems to me additional evidence of his critical distrust of Hasidism, the depth of his ethnological culture and the sceptical distance he assumed spontaneously, unlike Brod. The latter relates that he himself, in around 1914–15, frequented 'a "miracle-working" rabbi, a refugee from Galicia who lived [. . .] in the Prague suburb Zižkov':[173] 'Unusual circumstances of life had brought me near to a kind of religious fanaticism,' writes Brod.[174] He adds, proving his lack of understanding of Kafka's critical stance towards these Hasidic religious rituals:

> It is worthy of note that Franz, whom I took with me to a 'Third Meal' at the close of the Sabbath, with its whispering and hasidic chants, remained, I must admit very cool [. . . O]n the way home he said, 'If you look at it properly, it was just as if we had been among a tribe of African savages. Sheerest superstition.' There was nothing insulting, but certainly a sober rejection in these words.[175]

In other words, far from sharing Brod's naive infatuation with exotic religious rites, Kafka adopted an attitude of rationalistic scepticism and ethnological distancing, whereby he rejected adherence to a religious belief—even an 'authentic', Jewish one. He opted, as

Brod saw it, for a 'sober rejection' which, to say the least, indicated a marked difference in their two attitudes.

In this same period, in September 1915, Kafka reported in his diary another visit with Brod and Langer to a wonder-working rabbi. The latter's stay at the 'court' of such a rabbi in Galicia and his conversion to Hasidism made him a perfect informant for Kafka:[176]

> With Max and Langer at the wonder-rabbi's on Saturday [. . .] A lot of children on the pavement and stairs. An inn [. . .] A pale, dim room, whitish-grey walls, several small women and girls standing around, white kerchiefs on their heads, pale faces, slight movements. An impression of lifelessness. Next room. Quite dark, full of men and young people. Loud praying. We squeezed into a corner. We had barely looked round a bit when the prayer was over, the room emptied [. . .] We were pushed toward a table on the rabbi's right. We held back. 'You're Jews too, aren't you?' A nature as stongly paternal as possible makes a rabbi. 'All rabbis look like savages,' Langer said. This one was in a silk caftan, trousers visible under it. Hair on the bridge of his nose. Furred cap which he kept tugging back and forth. Dirty and pure, a characteristic of people who think intensely. Scratched in his beard, blew his nose through his fingers, reached into the food with his fingers.[177]

The interested distance shown in this quasi-ethnological description never subsides into empathic involvement or identification. And one can see Kafka taking rapid notes during the scene (the many sentences without verbs bear witness to this), seeking to understand, to grasp a logic, to describe so as better to remember, maintaining a spontaneous restraint and a rationalistic wariness. We should note also his extreme realism which stresses the details that render the adherence of the true believer impossible (the trousers, the hair, the dirt).

In July 1916, in a letter to Brod, Kafka related his visit in the company of the same Langer to the *rebbe* of Belz, one of Hasidism's highest dignitaries, when he was himself at Marienbad. The scene, as he saw it, was half-comical, half-ethnological. He did as much as he could to dispel any aura of enchantment around the doings of the famous rabbi and his disciples—that is to say, he described them as objectively and factually as possible. 'He looks like the Sultan in a Doré illustration of the *Münchhausen* stories which I often looked at in my childhood.'[178] The comparison gives an idea of the level of seriousness and 'profundity' Kafka attributed to these religious practices. Further on, referring to the questions the rabbi asked during a short walk in the street, Kafka writes: 'All in all, what comes from him are the inconsequential comments and questions of itinerant royalty, perhaps somewhat more childish and more joyous [. . .] Langer tries to find or thinks he finds a deeper meaning in all this; *I think that the deeper meaning is that there is none and in my opinion this is quite enough.'*[179]

With this key sentence Kafka marked the difference between his own attitude and the naivety of Langer's belief, asserting, as he does here, that he neither sought nor found any transcendence in these practices, any 'deeper meaning' or, in other words, any metaphysics. The use of the word childish betrays his attitude exactly: it was both distant and amused. He simply observed the practices of this group of Eastern Jews with the interested curiosity of an ethnologist attempting to decipher something that remained obscure. There follows a highly amusing description of the rabbi's curiosity about a building 'of a neutral style' and about a system of rain gutters previously unknown to him: 'He makes a detour in order to come close to a downspout that runs in a corner formed by a projection of the building. He is delighted at the water's thumping inside; he listens, looks up along the pipe, touches the pipe, and has the whole apparatus explained to him.'[180]

This sceptical irony and stress on material details were clearly incompatible with any belief of a mystical kind. Here lay the complexity and subtlety of Kafka's position: he was no believer in the magic of tradition and did not have an idealized view of Eastern Judaism. In a word, thanks to his initiation by Löwy, he avoided the trap of unrealistic nostalgia for the shtetl. Yet, at the same time, he believed in a renewed, living version of secularized Judaism.

His attitude towards the Easterners who had taken refuge at Prague during the war also attests to the difference in his approach from that of Brod. In March 1915, for example, he writes in his diary:

> Eastern and Western Jews, a meeting. The Eastern Jews' contempt for the Jews here. Justification for this contempt. The way the Eastern Jews know the reason for their contempt, but the Western Jews do not. For example, the appalling notions, beyond all ridicule, by which Mother tries to comprehend them. Even Max, the inadequacy and feebleness of his speech, unbuttoning and buttoning his jacket. And, after all, he is full of the best good will [. . .] I, as if made of wood, a clothes-rack pushed into the middle of the room. And yet hope.[181]

The realism of his view of the Eastern Jews—and, most importantly, of the view those in his close circle held of them—was so great that he saw and understood not just the contempt of the Westerners for the Easterners but the symmetrical contempt of the Eastern Jews for the Western. The hints of embarrassment felt by Brod at this meeting gives a good indication of the split—and even, in some respects, the complete rift—that occurred between them in this period. This constitutive misunderstanding and dissymmetry had many repercussions on their relationship, on the very writing of Kafka's texts and also, much later, on the way Brod interpreted his friend's writings. Their views of Judaism and the politics connected with that Jewish identity were irreconcilable and the moment of the encounter with the troupe of Yiddish actors attests to this more than any other. As a cultural and political movement, Yiddishism appeared to Kafka, at least in the first years after he discovered it, an almost perfect (at least theoretical) solution to the political problems that concerned him. It was as though he had found in that configuration tools that enabled him to assert and consolidate his social and political critique.

Drawing the consequences from the situation of the assimilated Jews of his generation, Kafka in his solitary state at Prague built up a strange party-less, programme-less position that was nonetheless astonishingly coherent, *Yiddishkeit* providing him with both the content of a social critique and the means to implement and express it.

'Sewn into their skins'

All these elements enable us to establish a parallel between Kafka's behaviour in this situation and that of certain small groups of radical Jews described by Aschheim, second-generation Zionists and/or critics of Zionism.[182] The American historian sees Kafka as a member of an informal group of non-Zionist intellectuals who enthusiastically venerated the *Ostjuden* and drew on the East European Jewish experience to mount a challenge to the Cultural Zionists.[183] This group was a tiny minority within the group of politicized Jews (themselves a very small minority), but they were highly influential at the turn of the century. Among them were Georg Wollstein and Gustav Landauer.[184] Within this tendency, a very powerful belief in the 'authenticity' of Eastern Jews was to emerge and social representations and identity projections were entirely inverted by it. It saw the Eastern ghettos as harbouring a real, living Jewish culture, with which it sought to align itself.[185] A genuine veneration thus emerged for everything relating to this form of life which was assumed to be more authentically Jewish—for a Judaism thought of as unaffected by assimilation. In revolt against German culture, these people had not only chosen *Judentum* over *Deutschtum* but had reversed the presupposition of Western superiority over the Easterners to such a degree that they were convinced the Westerners had everything to learn from those in the East. In other words, they rejected themselves as assimilated Jews, professing a kind of strange self-hatred not because of their Jewishness but of what they regarded as their loss of themselves as Jews, insofar as, at the end of the process of assimilation imposed by their parents, they were no longer sufficiently Jewish. Those who reached this degree of self-rejection as German Jews were very few in number, notes Aschheim. For these radicals, as he calls them, Jewishness and Germanness were (and were to remain) incompatible. The problem of the link to the Jewish East was indissolubly connected with assimilation. To venerate the Easterners was, for them, a way of expressing their refusal and rejection of assimilation. The forms of this fascination with the Jewish East were multiple and gave rise to internal debates in which infinite nuances of position, conviction and concrete practice (more or less extreme and more or less cautious) were expressed. The central question that arose for them was how to redefine an authentic Judaism when they experienced their own as something deformed, lost and dissolved within a process of integration imposed by their parents. Some, like Langer, effected a kind of reverse assimilation and moved from West to East. On his return to Prague, Langer continued to practice a Judaism akin to Eastern norms.[186]

Some of the positions adopted by Kafka in very diverse fields make it conceiveable that, without being clearly affiliated to any broad political movement professing these types of convictions or subscribing to any belief of a mystical kind, he was close, in his Prague solitude—and felt close to—the positions of this radical, critical minority. Among other things, he was close to them on all matters relating to education and teaching. Robert points out that he read everything new that was published in the field and attended several lectures on the subject at Prague.[187] At the time, the education issue was much debated among politically committed Jews (whatever their particular orientation), both in Western and Eastern Europe because it was directly linked to the nagging question of assimilation. In the categories of thought of the day, the question was: How was it possible for assimilated Jews to 'become Jews again'? And the most radical, who thought it too late for those who had been through the school system and acquired German values, asked whether it was possible, by means of a non-German education, to avoid German- or Austrian-born Jewish children meeting the same fate, and to create avenues for the education of unassimilated Western Jews. Zionist theorists worked on this issue. Aschheim also shows that, among those who saw the Eastern way of life as an instrument for the critique of the values, beliefs and ways of life of the Germanized Jewish bourgeoisie (and petty bourgeoisie), some went so far as to call for the formation of 'voluntary ghettos'[188] in order to isolate Western children until they acquired a genuine

Jewish identity—in other words, until they threw off their German trappings and became 'Jewish enough' to face contact with Germanness without the danger of dissolution.[189] Taking the inversion of the negative stereotype of the Eastern Jew to its logical conclusions, Wollstein wanted, for example, to make the Easterners the educators of the Westerners by inverting the customary relation of dependence between the two.[190]

Drawing on a very deeply held conviction, Kafka went so far, during summer 1921, as to ask his eldest sister to part from her 10-year-old son and send him to school away from the assimilationist environment of Prague. Seeking to convince her, he painted a terrifying portrait of the assimilated Jew, arguing that her child might have a chance of escaping this fate:

> Ten years are not many, but in some circumstances ten can be an advanced age [. . . T]hese ten years have been spent in Prague where prosperous Jews are affected by a particular spirit from which children cannot be shielded. I am not referring to individuals, of course, but to this almost tangible general spirit, which expresses itself somewhat differently in everyone, in each according to his character, which is in you as well as in me—this small, dirty, lukewarm, squinting spirit. To be able to save one's own child from that, what good fortune![191]

Between 1915 and 1923, educational institutions were founded by radical Zionist groups in Czechoslovakia, Austria and Germany. The Jüdisches Volksheim (Jewish Cultural Centre) was one of a number of reception centres and educational institutions for the children of Jewish refugees from Galicia. It was founded in Berlin by Siegfried Lehmann (1892–1958), a Buberian Zionist, with a group of students and the support of Max Brod, Martin Buber, Gustav Landauer and others.[192] The school (which had 250 East European pupils when it was opened in 1916) embodied the hopes of a small political group of dissenters from official Zionism and sought a path towards a renewal of the Jewish way of life.[193] As Lehmann saw it, the cultural centre was to represent a genuine vanguard within

the Jewish people at the heart of a process that was to transform
both Eastern and Western Jewish youth. Lehmann always stressed
the need for a mutual transformation.[194] The group's educational
project—or, rather, its educational utopia—lay in the hope of escaping
assimilation, which they regarded as a cultural and social tragedy,
and in finding pathways to a Jewish 'renaissance' for the generations
that would follow. Essential to this schooling and education was
what they imagined to be a return to origins and a learning of Jewish
ways of life and thought that should be dispensed by Eastern Jews.
It was to this institution, during the war, that Kafka's fiancée Felice
Bauer, then living in Berlin, decided to commit herself as a teacher.
Kafka greatly encouraged her and took a very close interest in the
activities of the centre. Some of his letters to Felice in 1916 give us
very clear signs of the importance he accorded to education as a
weapon in the struggle against assimilation. On that occasion, he
laid out the paradoxical reality and radicalism of his position on the
subject. On the one hand, he urged Felice to throw herself fully into
the activities of the centre—that is to say, to show her commitment
to the Jewish cause in practical terms; on the other, he was also
extremely hesitant about the reflex reactions of Western Jews in
Berlin, as manifested spontaneously by his fiancée, and he constantly
warned her against them.[195] He tried to explain his position by
choosing his words carefully, toning down his assertions and
employing euphemisms (it seems he was always afraid of shocking
Felice with his 'extreme' opinions and that he took great care not to
frighten her). In September 1916, he wrote to her:

> As far as I can see, it [aid to Galician refugees] is positively
> the only path, or threshold to it, that can lead to spiritual lib-
> eration. The helpers, moreover, will attain that goal earlier
> than those who are being helped. Beware of the arrogance of
> believing the opposite, this is most important. What form
> will the help in the Home [Cultural Centre] take? Since people
> are sewn into their skins for life and cannot alter any of the
> seams, at least not with their own hands and not directly,
> one will try to imbue the children [die Pfleglinge:[196] 'those we

take care of']—at best respecting their individual characters—
with the spirit and more indirectly the mode of life of their
helpers [*der Helfer*]. In other words one will try to raise them
to the standard of the contemporary, educated, West European
Jew, Berlin version, which admittedly may be the best type of
its kind. With that, not much would be achieved. If, for
instance, I had to choose between the Berlin Home and
another where the pupils were the Berlin helpers [*die Pfleglinge
die Berliner Helfer*[197]] (dearest, even with you among them,
and with me, no doubt, at the head), and the helpers simple
East European Jews from Kolmyja or Stanislawow, I would
give unconditional preference to the latter Home—with a
great sigh of relief and without a moment's hesitation. But I
don't think this choice exists; no one has it; the quality corresponding to the value of the East European Jew is something
that cannot be imparted in a Home.[198]

Kafka's conviction is entirely counter-intuitive (to us) and, in
any event, far removed from our ordinary notions and assumptions
in such questions. The historical detour I have had to make to clarify
the terms of this letter is a measure of the intellectual distance, the
difference in common background and the sheer gulf in understanding that separates our categories of thought from those of Kafka. If
the letter were not put into its historical context, we would be forced
to postulate a certain modesty on Kafka's part, a self-effacement that
would show a kind of unconditional, naive, ill-considered admiration
for deprived peoples, an intense feeling very like Christian charity
or akin to solicitude for the 'poor'. And this would lead directly to
the Brodian conception of a saintly Kafka. Yet Kafka is acutally
making clear here his indivisibly political and existential position
on a crucial point. However, as is often the case with his diaries or
letters, based as they are on historico-political assumptions shared
by both writer and addressee (or, rather, based on things that neither
was aware of knowing, so consubstantial were these assumptions
with their everyday lives), it never occurred to Kafka to spell out his
meaning or clarify certain points, which is precisely what is missing

for the contemporary reader. This is why the letter has to be para-
phrased if it is to be understood in all its dimensions.

So, what precisely is Kafka saying to Felice? First that, if one
were not careful and if one were not aware, one was so well 'sewn
into [one's] skin' as a Western Jew and could so little 'alter any of
the seams' of one's assimilated being that if one wanted to teach
young minds from the East something, one would succeed only in
transmitting one's own standard to them: namely, the 'standard of
the contemporary, educated, West European Jew, Berlin version'—or,
in other words, 'not much', even if this 'may be the best type of its
kind'. It was to be hoped, says Kafka, that those who went into transmission activities of this kind knew that 'simple East European Jews'
would be better teachers, better at 'impart[ing]' Jewish culture and
Jewish being than the Jews of Berlin. Here, in the West, no one could
impart anything of 'the quality corresponding to the value of the East
European Jew'. As a Germanized Jew, one could simply try to 'acquire'
what they possessed and what Westerners no longer had. Kafka
stresses his reluctance to sustain the dissymmetrical relationship
which seemed self-evident to Felice and argues for overturning the
relation of dominance which applied at the time between Westerners
and Easterners. The letter was in fact quite violent, opposing both the
Berlin *Volksheim* project and the illusions of Felice who was readying
herself, no doubt naively, to begin to give classes to children who
spoke little or no German. Kafka was trying to tell Felice that, though
the generosity of the project was admirable, in his view no one would
gain much from it if everyone held to their ordinary conceptions.

Once again the difference between Brod's convictions and
Kafka's is very clear here. Brod, almost systematically adopting moderate positions in keeping with his habitus, would become the
spokesperson for the most widespread Western beliefs, namely, that
the *Westjuden* had to impart to the Easterners the canons and values
of the German tradition in which he continued to believe. Consistent
with these beliefs, Brod taught literature classes in the refugee school
established at Prague during the war while Kafka did not.

Defence and Illustration of the Small Literatures

The other question which indicates that Kafka adopted 'pro-Eastern' positions concerns the place to be accorded to the Yiddish language and the use to be made of it. It seems that, generally, where political and linguistic questions were concerned, Kafka fell in with the most commonplace Yiddishist positions. We have, first, to understand his 'Introductory Talk on the Yiddish Language' as setting out a position.[199] The conviction which shows through in it, the care with which he develops his arguments and the highly skilled construction of his reasoning are indications of the fact that this was not a case of mere nostalgia for what he regarded as an archaic practice but a firm decision in favour of this popular language or, in other words, a Westernized transposition of the choices of the Yiddishists.[200]

We may see it, then, as the repository of everything he had read and heard on the subject which reinforced his belief in the truly 'popular' character of that language. We may hear it also as a set of rhetorical strategies aimed at trying to convince the audience—of Germanized Jews—that Yiddish was not a contemptible jargon but a Jewish national language worthy of the name.

Even in his introductory remarks, Kafka stresses the fact that the evening's audience were closer than they thought to that language —that is to say, closer than they thought to the Eastern Jews: 'I should like, ladies and gentlemen, just to say something about how much more Yiddish you understand than you think.'[201] He skilfully develops the argument that the public was not actually contemptuous of that language, as the thesis then most widespread at Prague had it, but 'frightened of Yiddish',[202] precisely because of the fact, as he implies, of this forgotten closeness. Without being explicit about it, he analyses this sense of fear as a product of assimilation or, in other words, as a kind of collective denial or repression in the psycho-analytic sense:

> But dread of Yiddish, dread mingled with a certain funda-
> mental distaste, is, after all, understandable [. . .] You begin
> to come quite close to Yiddish if you bear in mind that apart
> from what you know there are active in yourselves forces

and associations with forces that enable you to understand Yiddish intuitively [. . .] Then you will come to feel the true unity of Yiddish, and so strongly that it will frighten you, yet it will no longer be fear of Yiddish but of yourselves.[203]

It may be said, then, that a kind of collective cultural unconscious had continued to exist among German Jews despite assimilation, and Kafka suggests that hearing Yiddish poetry could suddenly bring these forgotten elements back into consciousness. He addresses assimilated Jews in this way in order to speak to them of assimilation itself as the forgetting and loss of their identity, but he speaks of it, too, with the hope that a kind of collective memory will enable them to recover an intuitive sense of the language.

As is to be expected, we can also detect arguments that come straight from the reading of Pinès's book. We find almost word for word, for example, the belief in a mobile, shifting tongue made up exclusively of borrowings because it was spoken by the people: 'It consists solely of foreign words. But these words are not firmly rooted in it, they retain the speed and liveliness with which they were adopted.'[204] We can see, incidentally, that the text is made up of numerous borrowings but what Kafka brings to it is the addition of a kind of enthusiasm and enchantment entirely absent from Pinès's thesis which, by contrast, bears the stamp of the austerity and seriousness of academic writing. Keen to foreground and high-light only the elements that make Yiddish an essentially popular idiom, a language free of any dependence on German and any cod-ification arising out of intellectual injunctions, Kafka selects from Pinès only such propositions as run in that direction. For example, when Pinès concludes that there has been a standardization of spelling which has assisted in the dissemination of literary works,[205] Kafka writes: 'Yiddish as a whole consists only of dialect, even the written language; though agreement has been largely reached as to its spelling.'[206] Similarly, with regard to grammar, whereas the Russian, in a highly nuanced argument, stresses the existence of a specific Yiddish grammar, Kafka for his part asserts: 'No grammars of the language exist. Devotees of the language try to write grammars, but Yiddish remains a spoken language that is in continuous flux. The people will not leave it to the grammarians.'[207]

However, in his contention that Yiddish was indeed a language— and not just a 'ghetto slang'[208]—Kafka relies on reasoning not found in Pinès's book. He draws on a much more sophisticated (though largely false) philological and genealogical argument which, as Bechtel has shown,[209] had wide currency in Germany at the time, to the effect that Yiddish and modern German were derived from a single language, Middle High (that is, mediaeval) German. Kafka writes:

> Yiddish originated in the period when Middle High German was undergoing transition into Modern High German. At that time there was a choice of forms, and Middle High German took one course and Yiddish the other. Or Yiddish developed Middle High German forms more logically than even Modern High German did [. . .] Or Yiddish keeps to Middle High German forms in spite of Modern High German.[210]

This 'Germanizing' approach to Yiddish is clearly most ambiguous, since it made the language dependent to a certain degree on German.[211] Understandably, the initial aim here was to reassure the Prague audience by affirming the closeness of Yiddish to the legitimate tongue. Moreover, though seemingly in contradiction with the argument (simultaneously developed by Kafka) that it was made up only of foreign terms, this point about the closeness of Yiddish to mediaeval German was central in the discussion with the pro-Hebrew faction since it sought to respond to their critique that presented Yiddish as an 'impure', hybrid language. According to Herderian conceptions, 'purity' of language was a necessary foundation for legitimate national claims. Yet the enemies of Yiddish defined it as a 'jargon' which, initially 'pure' German, had gradually deteriorated. The genealogical argument was aimed, therefore, at re-establishing historical purity for Yiddish which should no longer be regarded as a degraded form of German but a related language, derived from the same mediaeval German. This line of reasoning, which assumes a complete understanding of the linguistic struggles within Jewish political movements and, above all, great mastery of Yiddishist argumentation, could not have been elaborated within a few weeks by Kafka working alone. It required collusion with—and assistance from—Löwy.

The last sign of a conversion on Kafka's part to the Eastern stance is his analysis of the small or 'little literatures'.[212] After three months of discussions with Löwy and initiation into the various aspects of Yiddish literature, and after much reading on the subject, Kafka sketched out a sort of theory of the literatures of the 'small nations', basing himself on a comparison of the Czech and Yiddish literatures and the parallels between them. Bruce points out that this was a very common expression in the Austro-Hungarian Empire where, following Herderian categories of thought, the emergent literatures that accompanied the movements campaigning for national autonomy within the empire were dubbed *kleine Literaturen* or *Literaturen der kleinen Nationen*.[213] Instead of simply trying to characterize emergent Yiddish literature, Kafka sought the laws of that literature's functioning by the comparative route.

Klein (little, small) is clearly a relative term and has no actual content on its own. If there were 'small literatures', that was because they stood over against 'great literatures' [*grosse Literaturen*] in general, and, in particular, the literature that served as a standard of measurement in that part of the world: namely, German literature.[214] And recognizing points of similarity between them, despite their differences, Kafka deduced from these a certain number of general characteristics. There are several ways in which we may read this initial thinking on the differences between the 'great' and 'small' literatures as Kafka saw them in 1911. We may see it, as I have done elsewhere, as one of the first attempts at a general theory of the dominated literatures and one of the first realistic descriptions of the features of the emergent literatures that are found generally, whatever the context.[215] Kafka made a direct connection, leaving no room for doubt, between literature and the nation, between the appearance of a claim to nationhood and the development of a literature accompanying, reinforcing and consolidating that claim. This connection between literature and nation, regarded as the main characteristic feature of the 'small literatures'—

that is, of the dominated literatures—was a great theoretical advance on Kafka's part.[216] However, when we are looking to understand the later development of Kafka's work, these notes jotted down in haste may also be read as one of the first signs of his conversion to another type of literature. He was thinking, in the infinitely paradoxical terms of a writer belonging to a dominant literary space with a very long, rich and prestigious literary history, of the effects that would be produced by writing from another standpoint, from another conception of the literary art or of the real—realistic—working conditions of the writers producing in dominated languages. From his position as a German-language writer, Kafka was seeking to understand the position, the labour and the specificity of those who were writing with an opposite perspective; to gauge the differences between them and himself; to grasp, as if from the inside, what gave them their 'advantage' (*Vorteil*) and, as it were, to adopt their point of view. Kafka might be said, then, to have been a spontaneous theorist seeking out the ways to exploit the 'advantageous' characteristics of the small literatures practically in his writing. Now, their major feature—and also their very great originality—which he formulated in several ways, was their openly political character or, rather, the fact that there was a great interweaving in each of them of the political and the literary: ' "literary events" taken as "objects of political solicitude"; "literature [. . . disseminated within] a country on the basis of political slogans" ', writes Kafka.[217] In other words, to define the 'advantages' of literatures of this type is a way of both stressing their absence of autonomy (autonomy being understood here in the sense of an exclusive preoccupation with literature, a systematic depoliticization), and being content with, and even laying claim to, their heteronomous—that is to say, at once political and national—character.

This delight in their connection with politics was all the more striking for the fact that Kafka viewed the real literary life within these little worlds very harshly. He enumerated their faults and disadvantages. They were characterized, he said, by a lack of 'outstanding talents' or 'irresistible national models' and by 'mediocre talent'; theirs was 'a literature poor in its component parts', using 'mediocre material'.[218] There were neither 'great personalities to be studied' nor 'literary movements of great scope'; 'petty themes' are treated and 'insults, intended as literature, roll back and forth.'[219] In other words, he had no illusions about the literary quality of the products of these emerging universes, just as he was realistic about the quality of the Yiddish plays he had been watching since the beginning of October. But it was from just these weaknesses that Kafka drew the kind of certainty that the 'usefulness' of literary work—conceived as a service to the community—provided a much more thrilling conception of writing than was to be found in perpetuation of the grandeur of the German literary tradition.

The major advantage of literary work within a 'small literature', from the standpoint of a Kafka striving to adopt the perspective of the Yiddish writers, was its collective and hence combative character: '[E]veryone must always be prepared to know that part of the literature which has come down to him, to support it, to defend it—to defend it even if he does not know it and support it.'[220] Kafka also stressed the collective enthusiasm peculiar to these literatures, an enthusiasm he seemed to share, which suggested that there were indeed several 'benefits' to be had from working as a writer in these worlds: 'the stirring of minds', 'the liveliness of such a literature exceeds even that of one rich in talent,' 'there is universal delight in the literary treatment of petty themes.'[221] Above and beyond their political and combative definition, Kafka also stressed their popular character, which was congruent with their other distinctive features: '[L]iterature is less a concern of literary history than of the people [*als Angelegenheit des Volkes*], and thus, if not purely, it is at least reliably preserved.'[222] We find here undimmed his almost voluntaristic faith in the need to follow the people.

It seems to me that this famous text in which he ruminates on the *kleine Literaturen* is, for him, a way of preparing his own literary project. On the basis of this thinking, he would strive to adopt a dominated stance within a dominant literature, to introduce into the German language devices, endeavours and demands peculiar to the writers of the most dominated literatures, and to try to occupy (and hold) a position that is genuinely untenable, invisible or incomprehensible for his contemporaries.

It is impossible, lastly, to avoid mention of Gilles Deleuze and Félix Guattari's analysis in this connection. As is well known, their commentary was a critical milestone. I have to acknowledge, on the one hand, that they are right when they assert: 'Never has there been a more comic and joyous author from the point of view of desire; never has there been a more political and social author from the point of view of enunciation. Everything leads to laughter, starting with *The Trial*. Everything is political, starting with the letters to Felice.'[223] After this long labour of historical contextualization, it does indeed emerge that a politics on Kafka's part—or, rather, a labour of critique—is undeniably at work in his writings. They also have matters right when they state that the question of the language of the writing played a central role in his work and that the politics concerned was expressed in part in the diary entry of 25 December 1911 devoted to the analysis of the 'small literatures'.

However, driven by the—entirely legitimate—desire to defeat on their own ground 'the dreary psychoanalytic interpretations'[224] that ruled the roost within literary criticism in the 1970s, Deleuze and Guattari at best present only a number of historical intuitions. Admittedly, they deserve enormous credit for wresting Kafka from the clutches of psychological criticism, which, after setting out what it regarded as the ultimate truth of his work, laid claim to an interpretative monopoly. But their very sketchy conception of the 'minor literatures', their very vague view of the relations between Jews, Czechs and Germans in Prague and their belief that the adjective 'minor' described 'the revolutionary conditions for every literature'[225] provide no genuine content for Kafka's 'politics'. Most importantly, their minimal—if not, indeed, minimalist and, often entirely mistaken—reconstitution of the political and linguistic issues of turn-of-the-century Prague, discussed solely on the basis of the information found in Wagenbach (an important book, admittedly, but not one on which to base a reconstruction of the totality of the space),[226] make their *Kafka* more a sort of programmatic outline for a future criticism than a genuine instrument for a renewed approach to the reading of the texts. And although Deleuze and Guattari rightly stress the political character of the drives underlying Kafka's work (though they are wrong about the actual issues), they fail to spot the dual situation that arises out of his simultaneous membership of two worlds that place more or less contradictory demands on him. Kafka was preoccupied both with criticism and with literature (as stylistic and formal experimentation) and this is what the exclusively political readings of his work fail to see.

NOTES

1 We know that Kafka spoke Czech well, but that he took scant interest in Czech literary life. Unlike Brod, he had little knowledge of contemporary Czech authors. Cf. Zimmermann, 'Kafkas Prag und die kleine Literaturen' in von Jagow and Jahrhaus, *Kafka Handbuch*, p. 176.

2 Cf. Michel, *Prague, Belle Époque*, p. 67.

3 Along these lines, Anderson has shown that the young Kafka was fascinated by *Jugendstil* and by *fin de siècle* aestheticism (see 'Chapter 2: The *Jugendstil* Body: Reform Clothing and the Cultural Politics of the Kunstwart' in *Kafka's Clothes*, pp. 50–73). Robertson has also stressed the young Kafka's fascination with German literary culture, particularly the figure of Goethe, in *Kafka: Judaism, Politics and Literature*, pp. 7–9.

4 Franz Kafka, 'The Judgment' (Willa and Edwin Muir trans) in *The Complete Stories of Franz Kafka* (Nahum N. Glatzer ed.). (New York: Schocken Books, 1995), pp. 77–88 [originally written in 1912, 'Das Urteil' was published in 1913 in *Arkadia* (Leipzig: Kurt Wolff)]; all further mentions of *The Complete Stories* refer to this edition.

5 Löwy, *Franz Kafka, rêveur insoumis*, pp. 53ff.

6 Kafka, 'Letter to His Father' in *Dearest Father*, p. 145.

7 Ibid., pp. 161–2.

8 Rose-Marie Ferenczi, *Kafka: Subjectivité, histoire et structures* (Paris: Klincksieck, 1975), p. 22.

9   Elias Canetti, *The Conscience of Words* (Joachim Neugroschel trans.) (London: HarperCollins, 1979), p. 114.

10 Kafka, 'Letter to His Father' in *Dearest Father*, p. 162.

11 On the origin of his identification with the socialist stance, see also Robert, *As Lonely as Franz Kafka*, pp. 40–61.

12 Max Pulver, 'Spaziergang mit Franz Kafka' in Hans-Gerd Koch (ed.), '*Als Kafka mir entgegenkam.*' *Erinnerungen an Franz Kafka* (Berlin: Wagenbach, 2008), pp. 130–5; here, p. 131.

13 Klaus Wagenbach, *Kafka* (Eweld Osers trans.) (London: Haus Publishing, 2003), p. 35.

14 The Boer War (1899–1902) is regarded today as one of the great colonial wars of the modern era. It pitted Great Britain, then the principal world power, at the head of the largest, most powerful European colonial empire, against two Afrikaner republics of South Africa, Transvaal and the Orange Free State, populated by Boers—that is to say, Dutch and French settlers—who refused to be annexed by the British Empire. The dissymmetry in forces involved—the British deployed an army of some 500,000 men against very sparse bands of Boers—the unexpected resistance of the Boers, the brutality of the British, and the very high number of victims on both sides for a long time made this war a byword in socialist (or socialist-inclined) circles for popular resistance to colonial oppression.

15 Hugo Bergmann, 'Schulzeit und Studium' in Koch, '*Als Kafka mir entgegenkam.*', pp. 13–24; here, p. 21.

16 Ibid., p. 20.

17 Löwy, *Franz Kafka, rêveur insoumis*, pp. 19–50.

18 See Jürgen Born, *Kafkas Bibliothek: Ein beschreibendes Verzeichnis* (Frankfurt: Fischer, 1990).

19 Ibid., p. 19.

20 Brod, *Franz Kafka*, pp. 100–01.

21 Wagenbach, *Kafka*, pp. 72–3.

22 Löwy, *Franz Kafka, rêveur insoumis*, pp. 29–31; see also Wagenbach, *Franz Kafka: Biographie seiner Jugend*, pp. 162–4.

23 Löwy uses this term, referring to Kafka's 'romantic socialism of a libertarian cast' in *Franz Kafka, rêveur insoumis*, p. 39.

24 That is to say, the writings produced as part of his occupational activity [available in English as *Franz Kafka: The Office Writings* (Stanley Corngold, Jack Greenberg and Benno Wagner eds, Eric Patton and Ruth Hein trans) (Princeton: Princeton University Press, 2008); hereinafter referred to as Kafka, *The Office Writings*].

25 Wagenbach, *Kafka's Prague*, p. 78.

26 Ibid., p. 79.

27 Cf. Ernst Pawel, *The Nightmare of Reason: A Life of Franz Kafka* (New York: Vintage Books, 1984), p. 185.

28 Wagenbach, *Kafka*, p. 67. On Kafka's occupation, see also Robertson, *Kafka: Judaism, Politics and Literature*, pp. 40–2.

29 Quoted in Wagenbach, *Kafka*, p. 67.

30 Ibid., p. 69.

31 Gustav Janouch, *Conversations with Kafka* (Goronwy Rees trans.) (London: Quartet Books, 1985), p. 66.

32 Brod, *Franz Kafka*, p. 82.

33 Kafka, *The Office Writings*, p. 54.

34 Ibid., p. 61.

35 Ibid., p. 56.

36 See David, *Franz Kafka: Oeuvres complètes*, VOL. 4, p. 1177. This passage is not included in the English selection of *Office Writings*.

37 Kafka, *The Office Writings*, p. 66.

38 Ibid., p. 69.

39 Lily Braun, *Memoiren einer Sozialistin*, 2 VOLS (Munich: Langen, 1909–11).

40 Franz Kafka, 'Letter to Minze Eisner, November/December 1920' in Beverly Colman, Nahum N. Glatzer, Christopher J. Kuppig and Wolfgang Sauerland (eds), *Letters to Friends, Family and Editors* (Richmond: Oneworld Classics, 2011), p. 244. The letter to Ottla (Ottilie David), not included in this volume, was written around 1 May 1920. A French translation can be found in David, *Franz Kafka: Oeuvres complètes*, VOL. 3, p. 974. [Trans.]

41 Kafka, '11 September 1916' in *Letters to Felice*, pp. 614–15. [The second part of the passage is not included in this English translation of the letters. Trans.]

42 Kafka, 'Letter to Minze Eisner, November/December 1920' in *Letters to Friends, Family and Editors*, p. 244.

43 Cf. Bruce, *Kafka and Cultural Zionism*, pp. 125–6.

44 See Chapter 3, p. 257.

45 According to Gelber, Kafka became a Zionist in his last years, when he spoke of leaving for Palestine and took lessons in Hebrew. Cf. Mark. H. Gelber, 'Kafka und zionistische Deutungen' in von Jagow, and Jahraus, *Kafka-Handbuch: Leben-Werk-Wirkung*, pp. 293–303; here, p. 295. See also Robertson, who argues that Kafka felt a deep sympathy for Zionism in the last seven or eight years of his life (*Kafka: Judaism, Politics and Literature*, p. *viii*, pp. 13–14).

46 Gelber, 'Kafka und zionistische Deutungen' in von Jagow and Jahraus, *Kafka-Handbuch*, p. 302.

47 Cf. Binder, *Kafka-Handbuch*, VOL. I, pp. 435–7. Several of his diary entries are quite explicit on this. See, for example, 17 December 1913: 'Lecture by Bergmann, "Moses and the Present". Pure impression—In any event, I have nothing to do with it' (Kafka, *Diaries*, p. 249).

48 Kafka, 'Letter to Grete Bloch, 11 June 1914' in *Letters to Felice*, pp. 552–3.

49 Bruce, *Kafka and Cultural Zionism*, p. 203.

50 Bergmann, 'Schulzeit und Studium' in Koch (ed.) '*Als Kafka mir entgegenkam*', p. 17, p. 21.

51 Scholem, *From Berlin to Jerusalem*, p. 41.

52 After the First World War, Brod became a member of the Hapoel Hatzair (Young Worker) Party, in which the majority of Czechoslovakia's Zionists were enrolled and which had been founded in Palestine in 1906 by Aaron David Gordon. In 1920, he published two essays on the subject: 'Sozialismus im Zionismus', in order, as he put it, to deal with the social aspects of Zionism, and 'Im Kampf um das Judentum'. In the first he rejected the Zionism of Poale Zion (Workers of Zion), another socialist Zionist party, because it was Marxist (as part of this argument, he naturally also rejected the Bund for the same reasons). His political writings campaigned for the 'utopia', as he put it, of a non-Marxist socialism.

53 Löwy, *Franz Kafka, rêveur insoumis*, p. 67.

54 See Robertson, *Kafka: Judaism, Politics and Literature*.

55 See Gilman, *Franz Kafka: The Jewish Patient*, pp. 12–13.

56 Bokhove, ' "The Entrance to the More Important": Kafka's Personal Zionism' in Gelber, *Kafka, Zionism and Beyond*, p. 58.

57 Neumann, *Franz Kafka: Aporien der Assimilation*, pp. 29–32.

58 Löwy, *Franz Kafka, rêveur insoumis*, p. 39.

59 '[H]is attitude towards Zionism alternated between irony and scepticism to antagonism,' writes Bokhove (' "The Entrance to the More Important": Kafka's Personal Zionism' in Gelber, *Kafka, Zionism and Beyond*, p. 54).

60 Ibid., p. 57.

61 Löwy, *Franz Kafka, rêveur insoumis*, pp. 29–31.

62 [Franz Kafka, *The Metamorphosis* (Susan Bernofsky trans., David Croenberg introd.) (London and New York: W. W. Norton and Co., 1996); originally published in 1915 as *Die Verwandlung* (Leipzig: Kurt Wolff); Kafka, *Amerika: The Man Who Disappeared* (Michael Hofmann trans.) (London and New York: Penguin, 2007); originally published in 1927 as *Der Verschollene* (Leipzig: Kurt Wolff); Kafka, 'In the Penal Colony' (Willa and Edwin Muir trans) in *The Complete Stories*, pp. 140–67; originally published in 1919 as *In der Strafkolonie* (Leipzig: Kurt Wolff).]

63 This is also argued by Robertson in *Kafka: Judaism, Politics and Literature*, pp. 28ff.

64 Cf. Bruce, *Kafka and Cultural Zionism*, pp. 36–7.

65 Brod, *Franz Kafka*, p. 112.

66 On Kafka's relations with the Lemberg troupe, see Binder, *Kafka-Handbuch*, VOL. 2, pp. 390–5.

67 Kafka, *Diaries*, pp. 99–100.

68 Ibid., p. 65.

69 Ibid., p. 73.

70 Ibid., p. 77 (translation modified).

71 Ibid., p. 86.

72 Janouch, *Conversations with Kafka*, p. 70.

73 Kafka, '6 October [November] 1912' in *Letters to Felice*, p. 129.

74 Brod, *Franz Kafka*, pp. 110–11.

75 Ibid., p. 113 [see Franz Kafka, 'Introductory Talk on the Yiddish Language' (Ernst Kaiser and Eithne Wilkins trans) in *Dearest Father*, pp. 381–6].

76 Ibid., pp. 110–11.

77 [Heinrich Graetz, *History of the Jews*, 6 VOLS (Bella Löwy ed. and trans.) (Philadelphia: The Jewish Publication Society of America, 1891); originally published in 1887–89 as *Volkstümliche Geschichte der Juden*; Méir Pinès, *L'Histoire de la littérature judéo-allemande* (Paris: Jouve et Cie, 1911).]

78 Franz Kafka, '24 January 1912' in *Diaries*, pp. 172–3.

79 Franz Kafka, 'Concerning the Jewish Theatre' in *Dearest Father*, pp. 129–34. At Kafka's suggestion, Löwy tried to write his memoirs in order to publish them in *Der Jude*. Since, however, his mastery of German was far from perfect, he asked Kafka for some editorial assistance. Kafka accepted and when he received the manuscript from Löwy he appealed to Brod for help. He wrote to his friend at the end of September 1917: 'Löwy [. . .] sends me the opening of his essay for Der Jude. I consider the piece very usable but naturally it needs to be polished up grammatically ever so slightly and this would take an incredibly subtle hand. I will soon send you a typed copy of the piece (it is quite short) for your consideration. An example of the difficulties: He comments on the Polish theatre's audience, as opposed to the audience for the Jewish theatre: tuxedoed men and ballgowned ladies. Excellently put, but the German language balks. And there is a great deal like that; his highlights are the more effective since his language veers between Yiddish and German, inclining a bit toward the German. If only I had your skill at translating!' ('Letter to Max Brod, Zürau, end of September 1917' in *Letters to Friends, Family and Editors*, p. 148). It is not known why the text, extensively revised by Kafka, was not sent to Buber.

80 Ibid., pp. 132–3.

81 Ibid., pp. 133–4.

82 A political party created by Simon Dubnow in 1906. See Chapter 1, p. 86 note 101.

83 On the practical and material conditions of the organization of the conference and how it passed off in actuality, see Joshua A. Fishman, 'Attracting a Following to High-Culture Functions for a Language

of Everyday Life: The Role of the Tshernovits Language Conference in the "Rise of Yiddish"' in Joshua A. Fishman (ed.), *Never Say Die! A Thousand Years of Yiddish in Jewish Life and Letters* (*Contributions to the Sociology of Language*) (The Hague: Mouton, 1981), pp. 370–91. The conference simply enabled Yiddish to be recognized as *a* Jewish language among others.

84 Cf. Régine Robin, *L'Amour du Yiddish: Écriture juive et sentiment de la langue, 1833–1940* (Paris: Le Sorbier, 1984), p. 99.

85 Kafka, *Diaries*, p. 70.

86 Robin, *L'Amour du Yiddish*, pp. 280–1.

87 [Also available in two different translations as Samuel Frug, 'Sand and Stars' (trans. anon.) and 'As the Stars and the Sands' (Joseph Jasin trans.) in *The Standard Book of Jewish Verse* (Joseph Friedlander comp., George Alexander Kohut ed.) (New York: Dodd, Mead and Company, 1917), p. 700; p. 703.]

88 Robin, *L'Amour du Yiddish*, pp. 280–1.

89 Kafka, *Diaries*, p. 81.

90 Cf. Minczeles, *Histoire générale du Bund*, pp. 231–54.

91 The translation of the *Communist Party Manifesto* into Yiddish by Chaim Zhitlowsky dates from 1897.

92 And also their closest adversaries: the Socialist Zionists, the Poale Zion (or Poalei Tziyon), the anarchists, etc. Cf Minczeles, *Histoire générale du Bund*, pp. 255–85.

93 Ibid., p. 235.

94 Cf. Rachel Ertl, *Le Shtetl: La bourgade juive de Pologne* (Paris: Payot, 1986), pp. 163–4.

95 Cf. Henri Minczeles, *Vilna, Wilno, Vilnius: La Jérusalem de Lituanie* (Paris: La Découverte, 2000), pp. 237ff; Alain Dieckhoff, 'Litvakie: le terreau sioniste' in Alain Dieckhoff and Yves Plasseraud eds), *Lituanie juive, 1918–1940: Message d'un monde englouti* (Paris: Autrement, 1996), pp. 158–66.

96 Robin, *L'Amour du Yiddish*, p. 105.

97 Cf. Ariel Sion, 'Séculier et religieux: le paysage scolaire' in Dieckhoff and Plasseraud, *Lituanie juive, 1918–1940*, pp. 122–41; here, p. 123.

98 Dieckhoff, *L'invention d'une nation*, pp. 24–5.

99 See Minczeles, *Vilna, Wilno, Vilnius*, pp. 57–150, pp. 229–85. See also Dieckhoff, *L'Invention d'une nation*, pp. 22–8.

100 Cf. Jean Baumgarten, *Le Yiddish: Histoire d'une langue errante* (Paris: Albin Michel, 2002), p. 11.

101 Dieckhoff, *L'Invention d'une nation*, pp. 126–7.

102 Cf. Minczeles, *Vilna, Wilno, Vilnius*, p. 148.

103 Cf. Baumgarten, *Le Yiddish*, p. 21.

104 According to the sociolinguist Fishman, Yiddish is the only Jewish language of the diaspora through which intellectuals pursued the objective of a secularization of Jewish society. He argues that (fictional or scholarly) literature exerted a modernizing influence on the Jews themselves, particularly through what he calls the 'promotion of the modern author' who, in secular Jewish milieus, for the first time in the history of traditional Jewish communities, could claim to equal or even surpass the rabbis. See Joshua A. Fishman, 'Le yiddish: de la tradition à la modernisation' in Shmuel Trigano (ed.), *La Société juive à travers l'histoire*, VOL. 4 (Paris: Fayard, 1993), pp. 511–21.

105 Ertl, *Le Shtetl*, pp. 146–52. See also Rachel Ertl, 'La littérature yiddish: une littérature sans frontières' in Rachel Ertl (ed.), *Royaumes juifs: Trésors de la littérature yiddish*, VOL. 1 (Paris: Robert Laffont, 2008), *ix–lv*; here, pp. *xxvii–xxviii*.

106 Kafka, '26 January 1912' in *Diaries*, p. 174.

107 Kafka, who began to read Pinès's *Histoire de la littérature judéo-alle-mande* in the French edition in January 1912 (by 'Judaeo-German literature', it was Yiddish writing that was meant, not, as subsequent usage would have it, literature written by German Jews in German), noted down certain passages from it in his diary (see '26 January 1912', in *Diaries*, pp. 173–6).

108 Cf. Ertl, *Le Shtetl*, p. 177.

109 Kafka, *Diaries*, p. 174.

110 Cf. Ertl, 'La littérature yiddish', pp. *xl–xli*.

111 Cf. Robin, *L'Amour du yiddish*, pp. 49–50. [*Ahavat Zion* was translated into English by F. Jaffe in 1887 as *Amnon, Prince and Peasant: A Romantic Idyll of Judaea* (London: Simpkin, Marshall and Co.). Trans.]

112 Cf. Joseph Shatzmiller, 'Les limites de la solidarité: antagonismes au sein de la société juive ancienne et moderner' in Trigano, *La*

Société juive à travers l'histoire, VOL. 4, pp. 387–425; here, pp. 412–13. See also Laqueur, *A History of Zionism*, p. 60. Laqueur gives a figure of 400,000 Jews who are said to have emigrated to the US between 1903 and 1906.

113 Irving Howe, with the assistance of Kenneth Libo, *World of Our Fathers: The Journey of the East European Jews to America and the Life They Found and Made* (New York: Harcourt, Brace, Jovanovich, 1976), pp. 27–62.

114 Ibid.

115 Renée Poznanski, cited in Simon Dubnow, *Lettres sur le judaïsme ancien et nouveau* (Paris: Les Cerf, 1989), p. 380 note 6.

116 Minczeles, *Histoire générale du Bund*, p. 178. Between 64 and 71 per cent of Jewish immigrants settled in New York (Poznanzki cited in Dubnow, *Lettres sur le judaïsme*, p. 380 note 6).

117 Dubnow, 'Ninth Letter: A Historic Moment (The Question of Emigration)' in *Nationalism and History*, pp. 193–4.

118 Franz Kafka, *Letters to Milena* (Willy Haas ed., and Tania Stern and James Stern trans) (London: Vintage, 1999), p. 156.

119 Howe, *World of our Fathers*, pp. 81–2.

120 Ibid., pp. 104–06. Different socialist currents also developed in parallel with these. Cf. Baumgarten, *Le Yiddish*, p. 172. See also Jonathan Frankel, 'Chapter 9: Class War and Community: the Socialists in American-Jewish politics, 1897–1918' in *Prophecy and Politics: Socialism, Nationalism and the Russian Jews* (Cambridge, London and New York: Cambridge University Press, 1981), pp. 453–547.

121 Cf. Howe, *World of our Fathers*, p. 296.

122 Ertl, 'La littérature yiddish', pp. *xlvi–xlvii*.

123 These were published in Russian in 1897 and 1898 and translated into German by Israel Friedlander as Simon Dubnow, *Die Grundlagen des Nationaljudentums* (Berlin: Jüdischer Verlag, 1905).

124 The Introduction to the German translation is not contained in the English translation, *Nationalism and History*, and is here translated from Dubnow, *Lettres sur le judaïsme*, p. 479 [Trans.].

125 Kafka, *Diaries*, p. 86.

126 Ibid.

127 Ibid., p. 175.

128 Ibid., p. 86.

129 Cf. Howe, *World of Our Fathers*, pp. 434–5.

130 Pinès, *Histoire de la littérature judéo-allemande*, pp. 329–87.

131 Ibid., p. 330.

132 Ibid. [This translation of 'The Sweatshop' is taken from Marc Miller, *Representing the Immigrant Experience: Morris Rosenfeld and the Emergence of Yiddish Literature in America* (New York: Syracuse University Press, 2007), p. 78. Trans.]

133 Pinès, *Histoire de la littérature judéo-allemande*, p. 340.

134 Ibid., p. 497.

135 Kafka, *Diaries*, p. 132,

136 Ibid., pp. 175–6.

137 Seth L. Wolitz, ' "Le paon doré s'est envolé . . ." La culture ashkénaze, 1860–1940: une trop brève renaissance' in Nathalie Hazan-Brunet (ed.), *Futur antérieur: L'avant-garde et le livre yiddish (1914–1939)* (Paris: Flammarion, 2009), p. 18. This is the catalogue of an exhibition at the Musée d'Art et d'Histoire du Judaïsme, published in the 'Skira-Flammarion' collection.

138 Cf. Pinès, *Histoire de la littérature judéo-allemande*, pp. 497–8. The operetta is a show in which singing, dancing and sequences of dialogue alternate. Cf. Wolitz, ' "Le paon doré s'est envolé . . ." La culture ashkénaze, 1860–1940: une trop brève renaissance'.

139 Pinès, *Histoire de la littérature judéo-allemande*, p. 499.

140 Howe, *World of Our Fathers*, p. 474.

141 Kafka, *Diaries*, p. 176.

142 Howe, *World of Our Fathers*, p. 482.

143 Pinès notes that 'many of the couplets with their accompanying melodies went right round the ghetto and became truly popular' (*Histoire de la littérature judéo-allemande*, p. 497).

144 Ibid., 'Notes', pp. 500–01.

145 Kafka, *Diaries*, p. 88.

146 On 22 October 1911, Kafka wrote: 'Yesterday with the Jews. *Kol Nidre* by Scharkansky, pretty bad play . . .'. Ibid., p. 85.

147 Pinès, *Histoire de la littérature judéo-allemande*, p. 6. On Pinès's book and Kafka's notes, see also Robertson, *Kafka: Judaism, Politics and Literature*, pp. 16–21.

148 Kafka spoke of it in similar terms a few days earlier: 'Also, would like to know Yiddish literature, which is obviously characterized by an uninterrupted tradition of national struggle that determines every work.' Kafka, '8 October 1911' in *Diaries*, p. 70.

149 Pinès, *Histoire de la littérature judéo-allemande*, pp. 6–8. Pinès was a Russian Jew born in 1881 at Mogilev (Mahilyow). He left Russia in 1900 and went first to Berne, then to Paris to study. He was a member of the Zionist Socialist Party. Cf. Bechtel, *La Renaissance culturelle juive*, p. 279 note 85. His book came out of his doctoral thesis which was supervised by the Sorbonne professor Charles Andler who also wrote its foreword.

150 In particular, cf. Bechtel, for whom Pinès's work is 'quite a mediocre doctoral thesis [. . .] overloaded with commonplaces on Yiddish that were widely believed in Western Europe and peppered with factual errors' (ibid., p. 103).

151 Bruce also stresses that the book is one of the two first academic accounts of Yiddish literature (*Kafka and Cultural Zionism*, p. 52).

152 Pinès, *Histoire de la littérature judéo-allemande*, pp. 438–93.

153 Ibid., p. 484.

154 Among many others, Robin is convinced that Kafka went along with a 'anti-Haskalah vision of Yiddish literature' and that he had a 'Chagalian, nostalgic, populist, passéist tendency'. See Régine Robin, 'Le yiddish et l'allemand: la langue de l'autre, l'autre de la langue' in Max Kohn and Jean Baumgarten (eds), *L'Inconscient du yiddish* (Paris: Anthropos, 2003), pp. 61–77; here, p. 75.

155 Kafka, *Diaries*, p. 174.

156 Robin, *L'amour du yiddish*, p. 80.

157 Mendele Mocher Sforim, *Fishke the Lame* (Gerald Stillman trans.) (New York: Thomas Yoseloff, 1960); originally published in 1910 as *Fischke der Krumer* (Warsaw: Mendele).

158 Kafka, *Diaries*, pp. 174–5.

159 Ibid., p. 175.

160 Ibid., p. 176.

161 Robin, *L'Amour du yiddish*, p. 278, p. 279.

162 Ibid., p. 276.

163 Franz Kafka, 'Letter to Max Brod, June 1921, from Matliary' in *Letters to Friends, Family and Editors*, p. 289.

164 Howe, *World of Our Fathers*, p. 444.

165 Ibid., p. 429.

166 See pp. 156–61.

167 Gustav Janouch, *Conversations avec Kafka* (Bernard Lortholary trans.) (Paris: Maurice Nadeau, 1998), pp. 243–4. [This passage is not present in the English translation. Trans.]

168 Dieckhoff, *L'invention d'une nation*, pp. 71–2. And he adds that two major changes undermined the organization of the traditional shtetls: 'at the level of the elites, the consolidation of a secularized Jewish intelligentsia made up of students and young autodidacts as writers and journalists; at the level of the masses, the appearance of a proletariat more craft-based than industrial.'

169 Löwy, 'Tsvey Prager Dikhter', cited in Beck, *Kafka and the Yiddish Theater*, p. 222.

170 On this point, see Bechtel, *La Renaissance culturelle juive*, pp. 170–1.

171 Brod, *Franz Kafka*, pp. 110–12.

172 Max Brod, 'Eine Jargonbühne in Prag', *Prager Tagblatt* (27 October 1911). Cited in Bruce, *Kafka and Cultural Zionism*, p. 141.

173 Gradually, the Hasidim began to give their own 'lessons'. Cf. Ertl, 'La littérature yiddish', p. *xxv*. The 'miracle-working' rabbi, endowed with supernatural powers, was one of the central elements in the Hasidic belief system.

174 Brod, *Franz Kafka*, p. 153. It is evident that Brod maintained a relation of religious faith with this Hasidic world that is wholly removed from Kafka's attitude to these same practices.

175 Ibid.

176 In the ethnological sense. On Jiří Langer's conversion to Hasidism, see Chapter I, p. 54. Langer also gave Kafka some lessons in Hebrew. Like Martin Buber he later published collections of Hasidic tales and wrote several works on the Jewish tradition (cf. Bruce, *Kafka and Cultural Zionism*, p. 85; see also Robertson, *Kafka: Judaism, Politics and Literature*, p. 176).

177 Kafka, *Diaries*, p. 341.

178 Kafka, 'Letter to Max Brod, mid-July 1916' in *Letters to Friends, Family and Editors*, p. 121.

179 Ibid.; p. 122, my emphasis. The words 'more childish and more joyous' here translate as *kindlicher und freudiger*. See Max Brod (ed.), *Franz Kafka: Gesammelte Werke* (Frankfurt: Fischer, 1966), p. 145.

180 Ibid., p. 123.

181 Kafka, '11 March 1915' in *Diaries*, p. 332.

182 Binder also compares Kafka's attitude with certain figures in the Jewish political world—particularly Nathan Birnbaum (1864–1937). Cf. Binder, *Kafka-Handbuch*, VOL. 2, p. 392. Birnbaum, who was among the earliest Zionists, broke with Herzl in 1898 to become one of the theorists of diaspora nationalism and was one of the main organizers of the Czernowitz Conference in 1908. Birnbaum's most favoured target was precisely Cultural Zionism, which aimed to create a future Jewish culture, not recognizing, as he saw it, that such a culture had existed for many years. As a result, Buber was one of his opponents and Birnbaum accused him of having a backward-looking conception of an idealized Jewish people outside of any social reality. Cf. Aschheim, 'Chapter 5: Identity and Culture' in *Brothers and Strangers*, pp. 114–17. However, from the early days of the war, Birnbaum abandoned all secular, socialist concerns in favour of an orthodox religious view of the world. He could not, therefore, be a direct model for Kafka. Cf. Bruce, *Kafka and Cultural Zionism*, pp. 65–6.

183 Aschheim, 'Chapter 8: The Cult of the Ostjuden: The War and Beyond' in *Brothers and Strangers*, pp. 185–214; here, pp. 204–05.

184 Ibid., pp. 190 and 194–205 respectively.

185 Ibid., pp. 185–214.

186 See Chapter 1, p. 54 and Chapter 2, p. 145.

187 Robert, *As Lonely as Franz Kafka*, p. 116. Kafka's library includes many works on pedagogy (cf. Born, *Kafkas Biblothek*, pp. 109–47). On the Prague lectures, see Bruce, *Kafka and Cultural Zionism*, pp. 116–24. The 'meeting' between Kafka and Scholem, which occurred through the good offices of Felice, came about at a lecture given by Lehmann at the Jüdisches Volksheim on 'The Problem of Jewish Religious Education' which Scholem attended and criticized vehemently (Scholem, *From Berlin to Jerusalem*, pp. 78–80).

188 Aschheim, 'Chapter 8: The Cult of the Ostjuden' in *Brothers and Strangers*, pp. 190–1.

189 Ibid. Aschheim quotes Arnold Kutzinski, 'Freiwilliges Ghetto', *Der Jüdische Student* 15 (June 1917): 506–09.

190 Georg Wollstein, 'Neue Kompromisse', *Der Jüdische Student* 15 (January 1917): 353–4. Cited in Aschheim, 'Chapter 8: The Cult of the Ostjuden' in *Brothers and Strangers*, p. 190.

191 Kafka, 'Letter to Elli Hermann, Autumn 1921' in *Letters to Friends, Family and Editors*, pp. 240–1. The French edition of Kafka's correspondence suggests the letter was written in summer 1921.

192 Gustav Landauer (1870–1919) was a famous German anarchist and revolutionary. As one of the main theorists of libertarian socialism in Germany, he took part in the creation of the Munich Soviet Republic. He was appointed commissar for public education and culture, but subsequently killed by counter-revolutionaries in the streets of Munich in 1919. Martin Buber was named as executor in his will.

193 Cf. Aschheim, 'Chapter 8: The Cult of the Ostjuden' in *Brothers and Strangers*, p. 193.

194 Ibid., pp. 194–5.

195 Insofar as we can know the theoretical and political positions of the Centre's founders on the one hand, and Kafka's positions on education on the other, his fears in this regard seem to have been largely unfounded.

196 *Franz Kafka: Briefe an Felice und andere Korrespondenz aus der Verlobungszeit* (Erich Heller and Jürgen Born eds) (Frankfurt: Fischer, 1981), p. 697.

197 Ibid.

198 Kafka, '12 September 1916' in *Letters to Felice*, p. 617. ['Home' here refers to the same *Volksheim* rendered elsewhere in this text, following Harry Zohn's usage in his translation of Scholem, as 'Cultural Centre'. Trans.]

199 Even though Kafka had obtained the support of the Bar Kochba association which was usually more interested in literature written in Hebrew.

200 I should point out that there will be no question here of debating the real origins of Yiddish, its grammar or its syntax, nor even

flushing out mistakes that both Kafka and Pinès may have made with regard to that language. I intend to confine myself to the arguments advanced by Pinès, who was not a philologist, a fact he freely admits, and those developed by Kafka in his 'Introductory Talk'. In other words, I am trying to decipher the way Pinès and Kafka were instrumental in passing on a political belief that had crystallized around Yiddish. Admittedly, Pinès says nothing that the specialists in that language did not already know; he repeats a certain number of commonplaces about it in his work; and in Kafka's talk we find many traces of the notes he took while reading Pinès's book.

201 Kafka, 'An Introductory Talk on the Yiddish Language' in *Dearest Father*, p. 381.

202 Ibid., p. 382.

203 Ibid., pp. 382–6.

204 Ibid., p. 382.

205 Pinès, *Histoire de la littérature judéo-allemande*, p. 25.

206 Kafka, 'An Introductory Talk on the Yiddish Language' in *Dearest Father*, p. 383.

207 Ibid., p. 382.

208 Pinès, *Histoire de la littérature judéo-allemande*, p. 11.

209 Bechtel, *La Renaissance culturelle juive*, pp. 84–8.

210 Kafka, 'An Introductory Talk on the Yiddish Language' in *Dearest Father*, p. 383.

211 Cf. Bechtel, *La Renaissance culturelle juive*, p. 86.

212 Kafka, '25 December 1911' in *Diaries*, pp. 148–51.

213 Bruce, *Kafka and Cultural Zionism*, pp. 42–3.

214 These remarks are inspired in part by the new translation into French of the diary entry of 25 December 1911 by Marie-Odile Thirouin, 'Annexe' in Philippe Zard (ed.), *Sillages de Kafka* (Paris: Le Manuscrit, 2007), pp. 82–91.

215 Casanova, *The World Republic of Letters*, pp. 200–04.

216 Cf. Casanova, 'La guerre de l'ancienneté' in Casanova, *Des littératures combatives*, pp. 26–31.

217 Kafka, *Diaries*, p. 150.

218 Ibid., pp. 149–50.

219 Ibid., p. 150.

220 Ibid., p. 149. On the combative character of the 'small literatures', see Casanova, *Des littératures combatives*.

221 Ibid., p. 148, p. 149, p. 150.

222 Ibid., p. 149.

223 Gilles Deleuze, Félix Guattari, *Kafka: Toward a Minor Literature* (Dana Polan trans.) (Minneapolis: University of Minnesota Press, 1986).

224 Ibid., p. *xi*.

225 Ibid., p. 18. Robert's translation of the adjective *klein* here (which simply means 'small') as 'minor' (in David, *Franz Kafka: Oeuvres complètes*, VOL. 3, p. 194) is denounced by Bernard Lortholary as 'inexact and tendentious'. See Lortholary, 'Introduction' in Franz Kafka, *Un jeûneur et autres nouvelles* (Bernard Lortholary trans.) (Paris: Flammarion, 1993), p. 35.

226 Wagenbach, *Franz Kafka: Biographie seiner Jugend*.

Among Kafka's presuppositions, not the least is that the contemplative relation between text and reader is shaken to its very roots. His texts are designed not to sustain a constant distance between themselves and their victim but rather to agitate his feelings to a point where he feels that the narrative will shoot towards him like a locomotive in a three-dimensional film. Such aggressive physical proximity undermines the reader's habit of identifying himself with the figures in the novel.

Theodor Adorno, *Prisms*

Actually a single soldier would have been quite enough, such is our fear of them. I don't know exactly where these soldiers come from, in any case from a long way off, they all look very much alike [. . .] They are small, not strong but agile people, the most striking thing about them is the prominence of their teeth which almost overcrowd their mouths, and a certain restless twitching of their small narrow eyes.

Franz Kafka, 'The Refusal'

Let us now consider Kafka's place in the literary world. The galloping politicization of the small literary worlds of Prague, which I described in the first chapter, does not in any way mean that we should confound the literary world with the political, or feel justified in superimposing the one on the other. The fact that we see a progressive politicization of German-speaking Jewish writers—a previously depoliticized group—does not imply that we should interpret their literary position and undertakings in exclusively political terms. However, the political transformations I have just described mean that we have to take account of the progressive overlapping of political and literary spaces. As a result, I believe that if we are to understand the literary work of those concerned, we must not forget the intense politicization of the field in which they lived and produced, Kafka foremost among them.

Very often the critics see themselves as forced (believe themselves forced) to relate Kafka to only one of the two spaces: either to the world of political struggles, as is the case, for example, with Deleuze and Guattari, Löwy or Bruce, or—and this is the commonest temptation, given the habits of criticism—to the German (and even European) cultural space—in other words, to modernism, *fin de siècle* aestheticism or the modern novel. Anderson, for example, sees Kafka's fictions as 'pure' aesthetic objects: *The Metamorphosis* is, in his view, a call for autonomy;[1] and he suggests *Amerika* is to be understood in relation to the literary, artistic and philosophical movement which revolutionized the representation of both human beings and inanimate things throughout the European literary fields of the period.[2] Similarly, Kundera states that Kafka belongs 'to the generation of the great innovators—Stravinsky, Webern, Bartok, Apollinaire, Musil, Joyce, Picasso and Braque—all born, like him, between 1880 and 1883'.[3] In doing so, he seeks to relate Kafka's books to what he calls 'the *large* context of literary history (the history of the European novel)', not to the '*microcontext* of biography'.[4] In other words, the agencies of global consecration set up his stories as models of formal modernity: Kafka's work was evaluated by the aesthetic yardstick of the literary world which made the reputation of that work after the war—that is to say, by the literary standards of the most autonomous regions of the global literary space. And it was placed so high in the hierarchy of the founding works of novelistic modernity as to make it impossible to conceive that his stories had been written in a literary world operating in a quite distinct aesthetic context.[5]

It seems to me impossible to act as though Kafka and his contemporaries moved within a 'pure' literary world, as though their preoccupations were merely aesthetic or formal, as though, in a word, they were free of any political or even national concern (the question of national belonging forming the very substrate of political commitment in those years). Even if Kafka is less torn than his friend Brod because he was not nostalgic for German greatness, what is peculiar to Kafka is that he too belonged simultaneously to two literary spaces which were regarded as antagonistic. This dual membership means, then, that we have to study the two spaces between which he moved—the literary *and* the political—*at one and the same time.* To put it another way, he embodied in the literal sense the two poles and logics of the global literary field. By his double position, which produced a split literary habitus, Kafka experienced the contradictory forces of the global literary field within himself (as much as Brod, but in other forms, since he operated in a different zone of the political field). Just like Beckett, he was in an untenable position. By dint of his belonging to a dominant space, he had available to him the most sophisticated (formal, linguistic, syntactic, historical, etc.) resources, characteristic of a largely autonomized literary field. Through his belonging to a heteronomous space—that of Jewish political struggles—he also possessed a strong political and national drive, characteristic of that type of literary universe.

This being the case, then each time one wanted to describe one of Kafka's literary choices, one would have to describe it twice, in terms of two—supposedly antithetical—principles, as two versions of the same reality and the same work: once as the claiming of artistic independence or critical freedom and once as the assertion of the will to create a 'popular' work. Where these two fields intersect, he developed a novel stance quite unknown before him, which was highly innovative in political and, above all, literary terms, and challenged the divisions between literature and politics as these were tacitly understood among the German-speaking writers in Prague. In other words, the divided, duplicated structure of the literary space to which he belonged makes it impossible to attribute a single definition to his work. We must postulate, rather, that it is governed by two apparently competing logics which he nonetheless strove all his life to bring together or reconcile: the logic of a pure, solely artistic undertaking and that of a political and social commitment.

But Kafka did not just adopt the stance and options characteristically taken by writers coming from dominant (or autonomous) spaces: he stood at the intersection of two worlds far removed from each other in global space and endowed with differing degrees of autonomy. He therefore took each of these spaces and crossed it with the other, in terms of the demands imposed by—and the production expected of—each: he delivered highly sophisticated thoughts on the social world in forms usually reserved for the most popular literature—tales, fables, legends, myths, fantasy stories— and, conversely, produced a violent, radical social criticism in forms so sophisticated that they were not necessarily identifiable by those whom that critique was seeking to convince. The practice of this kind of chiasmus ('doing the splits', as it were) gives his texts the simultaneously enigmatic and miraculous character which defines those literary *oeuvres* whose existence is so improbable that it seems to reside entirely in their contradictoriness.

KAFKA IN THE LITERARY WORLD

The Last of the Krausians?

One of the ways of explaining Kafka's place in that world—of perceiving the nuances and complexities of his convictions and the positions he assumed within the Prague literary field—would be to compare it, *mutatis mutandis*, with that occupied by Karl Kraus at Vienna. There are copious clues to suggest that these were homologous in many respects, despite the profound differences and divergences between the two men. Taking into account the structure of dependence between the Viennese and Prague spaces, we might take the view that, all other things being equal, Kafka had a position at Prague close to Kraus' at Vienna. On this assumption, the structural homology might be thought to be the product of the exportation and reappropriation of the Krausian model. Kafka would actually have drawn on the model of criticism provided for him by Kraus to forge his own positions—and, most importantly, to sustain them— within the Prague field.

I state this comparison with the proviso that it must be made in measured, cautious terms. I am not at all trying to superimpose the two trajectories. Where political options and convictions are concerned, particularly with regard to Jewishness, the two men are at opposite ends of the spectrum: Kraus is a declared assimilationist and Kafka a radical anti-assimilationist. Kraus regards himself as a guardian of Germanic tradition but Kafka is looking for a way to free himself from the injunctions of Germanism. However, since the foundation of *Die Fackel* in 1899, Kraus became positively an institution of Viennese intellectual life within the entire German-speaking area, a charismatic, if not mythical, figure who, above and beyond his political convictions, transformed himself very quickly into someone who 'revealed the rules of the game' of the intellectual field.[6] Pollak clearly shows that the fascination Kraus exerted over a very broad audience was in no way reducible to the political stances he took. It was actually his strategy of internal critique of the intellectual milieu that earned him his enormous prestige. By breaking —through techniques of provocation (the use of proper names, personal polemics)—with the elementary rules of decorum that govern the ordinary relations and compromises within any intellectual milieu, Kraus brought out what normally remained hidden. He also whipped up excitement among intellectuals because, entertaining an active conception of the written text (which, through the rupture it produced or its violent condemnatory impact, he conceived as having rapid effects), he had an extraordinary influence on conflicts among intellectuals themselves.[7] It is in this sense, it seems to me, that Kraus was able, on occasion, to be either a model or a recourse for Kafka.

This role Kraus played for Kafka, though recognized by a number of specialists, has either been downplayed or seen as not redounding to Kafka's credit, given Kraus' poor posthumous reputation among the French and American historians of this period. Among these, David writes that Kafka 'took an interest' in Kraus, though, he adds, that it was 'tempered, apparently, with reserve'.[8] The Hungarian critic Andor (André) Nemeth, armed with the conviction that Kafka could not but be critical of Kraus, has produced a strange interpretation of 'Josephine the Singer, or the Mouse Folk'[9] which, in his view, represents the metaphorical transformation of the passionate, fascinated but baneful relations between Kraus and Austria's Jews.[10] As Anderson sees it, Kraus played a key role in the elaboration of Kafka's anti-ornamental aesthetic.[11] One of his biographers, Ernst Pawel, points out that Kafka took a very close interest in Kraus and his doings. He even notes that 'Kafka's own views [. . .] came remarkably close to those of Kraus, though he approached them from a different angle and drew from them radically different conclusions.'[12] Moreover, Gray, who has published a remarkable and fascinating study of Kafka's aphorisms, demonstrates at length the major role Kraus' own played in the writing of them.[13] Kraus was as much a leading light of the Prague intellectual and literary scene as he was of the Viennese.[14] His role as a critical intellectual was undisputed in Bohemia. Through the many readings and lectures he gave there,[15] his permanent presence in the press, the publication of his books and his connections (at least in 1910–14) with the Expressionist poets, he was regarded as a fully fledged member of the Prague intellectual field. He was read, discussed, respected, admired or hated there, as he was in Vienna; until 1911, he had collaborators and friends in the two cities. We know, for example, that between 15 and 20 November 1918, he gave a series of four readings in Prague during which he read scenes from *Die letzte Nacht* and the Epilogue from *The Last Days of Mankind: A Tragedy in Five Acts*.[16] And it is to Kraus that the famous line is attributed which evokes the allegedly frenetic literary activity of the city: 'Es werfelt und brodelt, kafkat und kischt,' which might be translated as 'They werfel and brodel, they kafka and kisch.'[17] Everyone followed the publications and polemics Kraus launched against sundry individuals. This ensued, of course, from the structure of domination internal to the Austrian political space, which made Prague dependent on Vienna, but was due also to the fact that Kraus himself took a great interest in everything that went on in Prague. He was a regular and assiduous reader of the German-language Prague press, particularly of the liberal-leaning *Prager Tagblatt*, whose literary critic Ludwig Steiner he admired.[18] Moreover, as he registered an interest over many years in Czech nationalism and as the development of the Czech Republic became one of his pet subjects after 1918, he was also regarded as a great intellectual figure by the Czech section of the Prague literary space. The Czech writers of Karel

Čapek's generation, in particular, revered him and nicknamed him in laudatory fashion 'the enemy of cliché'.[19] It must be said that, contrary to the great majority of German-language writers, Kraus recognized the independence and sovereignty of Czechoslovakia very promptly and did so without reservation.[20]

Kraus did not stand alone. The historian Allan Janik and the philosopher Stephen Toulmin, in a reinterpretation of Ludwig Wittgenstein based on a historicization of his work which covers the content of debates in turn-of-the-century Vienna and the interests at stake in them,[21] describe the characteristics of a group of intellectuals and artists who allegedly shared the same stance of critical radicalism in their respective fields and dub them the 'Krausians'.[22] All being greatly impressed by Kraus' personality and, most importantly, by the work he performed as a critic of journalism and literature, they wanted to import the same impulses and homological forms of internal criticism into their own artistic practice. Apart from Kraus himself, Janik and Toulmin argue that the (self-evidently informal) group included Adolf Loos, Arnold Schönberg, Oskar Kokoschka and Ludwig Wittgenstein. The Krausians were said to have shared a recognition of Kraus as a master who had exerted a considerable influence on them but also to have transposed—each in his own way—Kraus' critical stance and anti-ornamental aesthetic conviction into their own respective artistic fields (architecture, music, painting, philosophy and literature). Kraus himself had drawn inspiration, in his battle against literary journalism, from Loos' principle of architectural anti-ornamentalism. In other words, Kraus proceeded by homology and shifted the critique of ornamentalism from the architectural to the literary domain. Timms identifies a great many echoes of Loos' conceptions in the writings of Kraus.[23] The aphoristic style, insofar as it stands opposed almost point for point to ornamentalism, can be understood both in relation—and opposition—to the elaborate, adjectival, ornate style of the feuilletonists and by homology with Loos' struggle in the field of architecture—to the point where the latter became for Kraus much more than a friend. He was, in fact, a theorist who arrived at just the right moment to reinforce Kraus' own aesthetico-political convictions, and a kind of auxiliary in the development of his own style which may be regarded as an exact equivalent of the proclaimed architectural austerity (and famous non-facade) of the house in the Michaelerplatz.[24]

Bearing in mind this logic of the transposition of Krausian postures into different fields of artistic and intellectual creation, I propose to define Kafka here as 'the last of the Krausians'. If he is so, however, he is a Krausian who would reject the appellation. That is to say, he is a writer with the same critical (but not political) dispositions as the other members of that informal group. However, living in the provinces far from Vienna, in a much more politicized world, he found an artistic solution for his critical stance and his subversive habitus that was different from that of Kraus, despite the fact that it drew on the Krausian precedent for its expression. In other words, because of the dependence of Prague on Vienna and the very high degree of politicization of the Prague field—through the centrality of the national question at Prague—Kafka was not able to opt for the same forms of aesthetic criticism. He would retain Kraus' stance, his model of intransigent radicalism, the austerity of his language and his anti-ornamental, aphoristic style without adopting his political convictions. If Kraus practised a criticism of language, Loos a criticism of ornamental architecture and Wittgenstein a critique of the philosophical *doxa*, we may say that, on the basis of the same dispositions, Kafka developed a political criticism.

Kafka only seldom quotes Kraus in his diaries or correspondence. He mentions him once very briefly, as we have said, in March 1911, alongside Loos, writing of two lectures he attended: the one by Kraus—David believes this to be 'Heine and the Consequences' ['Heine und die Folgen']—which took place at the Lese- und Redehalle; and the other by Loos, which took place the next day, on the theme that made him famous, 'Ornament and Crime' ['Ornament und Verbrechen'].[25] Kraus is not mentioned again until 1921, at which point his name appears in the famous June letter to Max Brod and then in letters to Robert Klopstock, most notably in June 1922. While at Planá in southern Bohemia, staying with his sister Ottla, Kafka asks Klopstock (not Brod) to send him the latest issue of *Die Fackel*. When at Berlin in October 1923, he thanks Klopstock for sending a work by Kraus: 'I've received the Kraus book; it was kind, dear and spendthrift of you to have sent it. It's jolly, though only an afterbirth of the *Last Days*'.[26] David believes he is referring to a work by Kraus entitled *Untergang der Welt durch schwarze Magie* (End of the World by Black Magic), published in 1922;[27] Timms thinks the allusion is to *Wolkenkuckucksheim* (Cloud Cuckoo Land) which had just been published in Vienna.[28] We find other mentions of Kraus in Kafka's conversations with Janouch which confirm the Prague man's interest in the Viennese writer.

If one insists that the correspondence and the diary give a faithful, exhaustive account of reality, these mentions are insignificant both in number and the space Kafka afforded them. However, it is impossible to infer from the absence of mentions of Kraus from Kafka's diary over a period of some 10 years either that he did not read him or attend his performances. Kraus came to give public readings at least twice a year in Prague. Moreover, if we look at them carefully, these rare notes imply a deep interest in, and very thorough knowledge of, the Viennese intellectual's publications. For example, in the letter to Klopstock of June 1922 in which he asked him to send the latest issue of *Die Fackel*, he writes:

> Instead may I ask you for something else: If a new issue of *Die Fackel* has come out—I have not seen one for a long time—and it isn't too expensive, would you send it to me, after reading it yourself. I do not want to deny myself this tasty dessert made up of all the good and bad instincts.[29]

This provides proof: first, that he was sufficiently interested in *Die Fackel* to be concerned about its frequency of publication; second, that he knew that no issue had appeared for a long time; and third, that he missed it, even though he daily received copies of the *Abendblatt* which, he tells Klopstock, contained articles by Brod.

Furthermore, where Klopstock's sending of Kraus' book to him in 1923 is concerned, the critical note to the effect that it was a mere 'afterbirth' of *The Last Days of Humanity* presupposes, without any doubt, that Kafka knew that very long play by Kraus which had been published in a special number of *Die Fackel* in 1919.[30] The discussions between the two friends also imply that any comment in this regard was superfluous, given their knowledge of Kraus and their obvious admiration for him.

Doubtless, the deepest thing Kraus and Kafka had in common, which enabled Kafka to draw on Kraus as a precedent and a model, was how 'ill-disposed' they were towards their contemporaries or, to put it another way, how much they shared a criticism of the intellectuals around them. They felt so different from them that they were unable to join in with their most widely shared convictions. It seems to me that the homology of their positions could be founded on this 'ill-disposition' which might be said to lie at the origin of their common resolve to build their work on the criticism of the intellectualist positions of the Vienna and Prague theorists—a criticism hidden or partially veiled in Kafka's case but explicit in Kraus'.

From *Die demolierte Literatur* (Demolished Literature) of 1896 onwards, we know that Kraus' main targets in the Viennese literary world—at least up to the 1914 war—were the writers of the Jung-Wien group. If, as I have suggested earlier, we may understand the Prague Circle as a structural equivalent—at a 20-year interval—of the Jung-Wien group, Kafka's criticisms of these writers may be understood in exactly the same sense. They are an essential marker of the kinship that can be established between Kafka and the group of Krausians.

Aesthetic Aversions

Kafka, too, detested the aesthetic of the writers of Jung-Wien, a movement he knew very well. As he wrote to Milena,[31] he read Bahr's diary which appeared in serialized form in the *Neues Wiener Journal*; he knew the plays of Arthur Schnitzler—*Anatol, La Ronde*—and the novella *Lieutenant Gustl*.[32] He rejected this 'Aesthetic' aesthetic immediately and viscerally. He expressed himself very explicitly and, it might be said, without subtlety on this subject in his correspondence.

It is a trenchant, remorseless, determined rejection that can be seen from a letter to Felice of February 1913:

> But if you go to *Professor Bernhardi*,[33] dearest, you drag me along [. . .] and there is a danger that we both succumb to that kind of bad literature [*die schlechte Literatur*], which the greater part of Schnitzler represents for me [. . .] For I don't like Schnitzler at all, and hardly respect him; no doubt he is capable of certain things, but for me his great plays and his great prose are full of a truly staggering mass of the most sickening [*widerlichster*][34] drivel. It is impossible to be too hard on him [. . .] Only when looking at his photograph— that bogus dreaminess, that sentimentality I wouldn't touch even with the tips of my fingers—can I see how he could have developed in this way from his partly excellent early work (*Anatol, La Ronde, Lieutenant Gustl*) [. . .] Enough, enough! Let me quickly get rid of Schnitzler who is trying to come between us, like Lasker-Schüler the other day.[35]

His rapid analysis of the texts and plays of the most famous and recognized of the Viennese writers and dramatists of the age and the great violence of his language provide sufficient indication that he knew the texts and that his judgement was not based on a passing outburst of anger but on genuine reading. Kafka was asserting a contrary literary stance, irreconcilable with Schnitzler's.[36]

Obeying the same logic, he allowed his sense of repulsion at the literary choices of the Expressionists to surface through his criticism of a number of personalities in that group, whom he happened to mix with from time to time as a result of his acquaintance with Brod and Werfel. It was again in a letter to Felice that he displayed his 'repugnance' (*Widerwille*) for Else Lasker-Schüler:[37]

> And finally in yesterday's letter Lasker-Schüler was mentioned, and today you ask me about her. I cannot bear her poems; their emptiness makes me feel nothing but boredom, and their contrived verbosity nothing but antipathy. Her prose I find just as tiresome and for the same reasons;

it is the work of an indiscriminate brain twitching in the head of an overwrought city-dweller. But I may be quite wrong; many people love her, including Werfel, who talks of her with genuine enthusiasm. Yes, she is in a bad way; I believe her second husband has left her; they are collecting for her here, too; I had to give five kronen, without feeling the slightest sympathy for her. I don't quite know why, but I always imagine her simply as a drunk, dragging herself through the coffee-houses at night.[38]

In Lasker-Schüler, Kafka saw the pretentiousness and affectation that were features of city life. His violent, irrevocable rejection derived from the same anti-ornamental premises as espoused by the Krausians. One of the pieces of testimony on Kafka's life assembled by Hans-Gerd Koch also reports an anecdote about Lasker-Schüler. This is the text by Leopold B. Kreitner who, admittedly, offered one of the least credible memoirs among those collected by Koch, given the number of factual errors and approximations with which it is laced. However, the short anecdote concerning the Expressionist poet from Berlin matches up so well to the letter to Felice on this subject that it can, it seems to me, be reported here. I cite it because it puts another, unexpected and very aggressive slant on the story and attests to a great degree of hostility on Kafka's part. Kreitner here writes about Berta Fanta's literary salon, frequented by the young authors of Prague, to which a number of intellectual personalities were invited from time to time:

I believe it was an evening in 1913 when the German poet Else Lasker-Schüler was our guest of honour. She was very affected and outlandish. We all left the function around midnight (I recall that Franz Werfel and Egon Erwin Kisch were also present) and our visitor—she had given herself the name 'Prince of Thebes' and she was trying desperately to live up to it—having arrived at the marvellous square with its Gothic towers to left and right, which was bathed in almost supernatural moonlight, sank to her knees and began to recite an improvised ode. A policeman intervened and asked her who she was. She proudly rejoined, 'I am the Prince of Thebes,' at which point Kafka corrected her: 'She isn't the Prince of Thebes, but a cow from the Kurfürstendamm.'[39]

Kafka not only rejected the Viennese aesthetes but also turned his face against that same attitude when adopted by Praguers. This rejection is mentioned by Brod in terms that might suggest it was just a superficial, arbitrary assertion of particular tastes. But judging from his testimony with regard to their youthful years, it is clear that Kafka also rejected Jung-Prag aesthetic Decadentism and the affected style of the younger writers who were members of the Prague Circle.[40] 'In the authors of the "night side," of the decadence, he felt [. . .] not the slightest interest,' writes Brod.[41] 'At this time, [. . .] I welcomed everything that was out-of-the-way, unbridled, shameless, cynical, extreme, over-caustic. Kafka opposed me with calm and wisdom. For Meyrink he had no time [. . .] That sort of thing he considered too far-fetched and much too importunate; everything that suggested that it was planned for effect, intellectual or artificially thought up, he rejected.'[42]

Towards Otto Pick, a poet, journalist and translator close to the Prague Circle, Kafka felt some 'aversion', as he said on a trip to Vienna in 1913. And he adds, giving a portrait of Pick as a credulous Prague *littérateur* as he does so: 'Stupid prattling with Pick on literature. Quite a sense of aversion. Here is how one hangs (like Pick) on to the sphere of literature without being able to detach oneself from it because one has dug in one's fingernails, but in other respects one is a free man and wriggles about lamentably.'[43] These expressions of bad temper and assertions of difference and anti-aestheticism are merely markers of a virtually spontaneous hostility to the stances associated with the appeal to art for art's sake—or, to put it in Prague categories, of a hostility to Germanism. They all date from the years 1912–13, that is to say, from just after Kafka's 'Eastern turn'.

It is thus possible to understand the series of Kafka's linguistic and stylistic choices on the basis of his opposition to the Prague Circle. Since he rejected the extant, established aesthetic options and positions, he felt obliged to invent others. Like the Western Jew whom, by way of self-portrait, he described one day to Milena as a man who had not only to 'wash and comb himself' each day before going out but to 'sew his clothes as well, make his shoes, manufacture his hat, whittle his walking stick, and so on',[44] Kafka was a writer for whom (almost) nothing was given or who, in any event, gave himself the task of challenging the assumptions that were the 'natural' raw material of the other writers. He doubted the legitimacy of these principles, he rejected everything that was self-evident to others: language, style, narrative genre, the omniscient narrator, realism, etc. And, like René Descartes after the experience of radical doubt, he attempted to construct a literary project on the basis of new principles. He had nothing he could take for granted, as others did, or, at any rate, he always had problems and questions. In this impossible situation, the language of writing was clearly his first concern. As German was a necessity and not a choice, how could he write if it was as 'impossible to write in German' as it was to 'write any other way'?

THE LETTER OF JUNE 1921

In June 1921, while at the Tatranské Matliare (Matliary) sanatorium in the Tatras Mountains and a great distance from Prague, Kafka sent a long letter to Brod.[45] In it he gave a rather cursory description (as a prelude to criticizing it) of the literary world in which they both lived daily or, in other words, of the range of linguistic and literary choices open to them. Consequently, this famous letter represents a stand on Kafka's part on a question of enormous interest at the time to all protagonists within the Prague literary field: whether it was legitimate for Jewish writers to use the German language. It is, therefore, a crucial document for anyone attempting to decipher Kafka's position. It is one of the very rare overt and detailed explanations/clarifications of his resolute divorce from the German language and the connection he made between writing in German, his chosen literary aesthetic and the rejection of the cultural assimilation which had been inculcated in him.

However, everything (tacitly) being debated in that text is of the order of matters which neither the writer of the letter nor its addressee was aware that he knew. That is to say, it is of the order of the background knowledge which informs the whole letter. I have, therefore, striven here again to bring out as much as possible the unformulated, shared background in order to reconstruct the totality of the implicit reasoning—which is taken for granted in this text— and thus restore complete coherence to Kafka's remarks.

A proper understanding of this letter requires first that we take account of Kafka's interest in—not to say admiration for—Kraus. The older Viennese writer is actually very much present in the letter, through explicit references and in the form of quotations. Kafka had just read Kraus' 'magical operetta' *Literatur oder Man wird da doch sehn* (Literature, or We'll See about That), which brought the German literary 'space' at Prague onto the stage in order to poke fun at it. In Kafka's view, the play provided an excellent description of what he called 'this small world of German-Jewish writing' [*dieser kleinen Welt der deutsch-jüdischen Literatur*].[46] More than this, it seemed to him that it 'was exceedingly acute, piercing straight to the heart' [*ins Herz treffend*].[47] The two men had, naturally, heard about Kraus' satirical operetta and the circumstances of its writing. But the mere fact of drawing on the figure of Kraus in their discussion was already, on Kafka's part, something of a provocation towards Brod since the latter had hated the Viennese writer for many years.

A Long Quarrel

Brod had, in fact, been targeted by Kraus, having been an indirect victim of a literary polemic that ranged Kraus against Werfel over a period of almost 20 years.[48] Werfel, one of the group of Brod's close friends and a member of the Prague Circle, had published a book of poems in April 1912 entitled *Der Weltfreund*. He was initially supported and encouraged to a great extent by Brod who played a part in the publication of this first book and contributed substantially to its success.[49] Kraus also supported him initially, publishing a number of extracts from his texts in *Die Fackel,* and on several occasions expressed enthusiasm for the book. Within a few months Werfel became famous throughout the German area. He quickly came to be regarded as the young prodigy among the Expressionist poets in the way that Hofmannsthal had been within the Jung-Wien movement.[50] And he achieved genuine success, becoming the leading light of this emerging movement.[51]

However, Kraus soon distanced himself from Werfel. They subsequently exchanged polemical, mutually hostile writings through the columns of various literary magazines. In November 1916, Kraus published a parody of Werfel in Die Fackel entitled 'Elysisches' (In the Elysian Style), in which, as the biting irony of the title indicates, he mimicked with comic exaggeration the faults he found in Werfel's writing: grandiloquence, mannerism and affectation. Werfel replied in a publication edited by Brod with a direct attack on Kraus entitled 'Die Metaphysik des Drehs' (The Metaphysics of the Dodge), then with a play called Spiegelmensch (Mirror Man), subtitled 'A Magical Trilogy'.[52] The play featured the main elements of the Expressionist aesthetic and world view but it was also conceived as an attack on Kraus. The trilogy was staged at Leipzig in the following year and at the Vienna Burgtheater in 1922. However, in spring 1921, Kraus riposted with his 'magical operetta'. The Viennese wrote his play so quickly that he managed to read and present it at Vienna even before Werfel was able to put on his own. In other words, he pulled off the remarkable trick of satirizing a play that no one (including Kraus himself) had seen. He gave two readings of it in March and April 1921, scoring a very great success.[53] 'They said at Vienna,' reports Caroline Kohn, 'that you "died laughing" to hear Kraus speaking the typical language of the Neutöner,[54] his imitation unerringly accurate.'[55] This satire, directed against Werfel and the Expressionists, also had Bahr, [Franz] Blei, the psychoanalysts, the Dada movement and others among its targets.[56] The play drew large audiences because rumour had it that Kraus had achieved a kind of perfection in the satirical imitation of the Expressionists' stylistic tics. At all events, he lampooned their rhetoric in a manner highly convincing to contemporaries. Scholem recalls how Walter Benjamin and he 'choke[d] with laughter' to hear Kraus on that occasion.[57]

In *Literatur*, Kraus took up and parodied the theme of father–son conflict, which had become a veritable cliché in Expressionist writing.[58] The play depicts a group of writers/journalists in a cafe, speaking in pretentious, overblown language. Kraus was referring here to the Prague group. The Krausian parody in its entirety—and most of his comic effects for the German-speaking public—were based as much on exposing the ridiculous nature of poetic rhetoric as on the clash between the pronounced grandiloquence of the sons and the—heavily accented—ordinary spoken language, manners and expressions of the fathers.

Once battle had been joined between Kraus and Werfel, Brod, as a member of the Prague literary milieu which Kraus condemned in his operetta as egregiously superficial and bombastic, had himself become one of the Viennese intellectual's targets. The publisher of *Die Fackel* attacked him as the animating spirit behind that little world. He also held him responsible, because of his eminent place at Prague, for what he regarded as Werfel's aberrations. Brod, who had been the butt of his attacks for years, thus felt a particular hostility towards Kraus, particularly after the end of the war. He denounced his operetta as a malevolent caricature, pointing out the use of Austrianisms and 'vulgar' language.[59] Referring, for example, to the figure of Werfel's father in the play, he wrote: 'Kraus has him gibber in an ugly Judaeo-German that is drowning in business jargon. He doesn't get a single feature of the caricature right, but this one least of all. It is a total fabrication.'[60] His resentment was so great that he devoted a long chapter in his autobiography to the man he called 'the great polemicist'.[61] Accusing him of anti-Semitism and warmongering, at least in the early stages of the war, Brod was unable to contain his acrimony even in a book published in 1960, more than 45 years after the events.[62]

Kafka, Brod and Mauscheln

The mere fact of mentioning Kraus and stating that he had laughed as he read him was, then, for Kafka, a way of pointing up a disagreement between Brod and himself. Commenting on Kraus' play, he discerned three different elements in it: 'magnificent wit' [*Witz . . . allerdings prachtvoll*]; what he termed 'whimpering' [*Kläglichkeit*]; and its dose of 'truth' [*so viel Wahrheit*], 'at least as much truth as there is in this hand with which I write, just as distinct and frighteningly physical' [*deutlich und beänstigend körperlich*].[63] This undeniable, yet frightening, truth was the truth of the tragic consequences of the assimilation he was proposing to write about in the rest of the letter.

The word *Witz* means wit, repartee, jokes, humour. And Kafka attributed the *Witz* of Kraus' play—'magnificent wit, mind you'—to *mauscheln*. In other words, while not providing details that might irritate his friend, Kafka was stating, first of all, that he had appreciated Kraus' vein of parody. Above all, he was saying, this wit had to do entirely with the use of jargon (*mauscheln*), a usage that Brod had objected to as mere, base caricature. 'The wit [of the play *Literatur*] principally consists of Yiddish-German—*mauscheln*—no one can *mauscheln* like Kraus,' writes Kafka.[64] 'Although in this German-Jewish world,' he continues, 'hardly anyone can do anything else.'[65]

A clarification is needed here on the word *mauscheln*. As we have said, in Kraus' play the poets' fathers expressed themselves in a language often syntactically incorrect, borrowing many words and expressions from Yiddish or Hebrew—in short, using what German speakers call jargon or *mauscheln*. This representation of the language of the Jews was part of a long tradition. Gilman has shown that it mirrored one belief propagated by the Germans that Jews were incapable of speaking a truly correct German and another which supposed the existence of a 'hidden language of the Jews'. In the German-speaking countries from the second half of the nineteenth century onwards, *mauscheln* referred to the allegedly Jewish intonation of the German spoken by Jews who had been assimilated for several generations—what Kafka in his letter to Max Brod terms '*mauscheln*—taken in a wider sense'.[66] Since the beginning of the century, anti-Semitic Germans had spoken openly about Jews' usage of this allegedly 'degenerate', 'incorrect' German which they regarded as badly pronounced and poorly mastered and which functioned as a racial and racist marker. Liberal Jews themselves, who had in many cases accepted this assertion as truth, regarded the language question as a genuine obstacle to their assimilation. Gilman speaks of *mauscheln* as 'a creation of a German perception of the Jew', which he connects with their status as 'cultural pariahs', but he speaks of it also as the core of Jewish self-hatred.[67] Jewish milieus were themselves steeped in the phantasm of *mauscheln* and it was regarded as a kind of 'sign of membership' which efforts ought to be made to conceal.

It is disturbing, then, to note that we find in Kafka's argument most of the presuppositions of the anti-Semitic belief, as it expressed itself at the time in the German-speaking countries, that the Jews were incapable of speaking German without an accent or intonation 'revealing' them to be Jews. In the letter of June 1921, Kafka seems to accept as in some way self-evident that 'hardly anyone can do anything else' than *mauscheln* or, in other words, that the German-speaking Jews of Prague speak—and, consequently, write—in *mauscheln*, as though, like many of his contemporaries, he had internalized the racist categories of the biological discourse of his time.[68] He even gives a definition of it:

> This *mauscheln* [. . .] consists in [. . . an] appropriation of someone else's property, something not earned, but stolen by means of a relatively casual gesture. Yet it remains someone else's property, even though there is no evidence of a single solecism. That does not matter, for in this realm, the whispering voice of conscience confesses the whole crime in a penitent hour.[69]

This definition corresponds term for term with the ordinary representations of *mauscheln* at the time. It was generally accepted that the mother tongue of the Jews was not German and that, 'consequently', that language was for them a 'borrowed' one whereas for the Germans it was 'natural'. This is why the use of German by the Jews was assumed to be 'artificial' and 'poor'. It is in this sense that Kafka uses the word 'embers' and the expression 'a semblance of life' to describe the German of the Prague writers.[70] The metaphor of a language conceived as 'someone else's property [*fremder Besitz*]', acquired illegally, will recur at the end of the letter, when Kafka speaks very harshly of: '[A] gypsy literature [*eine Zigeunerliteratur*] which had stolen the German child out of its cradle [*die das deutsche Kind aus der Wiege gestohlen . . . hatte*][71] and in great haste put it through some kind of training, for someone has to dance on the tightrope. (But it wasn't even a German child, it was nothing; people merely said that somebody was dancing).'[72]

Kafka openly takes over the assumptions, then, which form the basis of the conviction that the Jews and the Germans are radically alien to each other. In other words, he takes the view that, for Jewish writers, the German language is, and will remain, try as they might, a foreign tongue,[73] and hence that they write—and can only write—a nameless literature in that language which has neither identity nor fatherland, because that is the ultimate criterion. It remains, for them, 'someone else's property', even if 'no evidence of a single solecism' is to be found in their texts.

How to Write in German without Writing in German?

Kraus and his parodic description of the Prague literary space were clearly not the real subject of the letter. Kafka analyses the situation of the writers depicted in the operetta differently from Kraus and is at odds with his position. Instead of mocking these writers' relationships with their fathers, he describes what he regarded as the awful consequences of a collective phenomenon: assimilation from the standpoint of its linguistic and, hence, literary effects. What is at issue in the letter is nothing less than the question of the legitimacy of the use of the German language by Jewish writers. The letter itself was part of a dialogue with Brod that had been going on for years.

In 1913, Brod published an article in a collective work under the auspices of the Prague Bar Kochba association which caused quite a stir. The volume, published by Kurt Wolff of Leipzig, bore the title *Vom Judentum* (On Judaism).[74] Contributors included some of the most notable personalities of the day and some of the most prestigious figures to have taken a position in this particular controversy, such as Jacob Wassermann, Hans Kohn, Martin Buber, Hugo Bergmann, Robert Weltsch, Moritz Goldstein, Arnold Zweig and

Nathan Birnbaum.[75] The work, 'which was inspired by Buber', notes Scholem, 'aroused violent controversies'.[76] In these years, it represented the political line and theoretical stance of the Cultural Zionists and was, at the same time, a target for attack from intellectual and political opponents in all camps. In his article, 'Der jüdische Dichter deutscher Zunge' [The Jewish, German-language Poet], Brod took a 'middle' path from the outset. Employing a subtle dialectic (which came close to being self-contradictory), Brod asserted that he did not wish to give up the German language. He developed an argument to the effect that, although for Jews German was undoubtedly, by his own terms, a *fremder Besitz*—that is to say, a resource they could not be said to have inherited from their ancestors—the very fact of the development of their own form of nationalism would give them the opportunity, through the establishment of Zionism, to accede to their own *Volkstum*, to their own non-German culture, and should 'consequently' and by a kind of analogy, enable them to make a new, properly Jewish use of the German language.[77] Like Kafka, Brod, as we see, accepted the idea of a German language which would remain foreign to the Jews, but he added:

> I am convinced that it is by deepening his national sense that the German-language Jewish writer has access for the first time to the true spirit of the German people and that in this way he will be able to realize the importance of the national language-values [*nationaler Sprachwerte*] and the responsibility which their correct usage entails. The enjoyment of one's own culture is more akin to the enjoyment of the culture of another people than to an attempt to lay hold of a foreign culture illegitimately.[78]

This 'middle' stance was in keeping with his position in the literary field: as a mediator and honest broker, his efforts were directed towards synthesis, attenuation, temporization. In another article published in the *Neue Rundschau* in 1918, Brod would assert his positions even more clearly: 'To give up the German language would amount to extracting a vital organ from my personality. It would be a lethal amputation.'[79]

Kafka, for his part, rejected this conciliatory logic. In the June 1921 letter, he twice employed exactly the expression that Brod used in his 1913 article: *fremder Besitz*. I do not claim by this that he was quoting from his friend's article which had appeared years before. It is simply that the expression was used on both sides of this raging controversy to undergird antagonistic positions. In a sense, Kafka was replying to Brod's public stances and statements with regard to the German language and, implicity, to a whole series of problems over which they disagreed. And, as Brod was an intellectual who took up public positions and was much more famous than he was, Kafka was referring tacitly to the texts published by his friend on this question which had long been a crucial, burning issue for the two of them. Whether they should regard themselves as foreigners in relation to the Germans was clearly central. Jewish intellectuals had to confront an implicit injunction addressed to them that they abandon one identity in favour of another.

In keeping with the logic of his steadfastly radical position, Kafka found other solutions than Brod's in his efforts to solve this dilemma. Along the Jewishness–Germanness scale, he shifted the cursor a very long way towards the Jewish end and asserted from the outset—from winter 1911–12 onwards—that there should be an irrevocable break between the two identities. From that moment on, he decided to turn his back on Germanness and the Germans, whom he spoke of as 'foreigners', and expressed very little nostalgia for that lost identity. In the June 1921 letter, he rejected radically and in the most implacable terms the possibility of a reappropriation of German by Jewish creative writers. This is why, knowing that he too could not turn his back on the German language for his writing, he was going to work at acquiring the greatest possible distance from— and to display the greatest possible mistrust towards—Germanism while remaining, from necessity, within the German language and sphere. In other words, he revisited his belief in the existence of *mauscheln*, turning it to his advantage.

Since he wished to demonstrate that Germans and Jews were alien to each other and did not speak the same language, Kafka took over the rhetoric of *mauscheln* which he borrowed for the occasion from Kraus. However, despite appearances, he used it to express exactly the opposite of anti-Semitic belief. The question for Kafka was not at all of a guilty relationship with German or of feeling in the wrong within it while wishing for a return to it but of an irrevocable break with that language which was, for him, simply a *fremder Besitz*. He thus stood on its head the argument—which admittedly seems so ambiguous and problematical to us today—of an innate 'flaw' on the part of the Jews, claiming this as the very token of their irreducible difference. The text is therefore tacitly—in the same spirit as Goldstein, for example—a plea for the founding of a Jewish literature which is entirely distinct from the German. Like Brod's article, the whole letter depends on the (folkist) belief that a literature, in order to be worthy of the name, should be 'national'—in other words, that it should be the emanation of a people whose difference and existence it would show and prove.

Gilman has shown that, beyond the ordinary forms of self-hatred, the reappropriation of the discourse on *mauscheln* by Western Jewish intellectuals (including, he says, Buber and Kafka) in the early years of the twentieth century represented a possibility for them (even a theoretical one) to free themselves from the belief that they spoke a damaged language.[80] Furthermore, Kafka is not at all critical of Prague's Jewish writers as 'guilty' of 'sinning' against German. He does not accuse them, as an anti-Semite would, of defiling the 'purity' of German. Quite the contrary, he speaks of a 'frightful inner predicament of these generations', of 'despair' and multiple 'impossibilities'.[81] He describes their condition as a tragic impasse for which they were not responsible. He also asserts—a very rare position among Germanized Jews—that he is not 'say[ing] anything against *mauscheln*.' '[I]n itself it is fine,' he continues. 'It is an organic compound of bookish German and pantomime [. . .] What we have here is the product of a sensitive feeling for language.'[82]

In the end, it was these writers' fathers whom he held responsible for the desperate situation in which they found themselves. For Kafka it was not at all the fact that they did not belong to 'German literature' that was problematical. The danger, rather, was that they wanted to deny or forget their Jewishness. 'Most young Jews who began to write German wanted to leave Jewishness behind them.'[83] Kafka deemed the fathers responsible for this desire for relinquishment. Of this relationship between Jewish fathers and sons he rejected from the outset the psychoanalytic explanation (which, as a good Austrian intellectual, he obviously knew). 'Psychoanalysis lays stress on the father-complex [. . .] In this case I prefer another version, where the issue revolves not around the innocent father but around the father's Jewishness.'[84] In other words, Kafka adopted another of the favourite stances of Kraus: the rejection of psycho-analysis as a pertinent explanation of behaviour, dilemmas or social and historical configurations. More than that, he objected to psycho-analysis on the grounds that it was an instrument for the depoliticization of the most contentious political and social situations.[85]

Most importantly, in his view, psychoanalysis absolved the fathers of responsibility: in the Oedipal conflict, as described by psychoanalysts, the father is innocent. For Kafka, however, the Jewish fathers were guilty. Guilty of letting their sons abandon Jewishness by their 'vague approval'—and he added, in an angry parenthesis, '(this vagueness was what was outrageous [*empörende*] to them).'[86] At the same time, he transformed the purely literary theme of the 'paternal complex', omnipresent among the Expressionists, into a social reality. This 'paternal complex' was, says Kafka, the literary transformation—the 'literarization'—of a tragic social reality: the 'flimsy' form and content of the Judaism bequeathed to these writers by their fathers in their haste to assimilate into German society. Kafka went on to say that, in order to understand the conflict of this generation of sons with their fathers, it was necessary to hypothesize that the fathers were guilty of having handed down only an evanescent form of Judaism to their sons and of thereby having encouraged them to deny their Judaism or, in other words, assimilate. In other words, the fathers were at fault in many different ways: for having bequeathed only 'an insignificant scrap' of Judaism to their sons; for having thereby placed them in psychological situations of great uncertainty and 'despair' in which they lacked a solid ground (*Boden*) to stand on, lacked an identity, a language, a heritage and any possible foothold in a past. The striking image he applies to these writers, comparing them implicitly to quadrupeds who are condemned to overbalance because, 'with their posterior legs they were still glued to the father's Jewishness,' while 'with their waving anterior legs they found no new ground,' is neither moral condemnation nor mockery.[87] It is simply, for Kafka, a way of describing, without pathos, the tragic inner rivenness of these intellectuals. For this reason, we may say that the real object of the letter is the description of the particular form of assimilation applying to writers. In Kafka's view, Jewish writers could not integrate into German letters and they were doomed to produce an affected literature that belonged to nothing and to no one.

More and more clearly, as it goes on, the letter becomes terribly pathos-laden because it is patent that Kafka begins to speak about himself and to do so in desperate terms. What he describes is not a situation capable either of a political or literary solution. These Jewish writers of Prague were caught in a situation from which there was no way out. No solution presented itself. And the situation was even worse for those who, like him, had understood that it was 'a literature impossible in all respects'.[88] Kafka here enumerates the three or four impossibilities which, when combined, produced this literature lacking in hope or prospects: 'They existed among three impossibilities [. . .] The impossibility of not writing, the impossibility of writing German, the impossibility of writing differently. One might also add a fourth impossibility, the impossibility of writing [. . .] Thus what resulted was a literature impossible in all respects.'[89] This famous phrase, transformed by Blanchotian criticism into the Mallarméan conviction of an *impossible de la littérature* is, in reality, a description of the Prague literary space from the standpoint of the politicized Jewish intellectuals. It is, in other words, a striking evocation of the various linguistic, cultural, political and national contradictions in which they were entangled. This stark summation of the situation of the assimilated writer, incapable of escaping the language of domination and unable to resort to the lost language of his ancestors, caught between the rejection of assimilation and the monolingualism it has inflicted upon him, shows him caught in a desperate, inescapable impasse. And, at the beginning of the letter, Kafka did indeed distinguish between three forms of appropriation of the German language, depending on the degree of denial of dependence—three stages which might also be three degrees of assimilation, from the most explicit to the most incorporated—using three adjectives: *stillschweigend* (tacit), *laut* (openly admitted) and *selbstquälerisch*[90] ('achieved at the cost of an internal struggle amounting to mental torture for the writer'[91]). This last was, in a way, the evocation of the quintessence of linguistic domination, when it is simultaneously rejected, incorporated, and a source of immense pain for the writer who cannot but employ it. It was no doubt with this word—*selbstquälerisch*—that Kafka best described his own position with regard to the German language.

At the same time, writing could be only an 'expedient' (*Provisorium*); it was something provisional, forever unstable and open to revision. And he added—and this says a great deal about Kafka's vision of writing—'an expedient that may well last a whole life'. To write as something provisional and in a provisional mode, in a 'borrowed' language; to write narratives outside all the prevailing norms, outside of any model established by one's peers, was the only conceivable way out (and hence not a way out at all) from this impossible situation. '[S]ince the despair could not be assuaged by writing,' he wrote in the same letter, it 'was hostile to both life and writing'.[92]

This attitude of refusal and despair was a new (negatively registered) mark of his resolve to reject the existing positions and to create an entirely novel one. Stylistically, the solution he chose could have been to attempt to write in German without writing in German. At the same time, the formal choices implied in this impossible writing project became immediately visible. This is the whole issue of what Arendt calls the 'style-less perfection' of Kafka's writing.[93]

The first Kafka, the one who wrote between 1904 and 1912, was interested in the language problems current within the Austrian Empire and was under the influence of the *Kunstwart* style. Connection has often been made between his earliest writings and Hofmannsthal's *Lord Chandos Letter*,[94] published in Berlin in 1902, on account of its questioning of language, its rejection of lyrical effusiveness and the connection it made between this suspicion of language and a vision of generalized mendacity. We also know that Kafka was very close to the Brentanist circle at Prague. Between 1902 and 1905 he attended the lectures of Anton Marty—a disciple of Brentano whose chief interest was in establishing the foundations of a philosophy of language—and the meetings at the Café Louvre.[95]

However, from 1911 onwards, the discovery of Yiddish language and literature, conceived as a 'combative' culture, radically changed his conception of language and, hence, of writing. From this point on, Kafka was to move from a questioning of the (suspect) nature of language, conceived as an abstract concept, to a questioning of language as a concrete notion and a 'political' object. In other words, he was moving away from an aesthetic, intellectual view of language towards a political view of it as the emanation of a people or, in its enforced use, as a pre-eminent marker of the domination of one people by another. At the point where Yiddish was revealed to him as the language of the Jewish people, German came to seem to be not *the* language of culture but the language forced upon assimilated Jews who had, in that same process, lost their own. This, for Kafka, marked a great political and linguistic divide. We can go further and say that we may deduce from the stylistic break evident in his texts from 1912 onwards the idea that German had become for him the language of the political 'lie', as opposed to Yiddish, which might be said to be the 'true' language of the Jews.[96]

In discovering Yiddish, Kafka also became aware of his ignorance of the language and his inability to write it. He realized, in other words, that assimilation was a collective process in which he had 'forgotten' that language. Yiddish was the language he had lost for ever and he would henceforth have to write in mourning for it. The famous passage in his *Diaries* in which he explains the incomplete love he felt for his mother in terms of a linguistic contradiction—which shows up intensely the central place of the missing maternal language and which is always analysed in exclusively psychological terms—derives, in fact, directly from his reflections on Yiddish. This analysis appears amid notes devoted to Yitzchak Löwy and his memories of the actor:

> Yesterday it occurred to me that I did not always love my mother as she deserved and as I could, only because the German language prevented it. The Jewish mother is no 'Mutter', to call her 'Mutter' makes her a little comic (not to herself, because we are in Germany), we give a Jewish woman the name of a German mother, but forget the contradiction that sinks into the emotions so much more heavily. 'Mutter' is peculiarly German for the Jew, it unconsciously contains, together with the Christian splendour Christian coldness also, the Jewish woman who is called 'Mutter' therefore becomes not only comic but strange.[97]

German, being simultaneously the mother tongue and a foreign, borrowed language, came to be seen as a language appropriated by assimilation. In the precise terms of the political discussion going on in Jewish circles throughout Europe, this made it a language 'filched' from others at the cost of a self-forgetting and a betrayal of Jewish culture.

Wagenbach was the first to stress the stylistic affinity between Kraus and Kafka. Speaking of Kafka's writing from 1912 onwards, he asserts: 'This attitude of Kafka's has its equivalent, all things considered, only in the fanatical purism of Karl Kraus.'[98] He points out the two men's shared hostility towards the poets of the Café Arco and their distrust and common rejection of the overblown aesthetic of the Prague School to explain their parallel recourse to an 'extremely austere' language. Being incapable of writing in Yiddish, Kafka found in Kraus one of the most austere forms of German; his was a style and a writing which, of themselves, represented a challenge to *fin de siècle* ornamentation. And yet, it does not seem to me that the two positions overlap exactly. As a result of adopting diametrically opposed stances on the question of assimilation, they also had divergent positions on the question of the German language:

Kraus opted for a highly conservative attitude, coming out in favour of a fanatical linguistic purism. In that respect he was as far removed as possible from the options taken by Kafka, who, for his part, rejected the Germanism of the liberal Jews.[99] However, drawing on Kraus' rigorism, though starting out from different premisses, his German would, from this point on, be impersonal and free of any traces of singularity, of any desire for originality. David notes that Kafka's vocabulary 'is small [. . .] the phrases are short and juxtaposed rather than subordinated to one another; the syntax seems as simplified as possible'.[100] Confronted with this language which does 'not belong' to him, he finds no other solution than a writing style as shorn of 'ornament' and 'artifice' as possible.[101] Arendt attempted to define this style-less style by means of the following analogy: 'Kafka's German is to the infinite plurality of possible linguistic styles what water is to the infinite plurality of possible beverages.'[102]

It was not Kafka's aim to flaunt, as Robert asserts, a kind of 'chancellery German', the official language of the empire and the tool of the insignificant 'functionary armed with his neutrality and his logic'.[103] In this 'plain' use of language, Kafka was looking, rather, for an instrument that could fit with his project of taking part in a collective literary work and, in contrast to an undertaking that would have subjectivity at its centre, seeking to give precedence to 'popular' literary genres. This implicit criticism of literary ornament, characteristic of the style and tastes of Kafka, assumes its full power of expression, its entire force of opposition and implicit violence only if we understand it for what it was: a relational choice—that is to say, a major divergence from the possibilities being explored at that same time by his friends and companions at Prague. This stylistic and aesthetic choice was, then, a rejection of the art for art's sake stance, a disavowal of aesthetic de-realization (personified by Werfel or Brod, for example), an implicit critique of the use of the German language by the Jewish writers of Prague and, lastly, a way of not writing in German. In other words, we may deduce from Kafka's syntactic options his resolve to construct—invisibly, secretly, ambiguously—a work of radical, violent criticism of the world in which he lived. The study of the entire literary space brings out his desire to forge a Prague *anti-style*, a radical *other side* to the Jewish German-language literature that he criticized in his June 1921 letter to Max Brod.

Yet, he did not always follow this rule of apparent neutrality. The short stories he wrote in late 1916 to early 1917, published in 1919 as *Ein Landarzt: Kleine Erzählungen* (A Country Doctor: Brief Tales), marked a break in terms of both style and language, shifting towards brevity, a sophisticated writing style and a studied construction, along with the choice of rare words and a preferred use of parataxis, enumeration, etc.[104] But this properly literary work was not at all akin to a rapprochement with the stylistic choices of the Prague Circle. On the contrary, it is as though Kafka were freeing himself increasingly—and ever more effectively—from the dominant aesthetic. We may note, moreover that he did not abandon his first style, particularly in the novels, and that the two styles competed in his work after 1917.[105]

UNRELIABLE NARRATORS AND AMBIGUOUS NARRATIVES

Suspending Belief

Pursuing his task of questioning the 'means employed' in literary writing and of undermining the aesthetic, linguistic and stylistic assumptions specific to his literary space, Kafka did not stop at the question of language. He also worked to perfect rhetorical and narrative devices which could be deployed as so many critical tools. Like Kraus, he turned his mind to texts that could have an immediate social impact. In other words, through literary 'attacks', he carried out a relentless tacit internal critique of what was being written at Prague at that particular moment while producing, through violently denunciatory content, an external, political critique of the social world in which he lived. And the construction of his narratives is so refined, their modes of narration are so novel and, at times, so perverse, that it is not possible to infer from their proximity to forms André Jolles has termed 'simple' any sort of literary simplicity whatever.[106]

I am aware that it runs pretty much counter to the mystique that has formed around Kafka to speak of narrative 'devices' where his fictions are concerned.[107] However, he himself clearly states in 1914 in his diary:

> [T]he best things I have written have their basis in this capacity of mine to meet death with contentment. All these fine and very convincing passages always deal with the fact that someone is dying [. . .] But for me [. . .] such scenes are secretly a game; indeed in the death enacted I rejoice in my own death, hence calculatingly exploit the attention that the reader concentrates on death.[108]

'Calculatingly' exploiting the attention of the reader, which is concentrated on some dazzling focus, as though in 'a game', while the story goes on elsewhere—this is precisely the definition of what I shall term here 'devices'. Kafka's writings teem with them.

In many cases, Kafka's narrative, fictional work consists of under-mining from within accepted social facts, a *doxa*, a collective belief. To set about such a gigantic undertaking, he resorts among other things to the questioning of one of the principles on which the edifice of Western literary narration rests—the function of the narrator. Ordinary habits of reading fictional texts presuppose the—unspoken but necessary—existence of an 'authorial point of view' which is most often assumed by the narrator or main character who thereby becomes a 'mouthpiece' for the author and, at the same time, a voice with which the reader is supposed to be able to identify. There is no reading of novels without a process of identification with one of the narrative voices (the first-person singular clearly facilitating the imme-diate adherence of the reader to the point of view expressed). Now, this habit of making the reader believe that a mirror-reading of literary fictions is the only truly legitimate reading enables them to be auto-matically dehistoricized (or depoliticized), by encouraging all readers to project their own representations, prejudices, fantasies, specific interests and personal histories onto texts, discounting all other pos-sible readings. Let us add here that these identificatory habits, under-stood as the foundation of all novel reading, are based in large measure on what Barthes called the 'reality effect' (very largely inherited from naturalism) and on the belief generated by texts which are assumed to 'resemble' the real. However, if one tries to analyse or understand texts which, like Kafka's, do not correspond to these criteria, which function neither in terms of the reality effect nor of naturalistic belief, and which expect from the reader not identification but, for example, a pedagogical effect or the understanding of a larger political or historical mechanism, then all attempts at clarification will run up against a total lack of understanding between scriptor and reader-interpreter. In shaking the foundations of the edifice of identificatory belief, Kafka at the same time mounts a powerful challenge to the very *doxa* he is seeking to condemn.

Thus, for example, one of his preferred narrative *dispositifs* is the depiction of an investigator who is supposed to be objectively reporting a reality unknown to the reader. Yet the character of the investigator ('Investigations of a Dog'), researcher ('The Great Wall of China'), traveller ('In the Penal Colony') or scientist ('The Village Schoolmaster'), who, in numerous Kafka stories is either the narrator or, if the narrative is in the third person, the one whose sole point of view is afforded to the reader through free indirect style (as in 'In the Penal Colony'), is very often what I propose to term an 'unreliable narrator'.[109] Hence a veritable trap is set for the reader. By placing the narrative in the hands of these 'investigators', Kafka is not allowing those with whom the reader should be able to identify 'naturally' to speak but, rather, those whose viewpoint he is criticizing or condemning. This narrator does not, as every reader accustomed to the codes of the naturalist story believes, embody the viewpoint of the author—a viewpoint on which the reader may lean to decipher the narrative—but, rather, the perspective Kafka wishes to condemn: the authoritarian stance of the Westerners, for example, who believe they can judge, understand and apportion or rescind legitimacy by the mere fact that they hold an undisputed monopoly of symbolic authority. Seeking to show that the dominant point of view, the *doxa*, is usually an intolerable perspective, Kafka reproduces this viewpoint, which is expressed 'naturally' in his narrative—as it is everywhere else in the social world—and therefore seems 'legitimate' to the reader at first sight. But he has that viewpoint appear in such a context that its legitimacy, potency and self-evident character collapse. In other words, one cannot see the critical violence of Kafka's texts unless one problematizes the ordinary terms of the naturalist narrative, unless one suspends one's belief in the unquestioned assumption of a shared outlook between a 'scientific Western' narrator and ourselves as modal Western readers, a belief which holds together virtually the entire Western literary edifice.

In 'In the Penal Colony', for example, while readers believe they can rely, as a long tradition of literary-ethnological narratives or travel writing encourages them to do, on the sincerity, honesty and rationality of the narrator—while, in other words, the readers believe they can, as in ordinary narrations, identify closely with the self-evident character of the viewpoint of this investigator/traveller/explorer, who is discovering the colony and its infernal machine at the same time as they are, and rely upon it—they will, in fact, fall immediately into the trap (a devilish one to be sure) which Kafka sets for them. The reader's quasi-immediate identification with the viewpoint of the explorer is the first narrative trap of this cruel tale. And it seems one cannot comprehend the cold condemnatory power of the story unless one supposes that the explorer is, in reality, a perfect representative of Western intellectuals in all their cowardliness and subordination to the social order and its violence: he will do nothing to stop either the killing machine or the infernal judicial machinery. The 'science' so frequently depicted by Kafka in his narratives (a metaphor, for him, for other authoritarian institutions like the Church) is a powerful symbolic authority, preserving the hierarchical order of the world, and underwriting, among other things, the dissymmetry between Westerners and Easterners, itself another form of the dissymmetry between Germans and Jews.

As though by the kind of naturalistic self-evidence I have just described, David, in his introductory comments to 'In the Penal Colony' in the French Pléiade edition of Kafka's works, immediately identifies the character of the traveller, through whose eyes the facts are obviously described, with the author of the text when he shows how—since 'the convictions the explorer will ultimately express owe nothing either to pity or charity'—we may logically deduce that he 'feels no sympathy for this condemned man who is a stupid-looking, wide-mouthed creature'. This is why, according to David, the text 'would seem to offer arguments to those who do not believe in the social and humanitarian concerns that some have attributed to Kafka'.[110] Given the paradoxically highly political yet radically reactionary—if not indeed racist—convictions David attributes to Kafka, the reader will understand that the preliminaries I am going through here on the presuppositions involved in every reading, are not mere methodological fastidiousness: it is the whole meaning of the work that is at stake. The interpretation of a 'literary politics' on Kafka's part is in play here.[111]

Arendt examines the question of identification in a very different way, arguing that there is no connection between it and the interpretation of the texts. She writes that: '[T]he purely passive reader, moulded and educated as he has been by the tradition of the novel, and active only in his identification with one of the characters, does not know what to do with Kafka [. . .] Kafka's stories [. . .] contain no elements of daydreaming and offer neither advice nor edification nor solace.'[112]

For Arendt, Kafka's stories, 'are far removed from reality in the sense given to it by realist novels', since Kafka was interested in the 'hidden structures' of the world and his narrative technique was akin to 'the construction of models'.[113] Comparing Kafka's work to that of architects, she uses the word in the sense of a scaled-down representation. 'These protagonists created by Kafka,' she continues, 'are not real persons [. . .] it would amount to hubris to identify with them [. . .] they are only models left in anonymity.'[114]

The do-nothing cowardice of the traveller/explorer of 'In the Penal Colony', who does not even manage to condemn the horrendous penal system in force within the colony, the hypocrisy of the plagiarist in 'The Village Schoolmaster', the mendacious exaggeration of the narrator of 'An Old Manuscript', etc., are so many forms of an authority we may term symbolic, insofar as it is exerted invisibly—that is to say, without coercion.[115] And yet it operates tyranically or, in other words, iniquitously, and to the detriment of the weakest. These are indeed 'models', in Arendt's sense, of Western intellectuals. In this same way, Kafka was able to describe Buber's 'translations' of the Hasidic tales as 'authoritarian adaptations',[116] as if for him the most tyrannical and unbearable forms of authority were the most surreptitious and the subtlest, those forms that are inbuilt in a system and hence unacknowledged. Similarly, he denounces in his stories the most invisible forms of authority when it turns despotic, as though what were at issue here were the only form of power which, by being almost imperceptible and hence not recognized, can perpetuate itself indefinitely without actually showing.

Another narrative trap very much present in Kafka's work and one related to a loss of the ordinary markers of identification is the use of 'I'—the first-person singular is a narrative mode widely employed in his short stories. We find it, most notably, in 'Memoirs of the Kalda Railroad', 'A Little Woman', 'The Burrow', 'Investigations of a Dog', 'A Report to an Academy', 'A Country Doctor' and 'An Old Manuscript'.[117] It is, in fact, one of the modalities of the 'unreliable narrator' arrangement, but it is even more disorientating for the reader who is immersed from the outset in the narrator's perspectives and arguments. The fact of knowing whether the person describing what we see is reliable is crucial in interpreting texts and assessing their degree of critical violence. The interpretation of texts written in the first person becomes an even more difficult question to unravel, given that it is overlaid by a large proportion of the history of commentary on Kafka's stories.

Since 1945, the interpretative *doxa* has, in fact, depended largely on the conviction that Kafka, as scriptor of his diary and correspondence, equates almost exactly with the first-person (and even third-person) narrators of his fictional writings. In other words, a biographical or autobiographical reading of the stories is favoured almost systematically. There are many reasons for this, which have to do, among other things, with the critical traditions that propose an author's biography as the only possible history of his or her work and are built on the idea that the only literary art worthy of the name is one in which the singularity of the author himself or herself is celebrated. In Kafka's case, this conceptual configuration is further reinforced by the confusion maintained between the autobiographical writings (the diary and the correspondence), the published narratives and the unfinished works, all of which together are taken to constitute the 'complete works'. Although they belong to entirely distinct genres or projects, these three types of writing are confounded and amalgamated in such a way that no distinction is made between a properly literary project or piece of work and diary writings that were not in any sense intended for publication, in which, of course, Kafka also uses the pronoun 'I'. Jacques Le Rider has shown that, so far as Kafka was concerned, writing his diary was not a literary endeavour; pouring out his feelings in his diary was, for him, at the opposite end of the spectrum from constructed, narrative work which, in his view, represented the only form of literary composition worthy of the name. The diary was, as Le Rider puts it, merely a 'substitute'[118] for writing, as Kafka clearly states on 25 December 1915: 'Open the diary only in order to lull myself to sleep. But see what happens to be the last entry and could conceive of thousands of identical ones I might have entered over the past three or four years. I wear myself out to no purpose, should be happy if I could write, but don't.'[119]

For French readers, this confusion has been perpetuated by the publication of Kafka's 'Complete Works' in the Pléiade edition.[120] The conviction that Kafka was speaking about himself in all his fictional writings is espoused more or less to the exclusion of all others by David, the editor of this particular translation of the 'Complete Works', who has played a crucial critical role for all francophone readers of Kafka. This exclusive hypothesis has served to evacuate history entirely (both Kafka's history and that of his literary and political world) and to foreground a representation of a writer occupied solely with his own person. And there are countless interpretative comments in this edition of the type: 'For Kafka, Russia was always the symbol of loneliness,'[121] or 'It would be wrong, however, only to see in this story one of the innumerable caricatures Kafka has left of himself.'[122] Referring to 'A Report to an Academy', David writes:

> To understand Kafka's at once crystal-clear and secretive story, it has to be put back into the time of its composition. In mid-April 1917, less than three months separated Kafka from his second engagement to Felice Bauer [. . .] We read, in the very second paragraph of 'A Report to an Academy', 'It is now nearly five years since I was an ape.' That is the time that separates Kafka from his first meeting with Felice.[123]

A relatively recent article by Fernand Cambon speaks of 'the fundamental humility of Kafka' which he seems to detect in 'A Hunger Artist', one of his last texts, written in the first-person singular, thus putting forward as a plain, unquestioned fact that Kafka's psyche expressed itself naively, unadorned and unfiltered, in his narratives.[124]

The French are not the only ones to have deliberately sought to confuse Kafka with his characters and hence to have regarded his fictional writings as biographical confessions. The best-known commentary to take this position is probably that of Canetti, in which he proposes, famously, to read *The Trial* as the transposition of the failure of Kafka's engagement to Felice. Canetti supposes that the novel actually originates in the events of 1 and 12 July 1914, the official engagement and its public termination. As Canetti sees it, the chapter depicting the arrest is a transposition of the engagement and the one depicting the execution can be seen as recounting its breaking-off, which also took place publicly in the form of a family gathering at the Askanischer Hof Hotel in Berlin attended by Felice, her parents and Kafka's.[125] Referring to this scene some days later in his diary, Kafka writes: 'The tribunal in the hotel. Trip in the cab. F.'s face. She patted her hair with her hand, wiped her nose, yawned. Suddenly she gathered herself together and said very studied, hostile things she had long been saving up.'[126]

Although many commentators have tried to show that the letter *K* is a very common initial in both Germanic and Slavic countries, the initial with which Kafka dubs his protagonist has clearly further contributed to drawing both *The Trial* and *The Castle* towards the realms of psychology and biographical confession. We may say then that, over time, an almost total superimposition of the person of Kafka onto his fictions has occurred. In other words, the writer and his protagonists have been presented as necessarily coinciding (with little mention even of Gérard Genette's hypothesis of a narrator introducing at least some distance between the writer and the character who presents himself through the pronoun 'I').

This interpretation, entirely in keeping with the habits of 'close reading' that prevail in literary studies—a close reading that finds all the elements supposedly adequate for the comprehension of a text within the confines of that text itself—has, paradoxically, the same assumptions at its origin as political criticism. With the fictional character Karl Rossmann's lack of interest in the workers' demonstrations in *Amerika* being both condemned and attributed immediately to Kafka himself, the Prague writer has been presented, plainly and simply, as an artist hostile to the working people! By the mere fact that the character never seems to take the side of the working class or of workers' struggles, it is 'logically' deduced that Kafka had no interest in the question—and even that he professed thoroughgoing contempt for this kind of battle.[127] But the fact is that, just as pure criticism always assumes that writers are apolitical and 'purely' interested in 'pure' literature, political criticism reduces the narrative to the author's presumed message which is supposedly delivered directly by a narrator always identified with the author and through a narrative always understood as 'realist'.

The Schoolmaster and Josephine: Scholem, Benjamin and Kafka
In order to convey what I mean by the notion of unreliable narrator, I propose to present a reading of two texts. One is, in appearance, obscure, austere and abstract and was written in December 1914. Kafka in his diary calls it 'The Village Schoolmaster' (Brod gave it

the title 'The Giant Mole'). The other was written in March 1924 at the end of his life and Kafka calls it 'Josephine the Singer, or the Mouse Folk'.

The first is an unfinished, abandoned text which combines the two forms of narrator I have just described, since it is both a first-person-singular narrative and a story told by a 'scientist'. It seems to me that one can find in it the reasons for Kafka's profound hostility towards Buber and, at the same time, read it as a precise, pointed and violent *prise de position* in one of the great debates with which the Jewish world was astir: the nature of the translations of the 'Hasidic' tales transposed by Buber, which were unanimously admired in Kafka's circle.

To characterize Kafka's attitude to Buber, we might say that it was halfway between Scholem's and Benjamin's. Whereas Scholem was at first fascinated 'like any self-respecting Zionist', as he puts it, by Buber's philosophy, he gradually moved away from it, probably under the influence of Benjamin whom he met in 1915 and who, for his part, was immediately very wary of Buberism.[128] Over many years, Benjamin and Scholem did, however, continue to read *Der Jude* regularly, to comment on the articles that appeared in it and (in Scholem's case) to publish in it or even, in the case of Benjamin in June 1916, to respond to it with polemical texts—proof, if such were needed, that Buber was nonetheless considered a worthy interlocutor. Benjamin's criticism related mainly, says Scholem, to the fact that 'every article it [*Der Jude*] published somehow presupposed Zionism and desired to improve and develop it [. . .] Most of all we discussed Buber, whom Benjamin criticized in sharp terms [. . . H]e told me [. . .] that if I should run into Buber I should hand him a barrel of tears in our names.'[129]

Scholem also recalls his annoyance at what he calls the 'effusions' of Buber's style, very much marked, as he said, by 'religious romanticism'. He did, however, express a great intellectual esteem for him, 'despite the far-reaching differences of opinion'[130] and continued throughout these years (*Der Jude* was published by Buber between 1916 and 1924) to write for the journal.

Very much like Scholem and Benjamin and for reasons similar to theirs, Kafka found it very hard to bear the atmosphere of empathic sentimentality that accompanied Buber's lectures. We do not know which of the three famous lectures given by Buber in 1909 and 1910 to the Bar Kochba association at Prague he attended. All that is known is that, unlike Brod, who 'converted' to Zionism as of the first of these, he was unmoved and remained very distant from—if not indeed distrustful of—this form of thinking. On 16 January 1913, he wrote to Felice that a lecture by Buber was being given that very evening. He explained that it had no attraction for him but that he would be attending part of the evening's event on account of the participation of an actress from Max Reinhardt's company whom he greatly admired: 'The thing is that Buber is lecturing on the Jewish Myth; it would take more than Buber to get me out of my room, I have heard him before, I find him dreary; no matter what he says, something is missing.'[131]

A few days later, Kafka was exasperated to learn that Felice had bought a book by Buber:

> The fact that you bought Buber's book is really curious! Do you buy books regularly or as the fancy takes you—and then such an expensive book! I know it only through a detailed review in which various passages were quoted [. . .] And then you speak of 'his' style, but I suppose these are translations? Unless it is one of his authoritarian adaptations [*oder sollten es so eingreifende Bearbeitungen sein*], which to my mind make his books of legends unbearable.[132]

In reality, in the previous letter, Kafka had made a sort of concession to Felice who, as a convinced young Zionist, was no doubt fascinated by Buber and had difficulty understanding Kafka's acerbic remarks. The writer had conceded, for example, that his *Chinesische Geister- und Liebesgeschichten* (Chinese Ghost and Love Stories), published in Frankfurt in 1911, was a fine work.[133] His obvious irritation when he learnt of Felice's purchase of the book, revealed the truth of his hostility towards the publishing enterprise associated with Buber's re-writing of the Hasidic tales.[134]

Biographical criticism feels free to assert that Kafka revised his judgement of Buber, since he seemed to find him pleasant company when he met him.[135] Yet, like Scholem, Kafka dissociated the man—whom he called 'as a person [. . .] lively and simple and remarkable'—from his work. In the same letter of 19 January 1913, he writes to Felice that Buber 'seems to have no connection with the tepid things [*lauwarme Sachen*] he has written'.[136] In fact, like Scholem, Kafka also sent texts to Buber in the hope of being published in *Der Jude*[137] which remained, as Scholem attests, one of the best German-language Jewish magazines and one of those which, as Scholem further states, 'fought for the emancipation of the Jews as Jews, a people among peoples',[139] a political line entirely congenial to Kafka.

We have a confirmation of Kafka's deep political (and we should no doubt also add, aesthetic) mistrust of Buber in a letter to Brod five years later in January 1918:

> I [. . .] am now reading Buber's most recent books, sent by Oskar. Hateful, repellent books, all three of them. To put it correctly and precisely, they are written—*Either/Or* especially—with the sharpest of pens [. . .] but they drive you to despair [. . .] even the healthiest lungs feel short of breath [. . .] As things are, their hatefulness grows under my hands.[140]

In any event, Kafka refused to join in with the collective fascination that had developed around Buber's person and work.

The Art of Plagiarism

'The Village Schoolmaster', written in December 1914, is a 'folk tale' in which it seems that Kafka is referring cryptically to Buber's *Tales of the Hasidim* and denouncing them as purloinings and misappropriations. But the force of the text and its disturbing effect derive, in large part, from the fact that—as in 'A Country Doctor', for example—it is precisely the first-person narrator who is the object of the criticism on which the text as a whole is founded. The entire narrative is, in fact, the *mise en scène* of the self-defence system of a narrator whose lying and hypocrisy are so patent that what is presented as obvious fact is gradually undermined from within. The entire narrative is the construction of an enormous lie and, under cover of enabling the narrator to justify himself, is in reality the deconstruction of a social hypocrisy and violence which show up so clearly only because the apparent discourse conceals (while exhibiting) a terrible social violence. The tale is built on the opposition between Eastern and Western Jews and on the ambivalent admiration the latter purport to feel for the former while laying hold, in the way Buber does, of their symbolic wealth (their folk tales, legends, stories, songs and rituals).[141]

The tale is the story of a village schoolmaster, which in this case means a poor stranger, bereft of any material or symbolic resources—one of a group of 'quite simple people', living in a remote village that 'could not be reached by the railroad'.[142] The discovery of a giant mole in his village is merely a pretext for describing the perverse and complex aspects of an oppression and misappropriation which present themselves in the guise of selfless interest.

The old village schoolmaster publishes a pamphlet recounting the discovery of this mole and it receives some public recognition. But the narrator produces a short text on the same subject in his turn, claiming that he wishes to defend the cause of the schoolmaster who had been attacked in scholarly circles and had 'suffered deeply from the cold attitude of the recognized authorities'.[143] Under cover of defending the unknown schoolmaster, a man devoid of influence, the narrator actually inserts into his narrative a whole series of indications discrediting him. The seemingly chivalrous semblance of the narrator's undertaking collapses quite quickly when we read of the schoolmaster that 'neither his abilities nor his equipment made it possible for him to produce an exhaustive description that could be used as a foundation by others, far less, therefore, an actual explanation of the occurrence'[144] or when, on the pretext of attempting to avoid being influenced in any way, the narrator decides not to read the teacher's contribution:

> To read his pamphlet could only have led me astray, and so
> I refrained from reading it until I should have finished my
> own labours. More, I did not even get in touch with the

teacher. True, he heard of my inquiries through intermediaries, but he did not know whether I was working for him or against him.[145]

The rhetorical character of the narrator's system of defences has a twofold goal: to convince the reader not only of his good faith but also of the quality of his discoveries about the giant mole. His own text, which allegedly owes nothing to the schoolmaster's discoveries, is supposed to be both far better and much more reliable in scholarly terms. This also enables him to leave the unknown teacher entirely in the shade: '[P]erhaps on this point indeed, I showed all too great a scrupulosity; from my words one might have thought nobody had ever inquired into the case before, and I was the first to interrogate those who had seen or heard of the mole, the first to correlate the evidence, the first to draw conclusions.'[146]

Protesting excessive scrupulousness, the narrator in this way justifies his plagiarism and misappropriation. Buber obviously comes to mind here. Making no reference to the work of the Yiddish writers and the collective development of a new literature in Yiddish, that writer found himself, thanks to his 'Tales', feted in the West for having 'discovered' the creativity of the Eastern Jews.

So as to change point of view without changing narrator, Kafka then very subtly constructs a part of his text in free indirect style, having the schoolmaster character speak through the mouth of the plagiarist.[147] The defensive system of the Eastern Jew protesting against the appropriation of his efforts and writings by his *soi-disant* Western defender is perfectly rational, deductive, logical and convincing: '[The schoolmaster said that] if I was really concerned solely to give publicity to his pamphlet, why had I not occupied myself exclusively with him and his pamphlet, why had I not pointed out its virtues, its irrefutability, why had I not confined myself to insisting on the significance of the discovery and making that clear.'[148]

And, further, 'For, in his heart, he was convinced that I wanted to rob him of the fame of being the first man publicly to vindicate the mole.'[149]

It appears that the schoolmaster is actually accusing the narrator of misappropriation and most importantly—this, as I see it, is the central plank of Kafka's argument—of total incomprehension of the material misappropriated. Whereas the Westerner describes the teacher throughout as a poor, powerless and irritable wretch of questionable personal hygiene (he carries his tobacco around 'loose in all his pockets'[150]), seeking only financial reward from his business, we can see that he is actually driven by beliefs and values far superior to those of the narrator which have a certain baseness about them:

> What did he care whether his honesty was vindicated or not? All that he was concerned with was the thing itself, and with that alone [these are assertions by the narrator, reporting the schoolteacher's remarks]. But I was only of disservice to it, for I did not understand it, I did not prize it at its true value, I had no real feeling for it. It was infinitely above my intellectual capacity.[151]

In other words, the teacher (the Eastern Jew) is himself asserting his contempt for the Westerner.

If Kafka is to pull off this narrative of virtuosic sophistication, the problem he sets for himself is that he has to articulate a discourse containing a double meaning—a discourse whose 'truth' must at no point escape the reader—while composing a mendacious surface monologue which, despite everything, retains its verisimilitude.[152] The double level of his text has to be perceptible throughout—on the one hand, as an allegedly objective report into a matter of scholarly reputation and, on the other, as a lie and a distortion of reality in the interests of plagiarism and misappropriation.

The main thing that sets Easterner against Westerner is symbolic power—that is, the latter's capability to make and unmake reputations, to lend the schoolmaster and his book existence among the 'city people'. Yet this protector, far from making the man known, helps consign him to oblivion. More than this, in the latter part of the text, 'science' is described as an implacable, insurmountable system of domination. The only thing the provincial teacher does not have is 'scientific' legitimacy—that is to say, the credibility and respect that ought to be due to him. He is forgotten because he is subject to pre-ordained scorn and discredit (this resembles the taint borne by the Eastern Jews), difficulties that are denied all along by those claiming to contribute to his fame. In the end, the narrator, after declaring amid much ambiguity that he was withdrawing from the business, tries to rid himself, hastily and with a kind of disgust, of the man who is for him merely a 'stubborn little old fellow':[153] 'I could not bear the stink of his tobacco,' says the narrator; 'But today his silent presence as he sat there was an actual torture to me.'[154]

At the centre of the short story, then, we find a tacit but firm—and, as it seems to me, formally very complex—defence of the Yiddish storywriters whom there were no grounds for 'transposing' and who should, rather, have been recognized by Westerners for their noble achievements. Everything turns on the question of fame usurped and the narrator's hypocrisy. ' "It is the aim of this pamphlet"—so I ended up all too melodramatically [. . .] "to help in giving the schoolmaster's book the wide publicity it deserves. If I succeed in that, then may my name, which I regard as only transiently and indirectly associated with this question, be blotted from it at once." '[155]

The above sentence is a declaration of intent that mimics Buber's assertions when he claims to pay homage to the Eastern Jews, to do justice to them and set his own reputation aside. Since, as Kafka saw it, it was largely on the strength of Buber's interpretation and commentary that the young Prague Zionists returned to their Jewish identity, we may, without straining this text, read it, I think, as a critique of the—largely Buberian—Cultural Zionism practised and developed at the time in the Bohemian capital.

Rather remarkably, the—at times very sharp—criticisms levelled at Buber regarding his conception of Hasidism (not of the Yiddish stories) and his 'transposed' tales, most notably by Scholem, related precisely to his appropriation (in other words, his entirely personal conception) of Hasidism. He was criticized for changing the texts, filtering them through his own vision as a Western Jew, oblivious of the social and cultural reality of that movement. He was said to have been selective with his material, to have retained only what suited him or what fitted with his expectations or desires and to have rejected everything too far removed from these. On the pretext that the transmission to a Western audience made 'adjustments' necessary, he was said to have gone a long way towards Westernizing (and hence in Scholem's view, betraying) Hasidic literature. Referring to Buber's tales, Scholem speaks of 'neo-Hasidism' and stresses the subjective character of the choices made within the texts.[156] Bechtel, who has made a detailed comparison of certain originals and Buber's transposed versions, finds in them deletions, a 'sentimentalization', a dramatization of the narrative, the presence of clichés relating to archetypal representations of Eastern Jews then current in Germany and Austria, the addition of secondary plots and characters and the decision to employ an affected language full of archaisms. In her view, the Buberian text is more to be 'ranged among the classics of German Expressionism' than set alongside the translation of traditional texts.[157]

'A Mere Nothing in Execution'

'Josephine the Singer, or the Mouse Folk' seems to me to be another—later and even more stinging—satire on Buber. On that assumption, this longer story can be seen as a darkly humorous, sarcastic indictment of the philosopher's project and a way of recounting his immense success (undeserved in Kafka's view) among Western Jews. Giving the folk in question an animal identity is perhaps, as Anderson asserts, a reference to anti-Semitic stigmatizations of the Jews but it is certainly not an acceptance or appropriation of that stigma. The mouse folk are described above all as frail and weak. They lead a 'hard' life, experience 'emergencies' with 'many worries and dangers', forcing them 'to take devious ways' when 'things are most upset'. In the midst of 'grave decisions', they live out a 'precarious existence amidst the tumult of a hostile world'.[158] This might well be a representation of the Jews but without the necessary pejorative implications; or it might be an inverted reprise of the cliché with the intention of undermining it.

The narrator, who belongs to the 'opposition', describes 'Josephine's art' in the most precise way possible. He provides the most apparently contradictory—that is to say, most damaging— definitions of it. After asserting, as early as the second sentence, 'the power of [her] song', he never misses an opportunity thereafter to point out its weaknesses: this 'delicate creature' has 'a frail little voice'; she emits 'a thin piping'.[159] That piping is perhaps not even of the order of song; it is perhaps just a 'usual workaday piping'. 'So is it singing at all? Is it perhaps not just a piping?' insinuates the narrator. 'If that were all true, then indeed Josephine's alleged vocal skill might be disproved, but that would merely clear the ground for the real riddle which needs solving—the enormous influence she has.'[160]

The narrator, claiming to be objective, is out to demonstrate three things that are apparently contradictory (or, at any rate, incomprehensible, if they are true *at the same time*), on which the entire unease generated by this text would appear to rest: first, Josephine's indisputable 'effect' on the public; second, the lamentable nature of her singing which brings her such great popularity; third, the taking up and appropriation by Josephine of a folk piping or whistling (hence a piping that properly belongs to the people) which she passes off as her own creation and debases as she practises it. Josephine is not acquiring sophisticated skills, nor is she creating new forms. She is merely picking up on extant popular traditions. And that is why she plays such a crucial role: 'We admire in her what we do not at all admire in ourselves; in this respect, I may say, she is of one mind with us.'[161] This formula enables us to understand precisely the connection between Josephine and Buber. The latter, as seen by Kafka—and to give a rapid summary of the story—is precisely practising an embezzlement of public property. And, just as Josephine lies to the people as she robs it of its resources, so Buber illicitly appropriates the people's artistic practices which have already been given form by the Yiddish writers.

In fact, Kafka continues, the Josephine/Buber effect can be explained only by seeing her—that is to say, by the spectacle she makes of herself. Kafka emphasizes the ridiculous nature of the affected pose she strikes as soon as she steps on stage. She 'was quite beyond herself, spreading her arms wide and stretching her throat as high as it could reach'.[162] And to gather the mass of the people around her, she 'needs to do nothing else than take up her stand, head thrown back, mouth half-open, eyes turned upwards'.[163] And this is why 'a mere nothing in voice, a mere nothing in execution, she asserts herself and gets across to us.'[164]

After what looks very much like a furious denunciation of the affectations of Josephine/Buber,[165] Kafka strikes a final symbolic blow at this great charismatic leader when he foretells her imminent demise. By a kind of perverse, sophistic reasoning, the narrator claims to be deeply affected by this while suggesting that her loss will not ultimately amount to much. If her singing was in reality a virtually inaudible 'piping', then 'was [. . .] not [. . .] Josephine's singing [. . .] already past losing?'[166]

These critical tales are not exceptional in Kafka's narrative production. Bruce has convincingly shown that there are many parodies and rather biting satires on Zionist discourse among his short stories.[167]

A 'POPULAR' LITERATURE

New Mythologies

Having the movement for the emancipation of Eastern Jews suddenly revealed to him presented Kafka with the possibility of a sort of out-line programme of work and enabled him to redefine his role as a writer: to give Western Jews a—literary and political—transposition of what the Eastern storytellers offered their readers; to set before them a fighting literature but also a literature of 'popular education', whatever the paradoxes of a position of this type in the Prague German-language space might be. By the same token, as he saw it, the task of the Western Jewish writer was to attempt to restore collective existence to a people that denied or failed to recognize its existence as a people. In this respect, it was closely akin to the task of popular pedagogy which the Bundists had set for themselves.

Hence, one of the literary paths opening itself up to him might well be the elaboration of a new mythology and, most importantly, the development of a tool of social and political criticism. This new literary form, built onto existing traditions and forged by and for the Jewish people of Western Europe, would be a specific instrument capable of speaking to that people of its own sufferings, its history and its self-forgetting through assimilation. Developing this new popular mythology required the takeover and use of 'popular' genres, forms and traditions which Kafka (himself also) 'misappropriated', as it were, and redirected into the service of this novel form of literature. In this way, he can be said to have chosen to leave himself wholly out of the picture, so as to speak not of and for himself (as is believed when Kafka is conflated with his first-person narrators) but for 'everyone'. Or, to put it another way, he shared with the Zionists the folkist convictions that put the 'people' at the centre of the writer's preoccupations and justified his existence. However, drawing on the Yiddishists, he radicalized this stance and attempted to import into Western Europe the *conatus*, the tendency and the form of the literary and political battles being fought in the East.

We may thus advance the hypothesis that genuine 'thought' was at work in Kafka's texts. Concerned as he was to discover, understand and explain both Jewish specificities and his own convictions with regard to the social group to which he belonged, he developed throughout his work his own—subtle, paradoxical and provocative—thinking on the Jewish question. In November 1920, he wrote to Milena:

> I have one peculiarity which in essence doesn't distinguish me much from my acquaintances, but in degree a great deal. We both know, after all, enough typical examples of Western Jews, I am, as far as I know, the most typical Western Jew among them. This means, expressed with exaggeration, that not one calm second is granted me, nothing is granted me, everything has to be earned, not only the present and the future, but the past too—something after all which perhaps every human being has inherited, this too

must be earned, it is perhaps the hardest work. When the Earth turns to the right—I'm not sure that it does—I would have to turn to the left to make up for the past. But as it is I haven't the least particle of strength for these obligations, I can't carry the world on my shoulders [. . .] Any attempt to get through this on my own strength is madness and is rewarded with madness [. . .] It's more or less as though someone, each time before taking a walk, had not only to wash and comb himself and so on—this alone is indeed tiresome enough—but he also (since, each time, he lacks the necessary for the walk) has to sew his clothes as well, make his shoes, manufacture his hat, whittle his walking stick, and so on. Of course he's not able to do this very well, perhaps they hold together for the length of a few streets, but when he reaches the Graben, for instance, they suddenly all fall apart and he stands there naked among rags and tatters. And now the torture of running back to the Altstädter Ring! And in the end he probably runs into a mob engaged in Jew-baiting in the Eisengasse.[168]

Once again, years after the self-portrait sent to Grete Bloch, he was defining his place and particularity on the basis of his belonging to a collective. Once again, it was as a member of the group of Western Jews that he understood himself and analysed his specificity and originality. From his point of view, what the Western Jewish writer lacked most was the 'past' or, in other words, inherited traditions. 'Earn[ing]' or recovering a people's past (tradition, history, culture, language) was an exhausting task for someone who perceived himself as assimilated—that is to say, as deprived of everything.[169] Bereft of what constitutes general humanity, he could manage only to keep 'rags and tatters' together. He was, literally, the most disinherited of all writers, since he could neither inherit nor bequeath his heritage; he could only try to write texts that would constitute future Jewish literature and hence the future heritage of the Jewish people. And this intrinsic fragility was constantly reaffirmed and reinforced by the power of rising anti-Semitism. In the Herderian 'constellation of thought', 'soil' (*Boden*)—a word found in many texts of a private nature, in the diary or letters—'past' and 'people' (*Volk*) are almost equivalent. Since no great accumulation of time had occurred before the artist's own efforts, he was condemned to nakedness and failure, and the assimilated Jews were doomed to the perpetuation of their social misfortune. In 1918, he attributed his 'failure' to the same evils: 'It is not inertia, ill will, awkwardness —even if there is something of all this in it, because "vermin is born of the void"—that cause me to fail, or even to get near failings: family life, friendship, marriage, profession, literature. It is not that, but the lack of ground underfoot, of air, of the commandment.'[170]

But he added immediately, defining precisely as he did so his task as a writer and the meaning of his entire project: 'It is my task to create these, not in order that I may then, as it were, catch up with what I have missed, but in order that I shall have missed nothing, for the task is as good as any other. It is indeed the most primal task of all, or at least the reflection of that task.'[171]

Salvation, as Kafka saw it, could come only from his people. Yet, no popular tradition in Western Europe could 'justify' his existence as a writer. He had neither been recognized as a writer by his people, nor had he been elected to be one, but he wanted, as it were, to work *as if* he had been 'mandated' for the task: 'I can by my nature only take up a mandate that no one has given to me. In this contradiction, always only in a contradiction, can I live.'[172]

Kafka's endeavours, which represented a total thinking because they were as much literary and political as social, as much historical and cultural as ethnological, can be said to have been a novel form of literary exploration, not for the stance he adopted—we know that all the writers from the emerging countries made comparable choices[173]— but for their form. Because he belonged simultaneously to two literary spaces which did not inhabit the same literary time zone, Kafka stood the ordinary assumptions of literary representation on their head and tried, through literary fictions, to raise virtually unprecedented political or anthropological questions—or, at least, questions that had not previously been posed in that form. Into a space that knew and recognized aestheticism and art for art's sake, he imported popular contents and genres which belonged to the most recent, most deprived literary spaces. In other words, it was only in a guise that was, in its refinement, the product of the German and Austrian tradition which he, alongside others, had inherited that he got these 'common' forms through. Each path explored, each successful experiment, each narrative can be said to be the product of this kind of 'layering'—a product of his tireless search for new literary models.

At the beginning of his book of memoirs, Brod stresses his friend's freedom with regard to literary hierarchies and prejudices:

> How remote from his way of looking at things was all the talk about the 'standards,' 'literary hallmarks,' 'distinction of rank.' In every case he hit upon the essential. He could be carried away by a turn of speech in a newspaper article; with passionate enthusiasm he would dilate on the crowded life, the eye for drama, in some novel by some author or other who was generally sneered at as 'cheap.' I remember how [. . .] he produced a novel by Ohnet[174] from the boarding-house library and, with great enthusiasm, read me a passage —a conversation—which he praised for its unforced liveliness. Odd passages in a musical comedy or a conventional film [. . .] could move him to tears [. . .] He was an entirely independent explorer, who had not the faintest idea of being tied down by the insensitive classifications of histories of literature.[175]

Apart from the confirmation they bring of Kafka's interest in popular literature and culture, these details about his tastes provided by Brod lend credence to the argument advanced by Robert, among others, that Kafka made a precise and conscious use of certain literary genres. Epic and myth, granted, but also the chronicle, the legal document, the *Erziehungsroman*, the detective novel, the thriller, stories of the supernatural, the folk tale, etc. This taste, which Brod attributed to his liking for 'simple things', also reflected the professional interest of a man looking for narrative models elsewhere than among the range of possibilities offered by the Prague literary field.

Kafka began his search among universal materials—Greek mythology, for example—which he looked to exploit in an often ironic or disillusioned vein. He recycled, as it were, and modernized the figures of Prometheus, Ulysses or Poseidon. He also worked on collections of folk tales. The list of the books in his library, which was first provided by Wagenbach in 1958, then taken up again and completed by Born in 1990, confirms his extensive knowledge in this field. Among them, we may note the important presence of anthologies of Jewish legends and folk tales: Alexander Eliasberg's *Sagen polnischer Juden*,[176] Micah Joseph Berdichevsky, Rahel Bin Gorion and Emanuel Bin-Gorion's *Die Sagen der Juden*,[177] the German translation of a collection of stories by Peretz entitled *Aus dieser und jener Welt: Jüdische Geschichten* and *Jüdische Helden*.[178] There are also books of popular religious history and, most importantly, collections of Chinese and Turkish tales,[179] of Arabic poetry[180] and stories of travel, most notably among the Eskimos.[181] This interest in a field that is today regarded as secondary from a literary standpoint might be badly misunderstood if we held to such an assumption. Yet it was through folk tale that Kafka found many opportunities to encounter ethnology in the form it assumed at the time within the German-speaking space.

We must remember that German ethnology was divided in those days into two distinct disciplines. On the one side stood *Volkskunde* (the 'science of the people', the 'science of Germanness' or 'folkloristic ethnology'),[182] the descendant of Herder's *Volksgeist*. It emerged progressively in the course of the nineteenth century, spread deeply and durably throughout the German language and cultural areas and concerned itself almost exclusively with the question of German identity, national unity and the definition of a German specificity through a definition of the *Volk*. Its aim was to know the 'German people' from within through its traditions, which were themselves supposed to give access to the *Volksseele* ('the soul of the people'). In parallel with this, there had developed an ethnology of *other* peoples, more akin to the English and French definitions of the subject, and this established itself under the name *Völkerkunde* ('science of peoples'), though it was also known among ethnologists and anthropologists as *Ethnologie*.[183]

Volkskunde permeated the totality of the German literary and intellectual space, leaving lasting effects. Indeed, it went beyond it into all the spaces where Herderian ideas became entrenched. At a very early stage, under the influence of the Brothers Grimm, *Volkskunde* set great store by transcribed oral traditions and anything that could in any way be part of a definition of popular literature, including songs and theatre, proverbs and riddles, tales and legends. We may speak of a kind of privilege accorded to the collection of material by philologists: since the Grimms, the 'spirit of the folk' was supposed to be expressed or asserted most 'authentically' in 'popular poetry'. The folk tale was, therefore, very widely regarded as giving privileged access to the 'soul'—and, hence, to the truth—of a people. In Jewish nationalist circles, for example, discourse around the *Ostfrage* was steeped in this omnipresent ethnology, whether it be essays, travel writing, polemical articles, arguments for or against Zionist convictions, or literary texts. *Völkerkunde* made its appearance at a later stage, in the second half of the nineteenth century. It shared a number of assumptions with *Volkskunde*, particularly the emphasis it placed on the need to gather oral legends and folk tales into published collections as a means of understanding each of the peoples studied. This widely shared interest enabled a whole generation of intellectuals, writers, dramatists, politicians and essayists to extend the ordinary field of investigation and acquire knowledge of tales and legends from distant peoples.

Although, like all his contemporaries, he was steeped in the folkist presuppositions specific to the Austrian *epistême* of the time, Kafka, seeking to escape the all-powerful German cultural model, turned deliberately towards *Völkerkunde*. In his conversations with Janouch, he referred to 'ethnological' interests in a way so lacking in naivety and so well-informed that he was surely attesting to an in-depth reading which reflected great interest. With regard to his little drawings, for example, Kafka is said to have told Janouch:

> My drawing is a perpetually renewed and unsuccessful attempt at primitive magic [. . .] When the Eskimos want to set fire to a piece of wood, they draw a few wavy lines on it.

That is the magical picture of fire, which they'll bring to life by rubbing their fire-sticks together. That's what I do. Through my drawings I want to come to terms with the shapes which I perceive.[184]

Along the same lines, Brod reports the following remarks, linked directly to Kafka's occupational activity, from the notes he claims to have taken of conversations with his friend: 'Insurance is like the religions of primitive peoples who believe they can ward off evil by all kinds of manipulations.'[185] One immediately begins to take a different view of his 'Chinese' stories and his transposition of Kabyle folk tales. And one begins to see his interest in Yiddish stories as so many borrowings, appropriations and garnerings from what was then regarded as ethnology.

The Choice of America

The Yiddish storytellers, for example, provided Kafka with the ideas for a certain number of plot lines and characters, and with a tone and a variety of forms totally absent from the range of literary possibilities at Prague in 1910–20.[186] Pinès's book, which Kafka says he read 'with [. . .] thoroughness', offered him the main models. Apart from the central role accorded to short stories which were akin to folk tales written in a comic vein, it seems to me that Kafka found first and foremost in that work the possibility of raising the debates, issues of the day and most burning political questions of the moment (anti-Semitism, Zionism, socialism, the West's relations with Eastern Jewry, etc.), but doing so in such a way as to escape the constraints of naturalism. For example, the stories of Sholem Aleichem had the very particular characteristic of addressing both the most crucial world political affairs of the day (the Dreyfus Affair, European diplomacy, the threats of war) and the political events internal to the Jewish community of Russia and Poland (the boycott of Polish shops by Jewish groups,[187] the stinging criticism—though in a comic vein— of assimilated Jews,[188] emigration to New York, the poverty of immigrant Jews, strikes and the power of American trade unions,[189] etc.). In his book, Pinès translated and published fragments from a short story by Sholem Aleichem entitled 'Dreyfus in Kasrilevke'—the fictional town where Sholem Aleichem's hero lived—taken from a volume of his works published in Warsaw in 1903:

> I wonder if the Dreyfus affair made such an impression anywhere in the whole world as it did in Kasrilevke? Paris, they tell me, boiled like water in an overheated kettle. But the agony, the pain and despair that Kasrilevke lived through from all this, that, I tell you, Paris will never match, not until the coming of the Messiah.[190]

Apart from the satirical and comic vein, what Kafka could not fail to notice in the analysis and the many quotations/translations of Yiddish texts provided by Pinès in his book—which was, in a sense, the opposite of the aesthetic literature produced by his friends—was the possibility of a writing oriented towards the collective. The Yiddish tales had protagonists who were not individuals equipped with a plausible psychology and personal history but mouthpieces for an entire group behaving as a collective. These protagonists (particularly those of Abramovitsh or Sholem Aleichem) presented a version of social reality that was itself satirical. They could be subject to tacit criticism, they were not heroic. For example, Sholem Aleichem's famous character is described as follows by Pinès: 'What characterizes Menachem Mendel is that, while assuming the grave, serious air of a man of "superior understanding", he understands nothing at all of what is going on around him [. . .] Menachem Mendel meddles in everything and sees everything superficially, without ever understanding the underlying nature of things.'[191] The marked failings of the various characters were not the product of a criticism with condemnatory intent; they were the consequences of a poverty, injustice and lack of social acceptance which were themselves relentlessly criticized by these writers, who saw their part in the struggle for the emancipation of their people as a 'useful' one. In this sense, the tales of the classic Yiddish writers were the exact opposite of Martin Buber's 'Hasidic' tales that were held out to the Prague intellectuals as the quintessence of Jewish art. They evoked the material miseries—hunger, cold and sickness—of a very real people.[192]

Furthermore, Kafka was also able to glean from this work the initial conceptions of narrative techniques which he was himself to use extensively, including the device of having animals speak. We know there are very many talking animals in his writings: mice, a cockroach, a dog, a mole, a horse, a lamb, a cat, a jackal and an ape, among others. It is a classic technique of folk tale and fable, but one Pinès studies with specific regard to the Yiddish novelists. For example, he analyses at some length Abramovitsh's novel *Di klyatshe* or *The Nag* (published 1873),[193] in which a skinny, hounded, talking mare embodies the destiny of the Jewish people.[194] It seems, then, that what was at stake for Kafka in his reading of Pinès's book was the choice of another type of literature through which the writer could produce a realist (though not a naturalist) vision—far removed from any political idealism and intellectualism—of a people and of the social and political questions confronting it.

Amerika: The Man Who Disappeared, written by Kafka mostly during autumn 1912, might thus be read in large part as a Yiddish tale or, at any rate, as a text possessing many characteristic features of the tales being distributed at that same date by the Yiddishists and Bundists to the Russian villages. On this assumption, we may suppose that Kafka drew as models more or less explicitly—and often ironically—on these tales, to write one of the first stories into which he put political themes and social descriptions with a conscious use of caricature. However, he left the work unfinished, no doubt because it was a novel that was still a little too close to the canons and conceptions of *yiddishkeit*. The arguments advanced were a little too rigid and lifted too directly from political discourse. All in all, the project itself perhaps mimicked too naively the practices of the socialist writers.

This first novel of Kafka's was begun in May 1912 or, in other words, in the months immediately following his encounter with the group of Jewish actors from Poland. Like all his writings, it has been subjected to many interpretations, mutually contradictory to varying degrees. The 'social' interpretation has largely been favoured:[195] *Amerika* is said to be a critique of 'technological' civilization, of the alienation and enslavement to which industrial society gives rise. Others have interpreted it in directly political terms as a satire of capitalist civilization.[196] For yet others, including David, it is a new form of *Bildungsroman*, not to be regarded as a novel of social criticism.

However, it seems to me that the mere fact of situating his first novel in America was a way for Kafka of evoking, first, a very precise social reality: that of Jewish immigration into the US. Making America his protagonist's destination was just one way of adverting again to one of the collective realities of the Jewish people at the time, the mass emigration of Russian Jews, the Kishinev pogroms perpetrated only seven years earlier[197] and the Eastern discussions on Jewish exile. In other words, in the Jewish social and political debate of the early years of the century, America wasn't just, in some banal fashion, the site of 'modernity' and of the confused, indeterminate triumph of 'technological civilization';[198] it was also, most importantly, the new destination for the Jews driven out by the Russian pogroms— and a hellish one in many respects, given the terrible living conditions that awaited them there. It seems to me, consequently, that the interpretation of the novel as a critique of capitalist society and of the intensifying exploitation of the working class can be maintained only on condition that we understand that this was not a vague, general condemnation but the precise criticism of a real social situation: the massive emigration of East European Jews to New York, which was a great subject of concern for all politicized Jews.

We know that Kafka was almost entirely ignorant of the US. Much of what he did know about it came from a book by Arthur Holitscher, a German Jewish writer and journalist, which he had just read. Holitscher was close to the socialist movements and had published, at exactly this same time—in 1911 and 1912—serialized impressions of his travels in the US and Canada in the *Neue Rundschau*.[199] The evidence of this prior reading on Kafka's part confirms the fact that he felt an affinity with this type of socialist view and conception of the world. Violently hostile to America, Holitscher describes the country as a sort of hell on earth, the last word in triumphant capitalism. He condemns working conditions there, the exploitation of children, anti-Semitism, the ghettos of the New York East Side, the poverty of the Blacks, etc.[200] We can see precisely (almost all the critics agree on this point) the marks left on Kafka's novel by his reading of Holitscher. However, in his comments on the text, David asserts that the novel is not about 'the Blacks or the Jews' and that 'the book's project was, therefore, certainly neither a critique of America nor even an overall description of the United States.'[201] Yet—and this is a point I shall return to—Holitscher stresses on several occasions in his book that Blacks and Jews met with a very similar fate in the US and that there was a solidarity between them.[202] David also assures his readers, without citing any precise historical fact whatever to support his argument, not only that the information provided by Holitscher's book was 'tendentious and excessive' (in reality, it was clearly socialist) but also that Kafka would himself have detected its 'extreme character'.[203] Going further, David argues in cut-and-dried fashion that, because of the implausibility of certain details (the assumption is, then, that verisimilitude was Kafka's concern), 'in 1912 America is, in the main, the inaccessible country, the almost legendary *terra incognita* [. . .] the image of the future awaiting the Europe of 1912,'[204] and that, 'by setting the plot of his book in the USA, Kafka sought to situate it at the ends of the earth, on the fringes of unreality.'[205] Now we are aware today, through the work of historians, of the nature of the working conditions of the Jewish immigrants and how they were exploited. They were crammed into East Side hovels, forced to work in garment workshops for 10 or 12 hours a day, accommodated in frighteningly unhygienic conditions and always underpaid.[206] We know, therefore, that, contrary to David's assertions, Holitscher was not being at all extreme when he described the 'East End ghetto with its unspeakable filthiness [. . .] and its foetid smells', etc.[207] Seen from this angle, America cannot be said in any sense to symbolize the legendary land of a radiant future. It was, in fact, the land where once again the exile/exodus of the Jews was being played out, after they had been driven, as ever in their history, out of the territory on which they were living. It was, therefore, also—and consequently—the country where the drama of assimilation would unfold once again.

Amerika is the 'real' and legendary history of the assimilation of modern Jewry, a transposed Yiddish folk tale recounting the eternal exile of the Jews in the form of their emigration to America. In it Kafka writes of a kind of mythic exodus embodying the destiny of the Jews, but also and most importantly, of a modernized form of the process, eternally recommenced, of their assimilation. The mention of the city of Rameses[208]—the city in which the 'Hotel Occidental' is supposed to be located—is, of course, an explicit reference to the biblical Exodus.[209] But it is, first and foremost, a way of comparing the enslavement of the Hebrews in Egypt with that of the Jews in America.

Kafka was attempting in this political tale to spell out in relatively simple form—linear, novelistic and easily accessible—questions that arose for everyone in his world. America was depicted as a kind of Far West,[210] a sort of caricature (in the sense of a magnified version) of the situation in which the Western Jews found themselves. With this kind of displacement of European reality effected with the aid of America, Kafka could evoke that reality but reduced to a kind of structure, to a powerful mechanism, much more powerful than the will or desire of his protagonist Karl Rossmann. In other words, he was narrating the social and psychological realities, both collective and individual, of assimilation—of what he saw as the 'disappearance' of the Jews as Jews—together with the personal consequences and the effects on the community.[211] The practices of ordinary literary realism (particularly of naturalism) and the critical habits which have ensued have given rise to a belief that the novelistic hero necessarily has a psychological reality and acts in terms of common psychological characteristics. Yet, as Anderson points out, throughout the novel the character of Karl Rossmann remains a sort of 'flat surface' without depth or individual psychology.[212] Walter Benjamin also observed that Rossmann was a figure 'entirely unmysterious, transparent, pure [. . .] without character'.[213] Why is this? It seems to me that it is precisely because he personifies a collective. He is a 'collective type' in the sense Pinès gives to that expression,[214] because he takes on the generic features of the group of immigrants. For this reason, Kafka depicts him entirely unrealistically, if not indeed as caricature.[215]

The few mentions of his fictional writings during his conversations with Janouch cast some valuable light on this question. With reference to 'The Stoker', the first chapter of *Amerika*, when Janouch asks him whether the character of Karl Rossmann had been inspired by a real individual, Kafka replies: 'I was not describing people. I was telling a story.'[216] And, to another question relating to the name of another of his protagonists, he pointed out that, 'Samsa is not merely Kafka and nothing else. *The Metamorphosis* is not a confession, although it is—in a certain sense—an indiscretion.'[217] In other terms, to take him at his own word, Kafka was asserting that he was not describing particular human beings and, above all, not speaking about himself: his was not a confessional literature. By his own admission, his narratives would not, therefore, take as their object either himself as an individual or particular persons endowed with individual characteristics. 'They are images,' he added, 'only images.'[218]

Karl Rossmann is a sort of Menachem Mendel. He is a chatty, scatterbrained, boastful young man, full of good intentions, but not very perceptive. As Christian Klein stresses, he is a simple-minded, passsive anti-hero.[219] And I would add that he is incapable of understanding what is going on around him, even though he is convinced, like Menachem Mendel, that he understands everything and can solve every problem, including remedying the injustices that befall those he meets along the way (as in the first chapter, in which he tries to come to the aid of the stoker and repair the injustice done to him).[220]

After committing an indiscretion, a young man, Karl is driven from his home by his parents, a point Kafka particularly underscores: '[M]y dear nephew has simply been got rid of [*beiseitegeschafft*] by his parents—yes, let's just use the phrase, as it describes what happened—simply got rid of, the way you put the cat out if it's making a nuisance of itself.'[221] Karl's banal 'transgression' was seduction by a maid whom he had made pregnant.[222] He is therefore driven out, as the Jews have always been and continue to be, and arrives in America 'with [. . .] lamentably inadequate provision'—that is to say, with a specific language and culture that are unpardonably inadequate.[223] He begins, moreover, by forgetting his 'suitcase'—that is to say, his past and everything attaching to his ancestral home—on the ship, even before he has disembarked. Bereft of it, and confused as his past increasingly retreats, he attempts 'a new birth'. To that end, he sets about learning English and manages ultimately to acquire only the rudiments of its commercial vocabulary. However, 'the more Karl's English improved, the more inclined the uncle was to introduce him to his circle of acquaintances.'[224] In other words, the more he becomes assimilated and forgets his mother tongue, the more he integrates into rich American society. He identifies so well with his uncle's interests, that is to say, with those of the big American industrialists (Kafka makes clear that his uncle's business 'involved buying, storing, transporting and selling on a vast scale'[225]) that when 'striking metal-workers' go by, with 'carriers of flags and banners spanning the whole street',[226] Karl 'rest[s] happily against the arm Mr Pollunder had thrown around him, the conviction that he would shortly be a welcome guest in a well-lit, high-walled, dog-guarded country house making him very happy'.[227] Kafka was intending to show here that assimilation was both a betrayal (as forgetting) of the past and also a betrayal of the political interests of the people —the workers—in favour of the interests of the bourgeoisie and the bosses, Jewish or otherwise.

However, his uncle Jakob also 'gets rid of him'. As the victim of a decision the narrator describes as 'secret and painful',[228] Karl goes off carrying only his poor suitcase in which is stored—as the sole trace of his past—a photograph of his parents frozen in a kind of artificial pose: 'it wasn't a good photograph.'[229] This photo might be what remains of Judaism when it is reduced to religious formalism, to the 'insignificant scrap' of the kind bequeathed to Kafka by his father, a sort of a fake heritage, frozen in a meaningless tradition such as the heritage that falls to the assimilated Jews of the Austrian Empire. A remnant of forgotten reality, a poor image for a poorly bequeathed past: Karl Rossmann remains a kind of eternal exile. He then meets two workers, an Irishman and a Frenchman, Robinson and

Delamarche, with whom a rudimentary solidarity is established. As they are all three looking for work, they run across trucks from Uncle Jakob's company carrying signs saying 'dock workers hired'. However, his companions decline the offer, explaining to Karl that 'that way of hiring people was a shameful swindle and Jakob's company was notorious throughout the whole of the United States.'[230] Falling in here with the political theories of the Jewish socialists—particularly, the Bundists—which he seems almost to be illustrating, Kafka thus rejects the priority accorded at the time by the Zionists to what they called 'national solidarity' or the 'Jewish union' argument and finds in favour of the Bundists for whom, conversely, the most important thing is class solidarity—that is to say, solidarity between Rossmann the German Jew, Robinson the Irishman and Delamarche the Frenchman. In the terms of the Bundist propaganda of the day, national solidarity—such as that uniting Uncle Jakob to his nephew, the penniless immigrant, at the beginning of the novel—merely veiled the reality of the interests of the bourgeoisie, as against those of the common people, Jewish or otherwise.

Robin reports, for example, that a number of Yiddish popular serials distributed by the Bund ventilated the great contentious issues within the Jewish political world. The novel *All Jews Are Friends*, for example, contested the notion of 'Jewish unity' and, adds Robin, the illusion of the non-existence of class in Jewish society. At the heart of the action in *The Strike* was an employer attempting, with the support of the local rabbi and the police, to break a strike. However, 'class solidarity' overcame the wicked employer.[231] In the same way, Kafka in this first novel was depicting political preoccupations very much akin to the concerns of the Bundists, but doing so in such a refined narrative, aesthetic and fictional form that we are no longer able—historical forgetfulness and denial aiding—to read it today as a political allegory and 'fable' addressed to the Jewish population of Western Europe.

Curiously, a critique of the Zionist belief in community solidarity, which denies the reality of the division of Jewish society into social classes, is to be found in a text as late as 'Investigations of a Dog'

(1922). The canine narrator relates in ironic vein both the representation the group of dogs has of itself and the divided reality of that
same society:

> One can safely say that we all live together in a literal heap,
> all of us, different as we are from one another on account
> of numberless and profound modifications which have
> arisen in the course of time. All in one heap! We are drawn
> to each other and nothing can prevent us from satisfying
> that communal impulse; all our laws and institutions [. . .]
> go back to this longing for the greatest bliss we are capable
> of, the warm comfort of being together. But now consider
> the other side of the picture. No creatures to my knowledge
> live in such wide dispersion as we dogs, none have so many
> distinctions of class, of kind, of occupation.[232]

Karl Rossmann arrives, then, at the Hotel Occidental. There is
no need of a more explicit paraphrase to convey that, in the categories
of thought which were those of Kafka and all his contemporaries, the
adjective 'occidental' can refer here only to supposedly assimilative
Western Europe, by contrast with the Eastern part, the repository of
Jewish traditions. That hotel is the Western world, of which America
is a kind of extension. Arriving at the buffet of the Hotel Occidental,
Karl tries to get served but finds himself jostled: no one notices his
presence. Squeezing through, he eventually finds 'a little space at the
buffet, although his view was restricted for a long time', but he still
does not manage to get served. 'New guests [. . .] simply cleared the
buffet, sat down on the tables, and toasted one another; they were the
best places, from there they could see across the whole room.'[233]

This rapid description of the 'buffet' which represents the
American social world is among the first explicit traces of Kafka's
work on domination—work he will pursue throughout his life in different forms. The very rapid adumbration of this 'space' Karl eventually
finds—'a little space at the buffet, although his view was restricted',
as opposed to the best positions from which 'they could see across
the whole room'[234] (occupied by the 'ordinary' customers, that is to
say the non-Jews)—is a magnificent definition of symbolic domination.

In the New World, as seen by Kafka, only subordinate, ancillary places are left for new Jewish immigrants who are stigmatized, despised, 'jostled', never 'served', invisible. They believe they are merely 'late-comers', that they have simply arrived after the others whereas in reality they are being granted only a little space because they are despised for what they are.

However, happy that these little empty spaces are being conceded to them, the Jews, driven by the desire to assimilate, are going to put a great deal of passion into that endeavour. '[H]e kept thinking that in their lives [the others] had an advantage over him, which he needed to make up for by greater industry and a certain self-denial.'²³⁵ And he eventually manages to get attention only from a woman who takes him through the cool storeroom behind the counter and offers to take him in and give him a job. This offer, which he takes for favourable treatment—whereas, in fact, she is belittling him and consigning him to a lower status than the other customers—puts an end to his solidarity with his fellows. ('All day long you've been walking behind me, you've held on to my coat-tails,' says Delamarche, the Frenchman, 'But once you think you've found some sort of sup-port in the hotel, you start making big speeches to us.'²³⁶) However, Karl accepts because the offer is formulated attractively. The Head Cook of the Hotel Occidental offers him a place as a lift boy, a job that is monotonous, exhausting and humiliating. Here, with a mix-ture of bluntness, realism and irony, Kafka is retracing the process of assimilation that enables Jews, in agreeing to begin at the bottom of the social ladder, to believe that they are integrating into a society which, in reality, exploits and despises them. We might decipher Karl Rossmann's successive adventures in this same way—and page by page. They follow the same general principle and are constructed on the same pattern, retracing, as they do, all the stages of the his-torical and social process of the assimilation of the Western Jews.

The chapter devoted to Brunelda, in particular, can be interpreted as an evocation of the transition from the state of the worker (charac-terized by—albeit minimal—forms of organization and solidarity) to the solitary, anomic, defenceless state of the domestic servant. Karl, under compulsion from his two friends, will enter the service of the corpulent Brunelda who, with her whims and threats, takes exploitation to the point of physical violence and the removal of all protection. There is much to be written about caricature in Kafka. In this context, the tyrannical Brunelda is probably a representation of the bourgeoisie as a class, drawn in deliberately crude and exaggerated fashion, akin to the caricatures of Georg Grosz which, at this same period, represent 'capitalism' as an obese individual weighed down by his profits.[237] Kafka was familiar with Grosz's political caricatures since he spoke of them in his conversations with Janouch.[238]

In these last chapters of the novel, Kafka relates the interlocking exploitations and dominations to which the American proletariat fell victim. Karl's two old friends have also lost any notion of class solidarity. Delamarche, the Frenchman, is entirely dependent on Brunelda. He is wholly subject to her demands and obeys the slightest of her whims in order to take advantage of her wealth. Robinson becomes her servant and is treated atrociously at her hands while Karl Rossmann, as a Jew, will have to become the servant's servant. The Jewish student Josef Mendel does, however, advise him to hold on to this job, in accordance with the mechanism of voluntary servitude that runs through the entire book. Karl's very condition (as the exploited individual among the exploited), his constitutive 'backwardness' with respect to all social positions and his need to subordinate himself make him a total victim. He is the victim of the exploiters and also the paradoxical victim of all those who advise him to accept the condition into which he is sinking. Thus, alongside the highly critical description of his protagonist's behaviour, Kafka provides the reasons for it: particularly, the endless dialectic between his condemnation to a kind of eternal, uncomprehending subservience and his desire to integrate and assimilate into the Western society which convinces him that everything is possible while keeping him in a permanent position of dependency and humiliation. He is granted a place, admittedly, but a 'place without visibility'.

The final chapter of *Amerika*, entitled by Brod *Das Oklahoma-Natur-Theater* (The Nature Theatre of Oklahoma), can be read, it seems to me, as a sort of metaphor of the great assimilative lie of America. The theatrical metaphor—'it's the greatest theatre in the world'[239]—(which is also very much present at the beginning of *The Trial*) is, in itself, a first denunciation of the semblance and the pomp, the fakeries and the language of a society that presents itself as egalitarian but in reality perpetuates inequality. There is the stage-set and there is its darker side. There are the angels, the gold and the trumpets, but the trumpets 'weren't playing in tune, there was just wild playing' and the angels are 'women dressed as angels [. . .] and their hair, which they wore loose, looked too short and almost laughable, hanging between the big wings and down the side of them.' They are mounted on pedestals hidden by their 'long billowing robes'.[240] Most importantly, there is a placard announcing 'All welcome!' and Karl Rossmann repeats this to himself three times to give him heart to make the trip to Clayton. 'We are the theatre that has a place for everyone, everyone in his place!'[241]

Now, this theatre, which has set up its offices on a racecourse, with its recruitment stations 'in the little booths where they usually take bets'[242] as though this were a kind of obstacle race, this theatre, which is 'almost boundless',[243] turns out to be a figurative representation of the social world—that is to say, it is a very precise representation of the modes of reproduction of the hierarchies and inequalities characterizing American society. It is the whole deception of the American language of success for all, of the American talk of a 'New World', of the 'self-made man' and the possibility of working one's way up from scratch that Kafka is condemning here. The Far West that is America reproduces all the pathways by which European societies perpetuate social inequality. Karl gets to Clayton first, showing initiative in doing so: he is the first to enquire about recruitment procedures and yet very quickly he will end up 'the last'.[244] To begin with, he has no identity papers and then, although he 'wanted to be an engineer', he has no higher education and that is why, despite all the euphemistic language which enables him to be relegated step by step, without his realizing it, down the social ladder—'No cause for disquiet. We can use everyone'[245]—he very quickly reaches the bottom of the pile. He begins by claiming the title of engineer, but passes from the 'office for engineers' to the 'office for people with technical qualifications',[246] then to the 'office for former secondary schoolboys' and finally to 'the office for people who had attended secondary school in Europe'.[247] This last description, absurd as it may seem, turns out to carry a particular stigma in this world: 'the secretary was of the opinion that coming from a secondary school in Europe was something so lowly that anyone claiming to fall in that category could be taken at his word.'[248]

As he is taken from one booth to another, Karl notices people who had arrived after him and are 'already hired'. He, by contrast, finally ends up at 'a booth on the very periphery, not merely smaller than all the others, but lower too [. . .] This office seemed to be the end of the line anyway.'[249] Even there, there was some quibbling before he was engaged. Then, when asked his name, he hesitates. '[H]e was reluctant to give his real name and have that entered [. . .] he had kept it secret for too long to betray it now.'[250] This reticence in giving out his name and the desire to hide it from his employers —which is, indeed, the only 'cunning' shown by this eternal *naïf*— are among the strongest indications of Karl's Jewishness. He would have no reason to hide his name, were he not Jewish. Yet he knows that this name will cause him to be further snubbed. And that is why, confirming his inability to lie, he gives himself the name Negro, as though in that way he had found an American equivalent of the word Jew. We know that in his book Holitscher wrote of the racism of American society, of the Black ghettos of New York and the solidarity between Blacks and Jews.[251] Kafka knew, then, that the Blacks had very low status and were subjected to a high degree of segregation in American society. 'Negro' is a naive, blunt way of raising a suppressed issue, of naming inequality and racism in a world—like this great theatre—of fake harmony and consensus, in which job candidates are led to believe that integration, assimilation and equality of opportunity are a reality.

Equipped in this way with the two most ignominious titles in the eyes of the society he is preparing loyally to enter, Karl Rossmann becomes 'Negro, European secondary school pupil'. Admittedly, the placard at the Theatre of Oklahoma announced a job for everyone, not equality for all—'a place for everyone!' was the slogan, as if suggesting that all would be 'put in their places'—but the propaganda euphemized and attenuated that aspect. Now, the questioning to which he is subjected is a mix of conformity to the egalitarian-seeming discourse of the official propaganda and actual submission to the most implacable social order. Karl, who thinks he has just been employed as 'an actor' is led to accept a menial job but in such a way that this does not seem to have been imposed upon him. He is led gradually and skilfully to consent to this. The Leader of the Theatre's 10th Promotional Team asks Karl some precise questions: 'the way he stared as he asked them [. . .] seemed to give them a special significance, which one couldn't understand, but some sense of which made one awkward and self-conscious.'[252] Implying that Karl's tastes and aspirations were going to be taken into account, the leader asks him, 'What sort of job do you think would suit you?'[253] But gradually he is led towards the truth of what fate has in store for him: '"We probably can't make an engineer out of you right away," he said, "but maybe it would suit you for the time being to work on some fairly simple technical tasks".'[254] Relieved, Karl accepts: 'He was very happy.'[255] Further accentuating the menial nature of the work he is going to be offered, the gentleman adds, though the question is no more than a watered-down order: 'Are you strong enough for such demanding work?'[256] And in this way Karl, who has become through the euphemistic description of these ancillary tasks 'Negro, Technical Worker',[257] is also, in all senses of the word, the very last in this social world in which he was the first to present himself.

This last chapter of *Amerika* was written in October 1914 at the same moment as *The Trial* and 'In the Penal Colony' and it is difficult not to see in the remarks of the attendant, who subsequently takes Karl to where he is to eat, an equivalent of the minor characters in *The Trial* who, by their insinuations and echoing of rumours, maintain the insecurity of the accused man: '"Hurry up, it took a very long time before you were taken. I expect they had their doubts?" "I really don't know," said Karl astonished, but he didn't think so. Always, even in circumstances that were clear as crystal, someone could be found who liked to alarm his fellow-humans.'[258] Here again, we may note in passing, we have one of the rhetorical devices most often used by Kafka: the free indirect style which, by its exclusion of the first-person pronoun, in a sense objectifies the subjective viewpoint of the character. Karl, while he does not feel the sense of humiliation Josef K. experiences, does not understand why 'they' would 'have their doubts' and thinks that the situation is 'clear as crystal', whereas the reader knows very well that Karl is wrong and they have all kinds of reasons to 'have their doubts' about his identity. This is a way of entering into the logic of a character and conveying the coherence of his behaviour while distancing oneself from his viewpoint.

As they are being fed, the future employees want to drink a toast to the Leader of the 10th Promotional Team who, from his distant platform, pays no attention to their loud ovation—a clear sign of the existence of rigid hierarchies in this society. Then views of the Theatre of Oklahoma are passed around. Only one of them reaches Karl: 'The picture showed the box of the President of the United States.'[259] This confirms that the theatre is a metaphor for American society. For Kafka, the social order depends largely on stage-sets and theatrical stagings of power. Or rather, in keeping with the way collective belief attributes an 'offence' to K. in *The Trial*, the social order depends *both* on grandiloquent stagings *and* on the belief (maintained by propaganda) to which these give rise among the common people:

> At first sight, one might think it wasn't a box at all, but the stage, so far did the curved balustrades jut out into empty space. The balustrades were entirely made of gold. In between little pillars that might have been cut out by the minutest scissors, there was a row of portraits of former presidents [. . .] It was hardly possible to imagine people in this box, so sumptuously self-sufficient did it look.[260]

Similarly, in *The Trial* a painting depicts the institution of justice as something infallible, set above human frailties and contingencies.

It represents a judge 'sitting on a high throne-like chair'. But we learn that, in reality, this judge is 'quite tiny' and 'sits on a kitchen chair with an old folded-up horse-blanket on it'.[261] The picture, like the views that are handed around, is a kind of theatricalization intended to maintain belief in the theatre of justice, on the one hand, and of governmental politics, on the other.

Karl observes as he is getting on to the train that among the entire group with which he is associated—doubtless workers—'no one had any luggage.'[262] In other words, all are in a situation of forgetting, and having to forget, their pasts to assimilate into this new society which is claiming to welcome them wholeheartedly. 'Suspicious, unpropertied people had assembled here, and had been so well received and looked after!'[263] This new remark by Rossmann, the eternal *naif*, delivered in free indirect style, is a masterpiece of propaganda and/or an attestation of the credulity required if the system of domination is to function. In a last vision of Karl and his friend Giacomo plunging into the depths of a gigantic, threatening America, the story ends on an evocation of the train journey that will take them to Oklahoma. The description of the mountains, flanked by 'narrow dark cloven valleys' and cut through by 'broad mountain streams', the 'chill breath of them' making 'their faces shudder,'[264] is the opposite of the triumphal celebration of entrance upon a new life. Karl is 'disappearing' once and for all. At the end of this journey he will be assimilated, will have lost his name for good, will have become 'Negro, Technical Worker' and an American. With no baggage and no memory of his past, no tradition, no language and no identity, he will, in other words, have 'disappeared' as a Jew.

Among other things, this reading might explain the apparent contradiction between Kafka's avowed socialism and his protagonist's repeated indifference to the fate of the workers and to workers' organizations or protest—trade unions, strikes or demonstrations—which has so troubled the commentators, particularly the most political of them. Kafka is not in any sense identified with his hero, since his very project is opposed to the staging of any kind of subjectivity: he is writing a collective story in the service of a collective. He is writing the critical fable of assimilation.[265] This, too, it seems to me, is the sense of the title of this first novel: *Der Verschollene* (The Man Who Disappeared or The Missing Person). This word, a past participle—commonly used as an adjective—of a verb whose infinitive is not used, refers to someone who has got lost in obscure circumstances and whose existence 'hangs in doubt',[266] someone 'who has gone missing'.[267] As Scholem implies each time he mentions the question, in the little world of Jewish nationalists in those days the term 'assimilation' was strictly equivalent to 'disappearance'. In other words, the title of the novel Brod calls *Amerika* (thus giving rise to countless misunderstandings) refers unambiguously to an assimilated Jew, that is to say, a Jew who has disappeared or is disappearing *as a Jew*. The whole meaning of the novel is made explicit here, provided that we restore its actual meaning to the discussion taking place at the time between politicized Jews. *Der Verschollene*: the man who has disappeared because he is forgotten and has had himself forgotten as Jew.

In recounting the—historical, structural, ethnological and social—reasons behind the assimilation of the Jews in Western Europe, Kafka was also attempting to condemn this mechanism, presenting it as a kind of limit-case of exploitation that was all the more effective for being accepted and for not being recognized as acquiescence in an unjust order.

Having said this, *Der Verschollene* is, after 'The Judgment', one of the first texts penned by Kafka in the wake of his meeting with Löwy. In this first attempt at a novel, he is still at a political—almost propagandist—stage; this is a basic level, if we dare put it that way, that will not be seen again in his later work. His thinking around identity—first Jewish identity, then more broadly, that of dominated groups—will gradually become more elaborate and complex over the years. And we can also read his *oeuvre* as the story of a reflection, which develops through the practice of writing, on what it is possible for him to do, on the range of literary and narrative choices available to him within the limits he sets himself. But it is in this novel that we find the very matrix of the entire extravagant, unprecedented, paradoxical political and literary project of Franz Kafka, angry Jewish poet.

Chinese and Nomads

Another way Kafka is able to use ethnography is in the depiction of a remote people—a people so remote that it is virtually fictional. The designation 'China' and the 'Chinese' is, for example, a way for him to simulate distance in time and space and to do so in order to raise questions that were very much contemporary and close to home. This is what, in a letter to Brod of June 1921, he calls *ethnographischen Reiz*, the charm or appeal of ethnography.[268]

In the 1910s, there was great interest in China throughout the Germanic space. This was the case for many reasons. In the realm of literature and philosophy, Buber published two anthologies in 1910 which had an enormous impact: *Reden und Gleichnisse des Tschuang Tse* (Talks and Parables of Chuang Tzu), the first anthology of the Chinese philosopher's work in German, and *Chinesische Geister- und Liebesgeschichten* (Chinese Ghost and Love Stories), to which we have already referred, which was also the first collection of its kind in German.[269] There were two other successful publications of the same type: *Chinesische Lyrik vom 12. Jahrhundert bis zur Gegenwart* (Chinese Lyric Poetry from the Twelfth Century to the Present), translated and edited by Hans Heilmann in 1905, and *Die chinesische Flöte* (The Chinese Flute) by Hans Bethge in 1907.[270] These books triggered a great fascination with China among poets, writers and musicians. Kafka himself cited many 'Chinese' poems, books and thoughts in his letters and his diary. In his letter of 24 November 1912, he sent Felice a Chinese poem with his own comments. David points out that it is taken from Heilmann's anthology which Kafka greatly liked.[271]

In his narratives, China seems to be used in various ways. At times the Chinese seem to be one of the possible ways of representing the Jewish people (in 'The Great Wall of China' or 'The Problem of Our Laws'); at others, China, as a powerful empire led by a distant, mysterious emperor, might be a transposition of the Austrian empire. This possible parallel between China and Austria was first drawn by Politzer.[272] Binder has shown that Kafka took many of the features attributed to China from his thorough reading of Heilmann's anthology[273] and also from Julius Dittmar's travel book *Im neuen China*.[274] And many characteristics of the Chinese empire as Heilmann described it (slow decline, hierarchical society, the assimilation of other peoples, etc.) made the parallel between the old Austro-Hungarian Empire and the declining Chinese empire described by Heilmann rather an obvious one for Kafka.

Writing from a New Historicist perspective, Rolf Goebel has provided a magnificent reading of Kafka's short story 'An Old Manuscript', written in March 1917 and included in the collection *Ein Landarzt*. His interpretation of this very short, highly enigmatic text lends it entirely unexpected political and cultural resonances.[275] This 'Chinese' text, which presents itself as a story found on an old sheet (*Blatt*)—that is an old manuscript—reports an invasion of 'nomads' into the capital (never named, though the 'imperial palace' is built there) of the Chinese empire. The facts are reported and commented upon by a tradesman, a cobbler, who has a 'workshop [. . .] in the square that lies before the Emperor's palace'.[276] Extending Edward Said's definition of the term 'orientalism' to the Far East, Goebel reads this narrative as a critique of the corrupt, declining Austro-Hungarian Empire. According to Goebel, therefore, in this story Kafka is stressing the radical gulf which is forming between, on the one hand, the values of the business world, the ancestral social order, commercial ambitions and the narrow world view of the Chinese tradespeople—whose single viewpoint he gives us—and, on the other, the nomads depicted as brutal, bloodthirsty, barbarous, bestial, etc. Goebel concludes that the text is a meditation on the difficulties of intercultural understanding and the impossibility of assimilating the otherness of foreign domination. And he adds that we have to see in it a precise comparison between the Austro-Hungarian and the Chinese empires, and a critique of European colonialist policy in China.

I admire the method and the deductions proposed by Goebel in his reading of this text which, at first glance, seems to rank, despite its brevity, among the most indecipherable of Kafka's writings and I concur with his interpretation which links it to a political argument.

I agree also with his conviction that the narrator's viewpoint does not deliver the truth about the nomads. However, I cannot follow him in his conclusions. Even when guided by his deductions with regard to the possible meaning of the text, I prefer to interpret 'An Old Manuscript' as a variation on a theme omnipresent in Kafka: the enquiry into the way stigmatization operates, the rejection of one people which is declared the enemy of another, the *diktat* of foreignness that implies denial, exclusion, racism, etc. As in many of his stories, Kafka is looking for ways to show that suspicion (which falls on the Jews but also on other peoples in the world) obeys general anthropological laws. Though claiming—simply with the words of the title, on which he does not comment further—that he is reporting a very ancient narrative regarding a far distant country, Kafka is in reality painting the damning portrait of a people of sedentary, timorous, fearful artisans and shopkeepers, a people that might be said to resemble the Germans as he sees them. Again he employs a favoured technique, which Goebel terms the 'mono-perspectival' viewpoint and which I propose to call that of the unreliable narrator, with a narrator who regards these nomads as potential enemies, even though they seemingly harbour no warlike intentions towards the inhabitants of the country. And he does so simply because they differ from him in their language, habits and food. He goes into detail, in fact, regarding the dirtiness of the nomads, their allegedly warlike behaviour, the terrifying grimaces they make when they speak and their repulsive way of eating raw meat. He particularly stresses both their indifference and the impossibility of communicating with them:

> Speech with the nomads is impossible. They do not know our language, indeed they hardly have a language of their own. They communicate with each other much as jackdaws do. A screeching as of jackdaws is always in our ears. Our way of living and our institutions they neither understand nor care to understand. And so they are unwilling to make sense even out of our sign language. You can gesture at them till you dislocate your jaws and your wrists and still

they will not have understood you and will never understand. They often make grimaces; then the whites of their eyes turn up and foam gathers on their lips, but they do not mean anything by that, not even a threat; they do it because it is their nature to do it.[277]

The Chinese tradesman is not a reliable narrator for the simple reason that his description of reality is skewed by his prejudice. This (clearly racist) description, denying the foreigners any possibility of access to language, consigning them to pure animality (to radical strangeness), reducing their language to incomprehensible, grimacing facial contortions and condemning their intrinsic incapability of communicating with others, is the heart of the story—evoking the theme of the designation and explusion of a social group marked out as foreign.

Kafka's potent irony is evident, it seems to me, in the description of the nomads' horses: the cobbler-narrator claims, highly improbably, that these horses also eat meat. This assertion, clearly open to question, casts doubt on all that follows which seems to belong largely to the realm of (racist) fantasy: 'often enough a horseman and his horse are lying side by side, both of them gnawing at the same joint, one at either end.'[278] Then the cobbler claims to have seen the nomads ripping to pieces a live ox, 'tearing morsels out of its living flesh with their teeth'.[279] In short, all these signs underscore the fact that what the cobbler says is to be understood as a tissue of lies and exaggerations, intended as condemnation of the nomads and to present them as bloodthirsty barbarians. The final paragraph is a critique by this small trader of the emperor's policy. It confirms the identity of the 'we' of the narration: 'It is left to us artisans and tradesmen to save our country.'[280] At the same time, the presence of this emperor who says nothing and merely allows things to happen is a relatively exact figuring of the Austrian government, which knows what is happening on its territory but never intervenes to protect the Jews, ostracized as they are by the anti-Semitic petty bourgeoisie that claims to be under threat: 'How long can we endure this burden and torment? The Emperor's palace has drawn the nomads here but does not know how to drive them away again.'[281] Kafka is, at the same time, satirizing the narrow, limited spirit of the small traders of Prague or Vienna, incapable as they are of imagining that other habits of life and other languages are possible and who, out of both cowardice and stupidity, transform the Jews into bloodthirsty foreigners. From this standpoint, 'An Old Manuscript' can be seen as a new interrogation of the bloodthirsty character of the anti-Semitic imaginary, an interpretation of the primary conditions, a sort of primal scene which might explain the fact that the Jews (poorly tolerated, like all nomadic peoples, by powerful sedentary ones) are regularly accused (as in the recent Hilsner Affair) of 'ritual crimes'.

A letter to Milena of June 1920 comes at the same kind of questions in similar terms, though in an ethnographic form which actually appeared so unseemly to Brod that it was partially cut from the 1952 edition of the letters, as though Kafka were saying shocking things in it. In reality he was simply writing in objectivistic, historical —and almost scientific—terms on a major anthropological question, and he was doing so without troubling to take rhetorical precautions with Milena who had doubtless questioned him on the subject. In the passage in question, he made reference to the Hilsner Affair and asked how it was possible to attribute such acts to the Jews and how Czechs could possibly believe in them. He replied first, therefore, from the supposed standpoint of the Czechs, from the perspective of anti-Semitic belief which he lent to his narrator in many of his stories:

> First of all, what most terrifies me about the story is the conviction that the Jews are necessarily bound to fall upon you Christians, just as predatory animals are bound to murder, although the Jews will be horrified since they are not animals, but rather all too aware [. . .] I don't understand how whole nations of people could ever have thought of ritual murder before these recent events [i.e. the Hilsner affair] (at most they may have felt general fear and jealousy, but here there is no question, we see 'Hilsner' committing the

crime step by step; what difference does it make that the virgin embraces him at the same time?).[282]

It seems to me that we see here, with the conversational naturalness typical of a letter to a close friend, the—very specific, very characteristic—way Kafka raised the most urgent questions in respect of both politics and identity. He did not cry scandal or engage in lamentation or condemnation. He asked himself what those who believed in ritual murders were thinking; he asked himself how—by what logic or form of thought—it was possible to attribute such horrendous behaviour to the Jews, behaviour that was so irrational and hence so difficult to believe, as the committing of ritual murder. And what seemed most terrible to him was the conviction that they were 'bound to fall upon you'.[283]

Cruel, Kabyle Tales

Kafka could also inject directly ethnographic readings and knowledge into his stories. Janouch reports, for example, that Kafka advised him to read an anthology of African legends produced by Leo Frobenius.[284] Apart from the fact that, given the precision of the reference, the appearance of this proper name cannot easily be something invented or distorted by Janouch, the mention of the man who was at the time one of the most famous ethnologists and who was seen as a liberator of African humanity, opens up some interesting perspectives on certain of Kafka's tales.

As a theorist of a unitary conception of African civilization now viewed as entirely outmoded, a representative of a *Völkerkunde* whose very assumptions are widely disputed, and a man accused of adopting certain racist positions in the 1930s, Frobenius (1873–1938) suffers from a (probably justified) negative posthumous reputation, which in part prevents us from understanding the role he played for the German-speaking intellectuals of the early twentieth century.[285] He was initially regarded as one of the great European discoverers of Africa and also as an author highly critical of Eurocentric prejudices. For the early-twentieth-century reader he made it possible for those peoples who had hitherto been regarded as lacking a history to be perceived for the first time—like others—as having a culture and hence a place in world history.[286] And because he demonstrated and asserted the existence of African civilizations before anyone else had done so, he was also regarded as the creator of African anthropology and, very soon, as an emancipator of the Africans. *Der Ursprung der afrikanischen Kulturen* (The Origin of African Cultures) was published as early as 1898. One of the books that made him famous in 1912–13, *Und Afrika sprach* (*The Voice of Africa*), was the account of the third expedition of the *Deutsche innerafrikanische Forschungsexpedition,* in which he told of his discovery of the civilization and culture of the Yoruba of Benin.[287] The book *Schicksalskunde im Sinne des Kulturwerdens,* published in 1932, would play an important role for African intellectuals, since the founders of the Negritude movement—Léopold Sédar Senghor, Aimé Césaire and Léon-Gontran Damas—regarded Frobenius at the time as a forerunner of their campaigns and an anthropologist who had restored humanity and dignity to Black people.[288]

The conversations between Janouch and Kafka took place between March 1920 and July 1922. Now, between 1921 and 1923, the first three volumes of Frobenius' gigantic *Atlantis: Volksmärchen und Volksdichtungen Afrikas* were published, a vast collection of African tales bringing together in 12 volumes, published between 1921 and 1928, all the folk tales he had gathered throughout Africa.[289] The *Volksmärchen der Kabyln* (Folk Tales of the Kabyles) make up the bulk of these first three volumes and Frobenius wrote a long introduction to the first volume, divided into 11 sections which each presented an aspect of Kabyle culture and civilization for the Western reader—cave paintings, funerary architecture, social structures, etc. The first section of this introduction is called 'Berber und Araber', the second 'Das Hinschmelzen der Berber in den Oasenländer'. In it, he wrote of the relations between Arabs and Berbers and tacitly justified his decision to give precedence to the Kabyles over the more numerous Arabs whose civilization was known to the whole world. The Berbers, explains Frobenius, are distinct from the Arabs not only in their language but also in the strength of their rootedness and attachment to their birthplace. They also differ in their relation to their religion. But if they are so different, this is chiefly because they are dominated by the Arabs.

> 'The Arab eats the Berber' [*Der Araber ißt den Berber*], says a North African proverb [. . .] This is true. In one oasis after another, one area after another, Tamazight and Schelha (Berber languages) are losing ground. The Arabic language is victorious almost everywhere [. . .]. The Arabs have become the masters of the Berbers [*wurden die Araber die Herren der Berber*].²⁹⁰

And, as if further to support his argument, he repeats the proverb a little later, this time putting it in the past tense: 'the Arab "ate" the Berber [*der Araber hat den Berber 'gegessen'*].' 'Berber culture', Frobenius concludes logically, 'is dissolving rapidly [*Das Berbertum schmilzt schnell dahin*].'²⁹¹

At this current point in my research I have not succeeded in proving categorically that Kafka could have had knowledge of an earlier version of these texts at the time of writing his short story 'Jackals and Arabs' in 1916–17. Yet certain facts are, nonetheless, very disconcerting. We can see how much Kafka could have taken from such reading. Through this objectivized description of the domination of a distant, exotic people over another, which results in the absorption of the Berbers into the Arab entity—the imposition of a dominant language leading to the disappearance of the subordinate people's idiom and the 'devouring' of the one group by the other—he might have been universalizing the particular case of the Jews. In other words, he might have been explaining how their assimilation was part of a more general process which could take other forms in other parts of the world while retaining its specific features in this case. Frobenius speaks of a mechanism of 'dissolution' (the verb *schmelzen* literally means 'melt' in the transitive or intransitive sense), a concrete term akin to the one employed by Scholem to describe the assimilation of the Jews and their absorption into the German people. The ethnological approach gave Kafka a sort of guarantee of objectivity regarding the situation of Western

Jews, a kind of distance as a result of the implicit comparison involved. It provided him with the means for analysing, interpreting and condemning the tragedy of the Jews, through roundabout, 'para-scientific' channels, as a way of seeking to combat it.

Ethnological and political comparatism thus seems to be at the heart of Kafka's approach. And it seems that we can take the narrator of 'The Great Wall of China' seriously (despite his mendacious iden-tity) when he asserts that, 'During the building of the wall and ever since to this very day I have occupied myself almost exclusively with the comparative history of races—there are certain questions that one can probe to the marrow, as it were, only by this method.'[292] For him, in other words, the equivalence of historical, critical, political and ethnological situations is not in doubt; and to equip oneself to understand and, most importantly, explain their history to readers who might have forgotten it, it was necessary to call on different contexts, cultural traditions and narrational exoticisms.

Moreover, Frobenius' 'scientific' approach gave him licence, as it were, to take that path, since his method consisted, among other things, in comparing term for term the cultural practices and beliefs of various social groups far removed from one another geographically.[293]

If we accept that Kafka might have read Frobenius' *Kabyle Tales* in a version earlier than that of 1921, then we offer ourselves a way of understanding that, concretely, at the point of writing his short story, he may have been drawing on Frobenius' title (*Berber und Araber*) and replacing the Berbers—the most recognizable element in Frobenius' text which he might wish to conceal—by jackals, thus giving *Schakale und Araber*. Apart from the fact that Frobenius argued that is 'the most primitive form' of the folk tale, the animal fable, also stands opposed in its 'simplicity' and 'naturalness' to the sophis-tication of the Oriental tales we encounter most notably in *The Thou-sand and One Nights*.[294] This is why he stresses that 'we may assert that the Kabyle fable is more akin to European and Germanic fables than to those of central Africa and Asia.'[295] Moreover, Frobenius does not conceal his admiration for the beauty of that form: 'The form of the oral poetry of the Kabyles is, therefore at times delicate and graceful [. . .] at times sinister and cruel [. . .], but it is always unpretentious and perfectly natural.'[296]

Kafka, who was on the lookout for this type of story in the years 1916–17, adopted the animal fable in its most primitive version, divested as much as possible of 'refined plots' and 'infinite embellishments', with no 'magic walls', 'secret exits' or any of the 'pomp of the marvellous palaces of Haroon al-Rashid'.[297] Above all, he adopted the central character of the Berber tales transcribed by Frobenius in the third volume he devoted to them (entitled *Das Fabelhafte*, the fabulous), namely, the jackal, whom Frobenius describes as the 'main hero' of the Kabyle fables, a fact confirmed by all contemporary specialists in Berber folk tales.[298] A reading of the stories collected by Frobenius reveals immediately that the jackal is a figure at once cunning and cruel. He terrorizes the skylark and devours its young, lies to the wild sow and swallows up each of its seven young boars, breaks all his promises, betrays his friends and rejoices in the misfortune of others.[299]

'Jackals and Arabs' is a short tale, written in the first person, in which the traveller-narrator reports that a 'spokesman' for the jackals has addressed him in the hope of having him carry out the murder of the Arabs. The scene is related from the standpoint of this traveller who is described as a Westerner ('We know [. . .] that you have come from the North,' one of the jackals tells the traveller).[300] Seen by this latter, the pack of jackals is described as consisting of repulsive animals ('jackals [. . .] swarming around me';[301] 'a rank smell which at times I had to set my teeth to endure streamed from their open jaws.').[302] In the detailed description which these animals give of the Arabs, Gilman has quite convincingly found a catalogue of the most widespread anti-Semitic commonplaces: 'Why, the mere sight of their living flesh makes us turn tail and flee into cleaner air [. . .] their beards are a horror; the very sight of their eye sockets makes one want to spit; and when they lift an arm, the murk of hell yawns in the armpit.'[303] It is also, in his view, a parodic text, a way of presenting ironically the Christian, anti-Semitic vision of the ritual murder attributed to the Jews or *shechitah*,[304] though this does not mean that the tale itself is anti-Semitic!

The jackals cannot bear the fact that the Arabs kill animals before going on to bleed and eat them. They are of the opinion that their own way of proceeding is hygienic and conforms to their ritual laws; for them it is necessary for 'every beast to die a natural death' and, most importantly, for there to be 'no interference till we [the jackals] have drained the carcass empty and picked its bones clean. Cleanliness, nothing but cleanliness is what we want.'[305] The Arabs cut the sheep's throat before eating them, which is contrary to the jackals' conception of 'cleanliness'. In other words, Kafka is depicting two social groups that are at odds over a ritual law. And, most importantly, he describes the jackal group as driven by obedience to an invisible but omnipotent power: 'lithe bodies moving nimbly and rhythmically, as if at the crack of a whip'.[306] The invisible whip that is driving the jackals is the exact metaphor for the law they are obeying, the law which explains their behaviour. But the jackals are detestable and mendacious only in the eyes of the Western traveller who spontaneously adopts the perspective of the dominant group in this region—which is to say, as Frobenius explained, the Arabs. This is why, when seen in the light of the preoccupations of Frobenius' ethnology, it seems possible to understand this text as a story that does not really concern either the Jews in their relations with the Germans or the opposition between Western and Eastern Jews, as Bruce suggests,[307] or indeed any identifiable nation whatsoever. 'Jackals and Arabs' can be said to describe, more broadly, the constitution of the spontaneous representations of all dominated, marginal peoples whose codes of behaviour are not spontaneously in accord with the dominant ones. Seen from this angle, Kafka is not producing an enchanted version of the life of dominated peoples but trying, rather, to provide an 'ethnological' vision that can explain not, as is too often believed, the behaviour of the jackals, but the spontaneously racist vision of the traveller. Whereas the jackals kill no one and eat only carrion, the dominant people construct a representation of the carrion-eater as hate-filled killer. This might explain the presence of the parodic, anti-Semitic clichés that function as so many signs of an ancestral hatred between these antagonistic social groups. As he often does, Kafka is seeking to construct a text that will produce immediate effects in his readers: in this way 'Jackals and Arabs' gives rise to an instantaneous sense of disgust and unease. Humour is clearly present in this absurd portrait of the blood-crazed 'underdog'[308] and in the disingenuousness of the Western traveller.

However, I am not absolutely certain of this reading and it seems to me another interpretation of 'Jackals and Arabs' is conceivable. I present here the two readings which seem possible: the narrative is so ambiguous that I cannot make my mind up between them and I leave it to the reader to decide.

'Jackals and Arabs' can also be understood, in effect, as a story that gives voice—the better to condemn it—to the viewpoint of the anti-Semite (this hypothesis has already been advanced by a number of commentators, most notably Politzer, though he postulates at the same time that Kafka is portraying what he interprets as the writer's hatred of his own Jewishness).[309] In this version, anti-Semitism is proposed as a kind of 'law' or belief governing the collective behaviour of a group called 'the jackals' (following this hypothesis, the 'Arabs' would stand for the Jews). That law is accompanied by the assertion of its arbitrariness which is both its chief mark of ignominy and its ordinary mode of justification. As he often does, Kafka hands the narration to a traveller who is reporting someone else's remarks—in this case the remarks of the anti-Semite—and allows him to develop the violence and implacability of the anti-Semitic hate-speech. By dint of its character as a law, this latter is conceived as an absolute (categorical) imperative and the jackals can do no other than obey it throughout all eternity. The jackal group is described as made up of repugnant, subservient, lying animals and they provide a kind of 'entertainment', as the Arab leader laughingly comments in the last part of the story.[310] They claim, in fact, that they have been waiting for this traveller since the dawn of time, whereas, as he insists, he is actually there entirely by chance: '[T]hat is very surprising for me to hear. It is by pure chance that I have come here from the far North, and I am making only a short tour of your country.'[311] They are also cowardly—expecting the foreigner to carry out the murder of their enemies in their stead—spineless and greedy, cringing before the lash of the Arab, while stating that '[N]ever in the history of the world has any jackal been afraid of an Arab'[312] and hurling themselves on the carcass of a camel that is thrown to them. In short, the jackals are objects of disgust.

But Kafka's laughter rings out in this portrait of the anti-Semite as blood-crazed carrion-eater, languishing under an absurd law as though under the lash of a whip. He leaves the last word to the object of the jackals' hatred, the fatalistic, laughing Arab, who knows how disgracefully the jackals can act but at the same time as he wields the whip treats them with a sort of realistic indulgence ('they are our dogs; finer dogs than any of yours'[313]): 'Marvellous creatures, aren't they? And how they hate us!'[314] Kafka is, in this story, reversing the relation of domination, since here it is the hated creature who actually holds the whip hand and keeps the jackals under.

NOTES

1   Anderson, 'Chapter 5: Sliding down the Evolutionary Ladder? Aesthetic autonomy in *The Metamorphosis*' in *Kafka's Clothes*, pp. 123–44. Similarly, 'In the Penal Colony' is, for him, an ironic text, a reflexive commentary on Kafka's relations to contemporary aesthetic questions, and the island is a metaphor for artistic autonomy (see Anderson, 'Chapter 7: The Ornaments of Writing: "In the Penal Colony"', pp. 173–93; here, pp. 184–5).

2   Anderson, 'Chapter 4: Kafka in America: Notes on a Travelling Narrative', pp. 98–122; here, p. 99. For his part, Robertson relates Kafka's project to the Expressionist movement—in *Amerika* at any rate. See Robertson, *Kafka: Judaism, Politics and Literature*, pp. 55–7.

3   Kundera, *Testaments Betrayed*, p. 44.

4   Ibid., p. 42.

5   Cf. Pascale Casanova, 'Le méridien de Greenwich: réflexions sur le temps de la littérature' in Lionel Ruffel (ed.), *Qu'est-ce que le contemporain?* (Nantes: Cécile Defaut, 2010), pp. 113–45.

6 Cf. Michael Pollak, 'Une sociologie en acte des intellectuels: Les combats de Karl Kraus', *Actes de la recherche en sciences sociales* 36–37 (February–March 1981): 87–103; here, pp. 87–8.

7 Ibid., p. 88.

8 David, 'Notes' in David, *Franz Kafka: Oeuvres complètes*, VOL. 3, p. 1327.

9 Franz Kafka, 'Josephine the Singer, or the Mouse Folk' (Willa and Edwin Muir trans) in *The Complete Stories*, pp. 360–76 [originally published in 1924 as 'Josefine, die Sängerin oder Das Volk der Mäuse' in *Prager Presse*].

10 André Nemeth, *Kafka ou le mystère juif* (V. Hintz trans.) (Paris: Jean Vigneau, 1947), p. 162.

11 Anderson, 'Chapter 7: The Ornaments of Writing: "In the Penal Colony"' in *Kafka's Clothes*, pp. 180–1.

12 Pawel, *The Nightmare of Reason*, p. 238.

13 See Gray, *Constructive Destruction*.

14 On Kraus' influence on Prague intellectual life, see Hartmut Binder, 'Unvergebene Schlamperei: ein unbekannter Brief Franz Kafkas', *Jahrbuch der deutschen Schillergesellschaft* 25 (1981): 133–8; here, pp. 135–6.

15 Timms estimates that he gave more than 70 public readings in the city between 1920 and 1936 (*Karl Kraus*, p. 51).

16 [Karl Kraus, *The Last Days of Mankind: A Tragedy in Five Acts* (Frederick Ungar ed., and Alexander Gode and Sue E. Wright trans) (New York: Continuum, 2000); originally published in 1918–19 as *Die letzten Tage der Menschheit* in special issues of *Die Fackel*.]

17 Brod, *Streitbares Leben*, p. 27.

18 Though born in Bohemia, Kraus had lived at Vienna since the age of three and thus had only a rudimentary knowledge of Czech (cf. Timms, *Karl Kraus*, p. 51).

19 Ibid.

20 In Austria Masaryk and his allies were regarded as traitors (ibid., pp. 52–6).

21 Allan Janik and Stephen Toulmin, *Wittgenstein's Vienna* (New York: Simon and Schuster, 1973). On this subject, see also Jacques Bouveresse, 'Les derniers jours de l'humanité', *Critique* 339–40 (August–September 1975): 753–805.

22 See Janik and Toulmin, 'Chapter 4: Culture and Critique' in *Wittgenstein's Vienna*, pp. 92–119.

23 See, for example, Timms, *Karl Kraus*, p. 119.

24 See Hubert Damisch, 'L'autre Ich ou le désir du vide: pour un tombeau d'Adolf Loos', *Critique* 339–40 (August–September 1975): 806–18; here, p. 814. Also drawing a parallel between the stances of Kraus and Loos, Anderson writes, 'In all probability Kafka saw himself as Loos's ideological companion in the struggle against the ornate forms of fin-de-siècle culture' ('Chapter 7: The Ornaments of Writing: "In the Penal Colony"' in *Kafka's Clothes*, p. 181).

25 The latter talk is translated into English in Ludwig Munz and Gustav Kunstler, *Adolf Loos: Pioneer of Modern Architecture* (New York: Praeger, 1966).

26 Franz Kafka, 'Letter to Robert Klopstock' in *Letters to Friends, Family and Editors*, p. 394. [By contrast with David's French edition of Kafka's correspondence, this English edition ascribes the letter to 'early November'. Trans.]

27 David, 'Notes' in David, *Franz Kafka: Oeuvres complètes*, VOL. 3, p. 1628.

28 Cf. Timms, *Karl Kraus*, p. 363. [Both *Untergang der Welt durch schwarze Magie* and *Wolkenkuckucksheim* were published in *Die Fackel*, Vienna and Leipzig.]

29 Franz Kafka, 'Letter to Robert Klopstock, 30 June 1922' in *Letters to Friends, Family and Editors*, p. 330.

30 Cf. Jean-Louis Besson and Henri Christophe cited in Karl Kraus, *Les Derniers jours de l'humanité* (Marseille: Agone, 2007), p. 783.

31 Kafka, '4 July 1920' in *Letters to Milena*.

32 [Arthur Schnitzler, *Anatol* (Frank Marcus trans.) (London: Methuen, 1982); Schnitzler, *La Ronde* (Frank Marcus and Jacquelline Marcus trans) (London: Methuen, 1982); Schnitzler's *Lieutenant Gustl* was originally translated by Richard L. Simon as *None But the Brave* (New York: Simon and Schuster, 1926.]

33 A play by Schnitzler produced in 1912. [Available in English in Arthur Schnitzler, *Professor Bernhardi: And Other Plays* (G. J. Weinberger trans.) (Riverside, CA: Ariadne Press, 1993), pp. 3–146.]

34 Franz Kafka, *Briefe an Felice: und andere Korrespondenz aus der Verlobungszeit* (Erich Heller and Jürgen Born eds) (Frankfurt:

Fischer Taschenbuch, 2009), p. 299. *Widerlich* may also be translated as 'repulsive' or 'repugnant'.

35 Kafka, '14–15 February 1913' in *Letters to Felice*, pp. 305–06.

36 To this consciously penned letter, we may add, by way of confirmation of his anti-Jung-Wien position, an amusing account of a dream, which can be quite easily deciphered once one has the key to his rejection of Schnitzler, at least at a literal level. I am referring to a dream reported in November 1911 in his *Diary*: 'Dream: In the theatre. Performance of *Das weite Land* by Schnitzler, adapted by Utitz. I sit right up at the front, think I am sitting in the first row until it finally appears that it is the second. The back of the row is turned towards the stage so that one can see the auditorium comfortably, the stage only by turning. The author is somewhere near by, I can't hold back my poor opinion of the play which I seem to know from before, but add that the third act is supposed to be witty.' Yitzchak Löwy appears a little further on in the account of the same dream as a kind of anti-Schnitzler: '[N]ear me, remarkably free, the actor Löwy . . . is standing' ('Sunday, 19 November 1911' in *Diaries*, pp. 119–20).

37 *Widerwille* may also be translated as 'distaste' or 'aversion'. Kafka, *Briefe an Felice*, p. 296.

38 Kafka, '12–13 February 1913' in *Letters to Felice*, p. 302.

39 Leopold B. Kreitner, 'Der junge Kafka' in Koch, 'Als Kafka mir entgegenkam.', pp. 52–8; here, pp. 52–3.

40 Cf. Runfola, *Prague au temps de Kafka*, especially, pp. 83–102.

41 Brod, *Franz Kafka*, p. 48.

42 Ibid., p. 44.

43 Kafka, diary entry for September–October 1913. Quoted in David, *Franz Kafka: Oeuvres complètes*, VOL. 3, pp. 309–10. [This passage does not appear in the English translation of the *Diaries*, presumably because Brod notes that he omitted 'scathing criticism of various people that Kafka certainly never intended for the public' ('Postscript' in *Diaries*, p. 489). Trans.] Kafka adds, 'Overall a very fine man. There has always been in his character a little disagreeable flaw and when you observe him uninterruptedly it is precisely from that flaw that the whole of him comes creeping out'. On Otto Pick, see Binder, *Kafka-Handbuch*, VOL. I, pp. 438–40.

44 Kafka, *Letters to Milena*, p. 175.

45 Kafka, *Letters to Friends, Family and Editors*, pp. 286–9.

46 Ibid., p. 288. He is referring, of course, not to Yiddish literature but to Jewish literature in the German language.

47 Ibid. Additional German text from Franz Kafka, *Briefe: 1902–1924* (Max Brod ed.) (Frankfurt: Fischer, 1966), p. 336.

48 On that polemic, see Michel Reffet, 'Pro Werfel contra Kraus. Eine alte Polemik aus neuer Sicht' in Kurt Krolop and Klaas-Hinrich Ehlers (eds), *Brücken nach Prag: deutschsprachige Literatur im kulturellen Kontext der Donaumonarchie und der Tschechoslowakei; Festschrift für Kurt Krolop zum 70. Geburtstag* (Frankfurt: Peter Lang, 2001), pp. 201–19. See also Caroline Kohn, *Karl Kraus: Le polémiste et l'écrivain, défenseur des droits de l'individu* (Paris: Didier, 1962), pp. 182–6.

49 Brod, *Streitbares Leben*, pp. 12–80.

50 Franz Werfel was born in 1890.

51 Cf. Timms, *Karl Kraus*, pp. 234–6.

52 Kohn, *Karl Kraus: Le polémiste et l'écrivain*, p. 182. [Franz Werfel, 'Die Metaphysik des Drehs: Ein offener Brief an Karl Kraus', *Die Aktion* 7(9–10) (1917): 124–8; *Spiegelmensch: magische Trilogie* (Leipzig: Kurt Wolff, 1920).]

53 Kohn, *Karl Kraus: Le polémiste et l'écrivain*, pp. 185–6.

54 In his play, Kraus called the poets and writers who pursued novelty at all costs *Neutöner*—new musicians—as a way of making them seem ridiculous.

55 Kohn, *Karl Kraus: Le polémiste et l'écrivain*, p. 186.

56 Ibid. note 144.

57 Scholem, *Walter Benjamin*, p. 82.

58 In *Spiegelmensch* there is even a scene of parricide.

59 Cf. Timms, *Karl Kraus*, p. 362.

60 Brod, *Streitbares Leben*, pp. 68–9.

61 Ibid., pp. 61–80.

62 Ibid., pp. 68–9.

63 Kafka, *Letters to Friends, Family and Editors*, p. 288.

64 Ibid.

65 Ibid.

66 Ibid.

67 Gilman, 'Chapter 4: The Drive for Assimilaion' in *Jewish Self-Hatred*, 139–208; here, pp. 141–2. Gilman has shown that, from the end of the nineteenth century onwards, the 'scientific' discourse used to 'demonstrate' the 'otherness' of the Jews created, among both Germans and Jews, powerful persuasive effects (see especially, 'Chapter 5: The Science of Race').

68 Ibid., see also Gilman, *Franz Kafka: The Jewish Patient*, especially pp. 25–33; Anderson, 'Chapter 8: "Jewish" Music? Otto Weininger and *Josephine the Singer*' in *Kafka's Clothes*, pp. 194–216; here, pp. 197–210; Anita Shapira, 'Anti-Semitism and Zionism', *Modern Judaism* 15(3) (October 1995): 215–32.

69 Kafka, *Letters to Friends, Family and Editors*, p. 288.

70 Ibid.

71 Kafka, *Briefe: 1902–1924*, p. 338.

72 Kafka, *Letters to Friends, Family and Editors*, p. 289.

73 On this theme, see Gilman, 'Chapter 5: The Science of Race' in *Jewish Self-Hatred*, pp. 226–7.

74 Max Brod, 'Der jüdische Dichter deutscher Zunge' in *Vom Judentum: Ein Sammelbuch* (Leipzig: Kurt Wolff and Verein jüdischer Hochschüler Bar Kochba in Prague, 1913), pp. 261–3. According to Wagenbach, the volume was to be found in Kafka's library. On this collective project, see Kieval, *The Making of Czech Jewry*, pp. 148–53.

75 Cf. Bechtel, *La Renaissance culturelle juive*, p. 152 note 26.

76 Scholem, *From Berlin to Jerusalem*, p. 55.

77 Cf. Spector, *Prague Territories*, p. 81. See also Bechtel, *La Renaissance culturelle juive*, pp. 154–5.

78 Brod, 'Der jüdische Dichter deutscher Zunge', cited in Vassogne, *Max Brod et Prague*, pp. 346–7. On this article, see also Bechtel, *La Renaissance culturelle juive*, pp. 154–5.

79 *Die Neue Rundschau* 29 (1918), pp. 1580–3, cited in Vassogne, *Max Brod et Prague*, p. 347. This conception of language as national 'property' was not specific to the German Jews in these years. Many dominated peoples in search of recognition of their specificity and identity in far distant geographical climes and in other periods have also regarded language as property, a property defined as legitimate if

and only if it could be described as 'national'. In the neo-Herderian system of thought, the 'lawful owners' of a language were, therefore, those who inherited it from their ancestors, who also belonged to the same nation. See Casanova, *The World Republic of Letters*, especially pp. 232–5.

80 Gilman, 'Chapter 5: The Science of Race' in *Jewish Self-Hatred*, p. 285. On the paradoxes of Jewish emancipation, see also Bruce, *Kafka and Cultural Zionism*, pp. 148–50. We may note along these same lines that Kraus' position towards *mauscheln* is not as simple as it might seem. His biographer Timms has shown that Kraus enthused at a very early stage about theatre which used *mauscheln*, a popular entertainment he had discovered at Vienna in 1911. This type of theatre developed at the time mainly as a 'Jewish vaudeville'. In June 1911 (that is to say, by a sort of strange objective chance, some months before Yiddish theatre revealed itself to Kafka), Kraus had discovered in the Leopoldstadt area the performances of the Budapester Orpheumgesellschaft which offered comic sketches in *mauscheln*. Although Kraus and Kafka both used the term *Jargontheater*, they were not talking about the same thing at all: Löwy's company played the Yiddish theatre repertoire in Yiddish, whereas the company discovered by Kraus played in *mauscheln*. They were, however, both susceptible to this theatre which depicted all the contradictions confronting the Jews of the Empire, who were called on to assimilate, yet prevented from achieving assimilation. In parodic and comic mode, this theatre told the experience of first-generation German-speaking immigrant Jews who had retained the accents of the Yiddish spoken in the villages of Bohemia or Galicia. Timms has shown that Kraus' theatre writing and practice was transformed by his discovery of the Budapester. Its influence is clearly very pronounced in the magical operetta (Timms, *Karl Krau*, pp. 361–2).

81 Kafka, *Letters to Friends, Family and Editors*, p. 288.

82 Ibid.

83 Ibid., p. 289.

84 Ibid.

85 By attributing to individuals and to particular situations what Kafka regarded as the product of a disavowed collective history, psychoanalysis provided tools for moral ennoblement for young

writers obsessed with their relations with their fathers. This possibility opened up by psychoanalysis of conjuring away the real social conditions of problems and regarding them as capable of being posed and resolved in individual (and universal) terms—thus enabling the historical dimension of certain problems to be dissolved by reducing them to dehistoricized universal structures—has been analysed by Schorske. He has shown that psychoanalysis itself won out in Freud's life at a point when a desire arose within him to forget, deny or dissolve the role of political agency. Cf. Schorske, 'Politics and Patricide in Freud's *Interpretation of Dreams*' in *Fin-de-Siècle Vienna*, pp. 181–207.

86 Kafka, *Letters to Friends, Family and Editors*, p. 289.

87 Ibid.

88 Ibid.

89 Ibid.

90 Kafka, *Briefe: 1902–1924*, p. 336.

91 David, 'Notices et notes' in David, *Kafka: Oeuvres complètes*, VOL. 3, p. 1086 note 3 and p. 1591.

92 Kafka, *Letters to Friends, Family and Editors*, p. 289.

93 Arendt, 'Franz Kafka: Appreciated Anew' in Gottlieb, *Hannah Arendt: Reflections on Literature and Culture*, p. 95.

94 Hugo von Hoffmannsthal, *The Lord Chandos Letter* (Russell Stockman trans.) (Vermont: Marlboro Press, 1986) [originally published as 'Ein Brief' in *Der Tag*].

95 Cf. Friedrich Schmidt, 'Sprache, Medien, und Kritik. Kafkas Sprachskepsis im Kontext ihrer Zeit' in Marek Nekula, Ingrid Fleischmann, Albert Greule (eds), *Franz Kafka im Sprachnationalen Kontext seiner Zeit. Sprache und nationale Identität in öffentlichen Institutionen der böhmischen Länder* (Cologne, Weimar and Vienna: Böhlau, 2007), pp. 31–60.

96 On the change in the style of Kafka's writing after 1912, see Beck, 'Chapter 3: The Change in Kafka's Style' and 'Chapter 4: Style and Structure before 1912' in *Kafka and the Yiddish Theater*, pp. 31–69.

97 Kafka, *Diaries*, p. 88.

98 Wagenbach, *Franz Kafka, Biographie seiner Jugend*, p. 89.

99 His whole life long he would express boundless admiration for Goethe but he would abandon the idea of being 'faithful' to a German literary tradition.

100 Claude David, 'Préface' in Franz Kafka, *Un médecin de campagne et autres récits/Ein Landarzt und andere Erzählungen* (Paris: Gallimard, 'Folio bilingue', 1996), p. 7

101 In the letter to Felice in which he writes of Lasker-Schüler, for example, he uses the expression *künstlicher Aufwand*, which the translators render as 'contrived verbosity' (Kafka, '12–13 February 1913' in *Letters to Felice*, p. 302).

102 Arendt, 'Franz Kafka: Appreciated Anew' in Gottlieb, *Hannah Arendt: Reflections on Literature and Culture*, p. 94.

103 Robert, *As Lonely as Franz Kafka*, pp. 160–1.

104 On Kafka's 'Up in the Gallery' [(Willa and Edwin Muir trans) in *The Complete Stories*, pp. 401–02; originally written in 1916–17 as 'Auf der Galerie' and published in the volume *Ein Landarzt: Kleine Erzählungen* (Leipzig: Kurt Wolff, 1920)] and 'A Country Doctor' [(Willa and Edwin Muir trans) in *The Complete Stories*, pp. 220–5; originally written in as 'Ein Landarzt' and published in 1919 in the collection *Ein Landarzt*], see Chapter 4, pp. 349–50 and pp. 350–1 respectively.

105 I thank Jean-Pierre Morel for drawing my attention to the existence of these two distinct styles in Kafka's *oeuvre*.

106 André Jolles, *Einfache Formen: Legende, Sage, Mythe, Rätsel, Spruch, Kasus, Memorabile, Märchen, Witz* (Leipzig: Halle, 1930). In the simple forms, Jolles includes legends, sagas, myths, tales, riddles, etc.

107 And this is the case even though Malcolm Pasley has interpreted some of Kafka's fictions as reflexive narratives that can be seen as evoking the very conditions of their writing and the way in which Kafka might be seen, as a result, to be freshening up his literary devices. See Malcolm Pasley, *'Die Schrift ist unveränderlich' . . . Essays zu Kafka* (Frankfurt: Fischer, 1995).

108 Kafka, '13 December 1914' in *Diaries*, p. 321.

109 [Franz Kafka, 'Investigations of a Dog' (Willa and Edwin Muir trans) in *The Complete Stories*, pp. 278–316 (originally written in 1922 as 'Forschungen eines Hundes'); Kafka, 'The Great Wall of China' (Willa and Edwin Muir trans) in *The Complete Stories*, pp. 266–77 (originally written in 1917 as 'Beim Bau der Chinesischen Mauer');

Kafka, 'The Village Schoolmaster' (Willa and Edwin Muir trans) in *The Complete Stories*, pp. 168–82 (originally written in 1914–15 as 'Der Dorfschullehrer'). All three stories were published in the collection *Beim Bau der Chinesischen Mauer* (Berlin: Kiepenheuer, 1931).]

110 David, 'Notice de La Colonie pénitentiaire' in David, *Franz Kafka: Oeuvres complètes*, VOL. 2, p. 957.

111 Robertson, who also denies that Kafka was at all close to any kind of socialism by equating his stance with Buber's positions (*Kafka, Judaism, Politics and Literature*, pp. 140–53), also suggests that Kafka subscribes fully and unreservedly to the iniquitous, barbaric, racist arguments of the former Commandant of the colony. Ibid., pp. 152–5.

112 Arendt, 'Franz Kafka: Appreciated Anew' in Gottlieb, *Hannah Arendt: Reflections on Literature and Culture*, p. 105.

113 Ibid., pp. 102–04.

114 Ibid., p. 109.

115 Franz Kafka, 'An Old Manuscript' (Willa and Edwin Muir trans) in *The Complete Stories*, pp. 415–17 (originally written in as 'Ein altes Blatt' and first published in 1917 in *Marsyas*).

116 See Kafka, '20–21 January 1913' in *Letters to Felice*.

117 [Franz Kafka, 'Memoirs of the Kalda Railroad' in *Diaries*, pp. 303–23 (originally written in 1914 as 'Erinnerungen an die Kaldabahn' and published in 1951 as part of Max Brod (ed.), *Tagebücher 1910–1923* (Frankfurt: Fischer, 1951); Kafka, 'A Little Woman' (Willa and Edwin Muir trans) in *The Complete Stories*, pp. 319–24 (originally written in 1923 as 'Eine Kleine Frau' and published in 1924 in the collection *Ein Hungerkünstler* [Berlin: Die Schmiede, 1924]); Kafka, 'The Burrow' (Willa and Edwin Muir trans) in *The Complete Stories*, pp. 325–59 (originally written in 1923–24 as 'Der Bau' and published in the collection *Beim Bau der chinesischen Mauer*); Kafka, 'A Report to an Academy' (Willa and Edwin Muir trans) in *The Complete Stories*, pp. 250–9 (originally written in 1917 as 'Ein Bericht für eine Akademie' and published in 1919 in the collection *Ein Landarzt: Kleine Erzählungen*).]

118 Jacques Le Rider, *Journaux intimes viennois* (Paris: PUF, 2000), p. 47. [Note: Le Rider's term is *succédané* which may in this case be translated as 'substitute' or, perhaps, 'pale imitation'. Trans.]

119 Kafka, *Diaries*, p. 353.

120 Lortholary points out this conflation in the preface he provides to his French translation of 'In the Penal Colony': he is astonished that, 'the same status and the same authority are conferred on all Kafka's texts without exception, whether or not he published them, whether or not he crossed them out or altered them, whether or not he disowned them and wanted them destroyed, whether they are fictional productions or writing of a private nature etc.' (Bernard Lortholary, 'Preface' in Franz Kafka, *Dans la colonie pénitentiaire et autres nouvelles*, Bernard Lortholary trans., Paris: Flammarion, 1991, p. 12).

121 David, 'Notes et variantes' in David, *Franz Kafka: Oeuvres complètes*, VOL. 2, p. 951.

122 Ibid., p. 1063.

123 Ibid., p. 1101.

124 Fernand Cambon, 'La soumission et la loi', *Europe* 923 (March 2006): 98–112.

125 Lahire's 'theory of literary creation' is based on this same superimposition, effected on the basis of the same assumptions that the meaning of Kafka's work is to be discovered in the twists and turns of his 'sociological' biography. On that basis, *The Trial* can be said to be a mere transposition of Kafka's relations with his father (as though Kafka had no other concern than to articulate with regard to himself the problems the commentators raise about him in categories which are precisely their own); the various characters can be seen as objectivations or dramatic representations of his mother or father; and virtually the sole referent of each fictional text would be the 'Letter to his Father', as though the only possible referential 'reality' were the 'biographical reality' (see, for example, Lahire, *Franz Kafka*, note 4 on pp. 522–3). The narrator's relations to the 'Little Woman' would be the staging of a conflict that can only be 'interior' (ibid., p. 456). And in 'In the Penal Colony', Kafka is allegedly speaking of 'the fact of having always felt guilty, without ever having known exactly what he had done wrong and what he was being accused of, but suffering in his flesh from an internalized, negative (essentially paternal) judgement' (ibid., p. 520).

126 Elias Canetti, 'Kafka's Other Trial' in Franz Kafka, *Letters to Felice*, pp. 7–94.

127 Kafka, '23 July 1914' *in Diaries*, p. 293.

128 Cf. David and Morel, *Le Siècle de Kafka*, pp. 187–95.

129 Scholem, *Walter Benjamin*, p. 7.

130 Ibid., pp. 28–9.

131 Scholem, *From Berlin to Jerusalem*, p. 72.

132 Kafka, *Letters to Felice*, p. 273.

133 Kafka, *Briefe an Felice*, p. 260.

134 [Published by Literarische Anstalt Ruetten und Loening.]

135 It is, in reality, understandable that Kafka was very cautious in all his statements when addressing Felice; one understands why he did not want to break too radically with the canons and framing ideas of Zionist thought for fear of shocking her (that is to say, of losing her). According to Gelber, Zionism as a subject of discussion was one of Kafka's ways of approaching women and even became, at the point when he met Felice, a strategy for wooing her. Cf. Gelber, 'Kafka und zionistische Deutung', p. 298.

136 Cf. David in David, *Franz Kafka: Oeuvres complètes*, VOL. 4, p. 1242 note 1.

137 Kafka, *Letters to Felice*, p. 278.

138 We know that two of his stories, 'Jackals and Arabs' and 'A Report to an Academy', would be published in *Der Jude* in October and November 1917. [Franz Kafka, 'Jackals and Arabs' (Willa and Edwin Muir trans) in *The Complete Stories*, pp. 407–10 [originally written and published in *Der Jude* in 1917 as 'Schakale und Araber'.]

139 Scholem, *From Berlin to Jerusalem*, p. 72.

140 Kafka, 'Letter to Max Brod, Zürau, middle or end of January 1918' in *Letters to Friends, Family and Editors*, p. 190.

141 Günther Anders had proposed a similar reading in demonstrating that the text set the 'cultured Jew' against the 'orthodox eastern European Jew.' However, he construed it as a sort of moral fable of generalized intent, relating to 'the . . . critical relation between culture and its content' and 'culture's bad conscience and self-humiliation *vis-à-vis* the "original text"' in which he is allegedly offering 'some explanation of why he instructed the executors of his will to destroy his works after his death.' Günther Anders, *Franz Kafka* (Cambridge: Bowes and Bowes, 1960), pp. 93–5.

142 Kafka, 'The Village Schoolmaster' in *The Complete Short Stories*, p. 168.

143 Ibid., p. 169.

144 Ibid., pp. 168–9.

145 Ibid., p. 170.

146 Ibid., p. 171.

147 The recurrent use of the device of free indirect style in many stories leads us to think that it is from the novels of Flaubert, one of the literary figures he greatly admired, that he borrowed this idea. We know that Flaubert made extensive use of this stylistic and narrative device. Cf. Pierre-Marc Biasi, *Gustave Flaubert: Une manière spéciale de vivre* (Paris: Grasset, 2009), especially pp. 186–8. Biasi stresses the 'new system' of writing Flaubert sought to perfect in which 'the first requirement is the non-intervention of the author.' This seems to me also to be one of the main constants of Kafka's writing in his fiction (cf. ibid., pp. 175–97). For Bruce, Kafka is a 'Jewish Flaubert' (*Kafka and Cultural Zionism*, p. 143).

148 Kafka, 'The Village Schoolmaster' in *The Complete Stories*, p. 172.

149 Ibid.

150 Ibid., p. 181.

151 Ibid., p. 173.

152 It was no doubt on account of this difficulty of construction that he abandoned it in January 1915. Cf. David, 'Notes et variantes' in David, *Franz Kafka: Oeuvres complètes*, VOL. 2, p. 974.

153 Kafka, 'The Village Schoolmaster' in *The Complete Stories*, p. 182.

154 Ibid., p. 181.

155 Ibid., p. 172.

156 Scholem, 'Martin Buber's Interpretation of Hasidism' in *The Messianic Idea in Judaism*, pp. 228–50.

157 Bechtel, *La Renaissance culturelle juive*, pp. 123–9.

158 Kafka, 'Josephine the Singer, or the Mouse Folk' in *The Complete Stories*, pp. 360, 364, 366, 367.

159 Ibid., pp. 360, 362, 367.

160 Ibid., p. 361.

161 Ibid., p. 362.

162 Ibid., p. 363.

163 Ibid., p. 364.

164 Ibid., p. 367.

165 Buber who, it will be remembered, was condemned by Benjamin for his tendency to burst into tears. See p. 215.

166 Kafka, 'Josephine the Singer, or the Mouse Folk' in *The Complete Stories*, p. 376.

167 She has pointed out, for example, that the 'two small [. . .] celluloid balls' that harass Blumfeld and leave him not a minute of peace in 'Blumfeld, an Elderly Bachelor', even lurking beneath his bed as he sleeps and 'jumping up and down side by side on the parquet' are 'white [. . .] with blue stripes'. They are, in other words, the colours of Zionism and the Jewish flag and could also stand for the Blau-Weiss (Blue-and-White), the first Zionist youth movement founded in Germany (see Iris Bruce, 'Jewish Education: Borderline and Counterdiscourses in Kafka' in Gelber, *Kafka, Zionism and Beyond*, pp. 107–46; here, pp. 131–6).

168 Kafka, *Letters to Milena*, pp. 174–5.

169 On this question, see Hartmut Binder, *Kafka in neuer Sicht* (Stuttgart: Metzler, 1976), p. 350.

170 Entry for 25 February 1918 in the fourth of the eight octavo notebooks in Kafka, *Dearest Father*, p. 99.

171 Ibid.

172 Kafka, *Dearest Father*, p. 270.

173 Cf. Casanova, *The World Republic of Letters*, especially Part II, Chapters 6–9, pp. 173–302.

174 Georges Ohnet (1848–1918) was a very successful French novelist. His most popular work, *Le Maître de forges* (1882), is a sentimental story employing the techniques of the serial and the melodrama.

175 Brod, *Franz Kafka*, p. 50.

176 Born, *Kafkas Bibliothek*, p. 81. [Alexander Eliasberg, *Sagen polnischer Juden* (Munich: G. Müller, 1916).]

177 Ibid., p. 84. [Micah Joseph Berdichevsky, Rahel Bin Gorion and Emanuel Bin-Gorion, *Die Sagen der Juden* (Frankfurt: Rütten and Loening, 1919).]

178 Ibid., p. 43. [Yitzkhok Leybush Peretz, *Aus dieser und jener Welt*: *Jüdische Geschichten* (Vienna and Berlin: Löwt, 1919) and Joseph Weigl, *Jüdische Helden* (Frankfurt: Jüdischer Volksschriftenverlag, 1911).]

179 Born cites a book by Theodor Menzel, *Der Zauberspiegel: Türkische Märchen II* (Hannover: H. Lafaire, 1924). Ibid., p. 85.

180 The volume in question is one that is reported by Wagenbach but not found by Born was Abu'l-Alâ, *Arabische Gedichten aus dem zehnten Jahrhundert* (Munich: P. Bruckmann, 1920).

181 Born, *Kafkas Bibliothek*, pp. 81–7. Born makes reference to Roald Amundsen's *Eskimoleben: Eindrücke von der Polarfahrt 1903–1907* (Cologne: Schaffstein, 1912). See, also the account of Kafka's personal book collection in Klaus Wagenbach, *Franz Kafka: Les années de jeunesse (1883–1912)* (Elisabeth Gaspar trans.) (Paris: Mercure de France, 1967), pp. 232–44.

182 This last is the translation proposed by Céline Trautman-Waller in *Quand Berlin pensait les peuples: Anthropologie, ethnologie et psychologie (1850–1890)* (Paris: CNRS, 2004), p. 9.

183 The Berliner Gesellschaft für Anthropologie, Ethnologie und Urgeschichte was founded at Berlin in 1869.

184 Janouch, *Conversations with Kafka*, p. 36. [In the French translation cited by the author, the German term rendered in the English as 'shapes' is translated as *personnages*—characters. Trans.]

185 Brod, *Franz Kafka*, p. 74.

186 Beck has formulated the hypothesis that one can find the structure and themes of the Yiddish plays Kafka saw in 1911–12 almost term for term in his short stories. She takes the view, for example, that the parallels it is possible to draw between the themes, plot details and structure of three of the plays watched by Kafka (Jacob Gordin's *Got, Mensh un Tayvl* and *Der vilde Mensh*, and Abraham Sharkanski's *Kol Nidre*) and 'The Judgment' are so explicit that they have to be regarded as direct sources for the writing of Kafka's story. Similarly, she is of the opinion that the opening paragraph of *Amerika*, which describes the Statue of Liberty carrying a sword instead of a torch comes directly from the prologue to Gordin's play *Got, Mensh un Tayvl*. It is obviously possible, given his great interest in these things, that Kafka borrowed certain features from the Yiddish plays, but it seems out of the question that one can find them quasi-mechanically

and exclusively imported into his fiction. Moreover, though Beck identifies this influence very (too?) systematically, she offers no other explanation for it than his 'deep interest in Judaism'. Cf. Beck, *Kafka and the Yiddish Theater*, p. 71, p. 125 and p. *xii*.

187 Sholem Aleichem, *La peste soit de l'Amérique* (Nadia Déhan ed.) (Paris: Liana Levi, 2005), pp. 68–9.

188 Ibid.

189 Ibid., pp. 42–9.

190 Sholem Aleichem, 'Dreyfus in Kasrilevke' (Hilde Abel trans.) in Irving Howe and Eliezer Greenberg (eds), *A Treasury of Yiddish Stories* (New York: Schocken Books, 1973), pp. 187–92; here, p. 187. Cited in Pinès, *Histoire de la littérature judéo-allemande*, pp. 413–14.

191 Ibid., pp. 421–2.

192 See, for example, ibid., p. 193: 'Abramovitsh was the first, and the only one, among the Maskilite ['enlightened'] writers to raise the problem of the *material* poverty of the Jewish people' (emphasis added).

193 Ibid., pp. 183–99.

194 Ibid., p. 184.

195 The critics have often put forward Dickens as one of the direct sources of this book and as a literary reference claimed by Kafka himself. However, that author was, perhaps, a model at one remove. Rather amusingly, Pinès takes the view that Abramovitsh's novels have several features in common with Dickens and he suggests the reference to the English novelist as one of the sources of the Yiddish tales (*Histoire de la littérature judéo-allemande*, p. 204). For their part, Gérard Rudent and Brigitte Vergne-Cain assert that *David Copperfield* is not in fact the source of *Amerika* (in Rudent and Vergne-Cain, 'Mai 1910-mai 1913: la percée' in *Franz Kafka: Récits, romans, journaux* [Paris: Livre de Poche, 2000], p. 201).

196 Cf., for example, Robertson, *Kafka: Judaism, Politics and Literature*, pp. 47–54.

197 The Kishinev pogroms occurred in 1903 and 1905.

198 David, 'Notice de *l'Amérique* [*L'Oubliée*]' in David, *Franz Kafka: Oeuvres complètes*, VOL. I, p. 828.

199 Arthur Holitscher, *Amerika heute und morgen: Reiseerlebnisse* (Berlin: Fischer, 1913). Wagenbach attests that this volume was present in Kafka's library.

200 Cf. David, 'Notice de *l'Amérique [L'Oubliée]*' in David, *Franz Kafka: Oeuvres complètes*, VOL. I, pp. 823–4.

201 Ibid., p. 825.

202 Cf. Anderson, 'Chapter 4: Kafka in America: Notes on a Travelling Narrative' in *Kafka's Clothes*, p. 113.

203 David, 'Notice de *l'Amérique [L'Oubliée]*' in David, *Franz Kafka: Oeuvres complètes*, VOL. I, p. 824.

204 This is a magnificent anachronistic cliché.

205 David, 'Notice de *l'Amérique [L'Oubliée]*' in David, *Franz Kafka: Oeuvres complètes*, VOL. I, p. 826.

206 Cf. Howe, *World of Our Fathers*.

207 David, 'Notice de *l'Amérique [L'Oubliée]*' in David, *Franz Kafka: Oeuvres complètes*, VOL. I, p. 825.

208 Kafka, 'The March to Rameses', *Amerika*.

209 'Therefore they did set over them taskmasters to afflict them with their burdens. And they built for Pharaoh treasure cities, Pithom and Raamses' (Exod. I:II).Cf. Philippe Zard, *La Fiction de l'Occident: Thomas Mann, Franz Kafka, Albert Cohen* (Paris: PUF, 1999), pp. 48–9. See also Jean-Pierre Gaxie, *L'Égypte de Franz Kafka: Une relecture* (Paris: Maurice Nadeau, 2002), pp. 29–48, pp. 73–90.

210 Cf. Philippe Zard, '*Der Verschollene*, un récit de l'exil occidental' in Maurice Godé and Michel Vanoosthuyse (eds), *Entre critique et rire: 'Le Disparu' de Franz Kafka* (Montpellier: Université Paul-Valéry de Montpellier, 1997), pp. 99–116; here, p. 100.

211 On the title Kafka gave to this novel—'The Man Who Disappeared'— see p. 248.

212 Anderson, 'Chapter 4: Kafka in America: Notes on a Travelling Narrative' in *Kafka's Clothes*, p. 107.

213 Walter Benjamin, 'Franz Kafka: On the Tenth Anniversary of His Death' in *Selected Writings, Volume 2: 1921–1934* (Michael W. Jennings, Howard Eiland and Gary Smith eds, Rodney Livingstone et al. trans) (Cambridge and London: Belknap Press, 1999), pp. 794–818; here, p. 801.

214 Pinès writes as follows about Abramovitsh's work: 'He is concerned, above all, to describe the life of the people, in its customs, habits, doings and institutions. The most characteristic types in his novels

are at the same time *collective types*. That is to say, their individuality is made up, above all, of features common to the mass of the people [. . .] Mendele the peddler himself, the most important and typical of his characters, is, after all, merely a *collective type*' (*Histoire de la littérature judéo-allemande*, pp. 206–07; emphasis added).

215 Even Bernd Neumann, who nonetheless offers an interesting political interpretation of *Amerika*, never postulates any distance (or humorous relation) between Kafka and his characters. He thus assumes that Karl Rossmann, who refers to himself in the novel several times proudly as a 'Prague German', is a mouthpiece for Kafka. This clearly has vast consequences for the interpretation of the novel with Neumann postulating at the same time that Kafka identified with the Germans of the Empire. See Neumann, *Franz Kafka: Aporien der Assimilation*, pp. 54–5.

216 Janouch, *Conversations with Kafka*, p. 31.

217 Ibid., p. 32.

218 Ibid., p. 31.

219 Christian Klein, 'Introduction: Incohérences et irritations: les impasses de la critique' in Godé and Vanoosthuyse, *Entre critique et rire*, pp. 9–22; here, p. 14.

220 Kafka, *Amerika*, pp. 8–18.

221 Ibid., p. 19. *Der Verschollene*, p. 33.

222 In the same way, in *The Castle*, the members of the Barnabas family have to live as outlaws because one of their daughters has rejected the advances of a powerful castle servant: 'it was because she didn't go that the curse was laid upon our family'. Kafka, *The Castle*.

223 Kafka, *Amerika*, p. 20.

224 Ibid., p. 32.

225 Ibid., p. 34.

226 Ibid., p. 38.

227 Ibid.

228 Ibid., p. 63.

229 Ibid., p. 69.

230 Ibid., p. 73.

231 Robin, *L'Amour du yiddish*, p. 103.

232 Kafka, 'Investigations of a Dog' in *The Complete Stories*, p. 279.

233 Kafka, *Amerika*, pp. 79–80. [The German here is 'man übersah den ganzen Saal' (p. 121), which is rendered by the French translator as 'on dominait toute la salle'. Trans.]

234 Ibid.

235 Ibid., p. 100.

236 Ibid., p. 84.

237 See, for example, the drawing by George Grosz, *Swamp-flowers of Capitalism*, reproduced in Cathérine Wermester, *Grosz: L'homme le plus triste de l'Europe* (Paris: Allia, 2008), p. 35.

238 Janouch, *Conversations with Kafka*, pp. 144–5.

239 Kafka, *Amerika*, p. 205.

240 Ibid., p. 203.

241 Ibid., p. 202.

242 Ibid., p. 206.

243 Ibid.

244 Ibid., p. 214.

245 Ibid., p. 209.

246 Ibid., pp. 208–09.

247 Ibid., p. 209.

248 Ibid., p. 210.

249 Ibid., p. 209.

250 Ibid., p. 210.

251 Cf. David, 'Notice de *l'Amérique* [*L'Oubliée*]' in David, *Franz Kafka: Oeuvres complètes*, VOL. I, p. 824.

252 Kafka, *Amerika*, p. 212.

253 Ibid.

254 Ibid., p. 213.

255 Ibid.

256 Ibid.

257 Ibid.

258 Ibid., p. 214.

259 Ibid., p. 215.

260 Ibid.

261 Kafka, *The Trial*, p. 76.

262 Kafka, *Amerika*, p. 217.

263 Ibid.

264 Ibid., p. 218.

265 Bernd Neumann has advanced an opposite interpretation of the novel, postulating that the last chapter presents a scenario of successful assimilation. *Franz Kafka: Aporien de Assimilation*, pp. 66–7.

266 Anderson, 'Chapter 4: Kafka in America: Notes on a Travelling Narrative' in *Kafka's Clothes*, p. 104.

267 See Rudent and Vergne-Cain, *Franz Kafka: Récits, romans, journaux*, note 455. See also Bernard Lortholary, 'Préface du traducteur' in Franz Kafka, *Amerika ou Le Disparu* (Paris: Flammarion 'GF', 1988), p. 5.

268 Kafka, *Briefe: 1902–1924*, p. 334.

269 See Adrian Hsia, 'China as Ethical Construct and Reflector of Europe's Self-Perception: a Historical Survey up to Kafka's Time' in Adrian Hsia (ed.), *Kafka and China: Euro-Sinica* 7 (Bern: Peter Lang, 1996), pp. 22–3. [*Chinesische Lyrik* was published in Leipzig and Munich by Piper and *Die chinesische Flöte* was published in Leipzig by Insel Verlag.]

270 Ibid.

271 To Felice he writes in mid-May 1916, 'I imagine if I were a Chinese and were about to go home (indeed I am a Chinese and am going home), I would make sure of returning soon, and at any price. How you would love it!' (*Letters to Felice*, p. 594). To Milena he writes on 1 June 1920, 'One really is terribly foolish. I'm reading a book about Tibet; at a description of a settlement near the Tibetan border in the mountains my heart grows suddenly heavy, this village seems so hopelessly deserted, so far from Vienna. What I call foolish is the idea that Tibet is far from Vienna. Would it really be far?' (*Letters to Milena*, p. 37).

272 Heinz Politzer, 'Zwei kaiserliche Botschaften: zu den Texten von Hofmannsthal und Kafka', *Modern Austrian Literature* 11(3–4) (1978): 105–22; here, p. 105.

273 Hartmut Binder, *Kafka: Kommentar zu sämtlichen Erzählungen* (Munich: Winkler, 1975), pp. 218–22.

274 Julius Dittmar, *Im neuen China: Reiseeindrücke von J. Dittmar* (Cologne: Schaffstein, 1912).

275 Rolf J. Goebel, 'Kafka's "An Old Manuscript" and the European Discourse on Ch'ing Dynasty China' in Hsia, *Kafka and China*, pp. 97–111.

276 Kafka, 'An Old Manuscript' in *The Complete Stories*, p. 416.

277 Ibid., p. 416.

278 Ibid., p. 417.

279 Ibid.

280 Ibid.

281 Ibid.

282 Kafka, *Letters to* Milena, p. 51. The passage is from a letter to Milena from Merano on 20 June 1920.

283 Ibid.

284 'Some time later he recommended me to read Frobenius's collection of African folk-takes and fairy stories.' Janouch, *Conversations with Kafka*, p. 95.

285 See Hans-Jürgen Heinrichs, *Die fremde Welt, das bin ich. Leo Frobenius. Ethnologe, Forschungsreisender, Abenteurer* (Wuppertal: Peter Hammer, 1998), p. 21–2.

286 Ibid., p. 23.

287 Leo Frobenius, *Der Ursprung der afrikanischen Kulturen* (Berlin: Bornträgger, 1898).

288 Jean Servier, 'Préface' in Leo Frobenius, *L'Atlantide: Mythologie et cultes* (F. Gidon trans.) (Paris: Éditions du Rocher, 1993), p. *xxiii*. See also Heinrichs, *Leo Frobenius*, pp. 19–20. [*Schicksalskunde im Sinne des Kulturwerdens* was published in 1932 in Leipzig by R. Voigtländer.]

289 Leo Frobenius, *Atlantis. Volksmärchen und Volksdichtungen Afrikas*: *Volumes I and II; Volksmärchen der Kabyln* (Jena: Eugen Diederichs, 1921).

290 Ibid., VOL. I, 'Das Hinschmelzen der Berber in den Oasenländern', p. 4.

291 Ibid., pp. 4–6.

292 Kafka, 'The Great Wall of China' in *The Complete Stories*, p. 242.

293 See, for example, Leo Frobenius, *Das Zeitalter des Sonnengottes* (Berlin: Georg Reimer, 1904). In this book, Frobenius undertakes a comparison between myths or legends collected in areas that are far removed from one another (the myth of the whale among Polynesians, Indonesians, North Americans and South Africans; the myth of immaculate conception in America, Africa, Asia and Europe), etc.

294 Leo Frobenius, 'Introduction' in *Contes kabyles*, VOL. 3 (Aix-en-Provence: Édisud, 1997), pp. 7–9.

295 Ibid., p. 8.

296 Ibid., p. 9.

297 Ibid., pp. 8–9.

298 Ibid., p. 8. See Tassadit Yacine-Titouh, *Chacal ou la ruse des dominés: Aux origines du malaise culturel des intellectuels algériens* (Paris: La Découverte, 2001).

299 'The man, struck on the head by a blow from the pick, fell pole-axed, stone dead. The jackal, which watched the scene from a distance, burst out laughing' (Frobenius, *Contes Kabyles*, pp. 11–26).

300 Kafka, 'Jackals and Arabs' in *The Complete Stories*, p. 408.

301 Ibid., p. 407.

302 Ibid., p. 408.

303 Ibid., pp. 409–10.

304 Gilman, *Franz Kafka: The Jewish Patient*, pp. 150–3.

305 Kafka, 'Jackals and Arabs' in *The Complete Stories*, p. 409.

306 Ibid., p. 407.

307 Bruce, *Kafka and Cultural Zionism*, pp. 154–7.

308 Ibid., p. 155.

309 Heinz Politzer, *Franz Kafka: Parable and Paradox* (Ithaca, NY: Cornell University Press, 1966), p. 90.

310 Kafka, 'Jackals and Arabs' in *The Complete Stories*, p. 410.

311 Ibid., p. 408.

312 Ibid.

313 Ibid., p. 410.

314 Ibid., p. 411.

'It was about midnight. Five men held me, behind them a sixth had his hand raised to grab me. 'Let go,' I cried and whirled in a circle, making them all fall back. I felt some sort of law at work.'

Franz Kafka, narrative fragment

Above and beyond the use of devices provided by ethnological narratives or folk tale, Kafka, as we have seen, invented the terms of a new ethnology, an ethnology of Western Jews. From his encounter with Eastern Jewry he adopted, in effect, a sort of remote empathy towards his contemporaries—a posture that enabled him to view Westerners in a way Easterners were ordinarily viewed at this period. This reversal of perspective, which enabled him to stand back from his own society, may also be compared with the way an ethnologist observes a distant people. Undertaking a description of the peculiarities of Western Jews, Kafka gave a detailed depiction of their behaviour, history, careers and social life. Without entangling himself in celebration or hagiography, he provided realistic descriptions—since they were experienced from the inside—of the real life of assimilated Jews. Let us remember that the dog who narrates 'Investigations of a Dog' described himself as 'born [. . .] a citizen of falsehood'.[1] Kafka might be said to be the ethnologist of a people which did not know or recognize itself as a people, the creator of an ethnology both parodic and serious. 'Kafka,' writes Gerhard Neumann, 'becomes the ethnographer of his own culture and the pitiless diagnostician of its rituals.'[2] His stories are part of a legendary corpus invented by his own hand. From folk tale to fantastical narrative, from the rewriting of mythological tales to novels, Kafka would gradually develop some quite novel literary devices. We can see the considerable extent to which his thinking and mastery of narration evolved from the somewhat naive narrative and political structure of *Amerika* to *The Castle*.

ASSIMILATION AS DOMINATION

Assimilation may be regarded as one of the foundational themes of Kafka's *oeuvre*. He is entirely at one on this question with his Zionist friends' denunciation of the phenomenon. Like them, he roundly criticizes the delusions and betrayals associated with assimilation which he regards as a submission on the part of the Jews to German domination. And, indeed, from its very inception, he took out a subscription to the magazine *Selbstwehr* published at Prague by the Zionist group there, which took this same line. But he adopted a much more radical stance than them. It is as though his thinking on this question would gradually take on substance and widen out to other areas over the years as he elaborated his narrative techniques.

It is, in fact, in his fiction much more than in his other statements that we can identify and grasp the refinements of his analyses of these problems. He seems to have examined the phenomenon of assimilation from all possible angles: as dead end, as betrayal, as loss, as guilt, as individual and collective tragedy, as violence exerted on one and all, as disavowed domination. It is present in many of his fictional writings at all periods of his life as a writer, from his first published stories, such as 'A Report to an Academy' to the very last, including 'A Hunger Artist' and 'A Little Woman'.[3]

In the stories and novels, particularly *The Trial*, the desire for assimilation is embodied in characters who obey a mandatory— though not explicitly stated—law which forces them to submit to the rules of a society that despises and humiliates them, despite the fact that no physical violence compels them to do so and they are not clearly aware of the law in question. It follows that the hidden centre of Kafka's *oeuvre* is a (highly critical) reflection on domination. He is interested in all forms of power but mainly the most invisible and surreptitious forms and often those which are most violent because most disavowed—the phenomenon Bourdieu has termed symbolic domination.

Having said this, it is not at all my intention to turn Kafka into a sociologist or philosopher and, even less, to present him as a political activist. I do not think what he gave us in his fictional texts were historical analyses or demonstrative reflections. He was conveying, by literary and narrative means, his own non-analytic vision of the way this kind of invisible, disavowed violence might be explained. It is the distinctive feature of the unacknowledged ethnology he practised that, though seeking as far as possible to reproduce the distant stance of the ethnologists, he was not, like the practitioners of *Völkerkunde*, describing an alien human group living in a far-off country but the social group to which he belonged. Describing the life and *mores* of an 'average' liberal Jew living in a European country, to use the word the ape employs in 'A Report to an Academy',[4] he very quickly understood that he could do no other than include himself in the picture. In other words, he practised reflexiveness in drawing on his own subjective knowledge of assimilation and its effects in order to represent it. We can go further and say that his descriptions of the most secret situations and deeply felt wounds might be thought so precise only because he knew from the inside everything he was describing. On these subjects he spoke of himself as a representative of a collective entity; in other words, he placed himself as far as possible outside the classical logic of the self-portrait. He chose, that is, to produce a group portrait by depicting himself (among others) as an ideal typical representative of a collective. Kafka practised collective autobiography. He used his experience and also his unrelenting observation of power relations in his own social world as a basis for a comprehensive expression— in the form of narratives—of his thinking, criticism and rebellion.

The first lines of the self-portrait he sent to Grete Bloch in 1914, to which I have already referred, are highly characteristic. He asks her to understand him (and hence to have Felice understand him) not as an individual but insofar as he was generic:[5] 'Now please disregard the recognizable characteristics that distinguish me as an individual, and take the whole as a typical case,' he writes to her.[6] It is, in fact, very remarkable (and something which recurs many times) that, even in the most private circumstances, Kafka very often spoke of himself not as a singular individual profoundly different from his contemporaries but as a representative member of a group or set. It seems to me that this virtually constant trait has to be attributed not so much to some effect of supposed modesty as to his view of the world. Far from thinking of himself (and his literary work) in the most ordinary categories (for us) of individuality and singularity, his style of thought led him to think about groups, classes and nations—assimilated Jews, liberal Germans, nationalist Czechs, etc., This comes as all the more of a surprise to us as twenty-first-century West European readers because of the way Kafka has pre-cisely been turned into the writer of private suffering and secrecy, the standard-bearer of psychological criticism and the personification of the solitary wordsmith.

We cannot grasp the importance for Kafka of this question of the fight against assimilation as choice, as political stance, as core of his active political commitment and as social disposition, unless we connect it to the other question with which it is precisely symmetrical and which also runs through his work: the question of the father.

A 'Scrap of Judaism': Fathers of Scholem, Brod and Kafka.

For Kafka, the social process of assimilation, as submission to the Germanic order, began with the meagre cultural heritage Jewish fathers bequeathed to their sons. As the transmission of Jewishness traditionally took place through the acquisition of religious belief and ritual, the fathers who, as Kafka says in his June 1921 letter to Brod, encouraged their sons to abandon their Jewishness by 'approv[ing] of this, but vaguely', were guilty of a betrayal of their 'nationality'.[7] In order to understand the reality of the 'scrap of Judaism' which Jewish fathers handed on to their children as their inheritance, let us attempt a comparison between the religious prac-tices of the families of Scholem, Brod and Kafka. They all belonged to the most numerous group described by Scholem,[8] the assimilated petty or middle bourgeoisie which had lost all real ties with Jewishness but continued to reproduce simplified religious rituals that had by then become incomprehensible.[9] The comparison between these three cases, though it obviously does not provide a representative sample of the population group in question, provides much material for understanding the situation of the three men—what they really knew about the religious practices of Judaism, the grounds for the conflictual relations with their fathers and their desire to be rid of what they regarded as the lie of assimilation. This (very rapidly sketched) comparison enables us, above all, to understand that Kafka's is far from an isolated case.

Scholem's family, as he himself says, 'had been residing in Berlin for three generations'.[10] It was, as a consequence, 'a typical liberal middle-class family in which assimilation to things German, as people put it at the time, had progressed quite far. In our home,' he goes on, 'there were only a few perceptible relics of Judaism.'[11] He tells how:

> As far as Jewish ritual was concerned, in our home only Friday evening, which was considered family night, and the Seder on the eve of Passover were observed. The *Kiddush*, the Hebrew blessing for the Sabbath, was still chanted, but only half understood. That did not keep people from using the Sabbath candles to light a cigarette or cigar afterwards. Since the prohibition to smoke on the Sabbath was one of the most widely known Jewish regulations, there was deliberate mockery in this act [. . .] On the most solemn Jewish holiday, Yom Kippur, which was still observed as a fast day by the overwhelming majority, my father went to work and no one thought of fasting.[12]

Brod also came from a family that had long been assimilated into Austrian society, since he makes clear that they had been resident in Prague over several generations. His father spent his whole career in banking, rising from lowly bank official to the highest echelons of his company.[13] In other words, he was a member of the upwardly mobile lower (and, subsequently, middling) middle class: his position in a major local bank assured him of an elevated and respected social position.[14] When Brod writes of his family's relationship with Jewish religious ritual, his recollections resemble those of Scholem and Kafka point for point. Speaking of his childhood, Brod remembers, for example, 'remnants of ceremonies from the "Feast of Tabernacles" that had been preserved for just a few years, *like shadows*, before disappearing entirely.' He adds:

> [A]t Pesach, there was unleavened bread or matzos. We ate the paschal lamb and drank the four goblets of wine [. . .] Many prayers were intoned incomprehensibly [. . .] On this occasion, it is true, there was much laughter among the children [. . .] and there was no one to bring the over-excited gaggle of children into line. And this was not only true in our house. In many homes in this transitional period, things were like this. And yet, and yet, as incredible and absurd as it seemed, this *total absence of tradition*—which, apart from the lack of intention and awareness might have been demonic blasphemy—this abasement of the proceedings [*diese Entwürdigung*], which on closer examination repre-sented *less than nothing*, was enough to keep alive in me and my brothers and sisters something resembling a sense of our own value as Jews and even a sort of pride.[15]

The passages in 'The Letter to His Father' on the subject of Judaism almost give the impression that Kafka has set out to illustrate Scholem's sociological description:[16]

> On four days in the year you went to the synagogue, where you were, to say the least of it, closer to the indifferent than to those who took it seriously, patiently went through the prayers by way of formality, sometimes amazed me by being able to show me in the prayer book the passage that was being said at the moment [. . . A]t home it was, if possible, even more poverty-stricken, being confined to the first evening of Passover, which more and more developed into a farce, with fits of hysterical laughter, admittedly under the influence of the growing children (Why did you have to give way to that influence? Because you brought it about in the first place.) And so there was the religious material that was handed on to me.[17]

And, a little before this, he writes:

> Later, as a boy, I could not understand how, with the insignif-
> icant scrap of Judaism you yourself possessed, you could
> reproach me for not (if for no more than the sake of piety,
> as you put it) making an effort to cling to a similar insignif-
> icant scrap. It was indeed really, so far as I could see, a
> mere scrap, a joke, not even a joke.[18]

We can see that the three men had very similar experiences,
that they all wrote of a religious formalism emptied of meaning and
that the terms in which Brod describes what had been handed down
to him—these 'remnants of ceremonies [. . .] preserved [. . .] like
shadows, before disappearaing entirely'—are astonishingly close to
Kafka's words. All three denounced this sham and refused to reproduce it. In different forms and by other means, they wanted to
return to a Judaism that was not so tenuous. Now, in all three cases,
the father was the central figure. He it was who forced the dissolution
of their Jewishness on them, who was at the heart of what was experienced as a loss of identity and who broke with tradition in the
name of assimilation which the sons regarded as a lie and a betrayal.
This was the origin of the conflictual relations narrated with some
precision by Kafka and Scholem. The great difference between them,
however, was that the one, Scholem, offered an objective, historical
analysis of this situation almost 30 years after the Second World War,
whereas the other, also basing his commitment on the refusal to
reproduce this situation, proposed a reflective analysis of it as it happened and while it was having immediate effects on his life. Kafka
understood very quickly that he was himself the product of this tragic
dissolution and was personally best placed to write *from the inside* on
the aporias of this submission to a despised order. Moreover, analysing
his individual case with the great clear-sightedness we know he
possessed, stressing the intense sense of guilt that arose from his
relationship with an authoritarian father and dissecting the complexities of his own relations with Judaism, Kafka did not dwell at
length on his own unhappiness or neurotic temperament. He understood this opposition as a social structure or, in other words, as a

collective fact. This is why he very quickly raised the question to a more general level. The link between the two letters he wrote on the subject (the one he addressed to his father but would never send and the one he sent to Brod in June 1921) enables us to understand all the implications of Kafka's position. Both letters, for different reasons and in different contexts, paint a group portrait of Jewish fathers guilty of having let their sons abandon Judaism. And both analyse the intellectual and psychological consequences of the assimilation process on the Jewish writers of his generation at Prague.

In the 'Letter to His Father', Kafka provides his father with social reasons, so to speak, for this neglectfulness of his origins: 'You had really brought some traces of Judaism with you from that ghetto-like little village community; it was not much and it dwindled a little more in town and while you were doing your military service, but still the impressions and memories of your youth did just about suffice to make some sort of Jewish life.'[19] Then, with some lucidity, he connects these family circumstances to a more general collective situation. 'The whole thing is, of course, not an isolated phenomenon. It was much the same with a large section of this transitional generation of Jews, which had migrated from the still comparatively devout countryside to the towns.'[20] And he adds, as though to confirm his description: '[H]ere too you were conforming to the general method of treating sons in the Jewish middle class, which was the measure of things for you, or at least [. . . you adopted] the values of that class.'[21] However, he also accuses his father of having passed on indifference, at the same time as neglectfulness of his origins:

> Even in this there was still Judaism enough, but it was too little to be handed on to the child; it all dribbled away while you were passing it on [. . .] It was also impossible to make a child, overacutely observant from sheer nervousness, understand that the few flimsy gestures you performed in the name of Judaism, and with an indifference in keeping with their flimsiness, could have any higher meaning.[22]

As a result, Kafka accuses his father of only ever having handed on to him the desire to renounce his Judaism:

I could not understand how, with the insignificant scrap of Judaism you yourself possessed, you could reproach me for not [. . .] making an effort to cling to a similar insignificant scrap [. . .] How one could do anything better with this material than get rid of it as fast as possible was something I could not [as a boy] understand.[23]

In parallel with this, and as if by a kind of inverted symmetry, it seems reasonable to conclude that one of the reasons for Kafka's fascination with Yitzchak Löwy might also have been the actor's conflict with his own father. The two men had, in fact, broken with their respective fathers over the new definitions each wished to give to their Judaism. In the East, Yiddishism also generated a significant generational conflict. Conflict between fathers (wedded to religious tradition, austerity and the restrictive rituals governing everyday life) and sons (active in a party not far removed doctrinally from Marxism, actively atheistic and refusing to obey the commandment to pray) even became a kind of literary theme, visible in Yiddish drama and stories.[24] On this, Kafka made some notes in his diary that give an idea of the extent of the break between Löwy and his father.

The first pages of his memoirs, rewritten by Kafka in 1917, attest to the kind of conflict Löwy experienced with his father over this new form of Jewish theatre which stood out against religious tradition. Admittedly, the father in question personified faithfulness to Eastern tradition and popular piety and had handed down to his son a traditional culture far removed from the 'scrap of Judaism' bequeathed by Kafka's father, all of which ought to have fired him with enthusiasm. Yet he too, as seen by Kafka and Löwy, was in the wrong: he was blind, stuck in the rut of religious tradition, incapable of achieving a secularized, modernized Judaism—and highly authoritarian to boot.

Kafka and the Liberal Jews

Kafka was so worried about the future of Western Judaism that he thought it was in danger of dissolution and that it had to be defended at all events against the power of assimilation. In a conversation with

Janouch, Kafka speaks of the art of the 'the poor Jewish actors who act for Jews in Jewish. By their art,' he continues, 'they sweep away the deposits of an alien world from the life of the Jews, display in the bright light of day the hidden Jewish face which is sinking into oblivion, and so give them an anchor in the troubles of our time.'[25] This 'hidden Jewish face which is sinking into oblivion' is, it seems to me, the precise evocation of Kafka's vision of Judaism. A passage from his diary, dated 24 December 1911, the day he attended his nephew's circumcision ceremony, confirms this explicitly:

> Today when I heard the *moule*'s assistant say the grace after meals and those present, aside from the two grandfathers, spent the time in dreams or boredom with a complete lack of understanding of the prayer, I saw Western European Judaism before me in a transition whose end is clearly unpredictable and about which those most closely affected are not concerned, but, like all people truly in transition, bear what is imposed upon them.[26]

One of the most visible forms of his rejection of assimilation is his hostility to those who, in Jewish nationalist circles at Vienna and Prague, are called 'German Jews'—that is to say, in the categories of the day, those Jews who regard themselves as Germans, the liberal Jews who stay faithful to the Empire. We find traces of this hostility in Kafka's biographical writings or in the testimony of those who knew him, but such manifest signs are quite rare.

During one of his conversations with Janouch, for instance, Kafka relates the circumstances in which, as a boy, his friend Oskar Baum lost his sight in a brawl between Germans and Czechs at the school gates. And he adds, 'The Jew Oskar Baum lost his eyesight as a German [. . .] As something in fact which he never was, and which he was never accepted as being. Perhaps Oskar is merely a melancholy symbol of the so-called German Jews [*deutschen Juden*] in Prague.'[27] With this apparently simple sentence, Kafka was evoking the period of his childhood, when young Czechs fought young Germans in street brawls, Jews being identified with Germans by the Czechs at that time. In doing so, he was carrying out a kind of quick-fire, yet very radical political analysis: he was asserting that his friend Baum had lost his sight in the name of an identity which, because of anti-Semitism, the Germans had never actually conferred upon him and that Baum was, in consequence, a sort of personifi-cation of Jewish misery.

Along these same lines, in a letter Kafka sent to Felice in February 1913, he painted the portrait of a Jew who 'feels German' [*fühlt sich als Deutscher*]:

> I'm thinking of what I felt the day before yesterday in the evening when I saw a man I know come out of a house. He's the owner, or rather the son of the owner, of a Jewish bookshop. He must be in his forties [. . .] He has always remained entirely submissive [*grenzenlos ergeben*[28]] to his parents [. . .] He has never been independent [*niemals selb-ständig*]; since he left school—that is to say, for almost a generation—he spends his time in the tiny shop, where there is just enough work for one person, and with the help of a servant dusts the prayer shawls on the shelves; when it is hot he stays in the doorway [. . .] when it is cold, he stands behind the book-lined door and looks out into the street through holes left between these—generally obscene—books. He feels German and is a member of the German Casino here, a club which is, admittedly, open to all, but is regarded as the most distinguished by the city's Germans. And every evening, when he has closed his shop and dined, he probably goes to the *Deutsches Haus*.[29]

This portrait of a lower-middle-class Prague Jew is also, we should note, a portrait of the submissiveness of a life dependent on family order. In other words, his submission indicates that there has been no conflict with his father, that he has reproduced the older man's assimilationist values and not rebelled against him, unlike those of his generation who rejected the paternal order. This mere note is, moreover, a further indication, *a contrario*, of the structural conflict with their fathers of all who rejected assimilation. The portrait is rounded off with the observation that the man was a member of the German Casino, a club 'regarded as the most distinguished by the city's Germans', a point which unambiguously denoted his allegiance to the German camp. The contrast between the reality of the life spent in that 'tiny shop' and membership of the German club was obviously the embodiment for Kafka of the blindness represented by assimilation. This portrait, which has often been interpreted by biographical critics in exclusively psychological terms, on account of the parallel (not at all self-evident, it seems to me) with Kafka's matrimonial history, makes of this character a kind of ghost, a representation of one of the countless possibilities open to Kafka, whereas what we have here is rather (and more simply) the accusatory portrait of a German Jew.

ENCRYPTIONS

Self-Hatred?

The exercise of self-analysis as a member of a group was all the more exhausting for Kafka as it involved nothing less than describing the impasses and lack of insight which prompted that group to abandon or deny its Jewish identity. On 7 February 1915, he produced a long analysis to this effect of his reluctance to speak about himself:

> At a certain point in self-knowledge, when other circumstances favouring self-security are present, it will invariably follow that you find yourself execrable [. . .] You will see that you are nothing but a rat's nest of miserable dissimulations. The most trifling of your acts will not be untainted by these dissimulations [. . .] The filth you will find [. . . will be at] the nethermost and the uppermost, and even the doubts self-scrutiny begets will soon grow weak and self-complacent as the wallowing of a pig in muck.[30]

Remarkable, from this point of view, is the self-portrait he composed for Milena in November 1920 of himself as an assimilated Jew convinced of his intrinsic incompleteness, weakness and, above all, perhaps, the danger of disappearing as a Jew—and his fear of doing so—if he were not attentive to all the outward manifestations in which he had, so to speak, to persist in his being. This doubtless explains, at least in part, Kafka's lifelong interest in diet, gymnastics and vegetarianism. Anderson has interpreted this aspect of his personality as hatred of himself as a Jew, a desire to shake off the stigma of being Jewish.[31] But it seems to me that it is precisely the opposite. I do actually believe it possible to speak of a form of self-hatred on Kafka's part but, far from rejecting himself *as* a Jew, he wanted, like many Jews of his generation, to combat a weakness which he thought ensued from his assimilation—ensued, that is, from what he experienced as a loss of his Jewishness. It cannot be denied that Kafka's relationship with his own body was problematical. However, the weakness and inadequacy he felt was expressed, paradoxically, only as a (admittedly supposed, fantasized) lack of Jewishness. In other words, if Kafka felt self-hatred, which is probable, that feeling was triggered by an effect opposite to the one usually described, inasmuch as he regarded himself as an assimilated bourgeois and hence defined by *a lack of* Jewishness. As a result, what was in play here was a self-hatred generated not by the fact of being Jewish but by regret at not being sufficiently Jewish and being doomed never to be so because he was 'assimilated' and felt convinced that he was for ever 'sewn into [his] skin', as he told Felice.[32] This form of self-rejection, as a member of a group that was held in contempt, was clearly the product of a kind of hostility that was difficult to deny, a paradoxical but real anti-Semitism. Moreover, Bruce has emphasized at length that, in this period, anti-Semitic discourse and the critical discourse towards the Zionists could be very similar in appearance and one therefore cannot, as many commentators have done, take as manifestations of simple, unambiguous self-detestation texts which are, in reality, tongue-in-cheek satires of anti-Semitic clichés.[33]

In this connection, let me say parenthetically, as it were, that it seems impossible to argue, as Anderson does, that in 'Josephine the Singer' Kafka is accepting, adopting and reproducing—even with some attenuation—the anti-Semitic verdict of Richard Wagner and Otto Weininger.[34] This interpretation of the short story has been so successful that I shall pause briefly to consider it. Wagner, among others, had written in 1850 in *Das Judentum in der Musik* that the Jews were characterized by their 'unmusicality'. Similarly, the mouse who narrates the story asserts at the very beginning: '[W]e are not in general a music-loving race,' and 'we are quite unmusical.'[35] Yet, if Kafka is working on the basis of a metaphorical or allegorical displacement and if the mouse people is a representation of the Jews borrowed from anti-Semitic discourse[36] (which remains to be proved), why should the discourse on music be taken simply at face value? We must clearly assume that both Josephine's 'singing' and the mouse people's 'music' are ways of speaking about something else. And if we are paying attention to Kafka's discourse on music, why not focus on another text written a few years earlier which, in a quite contrary way, celebrates the great musicality of another animal people? In 'The Investigations of a Dog', though the canine metaphor is also borrowed from anti-Semitic discourse, the dog who narrates that tale stresses on several occasions 'the creative gift for music with which the canine race alone is endowed'.[37] Quite apart from the fact that they are one further reminder that the distinction between fictional texts and autobiographical writing is absolutely crucial if we are not to confuse two different orders of phenomena, then whatever else they show, the apparent signs of Kafka's acquiescence in anti-Semitic representations in his fictional texts cannot be taken as proof of his self-rejection as a Jew.

Schnitzler writes of this same ambiguous sentiment in his novel *The Road to the Open*. Regarding his feelings towards other Austrian Jews, one of his characters, himself a Jew, exclaims:

But there are Jews whom I really hate, hate as Jews. Those are the people who act before others, and often before themselves, as though they did not belong to the rest at all. The men who try to offer themselves to their enemies and despisers in the most cowardly and cringing fashion, and think that in that way they can escape from the eternal curse whose burden is upon them, or from what they feel is equivalent to a curse.[38]

Schnitzler, like Kafka, is simply stressing the feelings of the person Sartre calls the 'authentic' Jew—that is to say, the one who asserts his Jewishness with pride—towards the 'inauthentic' one who, for his part, refuses to be numbered among the Jews.[39] Kafka is definitely an 'authentic' Jew in Sartre's sense. Nevertheless, the violence and cruelty of the various representations of assimilated Jews in his stories—aided by the refinements and perversity of the exercise of reflection—border upon a strange collective and individual detestation. The description of the paradoxical, monstrous, conflicted animal he depicts in 'A Crossbreed [A Sport]', for example, a creature half-cat and half-lamb, yet neither cat nor lamb, is so virulent that it allows us to gauge the degree of Kafka's anger, political indignation and general animosity towards that group of people.[40] The conflicts and strife besetting the animal are highly disturbing in their violence and cruelty and make the story almost unbearable.

That said, this paradoxical rejection of himself as a Western Jew could not be expressed without, at the same time, taking account of Kafka's stance and campaigning in favour of the emancipation of the same Western Jews. In most of his texts, assimilation is never presented, reflected on or described without the presentation, also, of the other side of its reality, the notion inseparable from it, its inverted double which is alone able to explain its failure: namely, anti-Semitism. The particularity of Kafka's 'narrativized thought' is that he always conceived and presented not a thesis but two sides of a single problem at once. In other words, his scathing attacks were not on the Germanized Jews as such: he was critical at the same time—and indissociably —of the horror of the Germans' anti-Semitism *and* the delusion of assimilation.

Critics have frequently raised the question of the absence from Kafka's writings (merely apparent, as we shall see) of any direct mention of the great anti-Semitic scandals in Czechoslovakia at the turn of the century, particularly the two Hilsner trials of 1899 and 1900.

Yet, it is certain that, from 1912 onwards, the obvious fact of daily anti-Semitism, combined with his Yiddishist enthusiasm, brought this question to the forefront of his preoccuptions. On several occasions in his diary and his letters to Felice, he mentions that he sobbed as he read the accounts of the trials or the books connected with these affairs. Above all, his 'investigations' forced him to return constantly to this central obstacle. Yet he did not pose the question in ordinary political terms. As an attentive reader of the ethnology of his day, he looked, as he pondered this stigmatization, for an anthropological law that might govern the behaviour of the two social groups concerned: first, the Germans and consequently, because they were victims of it, the Jews. 'Law' (*Gesetz*) is a polysemic term in both English and German; it applies as much to the legal process, to social codes of behaviour and to religious rituals as it does to the tacit rules of conduct by which the behaviour of diverse social groups are ordered, as described by ethnology. The initial establishment of the 'law' of anti-Semitism is lost in the mists of time; this is 'a very old quarrel', an 'old tradition', as the jackal says to the traveller, and everyone has forgotten how it began.[41] And yet everyone, in Western and Eastern Europe, was subject to it both individually and collectively. The magnificent expression Kafka employs at the beginning of 'Jackals and Arabs'—*wie unter einer Peitsche gesetzmäßig*[42]—seems to me more or less to represent Kafka's general thinking. The point is to describe people who act as though 'under the law (*Gesetz*) of a whip' and perhaps, even, under the whip of a law. In the very name of reason, Kafka was denouncing the arbitrariness and horror of that law. He was calling for revolt against the (unspoken, unformulated, irrational, but real and implacable) law which established the Jews as suspects or as guilty 'by their nature' and placed them in the impossible situation of assimilated 'pariahs', to use Arendt's term.[43] However—and Kafka stresses this in 'In the Penal Colony' in particular—this law was in no way either inescapable or insurmountable. It was not superhuman in nature. It was merely the product of a forgotten history. The strength of his 'literarized' reflection is that, by posing this question in terms of a law, he was showing both its collective operation and its historical character. In other words, instead of defining anti-Semitic behaviour as an elusive act conforming to an inexplicable—and hence insurmountable—tradition, instead of turning it into something inevitable, Kafka was transforming this 'curse' into history. He was stating that it was possible to reject it or, in other words, to put an end to the stigmatization of the Jews. And in providing, as it were, a new version of historicism, Kafka was constantly, in his own way, repeating the saying that 'what history has made, history can unmake.' Since what was at issue was a social law—an unquestioned collective assumption never stated as such but conformed to (unconsciously) by everyone because it was impossible not to go along with it—then only the new-found awareness of its arbitrariness, injustice and violence could bring this order of things to an end. Thus we can see Kafka as having turned ethnologist in order to provide assimilated Jews with an instrument of self-knowledge and restore their culture and identity while seeking to liberate them from the burden of social 'laws' weighing upon them.

Moreover, by formulating the questions that concerned him in terms of 'law', Kafka wrenched himself away from the unquestioned assumptions of common sense and the philosophy of consciousness. In his fictions, he did not denounce active and conscious—or consciously repugnant and cynical—anti-Semites. He denounced the arrogance and certainty of the dominant social group; he was painting in morally repugnant colours a number of ill-intentioned characters whom he openly accused of injustice, ignominy and racism. But they were collective figures who represented anti-Semitism as a collective behaviour fostered socially.[44] Knowing that he was dealing with mechanisms affecting the whole of the social body, Kafka described the forms—often subtle and virtually indescribable, such as suspicion—and the motives of repeated collective actions that were the object of sustained convictions. He depicted these as a belief system very deeply rooted in the life of each social agent or, in other words, as a kind of frame of thought governing social organization without the agents being aware of it—a kind of collective unconscious, acting as both an unquestioned assumption and a conviction.

This is why his ambition was immense. Apart from the work of building up a past, a tradition and a 'folklore'—all of which were necessary, as he saw it, for the Jews to enter the 'concert of nations'— Kafka had the idea that literature could and should be an instrument of pedagogy in the noble sense, a tool for producing collective awareness, a cathartic mechanism that could allow material to pass from the unconscious into consciousness and hence bring an end to the ceaseless repetition of the stigmatization of the Jews. We know that at a very young age he expressed the idea that literature was active, that it acted concretely on readers, that it had—or should have— powerful effects on them. He wrote in this vein to his friend Pollak in January 1904: '[W]e need the books that affect us like a disaster, that grieve us deeply, like the death of someone we loved more than ourselves, like being banished into forests far from everyone, like a suicide. A book must be the axe for the frozen sea inside us.'[45] And such, it seems to me, is one of the tasks Kafka set himself as a writer—to produce texts that would enable material to pass from the (social) unconscious into consciousness and would, at the same time, be tools promoting rejection of, and rebellion against, the stigmata imposed by the order of the world. 'For the first time in literary history,' writes Arendt, 'a writer requires his readers to engage in the very same activity that upholds both him and his work.'[46] Behind each of Kafka's stories and novels there is the idea that they could and should provoke in their readers a rebellion against the *diktat* of anti-Semitism or, more broadly, against the inequalities produced by the structure of symbolic domination. It was a question of working, in what were at times extremely violent critical fictions, to enunciate and denounce that law which indefinitely reproduced Jewish misery and, more broadly, the misery of dominated men and women.

This is why it seems to me that the critical violence of his fictions is often underestimated. One of the functions of the universalization of a literary *oeuvre* is very often the neutralization of the writer's aim by simply forgetting the precise conditions and circumstances of particular pieces. Because Kafka's real targets vanished at the same time as his world disappeared, his parodic, denunciatory, critical—

or merely mocking—intentions vanished with them. The tone, the veiled allusions, the polemical violence and the rage that went into condemning a particular social institution as guilty were also engulfed by that same process. And what often remains of Kafka is merely a rather soothing image, as though both his anger and the causes of his anger had been dissolved in the lukewarm water of global consecration.

Allegories

If we postulate that Kafka's texts are encrypted, then it is impossible to avoid the question of allegory which has been (and continues to be) lengthily debated among specialists. In reality, even though it still arises each time a new interpretation of Kafka's work appears, the hypothesis of an allegorical intention on his part is very often dismissed with horror by the commentators.

Why this virtual unanimity? Doubtless because the very idea that a text may have been conceived as an allegory—that is, endowed with a hidden but intended meaning—runs very deeply counter to the patterns of thought that govern the activity of literary criticism at a subterranean level. The possibility is quite simply contrary to the conception literary critics and theorists have of themselves. Allegory has a bad reputation because, unlike symbols, for example, which might be said to be open and indeterminate, allegory 'would confine meaning within the dogmatism of a translation'.[47] Northrop Frye pointed out brilliantly that, 'The commenting critic is often prejudiced against allegory without knowing the real reason, which is that continuous allegory prescribes the direction of his commentary, and so restricts its freedom.'[48] This means that if critics aspire to exercise their interpretative freedom without the restriction of any 'historical corrective', to borrow Erwin Panofsky's magnificent expression,[49] allegory seems an intolerable constraint. As Angus Fletcher puts it, for example, allegory dictates a general meaning and imposes significations in a quasi-authoritarian manner. In other words, it reduces the reader's freedom.[50]

Now, if we consent to let the critical freedom (and the freedom as critics) that we claim be restricted by the evidence of a literary project, it seems to me we can re-evaluate the notion of allegory. To be more precise about this trope, I shall draw here on the definition provided by Joëlle Gardes Tamine and Marie-Antoinette Pellizza from a linguistic perspective. These authors prefer the definition of allegory as a discourse *with a double meaning* over the canonical definitions which regard it either as a device that consists in saying one thing to mean another[51] or as a move from the abstract to the concrete. At first sight, allegory presents only one—literal—meaning. But in allegory, as distinct from metaphor, all the words have a literal and a figurative sense. However, one of the essential dimensions of allegory, which distinguishes it from both symbol and metaphor, is that the second meaning may possibly be neither perceived nor understood.[52] By the same token, the two levels do not coexist and the two meanings are not simultaneous: 'in all cases', assert the two linguists, 'there is allegory because the two series which the unfolding narrative brings into play are independent.'[53] Moreover, and contrary to some received opinion on the subject, allegory is not based on something preconstructed, on a stereotyped, fixed symbolism. Rather, it constructs a parallel, 'which we might term analogy, but which is the consequence, not the source, of the figure'.[54] This is why there is no confusion between the two series, since the two significations do not in principle have anything to do with each other. As a result, allegory is open and may give rise to contradictory interpretations. Gardes Tamine and Pellizza therefore provide another, more precise and restrictive definition of the trope: '[A]llegory is a particular style that involves writing with a double meaning, for which an entire linguistic unit—sentence, text fragment or text— serves to convey a second meaning which is not made explicit and may therefore remain virtual.'[55] They refuse to reduce it, on the one hand, to personification (which is, in their view, merely a particular case) or, on the other, to the shift from the abstract to the concrete:[56] 'Figuration, personification and concrete illustration are merely possible consequences of a mechanism of double meaning.'[57] On the other hand, they do establish a typology of its different forms. They separate explicit allegories from implicit. The former provide instructions for their decipherment and yield up the keys to the coded text; the latter, by contrast, are far more numerous and remain enigmatic. The interpretation of these implicit allegories can never be certain. We also meet with allegories of varying lengths and there is a contrast to be made between 'generalized allegories' (such as the Homeric epics or Saint-John Perse's *Anabase*) and 'minimal' or 'local allegories' (such as proverbs) and also 'intermittent allegories'. Given the need to explicate its meaning, every allegory represents a puzzle which, 'for the person who has perceived it, has to be solved since, insofar as it involves no syntax or rhetorical figure specific to it and deploys only a coherent literal meaning, it exists only *in potentia* and its second meaning may pass unnoticed by the unwary reader.'[58]

If we accept this restricted definition of allegory as a discourse with a double meaning which has a latent meaning independent of its manifest one, it seems clear to me that we have to regard Kafka's texts as allegories. Except for those who subscribe to the poststructuralist hypothesis of undecidable, random meaning, it is impossible not to regard them as narratives with a double meaning. Even those who favour biographical interpretation—seeing *The Trial*, for example, as a transposition of the breaking off of Kafka's engagement with Felice—assume that the texts are written with the intention of conveying a double meaning and that the literal sense conceals or encodes the second meaning—in this case biographical. But we must be clear right away that what are at issue here are implicit, generalized allegories and that Kafka, as a good allegorologist, is utilizing the various possibilities offered by the figure of allegory: personification (in 'A Little Woman', for example), generalized allegory (as in *The Trial*), the shift from the abstract to the concrete (as in 'In the Penal Colony' or 'The Village Schoolmaster'), etc.

Critics often refer to a letter from Kafka to Buber to 'prove' the inadmissibility of the allegorical interpretation of Kafka's texts. We know that, in the October and November 1917 issues of his magazine *Der Jude*, Buber published two stories by Kafka, 'Jackals and Arabs' and 'A Report to an Academy', under the title 'Two Animal Stories'. Now this general title appeared at Kafka's request, after he had rejected Buber's suggestion that he use the title 'Allegories [*Gleichnisse*]'.[59] In reality, it seems to me that this anecdote is to be understood at several levels. On the one hand, if Kafka sent his stories to the famous Zionist magazine, which had the emancipation of the Jews as its exclusive aim, we may legitimately take the view that the two stories can have no other subject than an examination (even an extended examination, as I have shown) of the question of Jewishness.[60] This interpretation applies to the two published texts and also to the others: Kafka had sent a dozen stories, inviting Buber to choose from among them.[61]

Moreover, the simple fact that Buber agreed to publish them and proposed to do so under the heading 'Allegories' proves that, in that context, their meaning was crystal clear and, in his view, they were not in any way ambiguous. The disagreement between Kafka and Buber did not relate to the meaning to be attributed to the texts but to whether they belonged to the genre of allegory. This disagreement— and it must be said that it was not total, as Kafka simply wrote to Buber that 'they are not really allegories [*Gleichnisse*]'[62]—bears, it seems to me, precisely on the fact of their being folk tales. Since Kafka is, among other things, transposing a Kabyle fable which relates the law of the tyranny of one social group over another, a thing he does in the mode of cruel irony, it is not, as he sees it, properly speaking, an allegory which, in the usage of the day, involved a desire to convey ideas or an abstract message figuratively (often through personification). In Kafka's eyes, these two 'animal stories' are, much more simply, fables or folk tales, a genre that no one would think to ennoble by honouring it with the name of allegory. The two stories are satirical, violent and cruel and their very tone is at odds with the seriousness of the 'message' involved in allegorical transposition as understood in Kafka's Austria. In other words, it seems possible to me to include Kafka's stories in the category of 'allegories' even though the author himself appeared to reject that label. We do not understand the term in quite the same way as he did and the simple principle that these were texts designed to be understood on the basis of a double meaning (without the second meaning being either explicit or obvious) seems beyond question to me.

Against the hypothesis of a 'symbolic' meaning, Adorno and Benjamin proposed to include Kafka's stories within the category of *parable*, a category very close to allegory, though in this case they regarded the parable as an indecipherable one. As Adorno saw it, for example, Kafka could be said to have produced 'a parabolic system the key to which has been stolen'.[63] Benjamin asserts that Kafka's texts are allegorical stories but, at the same time, that one should not attempt to interpret them. 'Kafka had a rare capacity for creating parables for himself. Yet his parables are never exhausted by what is explainable; on the contrary, he took all conceivable precautions against the interpretation of his writings.'[64]

THE TRIAL, OR HUMILIATION

The reader will, of course, have understood that I disagree profoundly with Benjamin's viewpoint on Kafka. And I should like to present a detailed reading of *The Trial* to this effect. I realize that it might appear presumptuous or naive to aspire to offer a new interpretation of *The Trial*, which is probably one of the world's most famous novels and has given rise to countless different readings. But the enormous detour I have made through the history of the Prague literary space and the space of Jewish literary struggles was intended solely to enable me to go back to the texts and provide tools for their interpretation. The reading I offer here is, so to speak, the culmination and product of this historical work and can be justified only if it becomes a genuine instrument for understanding the texts.

Michael Löwy has summed up the situation by showing that there are four main schools of interpretation of the novel. First, there are the religious interpretations, which see the tribunal as a divine authority to which man is required to submit. Second, there are the moral interpretations, which assume K.'s guilt and the legitimacy of his conviction. Then come the autobiographical and psychoanalytic interpretations, which relate the narrative to the breaking off of

Kafka's engagement to Felice Bauer. A fourth path has been sketched out by Arendt's interpretation, a position recently reinforced by Michael Löwy and Bernd Neumann among others: this is a political interpretation of the novel.[65] It is this path I shall take, though I shall diverge from preceding interpretations.

The Trial seems to me to be a text emblematic of the project of social criticism devised by Kafka, in which he worked on the two aspects of the social mechanisms that concerned him. I propose to regard it as a double narrative in which we see, on the one hand, anti-Semitic suspicion and designation—that is to say, the mechanisms of collective belief that enable anti-Semitic convictions to develop and perpetuate themselves in the social world—and, on the other, the—symmetrical—effects which this disavowed suspicion produces among those who are its victims. On this assumption, the novel can be said to be an almost theatrical staging of the (in Kafka's social world, relatively banal and everyday) situation of anti-Semitic denunciation and suspicion from the standpoint of the victim. As Arendt brilliantly points out in reference to The Castle, the character Josef K. is clearly a Western Jew, not because of any 'typically Jewish trait, but [because of] the fact that he is involved in situations and perplexities distinctive of Jewish life'.[66]

Continuing his 'ethnographic' project of describing the fate of Western Jews, Kafka, who initially, in 'In the Penal Colony', which was written at the same period, placed emphasis on the 'machine'— in other words, on 'judicial' organization and the avenues by which collective belief is perpetuated—concerns himself in The Trial with both the social workings of this same 'machine' and, most importantly, the effects of this law on the accused themselves. Politzer, for example, spoke of the novel as a 'Trial against the Court'.[67] K. takes the view rather early on that 'this court was just as repulsive on the inside as it was on the outside.'[68] This is also no doubt why the places dependent on the court, including the offices of the 'court officials' and Titorelli's studio, are described as confined, 'squalid', oppressive, 'horrible' and 'dirty',[69] as though Kafka were trying to make both his character (who experiences feelings of faintness) and his readers feel the age-old, changeless, eternal character of anti-Semitic condemnation.[70]

The Court

In the first place, the story postulates the existence of a 'parallel judicial system', as Jean-Pierre Morel puts it, possessing a specialized, hierarchical staff, a bureaucracy, judges, lawyers and other operatives (guards, 'thrashers' and executioners).[71] And Kafka stresses that this system—or 'organization' as Josef K. defines it in the third chapter[72]—is, despite its clear iniquity and violence, not at all incompatible with the *Rechtstaat* or 'state of laws'. More than this, Kafka seems to suggest that this organization, far from clashing with the prevailing order, actually prospers in this *Rechtstaat* which happily tolerates the injustice and violence of its methods being exerted against certain of its nationals. 'After all, K. had rights, the country was at peace, the laws had not been suspended—who, then, had the audacity to descend on him in the privacy of his own home?' he asks at the time of his arrest.[73]

Unlike ordinary judicial institutions, however, this organization which is known to all and accepted by everyone—a power before which everyone bows and to which all lend assent, a body with offices and tribunals—nonetheless operates on rumour and semi-official materials, and *in camera*. It is not genuinely secret since everyone seems to know of its existence and no one seems surprised by K.'s arrest; but it is neither entirely public nor wholly private, neither entirely official nor wholly unofficial. This kind of ambiguous status gives rise to a deliberately maintained ignorance which promotes fear. The court is shrouded in a sort of increasingly threatening halo of mystery. The law is not secret but people are kept ignorant of it. And K. is rapidly caught in the toils of the contradictions inherent in this ignorance: ' "That is not a law I am acquainted with," said K. [. . .] "Look, Willem, he admits he doesn't know the law and at the same time claims he's innocent".'[74] And further on, in the empty conference hall, when K. is refused permission to take a look at the books on the judge's table, he comments: '[I]t's part of this legal system that one is condemned when one is not only innocent, but also ignorant.'[75] The prosecution proceeds in the most opaque manner imaginable, the judgement is not communicated to the defendant ('The court's final decisions are not published,'[76] warns the painter Titorelli), the procedure is 'not in public', the indictment is 'not available' to the defendant and a defence counsel is 'only tolerated'.[77] The defendant is drawn into a process which is entirely obscure. He is unable to foresee how things will develop, he knows nothing, understands nothing and his fate depends not on his alleged 'offence' but on the arbitrary decisions of a totally opaque organization.

So much is this the case that we no doubt have to understand the court's task as the reverse of the action carried out by an ordinary judicial institution. It has often been pointed out that the German word Kafka chose as his title, *Der Prozess*, means not only 'trial' but also 'process' (among other things, a pathological process).[78] Keeping this meaning in mind, we may hypothesize that it is the court's task not to punish a prior offence but to organize a very powerful system, with the totality of the social world playing its part in this—a process aimed first at producing, then maintaining, all possible forms of social humiliation. The offence is not the event which, as in ordinary legal procedure, *prompts* the judicial institution to act. Quite the contrary: from the arrest onwards (and perhaps even before that, as all K.'s ambiguities seem to indicate—since he seems to know these mechanisms without entirely recognizing them), a system is put in place which *produces* his suffering *ex post facto*. The court chaplain comes near to acknowledging this explicitly when he meets K. in the cathedral, without K. apparently understanding quite what is being said to him: '[T]he verdict does not come all of a sudden, the proceedings gradually turn into the verdict.'[79]

We may have the impression, as has often been highlighted, that only more lowly employees of the court appear in the novel. In reality, one gradually comes to see that the court is everywhere. In other words, there are no lower or higher judges but all the members of the social body belong, in one way or another, to the court. As though Kafka were trying to show us that, in order for the mechanism of anti-Semitic belief to operate, it required the collaboration of the entire social machine. From the first chapter onwards, in parallel with the initial scene of his arrest, there is persistent emphasis on the presence of a kind of eager, voyeuristic audience watching through the windows what is happening to Josef K. Even before the guards who have come to arrest him knock on his door, he glimpses from his bed, 'the old woman who lived opposite watching with, for her, quite unusual curiosity'.[80] The group of onlookers at the window continues to grow as it becomes clearer that he is under arrest and they show their hostile intentions ever more overtly. The attitude of K.'s landlady herself, Frau Grubach, who listens at the door, then contrives things so that she does not have to shake his hand—as though he had suddenly become a pariah—reveals, despite all her denials and assurances of cordiality, that she is in on the proceedings.[81] At his first hearing, K. is faced with a 'throng'[82] of people who very much resemble the onlookers of the first scene. Kafka sketches quite a terrifying portrait of them: 'They were all of them older men [. . .] Small black eyes darting to and fro, cheeks drooping like a drunkard's, the long beards stiff and sparse, and if you stuck your fingers into one it was as if you were making it into claws.'[83] The three bank clerks, whom K. encountered at the end of the first chapter and who will reappear several times throughout the story—'these insignificant, colourless young men [. . .] Rabensteiner stiff, swinging his arms, Kullich, blond with deep-set eyes, and Kaminer with the intolerable smile caused by a chronic muscular spasm'[84]—represent for some intepreters the three components of Prague's population at the time: the Czechs, the Jews and the Germans (let us note, in passing, that two of their names begin with K). If we accept this apparently quite credible hypothesis, we may suppose that, through these three somewhat ridiculous characters, Kafka is attacking the Prague social body as a whole, with particular anger reserved for the Germans. The ironic reference to Kaminer's fixed grin—which 'unfortunately common humanity forbade making a joke about'[85]—is clearly a sideswipe against what Kafka sees as collective hypocrisy on the part of the Germans.

It is only gradually that K. comes to understand the omnipresence of the court. 'So many people have connections with the court!' he exclaims when the industrialist informs him that he too is aware of his trial. '[E]verything belongs to the court,' admits the painter, not just the priest but also the threatening, troubling girls besieging his studio. As Kundera points out, without attributing the actual structure of the narrative to the workings of anti-Semitism:

> [N]o one doubts that K. is guilty. Society has already adopted the accusation and added the weight of its tacit approval (or its nondisagreement). We would expect indignant surprise: 'How could they accuse you? And for what crime, exactly?' But the uncle is not surprised. He is only frightened by the thought of the trial's consequences for all the relatives.[86]

So far as the description of this strange judicial machine is concerned, the extent of Kafka's realism is striking. Contrary to appearances, this is not a fantastical tale in the sense of each element being only very distantly related to—or a distortion of—social reality. There are, in fact, quite a lot of allusions to precise social situations. Block's talk about his lawyers is, for example, a way of referring to real events. He explains to K. the difference between what he terms the petty and the great lawyers:

> 'The great lawyers?' asked K. 'Who are they? How do you approach them?' [. . .] 'There's hardly a defendant who, once he's heard of them, doesn't dream of them for a while. But don't be tempted. I don't know who the great lawyers are, and I presume you can't get to them. I know of no case where it can be said for certain that they took part. They defend some people, but you can't get them to do that through your own efforts, *they only defend the ones they want to defend.*'[87]

On the basis of the hypothesis I am arguing here, it is impossible to see these few lines as anything but a mocking description of the few great anti-Semitic trials in which a number of famous lawyers did indeed intervene, on their own initative, to defend and save the accused. Kafka must be thinking, in part, of Émile Zola's intervention in the Dreyfus Affair, but, above all, he will have in mind the much closer case of Tomáš Masaryk, the famous Bohemian politician and future first president of Czechoslovakia, who had acted as a defence counsel for Leopold Hilsner, condemned to death at his first trial. At a second trial in 1900, Masaryk managed to have the sentence reduced, though only to life imprisonment. Kafka is actually highlighting the fact that these interventions by major public figures in the most high-profile trials of Jews depend on the goodwill of these famous lawyers and merely mask the truth of the everyday cases in which defendants are convicted without any great ado. Most importantly, these very rare 'affairs' give the impression that the system is ultimately fair. In reality Kafka is arguing, through the way *The Trial* is constructed, that the existence or chance intervention of these great lawyers does nothing to alter the violence and routine unfairness of the court's workings.

The Defendant

As the power of this active but silent judicial machine unfurls, *The Trial* also tells the story of the inculcation of the law. That is to say, it relates the progressive submission of an assimilated Jew to the law of inequality and humiliation of which he had up to that point been unaware or feigned ignorance. The novel tells how a senior administrator in a bank, after initially treating his arrest loftily and contemptuously (not believing what is happening to him and feeling sure he is in the right), gradually goes into decline, loses his assurance, grows afraid and finds his professional ambitions threatened. Compare K.'s peremptory tone in the third chapter, his stinging, 'harsh' remarks to the examining magistrate[88] with the fear that begins gradually to overwhelm him from the seventh chapter onwards. By that point K. is literally obsessed with his trial: the idea that he should 'draw up a written statement and submit it to the court' invades his entire existence to the point where it threatens his career, which he can no longer pursue normally.[89] Gradually, the energy and concentration required to draw up a submission to the court and the general strain involved prevent him from working. His rival at the bank, the deputy manager (whom we may suspect of being responsible for K.'s trial and of having denounced him to the court in the first place), takes over some of his functions, steals his clients, invades his office and becomes openly contemptuous. As a realist, Kafka is hinting at the idea that, in addition to humiliation, the anti-Semitic suspicion that hovers over assimilated Jews in an ordinary professional career prevents them from being appointed to the highest positions, keeps them in subordinate roles and forces them to channel the energy required for success into other things that are both invisible and too shameful to mention. '[I]t was the whole trial, and it was impossible to say how long that would last. What an obstruction had suddenly been placed in the way of K.'s career!'[90] This idea is corroborated by what the corn merchant Block tells K. in the eighth chapter. He explains that he has sacrificed everything to his trial, that as a consequence he now has hardly any possessions and has given up all professional ambitions or commercial success to devote himself entirely to the judicial process which requires both his energies and his money. He lives today with the bare mini-mum: 'I've spent everything I possess on this trial. For example, I've taken all the money out of my business. Before, my offices took up almost a whole storey, today a box-room at the back of the yard is enough for me and an apprentice. It's not only the withdrawal of money that has caused the decline in my business, but also the withdrawal of my own labour.'[91] We can thus detect what one of K.'s possible futures would have been if he had not been condemned to a swift death: he would have been quickly outstripped by his rival, the deputy manager, and relegated to some lowly function. Kafka is also making reference to the assimilated Jewish middle and upper-middle classes and the specific forms of obloquy they suffer as a result of their ostracization. K. has a superior position. He is, as he tells the examining magistrate at his first hearing, 'senior accountant with a large bank'.[92] This explains his initial assuredness, his spontaneously hierarchical view of the world and his conviction that he should not speak with 'these lowest of officials' but 'with someone of my own kind'.[93] But his case is not unique: as he is walking through the offices with the usher, he sees queues of people consisting of defendants who, 'to go by their facial expressions, posture, beards, and many other imperceptible little details, belonged to the middle classes'.[94] These are the people primarily subject to humiliation, along with the commercial classes, as is underscored by the eighth chapter which centres on 'Block, the corn merchant'.[95] The moving scene of K.'s encounter with a 'man whose hair was almost grey already' stresses very concretely that their suffering and shame is all the greater for their belonging to the bourgeoisie. The man, paralysed by the fear of harming his own cause, cannot bring himself to reply to the questions K. asks, 'which was all the more embarrassing because he was obviously a man with experience of the world who, elsewhere, would surely be able to control himself and would not easily relinquish the superiority he had achieved over others'.[96] We see here the refined nature of Kafka's quasi-sociological analysis. This total loss of resources on the part of the defendants elicits condescension from the 'officials' or, in other words, that kind of pronounced 'amiability' shown to 'the suspects' by all the members of the court's staff—a courtesy and apparent neutrality which actually underpin the entire stigmatization process. They all pretend not to be personally involved or able to do anything about the situation ('I am exceeding my instructions in talking to you in this friendly manner, but I hope there is no one to hear it apart from Franz, who himself has behaved towards you in a friendly manner, contrary to all regulations,' says one of the guards who came to arrest K. in the first chapter).

It is at this point that we are able to glimpse the structure of the second strand of the book. Kafka, who is close to Scholem's position in this regard and feels something of the same political violence, also attacks the Germanized Jewish bourgeoisie which, because of its desire to 'disappear' as Jewish and to be like the Germans or Czechs, blinds itself to the real possibilities of its 'dissolution' or, in other words, its assimilation. For Kafka, it is because he is trying to be like everyone else, because he does not want to be noticed, because he does not want to be different in any way but, rather, to join the group from which he has been cut off and into which he wishes to be reintegrated, that the supposed offender, unwillingly designated as Jewish, accepts the very principle underlying his accusation and trial or, in other words, agrees to submit himself to the torment of shame. Assimilation is described by Kafka as a social trap from which there is 'no way out' and it consists for K.—that is, for Jews as a whole—in accepting the unjust fate meted out to him on pain of seeing his very assimilation cast into doubt once again. While he is being humiliated, he is also made to believe that, in order to have an (entirely illusory) 'chance' of being 'acquitted', it is better that he does not deny the charge against him, as unjust and arbitrary as it may be, on pain of being immediately and irremediably stigmatized —that is to say, of losing his trial and experiencing exclusion. The trial is, therefore, an instrument of systematic suspicion with regard to Jews, enabling an assurance to be extracted that they will not raise their voices against this procedure. '[D]on't go on about your feelings of innocence so much, it spoils the not exactly unfavourable impression you otherwise make,' K. is told by the guards who come to arrest him.[97] '[S]top being intransigent, no one can resist this court, you just have to confess. Confess at the next opportunity.'[98] 'The only correct approach', the lawyer advised him, 'was to accept things as they were [. . .] The essential things was not to attract attention, to stay calm, however much it went against the grain.'[99] In this way, Block is condemned to obeying the most absurd orders of his tyrannical lawyer and to indefinite enslavement to his so-called defence lawyer, because of the distant possibility of an allegedly favourable outcome to his trial and the restoration of his honour.

To his description of the mechanisms of the court, Block adds:

Acting in common gets you nowhere against the court, every case is examined on its own merits, it is a most meticulous court. So acting in common gets them nowhere, only an individual can sometimes achieve something in secret, but it's only after it's been achieved that the others get to hear about it, and no one knows how it happened. So there is no common ground.[100]

In other words, Kafka is stressing, no solidarity or collective action is ever mobilized in the struggle against the court. Among the Germanized Jews there is no form of solidarity that could enable them to rebel against, or protect themselves from, the fate reserved for them. Along these same lines, Arendt points out that in *The Castle* Kafka shows us a lone Western Jewish character, 'For insofar as the Jew seeks to become "indistinguishable" from his gentile neighbours he has to behave as if he were indeed utterly alone; he has to part company, once and for all, with all who are like him.'[101] Everyone undergoes this torment of 'accusation' alone and does so without any possible remedy or appeal to precedent or assistance. Preoccupied with having to 'justify' themselves or 'prove their innocence'—and hence be recognized as average Germans—they forget to defend themselves as a group, that is to say, to defend themselves on the very basis of their Jewish identity.

Humiliation

In *The Trial*, Kafka is describing the particular form of anti-Semitism propagated in Western Europe, where the Jews are striving to assimilate, where they are being encouraged to do so officially but are, in reality, prevented from doing so by a doublespeak we see at work throughout the book. The particular form of stigmatization Kafka observes and describes may be defined as permanent—though disavowed—rejection and suspicion which claim to be based on an unknown set of laws and derive powerful legitimacy from that fact. Kafka shows himself to be very close here to the positions of Bernard Lazare who wrote, for example, in *Le Fumier de Job* of 1928:

> We no longer fence off Israelites in the West. We no longer put chains across the ends of streets. But we do create a hostile atmosphere around them, an atmosphere of mistrust and latent hatred, of prejudices which are unspoken but all the more powerful for that—a ghetto much more fearsome than the one you could escape through rebellion or exile. Even if this animosity is concealed, the intelligent Jew is

aware of it; he feels a resistance; he has the impression there is a wall between him and the others in his environment.[102]

In its apparently indecisive form, K.'s arrest is quite simply the establishment of a dividing line between the accused and the others. It is merely the beginning of a long process that will ultimately give rise to a long humiliation, endlessly reinstated and reproduced with no prospect of remission or end, a kind of endlessly reiterated torment. Moreover, the text indicates in its fourth chapter, when K. is going through the offices, the absolute equivalence between arrest and humiliation. The men K. sees 'never stood completely upright, their backs were bowed, their knees bent, they stood there like beggars in the street'. 'How they must have been humiliated,' says K. ' "Yes," said the usher, "they're defendants, all those you see here are defendants".'[103] Though the court actually organizes the 'limitless' suffering of a section of the population of an indeterminate European constitutional state, as the 'Thrasher' chapter shows, the stigmatization never involves physical violence. Right up to his execution, K. is never whipped, manhandled or tortured physically. The system is much more perverse than that. What is involved is a—disavowed—process, allegedly unknown to the official institutions, proliferating in the shadows, in silence and in secrecy, but ultimately shored up by a 'law' which K., as he says at the beginning of the book, 'suspect[s] [. . .] only exists inside [their] heads',[104] and which underlies the collective humiliation of an entire social group.

Countless commentaries on *The Trial* speak of a 'sense of guilt' which purportedly explains K.'s behaviour. Referring to the fact that he accepts the verdict and colludes in his own execution, Arendt takes the view that, 'submission is obtained not by force but simply through an increase in the feeling of guilt roused in the accused K. by the baseless, empty accusation against him.'[105] Yet, remarkably, there is never any question in the text of an offence or guilt or, even less, a sense of guilt on K.'s part. In reality—and the text is very clear on this—what is at issue is, much rather, the inculcation or instilling in the accused of a sense of humiliation, followed by feelings of shame.

Bourdieu has, in his ethnological texts, clearly pointed out the differ-ence between shame and guilt. According to Bourdieu, 'shame [. . .] in contrast to guilt, is felt *before others.*'[106] This means, conversely, that guilt is experienced only in relation to oneself. Now, K. feels no private guilt; on the other hand, he very often undergoes humiliation in the presence of others. The precise definition of this feeling involves an external action aimed, as the three-volume *Dictionnaire Larousse* of 1966 puts it, at 'bringing public contempt on, belittling in the eyes of others or mortifying'. In the novel, humiliation is a first stage, imposed in a concerted way on the 'defendant' by the court. Then after humil-iation inflicted from the outside, K. arrives at a state of shame which is an internal matter. He is encouraged and, in a sense, condemned by the court—that is to say, by the entire social body—to experience, above and beyond humiliation, the embodied feeling and private con-viction of his own unworthiness. The court first humiliates him and thereafter the 'defendant' gradually moves to accept the stigma, to acquiesce in the sense of opprobrium. He begins to feel the shame that appears in the book's last sentence.

If shame is the 'reverse side' of honour,[107] and if honour is, to borrow Schopenhauer's definition, 'the representation of our value in the thoughts of others',[108] then the specific action of the court is to cause all those whom it designates, stigmatizes and condemns to lose their honour or, in other words, their social value. Schopenhauer notes specifically that 'honour, once lost, can never be recovered.'[109] This, he says, distinguishes it from all other goods and lends it a vir-tually absolute value. K. states the truth from the very beginning when he is still sufficiently lucid to understand what is happening: 'Naturally there was another purpose behind the presence of these [bank] clerks; like my landlady and her servant, they were to spread the news of my arrest, damaging my reputation and, especially, weakening my position at the bank.'[110] 'That is why,' he says further on, 'innocent people are humiliated before packed meetings.'[111] It is also why it is impossible to be genuinely acquitted, as the painter Titorelli explains to K. The mechanism of humiliation must be never-ending. Officially or, rather, according to what circulates officially about this semi-official institution, there are three possibilities, or, three possible outcomes to trials: 'genuine acquittal, apparent acquittal, and protraction of the proceedings'.[112] Now, Titorelli very quickly makes it clear that he has 'never come across a single genuine acquittal'.[113] 'People do say [. . .] that there have been such acquittals, only that's very difficult to ascertain.'[114] 'Apparent acquittal' remains, through which one can leave the court a free man, though, says the painter, 'you are freed from the charge for the moment, but it continues to hover over your head.'[115] Lastly there is protraction: 'Protraction is when the trial is kept permanently at the lowest stage.'[116] In this case, the trial is uninterrupted and is constantly being revived. Thus, the accused 'is almost as sure of not being condemned as if he were free', but he is 'never free'.[117]

Domination

What Kafka makes manifest are precisely the effects of that mysterious power exerted on minds and bodies which Bourdieu calls symbolic domination. This, says Bourdieu, is 'a social law converted into an embodied law'. It is a peculiarity of this form of domination, unlike all others, that it is exerted in the absence of any physical violence 'through the purely symbolic channels of communication and cognition (more precisely, misrecognition), recognition, or even feeling', as Bourdieu further elaborates. '[T]he only way to understand this particular form of domination is to move beyond the forced choice between constraint (by forces) and consent (to reasons), between mechanical coercion and voluntary, free, deliberate, even calculated submission.'[118]

In relation to Germans, liberal Jews, as Kafka describes them and thinks about them, were undeniably in a dominated position and suffering a symbolic violence of this kind—that is to say, an invisible violence whose effects were all the more pernicious for the fact that they themselves denied that violence (without totally failing to see it, as is indicated no doubt by K.'s strange admission in the first chapter: 'I am surprised, but I wouldn't go so far as to say I'm very surprised').[119] It seems to me that one of the great strengths of Kafka's story relates to the fact that he does more than just deliver a political message or narratively transpose a symbolism. He produces in literary form a very sophisticated analysis of the state of the real suffering of the Germanized Jewish communities of Western Europe in the first decade of the twentieth century. And, in doing so, he shows how and why the Jews are, so to speak, victims who at no point afford themselves the possibility of rebellion.

It seems to me it is only the conviction that he has to cope alone with a misfortune which is, in reality, a collective stigma that can explain why K. colludes in his own death. He is condemned by an external court in whose judgement he acquiesces as though he were, ultimately, being 'worked' by that court. It has such a hold on him that he anticipates its wishes. This is precisely what is registered in the famous last sentence of the text: 'It seemed as if his shame would live on after him.'[120] This is precisely the declaration of the 'law' in whose name K. is accused and condemned, the law everyone is expected to know, at the same time claiming not to.

As proof that Kafka is concerned with the question of symbolic violence overall, and not merely with the situation of Austrian Jews, he also provides some secondary plotlines that involve other powerful but invisible forms of domination. In particular, women are represented as subject to great violence very much akin to that meted out to Jews.

Like K., women are subject to the effects of rumour which can imperil their honour and deprive them of all 'social value'. In their behaviour they must at all times have regard to the opinion that will be formed of them. From the beginning, K.'s landlady Frau Grubach makes derogatory insinuations about Fräulein Bürstner. She claims to be reporting facts which are actually just malicious gossip aimed at damaging the young woman's reputation, and she does so in the classic mode of denegation: 'Far be it from me to do Fräulein Bürstner down [. . .] but one thing is true, she should have more self-respect, she should hold back more. I've twice seen her in out-of-the-way streets, and with a different gentleman each time.'[121] At these slanders, since that is no doubt what they are, K., who has just been arrested, exclaims: 'You're on the wrong track entirely.' '[F]urious and hardly able to conceal it,' he goes on: 'I warn you, and I mean it, not to say anything to her. You're completely wrong. I know the young lady very well, nothing of what you said is true.'[122] He seems to be reacting as though the fact of being arrested that very morning had suddenly made him sensitive to women's symbolic vulnerability.

The entire second part of the second chapter relating K.'s visit to Fräulein Bürstner seems intended to present two systems of honour in parallel or in competition; the two function differently but in each case honour is imperilled by the spreading of rumour and gossip. K. attempts to restore his reputation in Fräulein Bürstner's eyes, though she, not aware of his arrest, was not at all minded to form a poor opinion of him. In his efforts, K. tells the story and reconstructs the arrest as though it were a stage-play, making so much noise that the occupant of the next room bangs on the door. As a result, Fräulein Bürstner begins to fear for her own reputation. '[P]lease go, please go. What do you expect, he's listening at the door, he can hear everything. Why must you torment me so?' she exclaims.[123] Slow to leave the room, K. prevaricates, then kisses her lingeringly in the hallway —that is to say, in a place where they can be easily seen. In other words, K. subjects the woman to what he was himself subjected to that morning: he offends against her honour and casts suspicion on her, putting her social 'value' in question. Despite constant indications of reluctance, tiredness, lassitude and a desire to be left alone in her room, K. importunes her, forces her to see him at this late hour on trivial grounds and, most importantly, seriously imperils her reputation. He humiliates her. Returning, defeated, to her room, she adopts the posture which will be that of the defendants in the 'loft': 'She nodded wearily, letting him kiss her hand, though she had already half turned away, as if she were unaware of it, and went into her room, shoulders drooping.'[124] K. exerts a domination over this young woman that is akin to the domination inflicted on him. But he does so *as a man*, as though, having been dominated as a Jew, he is trying to prove to himself that he remains dominant, as a man, over a woman.

There is a parallel scene in the fourth chapter with the court usher's wife, who appeared in the previous chapter in the courtroom, where she had been dragged into a corner by a man who was 'pressing her to him'.[125] One week later, in the empty conference hall, she explains to K. that she is a married woman but that he has been pursuing her for a long time and she cannot refuse him because he is a law student and 'likely to become very powerful'.[126] The woman is saying that she is in a situation of dependence and has to submit to male violence and domination so as not to damage her husband's cause. Despite this—and no doubt because of it—she is very sensitive to the question of her honour or, in other words, to K.'s opinion: '[Y]ou can't go away with a wrong opinion of me. Could you really bring yourself to leave now? Do I mean so little to you that you won't even do me the favour of staying here a little longer?'[127] And when the student comes to fetch her, she says, 'Don't be angry with me, I beg you, and don't think ill of me, but I have to go to him now, to that horrible man.'[128] However, the description of their relationship is gripping, in part because K. yields very quickly to her attempt at seduction and in part because, though she is a victim of a violent, dominating relationship, the woman does not seek release from it. She does not want to be 'freed',[129] as K. himself tells her, from the 'tyranny'[130] the student exerts over her. Here, for the first time in the text, Kafka stresses one of the paradoxes of domination. The dominated are often so attached to their domination and so good at sustaining their own misfortune that no one can release them from it:

> 'And you don't want to be freed,' K. shouted, placing his hand on the shoulder of the student, who snapped at it with his teeth. 'No,' cried the woman, pushing K. away with both hands, 'no, no, that's the last thing I want, what are you thinking of! It would be the ruin of me. Let go of him, oh, please let go of him [. . .].'[131]

Her husband, himself humiliated by this situation, will remark further on that 'she's [. . .] most to blame. She threw herself at him,'[132] as though he were trying to repair the dishonour done to him by pointing to his wife, who is even more dominated than he, as the guilty party. It is as though Kafka were trying to show that even the most dominated of men themselves perpetuate other forms of domination, particularly on women who are right at the bottom of a virtual pyramid of power relations.

Physical and symbolic violence are all the time connected in *The Trial*. The guards being whipped in the lumber-room of the bank are much more afraid of the dishonour than the physical pain, and implore K. to spare them from such shame. The guard Franz says, for example, '[M]y reputation is unblemished [. . .] My poor fiancée's waiting outside the bank to see what happens. I'm so terribly ashamed.'[133]

However, as Kafka keeps his narrative demonstration under close control, with no single thread escaping his grasp, it is doubtless in the scene in the cathedral that he best manages to convey the connection between social and institutional structures and the perpetuation of forms of domination. Bourdieu stresses that, '[A] relation of domination that functions only through the complicity of dispositions depends profoundly, *for its perpetuation or transformation*, on the perpetuation or transformation of the structures of which those dispositions are the product.'[134] In other words, Kafka does not forget the proper order of priorities. He never forgets that violence and iniquity are, in the first instance, the product of social structures.

The Legend and the Cathedral

At the centre of this very ambitious denunciation of all the mechanisms that make the perpetuation of this 'judicial system' possible, Kafka depicts the institution underpinning and legitimating it: the Church. The cathedral is a figuring of the Church as an institution, the cornerstone of anti-Semitic condemnation, the immense spiritual and symbolic power which allowed it to operate. The Church is, so to speak, *the* social structure which, in Kafka's view, enables this system to be perpetuated. Within the logic of the narrative, it embodies the highest echelons of the court. Kafka's cathedral is remarkable for the almost total darkness in which it is plunged, the number of artworks visible there—or, in other words, its wealth: altarpieces, sculptures, silver statuettes, elaborately carved pulpits—and, most importantly, its immensity: '[T]he vastness of the cathedral seemed to be at the very limit of what was still bearable for human beings,' notes Kafka.[135] All these features show up the almost unlimited nature of the symbolic power and potency of the Church.

For K., the cathedral is also a troubling, solemn, obscure place. The dominant position the priest at first occupies, high up in his pulpit, beckoning to K. from the handrail, 'his forefinger pointing sharply downwards', so as to point out to him 'a place just in front of the pulpit',[136] clearly indicates the undisputed domination and highly authoritarian character of the Church. The whole ambiguity of this scene depends on the priest's doublespeak and K.'s blindness. ' "I'm not prejudiced against you," [says] the priest,'[137] but, quite remarkably, while keeping up a dialogue and showing apparent tolerance, he becomes increasingly menacing. He never denies either the existence of the court or the rightness of the charge levelled against K. Quite the contrary, he actually foretells K.'s death to him (though K. does not hear it): ' "How do you imagine it will end?" asked the priest [. . .] "Do you know?" [. . .] "No," said the priest, "but I fear it will end badly. They think you are guilty." '[138] He refers to K. as guilty and refuses to listen to the defence he essays on the grounds of their common humanity: ' "But I'm not guilty," said K., "it's a mistake. How can a person be guilty anyway? We're all human, every single one of us." "That is correct," said the priest, "but that's the way guilty people talk." '[139] This firm refusal to grant K. entry to the human community is both a disguised accusation and the marking of a boundary between the 'guilty' and the others. Then, while keeping up the dialogue, the chaplain constantly warns K. against his naivety and blindness and, at the same time, asserts himself as guardian of the order whose legitimacy is, so to speak, underwritten by the Church: 'You misunderstand the situation,' 'Can't you even see two steps in front of you?' 'You are deceiving yourself about the court,' 'First of all you must understand who I am.'[140] But K. remains deaf and blind to all the chaplain's warnings: 'At first you were very friendly [. . .] and explained everything,' he says as he leaves the priest.

Though she does not make the assumption that anti-Semitism is being condemned in *The Trial*, Arendt sees the chaplain, far more than the lawyer, as the agent of the organization and the representative of the 'order' urging submission upon K.: 'In other words, while the lawyer only tried to clarify the way of the world, the task of the chaplain employed by this very world is to provide proof that this is the world order [*Weltordnung*].'[141]

The 'legend' (that is to say, the text which Kafka referred to as such) plays a major role both in the conversation between K. and the priest and in the economy of the novel because it legitimates the latter's point of view by referring it to a very longstanding 'tradition'. It has given rise to even more commentaries and interpretations than *The Trial* itself and it is impossible to cover all of these here. We know that Kafka himself considered it particularly successful. It is the only section of the novel which he published in his lifetime— in *Selbstwehr* in September 1915, under the title 'Vor dem Gesetz [Before the Law]'.[142] Arendt finds in it the traces of a politics on Kafka's part (though the word itself does not figure in her account).

In this—familiar—text, we see depicted a 'man from the country' who is determined to be 'allowed into the Law' but is kept out by the doorkeeper [*der Türhüter*] who 'says he cannot let the man into the Law just now'.[143] The man decides to wait and, sitting on a stool near the ever-open door, he waits for years, making many requests to the doorkeeper and even trying to bribe him, but all in vain. The years go by and, as the man is nearing his end, the doorkeeper confides: 'No one else could be granted entry here, because this entrance was intended for you alone. I shall now go and shut it.'[144]

It seems to me that, in keeping with the whole of the novel, we have to read this as an anti-authoritarian fable. The legend would then be a way of duplicating the message of Kafka's book, in a different form: namely, that the greatest obstacle to freedom lies in submission to authority, in the symbolic potency of power, in the most dominated themselves internalizing a belief in the necessity of obedience to authority which consequently has no need to impose itself by force. The man from the country does not get through into the Law because he is a slave to power: he allows an arbitrary law to be imposed upon him because he agrees, without any physical constraint and while the door is all the time open, to believe the doorkeeper's threats, even though he has no evidence that they are true.

As a result, it seems to me that, rather than being a condemnation of K., the legend puts a strong critical stamp on the entire novel. It might be seen as a call to rebellion, an encouragement to reject the arbitrary injunctions of authority. In support of this argument, we find a number of narrative fragments in Kafka's diaries that make plain the man's relationship with the doorkeeper. In July 1914—that is, just before he begins writing *The Trial*—Kafka draws up one of the first outlines of the novel. In that sketch, the figures of Josef K. and the doorkeeper appear. The text is as follows:

> Josef K., the son of a rich merchant, one evening after a violent quarrel with his father, [. . .] went, with no definite purpose but only because he was tired and completely at a loss, to the house of the corporation of merchants which stood all by itself near the harbour. The doorkeeper made a deep bow, Joseph looked casually at him without a word of greeting. 'These silent underlings do everything one supposes them to be doing,' he thought. 'If I imagine that he is looking at me insolently, then he really is.' And he once more turned to the doorkeeper, again without a word of greeting; the latter turned towards the street and looked up at the overcast sky.[145]

We might understand this text as a 'non-legendary' version of the legend. It is a very rapid (and very brilliant) outline of the paradoxes of the authority relationship. The definition of the doorkeeper as 'underling' immediately implies that his authority is merely supposed, is merely the authority we attribute to him: 'We are,' says Paul Valéry, 'what others believe us to be.'[146] The doorkeeper's power depends on the belief of the person who appears before him. His strength is contained entirely within the person looking at him. On his own, he is empty (a 'silent underling'). In other words, it all depends on the person who comes before him or, more accurately, on the power that person attributes to him. They 'do everything one supposes them to be doing' or, rather, they do what one believes they do and, since they do nothing, their power depends on the interpretation we make of their lack of action. In the case of the legend, the doorkeeper's power is merely the power the man grants him. While no physical constraint prevents the man from entering, he believes the doorkeeper's power is such that he must respect his prohibition. Kafka transforms belief in power into one of the highest, most coercive, most potent forms of power. This belief is another name for the 'soft' domination exerted, without his knowing it, over the man from the country. Another very short text by Kafka, written in October 1920, presents quite a closely related idea:

> I ran past the first watchman. Then I was horrified, ran back again and said to the watchman: 'I ran through here while you were looking the other way.' The watchman gazed ahead of him and said nothing. 'I suppose I really oughtn't to have done it,' I said. The watchman still said nothing. 'Does your silence indicate permission to pass?'[147]

In this sense, the legend is a call to rebellion and insubordination, at the same time as presenting, through its very sophistication and the description of the infinite paradoxes of symbolic violence, the reasons why it is so difficult to rebel against the most insidious forms of domination. At any rate, it invites us to reread *The Trial* as a literary depiction of the idea that tyranny exists only for as long as its victims consent to believe in it.

The glosses and various contradictory interpretations that follow the telling of the legend round out this interpretation. First, the 'tradition'—that is to say, the legend accompanied by its canonical glosses—is referred to by the Catholic priest as the set of texts serving as preamble to the law. In other words, the legend belongs to a corpus of texts which legitimate and reinforce the law of stigmatization and humiliation. As Morel shows, K.'s immediate reaction to the telling of the story—'So the doorkeeper deceived the man'[148]—highlights the parallel between his own story and the legend:[149] like the man from the country agreeing to grant the doorkeeper total power over his own life, K. has agreed to submit to the arbitrary nature of the trial of which he is a victim. And, because of the proximity of his own case to the legend, he spontaneously produces the interpretation that seems inevitable from the victim's standpoint. His interpretation also stresses the self-evidence of the meaning of the legend—in its very simplicity—and the fact that the truth about the injustice done to the man is perfectly clear to the Church. Yet the priest rejects K.'s interpretation, asserts that there has been no deception and, against the obvious, simple truth of K.'s reading, immediately pits arguments that he takes from 'opinions' on the legend, all of which function to exculpate the doorkeeper (and hence to justify the social order and its injustice).[150] It is at this precise moment that we realize that he is, 'beneath an amiable exterior [. . .] the most dangerous of the representatives of justice'.[151] In fact, seen from the simplest standpoint (which is also K.'s), the doorkeeper in the legend, 'denies access to the Law, frightens the man, allows himself to be corrupted and reveals at the end that he afforded his victim no chance'.[152] Yet, as the priest forcefully contends, the doorkeeper does his 'duty' and 'respects his superiors'.[153] In other words, he respects the social order. At this point in his demonstration, the priest explains to K. what a relationship of symbolic domination is or, one might say, clarifies the effect that he himself exerts on K.: 'The assumption is that for many years, as many as it takes for a man to grow to maturity, his task was *purely symbolic*.'[154] Then he drives home what is the ultimate verity for those charged with the maintenance of the established order: 'one doesn't have to take everything as the truth, one just has to accept it as necessary.'[155] Arendt bases her interpretation of *The Trial* on this precise point. She sees in this declaration the description of a world in which arbitrary 'necessity' alone takes precedence over truth: 'The [judicial] machine is kept in motion by the lies told for the sake of necessity.'[156] According to Arendt, K. will be changed and shaped, 'until he is fit to assume the role forced upon him, which is to play along as best he can in a world of necessity, injustice and lies'.[157]

However this may be, K. has the last word. He closes the discussion resoundingly, with the words: 'A depressing opinion [. . .] It means that the world is founded on untruth.'[158] And this is the world view underlying *The Trial*: the law as lie and lying as law. The truth is that the man from the country is deceived, but the deception (the injustice, stigmatization and humiliation) is both denied and endlessly repeated because it is seen as 'necessary' for the order of the world. This is doubtless also the metaphorical reason why the cathedral becomes constantly darker and darker. After this episode, K. and the chaplain do, indeed, walk in darkness and K. is completely lost 'in the dark'.[159]

It seems to me that if this interpretive hypothesis is accepted, we rediscover the critical thrust of the book. In many respects the story is often violent. Kafka's call to rebellion in this novel is also a call to freedom. But the power of the mechanism of the forgetting of history, which always accompanies the universalization of a text, has been so great in the case of this globalized narrative that its subtle narrative strategies, dependent on the location of the Prague literary field within the global literary space of the time, have been lost. Once Kafka's world and its great complexity disappeared, the—very particular—conditions for understanding his texts were also lost. And what has vanished, most importantly, is the writer's anger, his analysis of a political situation and his rebellion.

We find condemnations of the Catholic Church or, more broadly, of Christianity in several texts and in very different forms. The Church was, in fact, the Western institution which played a central role in the social and political life of Austria,[160] in the dissemination of anti-Semitism and in the acculturation of colonized populations that were abandoning their original cultural identities.

At the biographical level, when Kafka discovered the plays of the Yiddish theatre repertoire, the first thing that excited him and seemed highly innovative was the guilt-free relationship of the Jewish characters with the Christians: 'Some songs, [. . .] some of this woman's acting (who, on the stage, because she is a Jew, draws us listeners to her because we are Jews, without any longing for or curiosity about Christians) made my cheeks tremble,'[161] he notes in his diary on 5 October 1911, the day of the first performance he attended. He returned the next day and in his diary summarized the play he had just seen. It tells the story of a converted Jew who has renounced his Jewishness: 'Twenty years ago Seidemann, a rich Jew, obviously having marshalled all his criminal instincts towards that end, had himself baptized [. . .] In the last act the presiding judge is again the eternal Dragomirow (in this, too, contempt is revealed for the Christian . . .).'[162] Peter Sprengel notes that generally in the Yiddish theatre (but particularly in the two plays Kafka saw on 4 and 8 October 1911, Abraham Sharkanski's *Der Meshumed* and Joseph Lateiner's *Die Seydernacht*[163]) the conflicts between Jews and non-Jews were staged in such a way as to reverse the European theatrical cliché of the Jewish character (embodied preeminently in Shylock).[164] The 'villains of the piece' were Christians or converted Jews. This theatrical reversal of the ordinary balance of forces (shown routinely in Czech or German theatre) obviously played a key part in making these plays immediately attractive to Kafka (together with the Jewish actresses who were on stage, with whom he instantaneously fell in love).

This is why, when it comes to his fiction, it seems entirely possible to adopt anti-Christian interpretations of certain of his texts, interpretations which are most often dismissed on the grounds that this is to read too explicit a meaning into them. For example, with regard to 'In the Penal Colony', David writes: 'The epilogue devised by Kafka [. . .] runs the risk of giving the whole piece an anti-Christian coloration that would distort its meaning: the faith conjured up by the story must remain imprecise.'[165] But why should it? That epilogue, which alludes in a quasi-transparent way to the Christian belief in resurrection, has to be taken into account, it seems to me, and this enables us to see the meaning of the text quite simply, even though Kafka expressed the opinion on several occasions that he was not happy with it. In that epilogue to the published version of

'In the Penal Colony', the Commandant's grave, which now lies hidden because his supporters have gone underground, bears the following inscription: 'Here rests the old Commandant. His adherents, who must now be nameless, have dug this grave and set up this stone. There is a prophecy that after a certain number of years the Commandant will rise again and lead his adherents from this house to recover the colony. Have faith and wait!'[166] I believe this derisive, comical, highly blasphemous version of the Christian message of the resurrection and, subsequently, of the triumph of Christ— reduced, in this case, to the reconquest of a wretched colony to be ruled by an absolute order of colonial oppression and domination— lends 'In the Penal Colony' its full meaning and restores the harshness of its polemical, political intention. And there has perhaps been a little too much emphasis on Kafka's (apparent) discontent with it, precisely so as not to hear what the story was saying.

Similarly, if the second interpretation I have proposed of 'Jackals and Arabs' is adopted, that too can be seen as a parody of Christian prophecy. The cowardice of the jackals is such that they implore the explorer to kill the Arabs for them. But they do so on the pretext of an ancient tradition: '[W]e have been waiting endless years for you; my mother waited for you, and her mother, and all our foremothers right back to the first mother of all the jackals. It is true, believe me!'[167] This belief on the part of the jackals, which inverts the Christian dogma of the 'Father',[168] is also mendacious, since the explorer replies:

[T]hat is very surprising for me to hear. It is by pure chance that I have come here from the far North, and I am making only a short tour of your country [. . . W]hat you have just said agrees with our old tradition [. . .] And so, O lord, and so, O dear lord, by means of your all-powerful hands slit their throats through with these scissors.[169]

The European is transformed by the jackals into a prophet destined from all eternity to rid them of the Arabs. In a mode that parodies Christian prayer, the jackals turn the traveller into an instrument of their hatred by a kind of derisive, cynical, sanguinary

displacement of the functions of the Christian prophet who is supposed to have to come to 'save' the believers, incapable as they are,
given the state of subordination in which they find themselves, of
fulfilling the prophecy themselves. The jackals' 'prophet' is a chance
traveller and the text parodies Christian messianism.

A Prophetic Little Woman

One of the stories in which the two inseparable aspects of Kafka's
anger—relating to anti-Semitism and assimilation—appear most
clearly is probably 'A Little Woman', one of the last texts he wrote in
Berlin a few months before he died. Contrary to Brod's claim, it is
unlikely that Kafka met any 'quite slim [. . .] tightly laced' little woman
when he moved to Berlin in 1923. Or perhaps this is actually the portrait of the woman who was Kafka and Dora Diamant's landlady at
Berlin in September 1923 and who gave them notice to quit in the
November of that same year. The little woman both exists and does
not exist. She does not refer to anyone in particular and could be anyone herself. Presenting a collective entity while appearing to describe
a particular individual is a technique Kafka had fully mastered by this
point. The little blonde woman is a 'perfectly normal' Berliner. The
little blonde hatless woman dressed in grey is in no way remarkable,
except perhaps for the discontent she feels with the narrator. Kafka
hides as much as he shows, dissimulates even as he reveals and drives
home his point without ever mentioning the key word around which
his story revolves. He does much more than tell a story; he sets
out the reality of a social relationship consisting of hatred, rejection,
distaste and lack of understanding.

In two pages he puts in place the central configuration of the
story: the arbitrary, unjustified and yet undoubted 'torment' the narrator causes this little woman and the negative judgement public
opinion passes on the narrator because of these aspersions that are
cast so underhandedly. In other words, by way of this interior monologue, Kafka describes both the forms of an inexplicable ostracism
and, conversely, the effects of the internalization and acceptance of
this permanent violence by the victims. Kafka gives a rapid, yet detailed,

description of the paradox of the relationship connecting the little woman and the narrator. He stresses that the two protagonists are at once strangers to each other and yet linked by their mutual rejection. However, placed in a position in which he is accused in this way, the narrator is beginning to fear 'the court of public opinion'. He is fearful the world will ask him, 'why am I tormenting the poor little woman.' He wonders, then, if he shouldn't 'change [him]self [. . .] to lessen the little woman's rancour'.[170] He rejects the advice of one of his friends that he should 'go away for a short time', insisting that he is intent on 'keeping the affair within its present narrow limits which do not yet involve the outside world'.[171] He has just one strategy, which is 'to stay quietly where I am' and prevent the affair causing any significant, noteworthy changes to his life, which also means speaking to no one about it. Gradually the narrator elevates the little woman into his 'judge [*Richterin*]'.[172] Like K. during his trial, he hopes therefore that she will allow him to 'justify himself', as though he were playing an active part in her torment. Alas, nothing of the kind happens: '[T]here was no decisive moment, no justification.'[173]

As the reader will see, this short story reproduces exactly the situation of *The Trial*, though it reduces the confrontation to two characters. It seems to me the little woman personifies German anti-Semitism and the narrator the paradoxical position of the liberal Jews who not only accept this injustice and violence but indeed set about incorporating it into, and turning it against, themselves. Like K., the narrator is dead set on convincing himself, against all the evidence, that this is a 'trivial, purely personal matter', that he is going to be able to 'justify himself', that it is just a question of 'keep[ing his] hand over it, even quite lightly' and that, in this way, he will 'continue to live [his] own life for a long time to come, untroubled by the world'.[174] But Kafka is not re-writing *The Trial* here: within the same political configuration he introduces a new, decisive element. We know that he wrote this short story between mid-October and mid-November 1923. He had just moved to Berlin with Dora Diamant and the story can be read as the deep analysis of a political and social situation he was observing at very close quarters.

I am not confusing Kafka with his narrator, and, since the text is a
double-layered critique, I do not think it can be supposed that this
monologue is spoken by a mouthpiece for Kafka or by his double
but this narrator understands, as does Kafka, that the tension is
rising. And he draws opposite conclusions from it. Over the years
this confrontation has been going on between the little woman and
himself, the narrator notes that 'such occasions have repeated themselves [. . .] And that people are hanging around in the offing and
would like to interfere if they could find some way of doing it.'[175] He
feels that the affair is 'having wider repercussions'. Of course, '[T]he
situation was always like that [. . .] always provided with superfluous
bystanders and nosy onlookers [. . .] The only difference is that I
have gradually come to recognize them.'[176] And he is worried about
this. At the beginning he believed 'the affair was having wider repercussions, which would themselves compel a crisis.'[177] What he is
sure of, at any rate, is that 'If it ever should happen—and certainly
not tomorrow or the day after tomorrow, most likely never—that
public opinion concerns itself with the affair, which [. . .] is beyond
its competence, I certainly won't escape unharmed.'[178] 'A Little
Woman' is perhaps Kafka's only really 'prophetic' text: it announces
in astonishingly precise terms the rise of anti-Semitism and the
possible elevation of hatred to the status of authorized public discourse. And it seems that one can, without forcing the text, understand Kafka's *Entscheidung* (rendered in the English text as both
'decisive moment' and 'crisis')—something both expected and feared
by the narrator—as the awareness that an explosion of hatred towards
the Jews might very well occur, an emergence into the open of something previously hidden. In reality, in 1923, 10 years before the Nazi
accession to power, Kafka was simply delivering a political analysis
of the German situation as it appeared to him that is highly impressive in its complexity and perceptiveness.

THE '22 CHRISTIAN NEGRO YOUTHS IN UGANDA'

Having, as it were, dissected the evils of Western Jewish society and
become aware, also, that symbolic domination was exerted on many

social groups in quite similar forms, Kafka extended his field of enquiry—his 'investigations'—and applied his mode of questioning to other forms of invisible ascendancy over people.

From 1912 onwards, he mentioned Africa on several occasions and seemed to take an interest in it as a parallel to other political situations. In a letter to Felice on 24 November 1912, he wrote, for example:

> For a long time now I have planned [. . .] to cut out and collect from various papers news items that astonished me for some reason, that affected me, that seemed important to me personally for a long time to come; at a glance they were usually quite insignificant, for instance just recently 'The beatification of 22 Christian Negro youths in Uganda' [. . .] I find something of the kind in the papers nearly every other day. News which seems to be meant only for me.[179]

Kafka, who seemed interested in what today we term 'current affairs'—that is, the things that were happening around him, far from Prague—identified what might appear to us a mere trivial news item as being of very 'special' personal interest and sent it to Felice. A little further on in the letter he emphasizes this aspect: 'I am sure everyone feels there are certain news items not meant for every reader, but aimed only at certain readers here and there, in which the outsider could detect no reason for special interest.'[180] This particular item interested him so much, indeed, that he returned to it almost two months later, urging that Felice should not lose the clipping which came from the *Prager Tagblatt*: 'You send me so few newspaper clippings, and I have sent you such a nice one again. In closing, I trust you haven't lost the clipping on the beatification of the 22 Negro youths in Uganda?'[181] How are we to understand this 'quite insignificant' item about the '22 Negro youths' being 'meant only for' Kafka? Research in the newspaper's archives has shown that the article was published on 25 September 1912, two months before he sent it to Felice. This goes to show that he attached considerable importance to it, since he kept it all that time and felt it so worthy of attention as possibly to interest Felice insofar as it would speak of him, Kafka, as a particular individual. The article was enti- tled: 'Beatification of the Martyrs of Uganda' and read as follows:

A decree of the Congregation of Rites of 13 August announces the beginning of the process of the beatification of those known as the 'Uganda Martyrs', 22 Christian Negro youths who suffered death at the stake for their faith 26 years ago. As is reported in Rome, at the headquarters of the brotherhood of Saint Peter Claver, the cardinals who had to deliberate on this matter were moved to tears by the heroism of the young martyrs. The news of the beginning of the beatification process unleashed very great joyfulness among all the negro tribes, particularly those of North-Victoria-Nyasa, the native land of the first martyrs, a joyful- ness they expressed by dancing and leaping.[182]

One of the only—historically justified—ways of understanding Kafka's interest in this news item, a matter distant from him geo- graphically and, on the face of it, far removed from his concerns, is to connect it with the thinking he had been engaged in for about a year (and no doubt longer) on the questions of assimilation, domination and the 'disappearance' or dilution of a (communal or cultural) identity into another which dominated it symbolically. That young African converts to Christianity—that is to say, people who, in Kafka's terms, were also victims of the process of assimilation and acculturation characteristic of colonization—should accept death at the stake for their Christian faith (that they should deny their culture and religion to become Christian martyrs) could only appear to Kafka, particularly at this period, as one of the most extreme forms of assimilation which is here another term for the forgetting of self or the disappearance of self as a member of another dominated, subjugated community. To put it another way, there can be little doubt that Kafka immediately made the connection between the situation of the Jews in the Austrian Empire (and, more broadly, in Western Europe) and all other situations of symbolic domination, particularly those engendered by European colonization, which was then at its height. All the details of the article cut out by Kafka are illuminating if we attempt to see them from his standpoint, including the symbolic power of the Church accompanying the process of colonization and the compassion of the cardinals who are ready to reward such great submission to the Church's commands with beatification. The mention of the 'joyfulness' unleashed within 'all the negro tribes' by the news of these men's future elevation, a joy expressed not in European terms but 'by dancing and leaping'—that is to say, through the specific resources of a non-colonized African identity or what remains of it after assimilation into the culture of the colonizer: *ghostly remnants* or 'insignificant scraps' of an African religious tradition—must inevitably have aroused Kafka's attention. From this very broad interest in all situations of cultural domination and this 'comparative' impulse which seems to be at the origin of many of his texts, we may deduce that Kafka was not driven merely by the wish to 'illustrate' or explain the fate of Western Jews and the tragic aporia besetting them. He was trying, through all these texts, to understand, explain and expose every situation of domination.

This is why it seems to me we can interpret a number of his major texts as attempts to universalize the situations described. If, following this logic, *The Trial* is the minutely detailed description of the 'secret' mechanisms of anti-Semitism and all the effects it exerts on the Jews themselves in Western Europe, it is also the universal history of all the effects brought about by all collective, socially maintained humiliations—that is to say, all the forms of symbolic domination to which attention is not ordinarily drawn. It is the uncompromising narrative, reduced as it were to the bare bones, of the collective mechanisms that make the dominated both subjects and objects of dependency. Kafka is probably one of the first writers to have recognized that the mere description or condemnation of domination were not in themselves sufficient to bring an end to it. Because it is reproduced and renewed, shouldered and embodied both by those who are driving it and those who are its first victims, the subtlety of its mechanisms has to be understood before one can claim to free oneself from it. The modernity and refinement of his descriptions make Kafka one of the liberators of dominated humanity. He is no detached observer of facts, he calls for rebellion and insubordination.

'In the Penal Colony' comes at this question from the angle of the belief of the dominant and their conviction that the law must be obeyed. The story was written in 1914 or, in other words, at the same time as *The Trial* and the final chapter of *Amerika*.

'In The Penal Colony' or What Does It Mean to Obey?

Showing that Kafka substantially expanded the range of his concerns and political thinking after 'The Judgment' and *Amerika*, 'In the Penal Colony' presents a situation of colonial domination and is set in an unspecified location within the French colonial empire.[183] It is as though Kafka had very quickly made the connection, after writing *Amerika*, between invisible situations of political oppression—such as those affecting the Jews of Eastern Europe—and colonial situations. The connection between the two is not, however, exclusively political: the penal colony is a sort of horrendous laboratory showing up, as under a magnifying glass or microscope, the mechanisms which make it possible to produce a blatant situation of explicit oppression and racism that takes the inviolable, inescapable form of a Law which 'has to be respected'. In other words, this is clearly, as Michael Löwy observes, a text which stages several forms of power and authority—mainly in a colonial, military and bureaucratic guise[184]—but more profoundly, as it seems to me, a text which attempts to describe the mechanisms by which it is possible for the torturers to submit to regulations and go along with a cruel, unjust verdict which ought to be unacceptable and yet is regarded as a 'law' to be respected (and therefore applied) by all. Hence colonialism is as much at issue here as anti-Semitism. Such critical thinking, as Michael Löwy rightly stresses, is very uncommon in this period.[185]

However, the great violence and Kafka's manifest desire to provoke a kind of political shock-effect are, as it were, curiously attenuated by the discomfort engendered by the very process of reading. 'In the Penal Colony' sets in train a very powerful mechanism which disrupts reading practices and disturbs the structures of ordinary narrative. All the stances and characters in the text are at once explained for what they are, resituated in their historical context and criticized successively. As a result, readers lose their bearings. They do not know how to take the story since there is no mouthpiece explicitly to state the author's point of view. The effect of violence is present also in this kind of abandonment of the readers to pure cruelty or in the disgust they experience at each of the characters who turn out, one after the other, to infringe the most basic moral codes.[186]

Kafka seems to have worked here on the basis of taking the ordinary violence done to dominated groups, so to speak, which in the countries of Western Europe most often remains invisible, and making it concrete. In a sense, the killing machine lends material existence to social violence; it renders it visible with the resources of fable. We may also assume that, in order to convey the concrete reality of symbolic violence, Kafka needed a colonial context in which domination is commonly expressed in physical form.

The condemned man in 'In the Penal Colony' does not know he has been condemned, is unaware of his sentence, has had no opportunity to defend himself and is condemned by the so-called guiding principle of the 'law' underlying the judge's decisions, which is that 'Guilt is never to be doubted.'[187] By way of the 'Harrow' which will write them on his skin, he is going to 'learn [. . .] on his body' both his sentence and the commandment he has disobeyed. The story first relates the—unprecedentedly violent—process of the inculcation of the imperative to obey or, in other words, the learning of the law. In this way the Jews and colonial subjects gradually learn the unavoidability of the secret, inexplicable, inexpiable guilt with which they are burdened, whatever they do. And since no one knows what they are guilty of, there is no one who can understand the iniquitous punishment that ensues and rebel against it. But at the centre of the text lies not the murderous machine which, so to speak, blinds the character of the explorer as much as it does the reader but the great abstract judicial machinery which has established an inviolable 'law' enabling that deadly 'apparatus' to have been invented, perfected *and* maintained (as the zealous officer never fails to remind us). This killing machine is accepted as the legitimate means for enacting the sentences of the colony's institutions of justice. What is going on in the text, then, is nothing less than the description of the operation of a strange judicial institution, the greatest mystery of which is that some people not only agree to make it function but believe it their duty to do so.

In this sense, the text is itself a sort of infernal machine, its workings largely hidden, which radically challenges the inviolable, superhuman character of the social 'laws' underpinning the legitimacy of authority and, as a consequence, of domination. While the killing machine is merely a human invention and hence historical and modifiable or reversible, it has mutated, says the officer, into something 'so perfect' that, on grounds of social order, it has become necessary to obey it or impossible not to submit to it. 'Up till now a few things still had to be set by hand, but now it works all by itself.'[188] In other words, there is no need to act any more to make the mechanisms of the stigmatization of Jews or colonial subjects operate collectively. Persuasion and integration have now reached such levels that the machinery functions without the intervention of anyone's will.

The Machine

The short story features two executioners, one human, the other mechanical. The second merely carries out the sentences. It inscribes the law on the bodies themselves, the point being to apprise the condemned man of his 'guilt'. Such knowledge through the body is explicitly stressed in the text and is even one of the reasons given in justification of the condemned man not knowing his sentence: 'There would be no point in telling him. He'll learn it on his body,' states the officer.[189] 'Our sentence does not sound severe. Whatever commandment the prisoner has disobeyed is written upon his body by the Harrow.'[190] In other words, we are not just dealing here with an ordinary—or even iniquitously ordinary—sentence but one written on the condemned body itself, become part of it: it is the inscription of the law upon the body. Kafka is, in fact, careful to stress the slow, painful, self-destructive character of this inculcation. The condemnation is designed in such a way that the process of inscribing the law onto the condemned man's flesh lasts long enough for him to have time to understand, before he dies, what is being carved on his back:

> Enlightenment comes to the most dull-witted [. . . T]he man begins to understand the inscription, he purses his mouth as if he were listening. You have seen how difficult it is to decipher the script with one's eyes, but our man deciphers it with his wounds. To be sure, that is a hard task; he needs six hours to accomplish it.[191]

Kafka takes as his example a commandment which, when stated simply, sums up the unbearable arbitrary power wielded by the social order: 'Honour thy superiors.'[192] It will be engraved on the condemned man's body as the basis of the hierarchical order of the world and one of the possible ways of expressing symbolic domination. If we think of The Trial, written at this same period, we can see that the application of the law by its inscription deep in the flesh and the mind—along with this colony's justice mechanism, summed up in the simple formula 'Guilt is never to be doubted'—belongs precisely to the same types of dispositions, of successive instances of collective belief, of fear-ridden respect for the law, of mystery around a crime that is both unknown and yet seemingly indubitable and of terrible verdicts which no one either rebels against or condemns.

However, in 'In the Penal Colony', Kafka particularly stresses the viewpoint of the executioner or, in other words, of the man who firmly believes the condemnation to be soundly based. In a word, what he is describing in this kind of fable is another sort of incorporation and inculcation practised on the persecutor himself, the sort impressed upon him by tradition. He is relating the persuasive power of tradition which succeeds, without the involvement of any form of coercion, in convincing the persecutors (the dominant, the Germans, the colonialists) that the injustice they are turning into law is soundly based and legitimate. The power of the collective belief in tradition is such that the persecutor is persuaded, on the one hand, that it is legitimate to punish the condemned man—even in this terrible way and, indeed, most particularly in this way—and, on the other, that only the incorporation of the law into the condemned man's body is efficacious.

In the text Kafka undertakes a highly elaborate 'narrativized analysis'. Rather than simply denouncing the ignominy and injustice of domination, he shows in a paradoxical and almost unbearable fiction that the question cannot be resolved by a mere denunciation of the cowardice of individuals, an appeal to courage or a political stance. What are needed are analyses (which remain narrations) that describe the deepest mechanisms of the social world. In his view, tradition is transformed into law and that law is obeyed only if the obedience is not produced in a conscious way and arises from a conviction that renders the mechanism unconscious and invisible. If everyone is persuaded that the legitimacy of the law is self-evident, then the whole of the social world accepts obedience to it as self-evident (and the machine operates without anyone seeming to work it). By dint of this inculcation, the law is one of the most difficult things to express and to extirpate.

Judicial Power

The story presents not only power as it is exercised but the rich fabric of history which permits it to perpetuate itself while undergoing change: history may even be said to be the indispensable condition for the universal acceptance of the legitimacy of law and authority. This history is presented as two different phases of power.

First, there is the founding period, the one the zealous officer calls 'the golden age', in which the former Commandant, the inventor of the machine and organizer of the colony, held sway. It was the time when 'respect' for the law was at its most rigid and the cruelty of the punishments meted out to the condemned at its height, with acid added to the needles, new straps provided, machine parts changed for each execution, etc. The description of that 'golden age' is a magnificent parody in which Kafka sets his black humour to work ('The machine was freshly cleaned and glittering [. . .] The Commandant in his wisdom ordered that the children should have the preference [. . .] What times these were, my comrade!').[193] But this period is evoked only as a counterpoint to the present time of the narration. The officer states that he is devoting all his energies to maintaining what already exists or, in other words, to the established order. But today everything is changing. A new Commandant heads the colony and is of a mind to 'bring in [. . .] a new kind of procedure'.[194] He is 'always looking for an excuse to attack our old way of doing things'.[195] He is trying to 'soften' the existing system without calling it into question: '[O]ur new mild doctrine thinks otherwise. The Commandant's ladies stuff the man with sugar candy before he's led off,'[196] and 'the machine can no longer wring from anyone a sigh louder than the felt gag can stifle.'[197] In his comparison of the two periods Kafka describes the false challenges to the law, the pseudo-softenings of verdicts, sentences and executions and the transition from physical to symbolic violence which apparently make these bearable but do nothing to alter their existence or prevent them being perpetuated.

Above all, as in other later texts, Kafka shows that forgetting is one of the paradoxical conditions for the reproduction of the law by some and conformity to that law by others: the fact that it was established in the mists of time renders the law even more powerfully ineluctable. It is time which enables the arbitrary nature of the introduction of a law to be forgotten or become invisible and promotes belief in its sacrosanct and hence inviolable (inevitable) nature.

Sketched out in the so-called third octavo notebook in January 1918, one of his short stories, which ostensibly relates four versions of the Prometheus myth, takes up exactly this same question within a different narrative framework. Kafka's *détournement* of one of the great myths of the Western literary tradition enables him to take his condemnation of tradition as an instrument of the perpetuation of social suffering further and to raise the question of the origin of the law and of collective conformity to it. It is not, as Robert argues, that these four versions 'introduce the accidents of time into the eternity of the event'.[198] They are, rather, a sort of summarized history of its transmission—that is to say, they are the story of the forgetting of history. What belongs to tradition is, as it were, wrenched from history and presented as an eternal truth which it consequently becomes impossible to question. In traditional tales, mythologies, religious narratives and legends that speak of the mists of time, what is transmitted is both an injunction and a forgetting. Myth hands down to us the command to conform to a particular prohibition, taboo or belief but at the same time transmits the forgetting of the historical conditions which enabled it to emerge. Belief and collective conviction are the unexplained, almost forgotten traces of the past, arbitrary traces almost devoid of meaning. Yet they continue to leave their obscure imprint on the present without anyone knowing why. Kafka thus turns Prometheus—his first appropriation of him for his own ends—into an emblem of the perpetuation of dependency, a representation of domination. However, none of the variants of the myth says anything precise about the man condemned to eternal punishment who therefore finds himself in exactly the position of the Jews or of colonial subjects.

In the first—canonical—version of the legend, Prometheus is said to have betrayed the gods to men. This is why he was chained to a rock in the Caucasus and condemned to have his perpetually renewed liver devoured. The second evokes a Prometheus who, to escape his agony, disappears, pressing deeper and deeper into the rock until he becomes 'one with it'.[199] According to the third narrative, all the protagonists forgot Prometheus' original betrayal over the passing millennia: '[T]he gods forgot, the eagles forgot, he himself forgot.'[200] The fourth has it that '[E]veryone grew weary of what had become meaningless. The gods grew weary, the eagles grew weary, the wound closed wearily.'[201] Little by little, then, the origin of the punishment was forgotten. But '[w]hat remained was the inexplicable range of mountains' or, in other words, tradition. Or the plain fact of the reality of an ever-renewed punishment for a crime which is still averred, though long since forgotten.

The Condemned Man

When, at the beginning of 'In the Penal Colony', they read the story of the man's 'crime', as told to the explorer by the officer, who soon shows himself to have a 'narrow mind',[202] readers, working on the 'double-meaning' principle on which the whole text is built, fully understand that this condemned soldier rebelled in a legitimate but solitary fashion against an absurd order ('[every night], it is his duty, you see, to get up every time the hour strikes and salute the captain's door')[203] and against the unjust violence exerted on him the moment he forgot it ('[the captain] took his riding whip and lashed him across the face. Instead of getting up and begging pardon, the man caught hold of his master's legs, shook him and cried: "Throw that whip away or I'll eat you alive." '[204]). But the condemned man distinguishes himself first by his submissiveness, which is stressed on several occasions in a way that is almost shocking ('the condemned man, who was a stupid-looking, wide-mouthed creature with bewildered hair and face [. . .] looked so like a submissive dog that one might have thought he [. . .] would only need to be whistled for when the execution was due to begin'[205]). From this disparaging, if not indeed xenophobic description, some commentators have seen fit to conclude, as I mentioned above, that Kafka 'feels no sympathy for this condemned man with his animalistic face and dull-witted mind'.[206] And, further on, the explorer, observing the condemned man, says to himself: 'Yet the movement of his blubber lips, closely pressed together, showed clearly that he could not understand a word.'[207] This is again a description of the accused man as seen by the explorer, who bases his various certainties on a physical portrait and prejudices that are explicitly racist, and the whole of the narrative, composed almost entirely in free indirect style, is written exclusively from the explorer's standpoint which is why we may conclude that it merely conveys that character's contemptuous view.

Even more doubt can be cast on the idea of Kafka's personal commitment to these remarks if we look at some of Frobenius' earliest writings which Kafka may very possibly have read before writing this story. In those writings we find the ethnologist listing some of the characteristics ascribed to the condemned man, though doing so only to pour scorn on them. In 'The Origin of African Civilizations', mocking the clichés widely applied to Africa and Africans, Frobenius writes:

> Open an illustrated geography and compare the 'Type of the African Negro,' the bluish-black fellow of the protuberant lips, the flattened nose, the stupid expression and the short curly hair, with the tall bronze figures from Dark Africa with which we have of late become familiar, their almost fine-cut features, slightly arched nose, long hair, etc., and you have an example of the problems pressing for solution [. . .] A stroll through the corridors of the Berlin Museum of Ethnology teaches that the real African need by no means resort to the rags and tatters of bygone European splendor. He has precious ornaments of his own, of ivory and plumes, fine plaited willow ware, weapons of superior workmanship. Justly can it be demanded 'What sort of civilization is this? Whence does it come?'[208]

Frobenius also entitles the introduction to his book *Und Afrika sprach* (1913) 'Fiat Lux', with the aim of at last shedding light on (or bringing out of the shadows) that portion of the globe the explorer Henry Morton Stanley dubbed 'darkest Africa', those children we commonly view as 'naturally servile' and those peoples without attested history who are thought to be able to exercise power only in the debased form of brute force. 'Let there be light!', writes Frobenius in what is also a direct protest against the Church, which had asserted that 'negroes' had no souls.[209]

By way of the unreliable-narrator technique described above and the double meaning that ensues, Kafka makes it plain throughout his story that the explorer's viewpoint is entirely misleading and, far from the dog-like submissiveness attributed to him at the beginning, the condemned man will rebel against the colonial order and the fate meted out to him and will seek to avenge himself and escape this hellish colony.

That undisciplined soldier, who does not speak the language of those condemning him to death, who does not even know he has been sentenced, is in a situation very much akin to that of K. in *The Trial*. Like K. attempting to understand the mechanisms of the court in which he stands accused, we see this condemned man striving to decipher what is said about the killing machine and the fate that awaits him, despite his ignorance of French. We see him striving to observe the harrow and the needles. In so doing, contrary to what the explorer believes, he demonstrates a total absence of submissiveness. Once freed, and at the point when the officer submits himself to the harrow, he shows he feels avenged: 'Although he himself had not suffered to the end, he was to be revenged to the end. A broad, silent grin now appeared on his face.'[210] This idea of vengeance is wholly at odds with the feelings attributed to him by the explorer who views him as moronic, stupid or incapable of reactions worthy of a human being. And during the officer's torment, while the machine is malfunctioning and falling apart, the 'condemned man' is not stirred as the explorer is but observes the whole process impassively. He even refuses, as does the soldier, to extract the officer's body from the clutches of the machine, as the explorer asks him to.[211] Then, in a final moment of rebellion on the part of these two characters, who represent dominated individuals from a colonized people forcibly enrolled in the army in the service of the colonial power, they attempt to escape and the explorer unambiguously prevents them from doing so.

The Explorer

The last of the core elements of the narrative is the explorer, whose role, as the officer explains to him at length, could be essential in calling into question the 'traditional mode of execution'[212] or even causing it to be abandoned. The explorer, at first indifferent, then concerned, then cautious and, in the end, plainly cowardly, is clearly not a mouthpiece for Kafka. The whole of the scene is perceived and described from his virtually unique viewpoint. Kafka makes copious use of the technique of free indirect speech to convey the idea that he is simply revealing the very specific view of the explorer who is all the time weighing up his decision, hesitating and concocting reasons not to act. 'The explanation of the judicial procedure had not satisfied him. He had to remind himself that this was [. . .] a penal colony.'²¹³ He is very soon in no doubt about what he is seeing: '[H]e found himself strongly tempted. The injustice of the procedure and the inhumanity of the execution were undeniable.'²¹⁴ Yet he prevaricates: 'The explorer thought to himself: It's always a ticklish matter to intervene decisively in other people's affairs. He was neither a member of the penal colony nor a citizen of the state to which it belonged. Were he to denounce this execution or actually try to stop it, they could say to him: You are a foreigner, mind your own business.'²¹⁵

However, the officer, who attempts to have him intervene in favour of this procedure, explains how precious his public support would be and how it would play an irreplaceable role in the perpetuation of the system. The explorer (and the reader) then understands that, conversely, his public condemnation of the 'machine' could contribute substantially to getting this barbarous practice abandoned ('his influence cannot be rated too highly').²¹⁶ In other words, through the double-meaning technique, the explorer hears himself state all the reasons that ought to prompt him roundly to condemn the operation of this 'justice'. The explorer (and, with him, the reader) understands, among other things, that the new Commandant of the colony brought him there in the hope that he might make use of his opinion as a way of abolishing this 'traditional' procedure once and for all, even if it meant lying about his identity and his genuine area of expertise, presenting him as 'a famous Western investigator, sent out to study criminal procedure', when he is in fact merely 'a private individual'.²¹⁷ 'You believe your influence is insufficient. I know that it is sufficient,' insists the officer.²¹⁸ Yet, even though the explorer is convinced that he is himself 'fundamentally honorable and unafraid', even though he 'had no doubt about what answer he must give', even though he tells the officer, 'I do not approve of your procedure,'²¹⁹ he decides to do nothing or, rather, to act in such a way that his opinion remains private and the Commandant cannot make use of his criticism: 'I shall tell the Commandant what I think of the procedure, certainly, but not at a public conference, only in private.'[220] In other words, he will make no significant intervention at all and his condemnation will have no effect.

Kafka rounds off his denunciation of European cowardice in the last paragraph by describing how the explorer prevents the soldier and the condemned man—that is to say, members of this colonized people who understand that they must at all costs leave the island to have a chance of living a free life—from getting into the boat that is taking him away. And the story's last sentence rings out a like a kind of second sentence on the temporarily reprieved condemned man: 'They could have jumped into the boat, but the explorer lifted a heavy knotted rope from the floor boards, threatened them with it, and so kept them from attempting the leap.'[221]

Unhappy with this first version of the conclusion to his text, Kafka looked for other solutions which we find roughed out in his diary during August 1917. In the main they concern themselves with the cowardice of the explorer, as though this were the true heart of the narrative. The first provides a more explicit version of his guilty repudiation of the condemned man. Instead of driving back the two colonials who are trying to escape this hellish island, the explorer proclaims (to himself and the others) that he cannot tolerate this injustice any longer: 'I am a cur if I allow that to happen.'[222] And, as in animal fables, the character's prophetic words immediately come true, thus confirming that he was indeed willing to allow the intolerable situation to persist. He is thus immediately changed into a dog ('he [. . .] began to run around on all fours') while he touchingly and comically feels sorry for himself ('he [. . .] threw his arms around the neck of one of the men, and tearfully exclaimed, "Why does all this happen to me!" and then hurried to his post').[223] As a caricatured portrayal of a 'Western' explorer who is entirely aware that he is confronted with something intolerable but will do nothing to upset the social order, this epilogue confirms that Kafka did not necessarily attribute to his story the macabre and tragic character we see in it today. The third outline of an ending goes back to the condemned man and the soldier. This time, instead of being prevented by the explorer from leaping into the potential getaway boat, they are attacked even more violently: '[H]e [the explorer] dismissed the soldier and the condemned man with a gesture of his hand; they hesitated, he threw a stone at them, and when they still deliberated, he ran up to them and struck them with his fists.'[224] The fourth version sketches another possible way out for the explorer along lines already indicated in the first fragment: the explorer deceives himself, feigning climate-induced despondency and mental confusion. This enables him to exculpate himself quite comically once again while carefully refraining from action ('Who can penetrate the confusion? Damned, miasmal tropical air, what are you doing to me? I don't know what is happening. My judgement has been left back at home in the north.').[225]

Good Reasons and Bad Faith

Looking at Kafka's writings generally, many characters employ evasiveness to terminate an asymmetrical relationship or deny their guilt with absurd arguments because they are perpetuating injustice or prolonging hardship. In each case, it is a question of exploring power relations in their most unexpected forms and the paradoxes and injustices that arise from a domination that feeds on the bad faith of those perpetuating it. Kafka often depicts this bad faith in the guise of passivity or in the form of inaction explained away with innumerable excuses.

The magnificent story 'Up in the Gallery', for example, lays before us in a very finely wrought narrative the bad reasons 'a young visitor to the gallery' advances for not intervening to rescue a 'frail [. . .] equestrienne'.[226] Everything rests on the syntax of the two paragraphs which are organized around a chiasmus that generates both meaning and ambiguity. The first paragraph describes the reality of the young horsewoman's situation. She is a 'frail, consumptive equestrienne in the circus [. . .] urged around and around on an undulating horse for months on end without respite by a ruthless, whip-flourishing ringmaster, before an insatiable public'.[227] But this paragraph is, in fact, built on a number of conditional propositions, as though, instead of a factual description, we had before us a series of suppositions: 'If some frail, consumptive equestrienne in the circus were to be urged around and around [. . .] and if this performance were likely to continue in the infinite perspective of a drab future to the unceasing roar of the orchestra and hum of the ventilators'.[228] This is tantamount to saying that this description of reality is mere reverie. If this were the situation, then 'perhaps a young visitor to the gallery [through whose eyes this entire scene is described] might race down the long stairs [. . .] rush into the ring, and yell: Stop!'[229]

There then follows a second paragraph describing the illusion of reality as it appears to the onlookers, embellished by the footlights and all the decorum of the circus. But producing, as it were, a new version of the Platonic myth of the cave, this embellished, illusory reality is narrated in the present, as though it were reality itself: 'a lovely lady, pink and white, floats in between the curtains, which proud lackeys open before her; the ringmaster, deferentially catching her eye, comes toward her breathing animal devotion.'[230] This entire paragraph is constructed in the form of a series of purely enunciative propositions: they stand in direct, one-to-one opposition to those of the preceding paragraph: 'But since that is not so; [since] a lovely lady [. . .] floats in between the curtains; [since] the ringmaster comes toward her breathing animal devotion [. . .] the visitor to the gallery lays his face on the rail before him and, sinking into the closing march as into a heavy dream, weeps without knowing it.'[231] In other words, while he knows the miserable reality of the horsewoman's condition, while he dreams of wresting her from her actual destiny, the visitor inverts the order of the beautified illusion of the real and the miserable truth of reality in order to avoid having to act. And Kafka transposes the available syntactic resources, reserving conditionality for the description of a true reality and putting the stamp of the objective account on the description of an illusory one.

Beneath its fantasy-story exterior, we have before us in 'A Country Doctor' the parodic account of a physician who, angered at being called out, announces that a seriously ill patient, whom he has barely examined, is in good health. Here again the text is constructed from the central character's point of view and hence on the basis of his bad faith and all the false arguments he develops to justify his failing to perform his task. Judging himself too poorly paid by the district to attend to this patient's case properly, he tries to persuade himself that this is a false alarm from his 'night bell' and his one intent is to return home. Faced, however, with the dismayed family, he finally consents to take another look at the patient: 'I was somehow ready to admit conditionally that the boy might be ill after all [. . .] and this time I discovered that the boy was indeed ill.'[232] Discovering the patient has a deep wound, in which he can see worms, the doctor finds him 'past helping'. Indifferent to the sufferings of the family and their hopes of seeing the patient cured, he feels sorry only for himself and refuses to act ('That is what people are like in my district. Always expecting the impossible from the doctor'[233]). Without attempting either to treat him or relieve his pain, the doctor showers the boy with fine words that are so many lies designed to enable the physician to return home as quickly as possible ('I have been in all the sickrooms, far and wide, and I tell you: your wound is not so bad'[234]). The story ends with the naked, shivering doctor returning home, continuing his monologue as he does so and—in an inversion of the real situation of domination and dependence—continuously complaining and bemoaning his fate: 'Naked, exposed to the frost of this most unhappy of ages [. . .] old man that I am, I wander astray [. . .] and none of my limber pack of patients lifts a finger.'[235]

The humour running through Kafka's short narratives can only emerge if the reader agrees to countenance a comic intention on his part—for example, in those details of his story that seem at times the most horrific (in other words, details that are not presented entirely— or in any sure way—as comical). In 'A Country Doctor', the delectation in the description of the wound, with its complement of worms, seems to us today more like sordid realism than comedy. Yet, if it is true that Kafka is satirizing the doctor, the fact of not noticing—and not treating—a visible, gaping wound of this kind is such an obvious mistake that we have in my view to regard it as an element of parody. The oozing wound is described at some length: 'Rose-red, in many variations of shade, dark in the hollows, lighter at the edges, softly granulated, with irregular clots of blood, open as a surface mine to the daylight. That was how it looked from a distance.'[236] Then, from closer-up, other gruesome details become visible. 'Worms, as thick and as long as my little finger, themselves rose-red and blood-spotted as well, were wriggling from their fastness in the interior of the wound toward the light, with small white heads and many little legs.'[237] Ultimately, we should see Kafka's humour as one form of the violence-effect his narratives exert on us or, more precisely, as one of the reasons for the sense of turmoil that wells up in us as we read them—a sense that underlies the suggestive power of his work, as though it were precisely the undecidable or poorly defined character of that humour (for today's reader) that gave us to believe, wrongly, in a tragic intention on his part.

NOTES

1   Kafka, 'The Investigations of a Dog' in *The Complete Stories*, p. 312.

2   Gerhard Neumann, 'Kafka ethnologue', *Europe* 923 (March 2006): 253–71; here, p. 260.

3   In this connection, Gerald Stieg has shown that *The Castle* can also be interpreted as a fable depicting the question of the assimilation of the Jews. See Stieg, 'Wer ist Kafkas Bote Barnabas?', *Austriaca* 17 (1983): 151–6.

4   Kafka, 'A Report to an Academy' in *The Complete Stories*, p. 258.

5   See Chapter 2, p. 112.

6   Kafka, 'Letter to Grete Bloch, 11 June 1914' in *Letters to Felice*, pp. 552–3.

7   Kafka, *Letters to Friends, Family and Editors*, p. 289.

8   Gershom Scholem, 'On the Social Psychology of German Jews between 1900 and 1930' in David Bronson (ed.), *Jews and Germans*

from 1860–1933: The Problematic Symbiosis (Heidelberg: Carl Winter Universitätsverlag, 1979), pp. 9–32.

9 See p. 292.

10 Scholem, *From Berlin to Jerusalem*, p. 3.

11 Ibid., p. 9.

12 Ibid., p. 10.

13 Brod, *Streitbares Leben*, p. 114.

14 Michel, *Prague, Belle Époque*, p. 67.

15 Brod, *Streitbares Leben*, pp. 223–4.

16 Scholem, 'A propos de la psychologie' in *De la Création*. For more on this study, see Chapter 1, pp. 42–4.

17 Kafka, 'Letter to His Father' in *Dearest Father*, pp. 172–3.

18 Ibid., p. 172.

19 Ibid., p. 173.

20 Ibid., p. 174.

21 Ibid., p. 177.

22 Ibid., p. 174.

23 Ibid., pp. 172–3.

24 For example, Pinès mentions a play by Sholem Aleichem, *Zeseit un Serspreit* ['Scattered and Dispersed'], published in 1903, which deals with 'the struggle between fathers and sons in the ghetto' and depicts 'quite a rich Jewish merchant and his children, some of whom are committed to the revolutionary, national movement' in Pinès, *Histoire de la littérature judéo-allemande*, p. 507.

25 Janouch, *Conversations with Kafka*, p. 69.

26 Kafka, '24 December 1911' in *Diaries*, p. 147.

27 Janouch, *Conversations with Kafka*, p. 114. The German is from Gustav Janouch, *Gespräche mit Kafka: Erweiterte Ausgabe* (Frankurt: Fischer, 1968), p. 67.

28 *Ergeben* also means 'devoted'.

29 Kafka, '23–24 February 1913' in Erich Heller and Jürgen Born (eds), *Franz Kafka: Briefe an Felice und andere Korrespondenz aus der Verlobungszeit* (Frankfurt: Fischer, 1981), p. 313. [This letter is not included in the English edition edited by Heller and Born. Trans.]

30 Kafka, '7 February 1915' in *Diaries*, p. 330.

31 Anderson, 'Chapter 3: Body Culture: J. P. Miller's Gymnastic System and the Ascetic Ideal' in *Kafka's Clothes*, pp. 74–97. See also Gilman, *Franz Kafka: The Jewish Patient*.

32 See Chapter 2, pp. 148–53.

33 Bruce, 'Jewish Education' in Gelber, *Kafka, Zionism and Beyond*, pp. 130–1.

34 Anderson, 'Chapter 8: "Jewish" Music? Otto Weininger and *Josephine the Singer*' in *Kafka's Clothes*'.

35 Kafka, 'Josephine the Singer, and the Mouse People' in *The Complete Stories*, p. 360.

36 Cf. Bruce, 'Jewish Education' in Gelber, *Kafka, Zionism and Beyond*, p. 139.

37 Kafka, 'The Investigations of a Dog' in *The Complete Stories*, p. 281.

38 Schnitzler, *The Road to the Open*, p. 154.

39 Jean-Paul Sartre, *Anti-Semite and Jew* (George J. Becker trans.) (New York: Schocken Books, 1948), pp. 90–100.

40 Franz Kafka, 'A Crossbreed [A Sport]' (Willa and Edwin Muir trans) in *The Complete Stories*, pp. 426–7; here, p. 426 [originally published posthumously in 1931 as 'Eine Kreuzung' in *Beim Bau der Chinesischen Mauer*].

41 Kafka, 'Jackals and Arabs' in *The Complete Stories*, p. 408.

42 Kafka, 'Schakale und Araber' in *Ein Landarzt und andere Drucke zu Lebzeiten*, p. 213.

43 See, especially, Hannah Arendt, 'Active Patience' in *The Jewish Writings* (Jerome Kohn and Ron H. Feldman eds) (New York: Schocken Books, 2007), pp. 139–42.

44 Like the 'older men' looking on at K.'s first hearing in *The Trial*, whose 'long beards stiff and sparse' took the shape of 'claws' (Kafka, *The Trial*, p. 38). Or like the 'ill-pleased' little woman, annoyed 'at every step', who always finds 'something objectionable in' the narrator. Kafka, 'The Little Woman' in *The Complete Stories*, p. 317.

45 Kafka, 'Letter to Oskar Pollak, 27 January 1904' in *Letters to Friends, Family and Editors*, p. 16.

46 Arendt, 'Franz Kafka, Appreciated Anew' in Gottlieb, *Hannah Arendt: Reflections on Literature and Culture*, p. 104.

47 Joëlle Gardes Tamine (ed.), *L'Allégorie corps et âme: Entre personnification et double sens* (Aix-en-Provence: Publications de l'université de Provence, 2002), p. 5.

48 Northrop Frye, *Anatomy of Criticism* (Princeton: Princeton University Press, 1957), p. 90.

49 Erwin Panofsky, 'Zum Problem der Beschreibung und Inhalts-deutung von Werken der bildenden Kunst' in H. Oberer and Egon Verheyen (eds), *Aufsätze zur Grundfragen der Kunstwissenschaft* (Berlin: E. Verheyen, 1974), pp. 85–97.

50 Angus Fletcher, *Allegory: The Theory of a Symbolic Mode* (Ithaca, New York: Cornell University Press, 1964), p. 305.

51 See, for instance, Jean Pépin, *Mythe et Allégorie* (Paris: Études augus-tiniennes, 1976), p. 89.

52 Joëlle Gardes Tamine and Marie-Antoinette Pellizza, 'Pour une défi-nition restreinte de l'allégorie' in Joëlle Gardes Tamine, *L'Allégorie, corps et âme*, pp. 9–28; here, p. 10.

53 Ibid., p. 13.

54 Ibid., p. 14.

55 Ibid., p. 15.

56 As is often done. See, for example, the definition given by Henri Morier: 'Allegory is a description or a narrative expressing familiar, concrete realities in order to convey, metaphorically, an abstract truth'. *Dictionnaire de poétique et de rhétorique* (Paris: PUF, 1981), p. 65.

57 Tamine and Pellizza, 'Pour une définition restreinte de l'allégorie', p. 17.

58 Ibid., p. 25.

59 Cf. David, 'Notice de *Chacals et Arabes*' in David, *Franz Kafka: Oeuvres complètes*, VOL. 2, p. 1062.

60 According to David, however, 'This story is not in any way about Judaism' (ibid.). By contrast, Spector, while proposing an interpre-tation of this narrative different from mine, stresses that the context of the publication of these two stories cannot be insignificant (*Prague Territories*, pp. 190–2).

61 Cf. Kafka, 'Letter to Martin Buber, 22 April 1917' in *Letters to Friends, Family and Editors*, pp. 131–2. See also David, 'Notice de *Chacals et Arabes*' in David, *Franz Kafka: Oeuvres complètes*, VOL. 2, p. 1062. The tales would all be published by Kurt Wolff in the collection *Ein Landarzt* in 1920.

62 Kafka, 'Letter to Martin Buber, 12 May 1917' in *Letters to Friends, Family and Editors*, p. 132 (translation modified).

63 Theodor Adorno, 'Notes on Kafka' in *Prisms* (Samuel Weber and Shierry Weber Nicholson trans) (Boston: MIT Press, 1981), pp. 243–71; here, p. 246.

64 Benjamin, 'Franz Kafka: On the Tenth Anniversary of his Death' in *Selected Writings, Volume 2*, p. 804.

65 Michael Löwy has suggested, rightly as it seems to me, that the major anti-Semitic trials Kafka could have known, such as the Tisza trial (Hungary, 1882), the Dreyfus Affair (France, 1894–99), the Hilsner trial (Bohemia, 1899–1900) and the Beilis trial (Russia, 1912–13) may have directly inspired the writing and structure of *The Trial* (Löwy, *Franz Kafka, rêveur insoumis*, pp. 89–93). Having said that, he does not countenance the view that the book might be about anti-Semitism. Gilman, for his part, asserts that, more than anything else, the Dreyfus Affair provided the model for the book but he does not provide any convincing evidence for this (*Franz Kafka: The Jewish Patient*, pp. 68–87). Bernd Neumann presents *The Trial* as a First World War novel constructed entirely on the basis of the anti-Semitic trials that took place during that period (Neumann, *Franz Kafka: Aporien der Assimilation*, p. 113) and he sees it as a parable of the failed assimilation of Austrian Jews (ibid., pp. 113–74).

66 Arendt, 'The Jew as Pariah: A Hidden Tradition' in Gottlieb, *Hannah Arendt: Reflections on Literature and Culture*, pp. 69–90; here, p. 84.

67 Heinz Politzer, *Franz Kafka, Parable and Paradox* (rev. expanded edition; Ithaca, NY: Cornell University Press, 1966), p. 163.

68 Kafka, *The Trial*, p. 53.

69 Ibid., pp. 40–1.

70 In 'In the Penal Colony', the explorer, as he enters the teahouse, breathes its *dumpfige Luft* (stale air). Franz Kafka, *Die Erzählungen. Originalfassung* (Frankfurt: Fischer Taschenbuch, 2002), p. 197.

71 Jean-Pierre Morel, *Le Procès de Franz Kafka* (Paris: Gallimard 'Folio', 1998), p. 24. Bernd Neumann takes the word 'trial' literally and thinks that the book refers to actual changes in the administration of justice in Bohemia in 1914 as a result of the anti-Semitic trials (Neumann, *Franz Kafka: Aporien der Assimilation*, pp. 127–32).

72 Stressing the kinship between *The Trial* and 'In the Penal Colony', Arendt refers to this judicial apparatus as a 'machine' ('Franz Kafka, Appreciated Anew' in Gottlieb, *Hannah Arendt: Reflections on Literature and Culture*, pp. 96–7).

73 Kafka, *The Trial*, p. 7.

74 Ibid., p. 9.

75 Ibid., p. 40.

76 Ibid., p. 110.

77 Ibid., p. 81.

78 Cf. Morel, *Le Procès de Franz Kafka*, p. 49.

79 Kafka, *The Trial*, p. 152.

80 Ibid., p. 5.

81 Ibid., p. 19.

82 Ibid., p. 38.

83 Ibid., pp. 34–8.

84 Ibid., p. 15.

85 Ibid., p. 16.

86 Kundera, *Testaments Betrayed*, p. 211.

87 Kafka, *The Trial*, p. 128.

88 Ibid., pp. 32–4.

89 Ibid., p. 80. 'He couldn't get the trial out of his mind any more.'

90 Ibid., p. 95.

91 Ibid., p. 124.

92 Ibid., p. 33.

93 Ibid., p. 9.

94 Ibid., p. 50.

95 The change of the name of this character to 'Kaufmann Beck' (that is to say, a non-Jewish name), as shown in the facsimile historical-critical edition, proves that Kafka is torn between a logic of explicit

denunciation, in which his intentions would be clearly emphasized, and a logic of ambiguization that would conceal the principle of the text's construction. With *The Trial*, we can see that he did not make the choice but wavered between the two possibilities.

96 Ibid., p. 50.

97 Ibid., p. 13.

98 Ibid., p. 77.

99 Ibid., pp. 85–6.

100 Ibid., p. 125.

101 Arendt, 'The Jew as Pariah' in Gottlieb, *Hannah Arendt: Reflections on Literature and Culture*, p. 85.

102 Bernard Lazare, *Le Fumier de Job* (Strasbourg: Circé, 1990), p. 99.

103 Ibid., p. 50.

104 Ibid., p. 9.

105 Arendt, 'Franz Kafka, Appreciated Anew' in Gottlieb, *Hannah Arendt: Reflections on Literature and Culture*, p. 96.

106 Pierre Bourdieu, *Masculine Domination* (Richard Nice trans.) (Stanford, CA: Stanford University Press, 2001), p. 52.

107 Ibid.

108 Arthur Schopenhauer, *Die Kunst sich Respekt zu verschaffen* (Munich: C. H. Beck, 2011), p. 11. Seeking to describe the point of honour in Kabyle society, Bourdieu gives a definition of *nif* that is very close to Schopenhauer's definition of honour: '*nif* is, first and foremost, what leads one to defend at any price a certain self-image directed towards others'. See Pierre Bourdieu, 'Le sens de l'honneur' in *Esquisse d'une théorie de la pratique: Précédé de Trois études d'ethnologie kabyle* (Paris: Seuil, 2000), pp. 19–60; here, p. 38.

109 Arthur Schopenhauer, *The Wisdom of Life: The Essays of Arthur Schopenhauer* (T. Bailey Saunders trans.) (Fairford: The Echo Library, 2006), p. 38. Kafka had many of Schopenhauer's works in his possession. Jürgen Born lists nine in *Kafkas Bibliothek* (Frankfurt: Fischer, 1990), pp. 128–30.

110 Kafka, *The Trial*, p. 36.

111 Ibid., p. 37.

112 Ibid., p. 109.

113 Ibid., p. 110.

114 Ibid.

115 Ibid., p. 113.

116 Ibid., p. 114.

117 Ibid., p. 115.

118 Bourdieu, *Masculine Domination*, p. 37.

119 Kafka, *The Trial*, p. 12.

120 Ibid., p. 165.

121 Ibid., p. 20.

122 Ibid.

123 Ibid., p. 25.

124 Ibid., p. 26.

125 Ibid., p. 38.

126 Ibid., p. 41.

127 Ibid., p. 43.

128 Ibid., p. 45.

129 Ibid., p. 46.

130 Ibid., p. 45.

131 Ibid., p. 46.

132 Ibid., p. 49.

133 Ibid., p. 60.

134 Bourdieu, *Masculine Domination*, p. 42.

135 Kafka, *The Trial*, p. 150.

136 Ibid., p. 151.

137 Ibid., p. 152.

138 Ibid., p. 151.

139 Ibid., p. 152.

140 Ibid., pp. 152–3 and p. 160.

141 Arendt, 'Franz Kafka, Appreciated Anew' in Gottlieb, *Hannah Arendt: Reflections on Literature and Culture*, p. 96.

142 In the English translation I am using here, Mitchell translates *Vor dem Gesetz* as 'Outside the Law' (Kafka, *The Trial*, p. 153). [Trans.]

143 Kafka, *The Trial*, p. 153.

144 Ibid., p. 155.

145 Kafka, *Diaries*, p. 297.

146 Paul Valéry, *Oeuvres*, VOL. 2 (Paris: Gallimard, 'Bibliothèque de la Pléiade', 1960), p. 1120.

147 Kafka, 'On the Material Included in this Volume' in *The Complete Stories*, p. 467.

148 Kafka, *The Trial*, p. 155.

149 Morel, *Le Procès de Franz Kafka*, pp. 76–7.

150 Ibid., p. 78.

151 Ibid., p. 80.

152 Ibid., p. 75.

153 Kafka, *The Trial*, p. 155.

154 Ibid., p. 158.

155 Ibid., p. 159.

156 Arendt, 'Franz Kafka, Appreciated Anew' in Gottlieb, *Hannah Arendt: Reflections on Literature and Culture*, p. 96.

157 Ibid., p. 97.

158 Kafka, *The Trial*, p. 159.

159 Ibid.

160 Michel notes the particular importance of the Church in Bohemia at the turn of the twentieth century and reminds us that in the 1910 census Catholics represented 92.6 per cent of the population (*Prague, Belle Époque*, p. 30).

161 Kafka, '5 October 1911' in *Diaries*, p. 65.

162 Ibid., pp. 66–8.

163 Die Seydernacht is a play in which the action involves a plot to accuse Jews of ritual murder, a stratagem that is uncovered just in time by those who were about to fall victim to it. Cf. Bruce, *Kafka and Cultural Zionism*, p. 38.

164 Peter Sprengel, *Scheunenviertel-Theater. Jüdische Schauspieltruppen und jiddische Dramatik in Berlin (1900–1918)* (Berlin: Fannei & Waltz, 1995), p. 13.

165 David, 'Préface' in Franz Kafka, *Un médecin de campagne et autres récits*, p. 12.

166 Kafka, 'In the Penal Colony' in *The Complete Stories*, p. 167.

167 Ibid., p. 408.

168 And one can see in this inversion both Kafka's irony and his anger towards all 'fathers'.

169 Ibid., pp. 406–08 (translation modified).

170 Kafka, 'A Little Woman' in *The Complete Stories*, p. 321.

171 Ibid.

172 Unfortunately, the English translation renders 'meine kleine Richterin', which has clear legal overtones, as 'my small critic'. [Trans.]

173 Ibid., p. 322, translation modified [Kafka's original German here is: 'Aber nichts von Entscheidung, nichts von Verantwortung'. The French version which Casanova uses here runs: 'Mais de décision, point ; de justification, point' and I have modified the standard English translation to take account of this. Trans.]

174 Ibid., pp. 323–4.

175 Ibid., p. 322.

176 Ibid.

177 Ibid., pp. 322–3.

178 Ibid., p. 323.

179 Kafka, '24 November 1912' in *Letters to Felice*, pp. 167–8.

180 Ibid., p. 168.

181 Kafka, '24–25 January 1913'. [This passage is not included in the Heller and Born edition of the correspondence. Trans.]

182 From the *Prager Tagblatt* of 25 September 1912. Cited in David, *Franz Kafka: Oeuvres complètes*, VOL. 4, p. 1229.

183 Kafka specifies that 'the officer was speaking French' ('In the Penal Colony', p. 142). According to Gilman, the Dreyfus Affair forms the backdrop to the entire story and the island described by Kafka is directly inspired by Devil's Island to which Dreyfus was sent to serve his sentence (Gilman, *Franz Kafka: The Jewish Patient*, p. 81).

184 Löwy, *Franz Kafka, rêveur insoumis*, p. 70.

185 Ibid., p. 71.

186 In other words, it seems to me that Kafka does indeed have a point of view, but it can emerge only if the specificity of his position in

the Prague literary space is restored. For Anderson and Gilman, on the other hand, it is not possible to assign a definite position to Kafka in this text. For the one, he 'is everywhere in his text at once—the machine, the officer, the European explorer, the Former Commandant, even the "stupid-looking, wide-mouthed" prisoner' (Anderson, 'Chapter 7: The Ornaments of Writing: "In the Penal Colony"' in *Kafka's Clothes*, p. 193). For the other, he is as much the creator of the machine as its victim (Gilman, *Franz Kafka: The Jewish Patient*, p. 87).

187 Kafka, 'In the Penal Colony' in *The Complete Stories*, p. 145.

188 Ibid., p. 141 (translation modified).

189 Ibid., p. 145.

190 Ibid., p. 144.

191 Ibid., p. 150.

192 Ibid., p. 144.

193 Ibid., pp. 153–4.

194 Ibid., p. 146.

195 Ibid., p. 151.

196 Ibid., p. 152.

197 Ibid., p. 154.

198 Robert, *As Lonely as Franz Kafka*, p. 167.

199 Kafka, *Dearest Father*, p. 84.

200 Ibid.

201 Ibid.

202 Kafka, 'In the Penal Colony' in *The Complete Stories*, p. 146.

203 Ibid., pp. 145–6.

204 Ibid., p. 146.

205 Ibid., p. 140.

206 David, 'Notice de *La Colonie pénitentiaire*' in David, *Franz Kafka: Oeuvres complètes*, VOL. 2, p. 957.

207 Kafka, 'In the Penal Colony' in *The Complete Stories*, p. 144.

208 Leo Frobenius, 'The Origin of African Civilizations' in *Annual Report of the Board of Regents of the Smithsonian Institution for the Year Ending June 30, 1898* (B. Hoepffner trans.), p. 637. This translation is based

on a *Sonderabdruck* from the *Zeitschrift der Erdkunde*, VOL. 33 (Berlin, 1898). This was an initial outline of a work by Frobenius that would be published some months later as *Der Ursprung der afrikanischen Kulturen* (Berlin: Gebrüder Borntraeger, 1898).

209 Leo Frobenius, 'Fiat Lux', *Und Afrika Sprach. Bericht über den Verlauf der dritten Reise-Periode der D. I. A. F. E. in den Jahren 1910 bis 1912* (Berlin: Vita, 1913), p. 9.

210 Kafka, 'In the Penal Colony' in *The Complete Stories*, p. 163.

211 Ibid., p. 166.

212 Ibid., p. 158.

213 Ibid., p. 146. The use of free indirect style makes for greater lightness of syntax than indirect style. This last sentence, for example, had it been written in indirect style, would be phrased as follows: 'He told himself that he had to remember that . . .' However, it also enables a kind of ambiguity to be maintained regarding the status of the speaker.

214 Ibid., p. 151.

215 Ibid.

216 Ibid., p. 157.

217 Ibid., p. 156.

218 Ibid., p. 157.

219 Ibid., p. 159.

220 Ibid., p. 160.

221 Ibid., p. 167.

222 Kafka, *Diaries*, p. 380.

223 Ibid.

224 Ibid.

225 Ibid.

226 Kafka, 'Up in the Gallery' in *The Complete Stories*, pp. 401–02.

227 Ibid.

228 Ibid.

229 Ibid.

230 Ibid.

231 Ibid., pp. 401–02.

232 Kafka, 'A Country Doctor' in *The Complete Stories*, p. 223.

233 Ibid., p. 224.

234 Ibid., p. 225.

235 Ibid.

236 Ibid., p. 223.

237 Ibid. Attributing little legs to the worms clearly adds to the parodic comedy of the description.

I am aware of having sketched a portrait in this book of an unfamiliar Kafka, a Kafka apparently foreign to most of his readers, a writer so dependent on the political and social configuration of turn-of-the-century Prague that it seems difficult for us still to identify with his dilemmas, his heartaches, his humour and his closely held convictions. But that is not the case at all. This book is not a manifesto which would require Kafka's particularization or his removal from the literary pantheon on grounds of a damning dependence on history. The unfamiliarity which may initially be engendered by his reinscription in the world in no way diminishes his universal value. The error of perspective (the *trompe-l'oeil* effect, as it were) would be to conceive the question of universalization as involving a choice between two exclusive terms: either Kafka would be linked to the history of the European Jews of the early part of the twentieth century, in which case he could be understood only if we restored the extreme particularism of his work; or he would, in a vague, general way, reflect a moral philosophy available to all, in which case he would be celebrated along the lines of a vague universalism. I think we have to proceed in terms of both these assumptions at once. He is both a deeply Jewish writer, enquiring into the aporias of his own existence, and the thinker of a dominated humanity defined as a universal—and the two things are indivisible.

This angry Kafka is, in reality, very close to us. More exactly, he emerges as someone all the closer to us once we have gauged the full extent of the distance separating us from him. The historicization I have attempted to carry out here is, admittedly, an indispensable instrument for ridding ourselves of projections, and of illusions that his texts are immediately understandable. But it is also, ultimately, an immense detour by which to reappropriate, in a different way, the meaning of a literary undertaking. Far from marginalizing Kafka's texts by an interpretation that would confine them to narrow historical limits, my interpretive hypothesis allows us better to understand one of the reasons why they have been canonized in such an extraordinary way. It seems to me, in fact, that Kafka's hidden universality is the precise and particular object of his anger: it is his novel thinking on the paradoxes of authority and the universal question of domination that have earned him this virtually unconfined recognition. Symbolic domination is the commonest thing in the world and the confrontation between Jews and Germans at Prague was not the exclusive object of his anger. The most fascinating thing, when one tries to reconstruct Kafka's position—to reconstruct the series of problems with which he concerned himself—is that one finds, despite the extreme intellectual solitude in which he found himself, that he extended his field of investigation by producing, as he went along, a kind of freshly minted comparativism and interesting himself in all forms of social domination, particularly the most invisible.

This is why, against the clichés of saintliness and withdrawal from—or indifference to—the world that are foisted on him, I would like to highlight another feature of his character, which is in many ways also universal: his combative urge. By a kind of reflex reaction, linked to the categories and periodizations of literary history, critics habitually purse the question of his links to aesthetic modernity and modernism. In reality, as I see it, Kafka's great modernity lies in the fact that he was a fighting writer. His despair arose in large part from his extreme awareness of the dissymmetry in the balance of forces. In no way did he harbour the illusion that he would win out. His last will and testament bears witness to this. But the idea—constant, insistent and consubstantial with his literary urge—that writing is a battle and literature a fierce weapon in a merciless struggle that is as unequal as it is fierce, is one of the central definitions of his literary labours. He created totally new literary devices, previously unseen ways of disturbing his readers, of undermining narratorial omniscience, of putting an unreliable narrator on the scene; he also reflected on the features common to all the 'small literatures' and this makes him one of the first theorists of the dominated literary worlds. He was, in short, the first to equip himself with all the specific instruments of literary struggle which the dominated writers of the world republic of letters have repeatedly taken up again in his wake, without giving him his due for their creation. This is why, throughout the work on this book, Kafka has been for me a sort of extraordinary individual case in whom was embodied, probably more than in any other writer, the unforgiving structure of the global literary space. And his textual weapons are probably among the sharpest (that is to say, the most formidable). They are the great secret of the war Kafka conducted alone. Perhaps the core of his anger.

Most movingly, in the very last pages of his diary, shortly before illness prevented him from writing, he noted:

> More and more fearful as I write. It is understandable. Every word, twisted in the hands of the spirits—this twist of the hand is their characteristic gesture—becomes a spear turned against the speaker [. . .] More than consolation is: You too have weapons.[1]

NOTE

1   Kafka, *Diaries*, p. 423.

Bibliography

PRIMARY SOURCES

Amerika: The Man Who Disappeared (Michael Hofmann trans.). London and New York: Penguin Books, 2007.

Briefe: 1902–1924 (Max Brod ed.). Frankfurt: Fischer, 1966.

The Castle (Willa and Edwin Muir trans). London: Vintage Books, 2005.

The Complete Stories of Franz Kafka (Nahum N. Glatzer ed.). New York: Schocken Books, 1995. See, especially, the following (all translated by Willa and Edwin Muir):

'The Judgment', pp. 77–88.

'In the Penal Colony', pp. 140–67.

'The Village Schoolmaster', pp. 168–82.

'A Country Doctor', pp. 220–5.

'A Report to an Academy', pp. 250–9.

'The Great Wall of China', pp. 266–77.

'Investigations of a Dog', pp. 278–316.

'A Little Woman', pp. 319–24.

'The Burrow', pp. 325–59.

'Josephine the Singer, or the Mouse Folk', pp. 360–76.

'Up in the Gallery', pp. 401–02.

'Jackals and Arabs', pp. 407–10.

'An Old Manuscript', pp. 415–17.

'A Crossbreed [A Sport]', pp. 426–7.

Dearest Father: Stories and Other Writings (Ernst Kaiser and Eithne Wilkins trans). New York: Schocken Books, 1954. See, especially, the following:

'Concerning the Jewish Theatre', pp. 129–34.

'Letter to His Father', pp. 138–97.

'Introductory Talk on the Yiddish Language', pp. 381–6.

'Ein Hungerkünstler' in Hans-Gerd Koch (ed.), *Franz Kafka: Gesammelte Werke in zwölf Bänden, Volume I: Ein Landarzt; und andere Drucke zu Lebzeiten*. Frankfurt: Fischer Taschenbuch, 2008, pp. 261–73.

Franz Kafka: Briefe an Felice und andere Korrespondenz aus der Verlobungszeit (Erich Heller and Jürgen Born eds) (Frankfurt: Fischer, 1981), p. 697.

Franz Kafka: The Office Writings (Stanley Corngold, Jack Greenberg and Benno Wagner eds, Eric Patton and Ruth Hein trans). Princeton: Princeton University Press, 2008.

'A Hunger Artist' in *The Complete Short Stories of Franz Kafka* (Nahum N. Glatzer ed., Willa and Edwin Muir trans). London: Vintage Books, 2005, pp. 268–77.

Letters to Felice (Erich Heller and Jürgen Born eds, James Stern and Elisabeth Duckworth trans). New York: Schocken Books, 1988.

Letters to Friends, Family and Editors (Beverly Colman, Nahum N. Glatzer, Christopher J. Kuppig and Wolfgang Sauerland eds). Richmond: Oneworld Classics, 2011.

Letters to Milena (Willy Haas ed., Tania Stern and James Stern trans). London: Vintage Books, 1999.

'Memoirs of the Kalda Railroad' in Max Brod (ed.), *The Diaries of Franz Kafka 1910–1923* (Joseph Kresh and Martin Greenberg trans). Harmondsworth: Penguin Books, 1972, pp. 303–23.

The Metamorphosis (Susan Bernofsky trans., David Croenberg introd.). London and New York: W. W. Norton and Co., 1996.

The Trial (Mike Mitchell trans.). Oxford: Oxford University Press, 2009.

SECONDARY SOURCES

ABU'L-ALĀ. *Arabische Gedichten aus dem zehnten Jahrhundert*. Munich: P. Bruckmann, 1920.

ADORNO, Theodor W. 'Notes on Kafka' in *Prisms* (Samuel Weber and Shierry Weber Nicholson trans). Boston: MIT Press, 1981, pp. 243–71.

ALEICHEM, Sholem. 'Dreyfus in Kasrilevke' (Hilde Abel trans.) in Irving Howe and Eliezer Greenberg (eds), *A Treasury of Yiddish Stories*. New York: Schocken Books, 1973, pp. 187–92.

———. *La peste soit de l'Amérique* (Nadia Déhan ed.). Paris: Liana Levi, 2005.

ALT, Peter-André. *Franz Kafka: Der ewige Sohn*. Munich: C. H. Beck, 2008.

AMUNDSEN, Roald. *Eskimoleben: Eindrücke von der Polarfahrt 1903–1907*. Cologne: Schaffstein, 1912.

ANDERS, Günther. *Franz Kafka*. Cambridge: Bowes and Bowes, 1960.

ANDERSON, Mark. *Kafka's Clothes: Ornament and Aestheticism in the Habsburg Fin de Siècle*. Oxford and New York: Oxford University Press, 1992.

APOLLINAIRE, Guillaume. *L'Hérésiarque et Cie*. Paris: Stock, Delamain et Boutelleau, 1910.

———. 'The Wandering Jew' (1902) in *The Wandering Jew: And Other Stories* (Rémy Inglis Hall trans.). London: Rupert Hart-Davis, 1967, pp. 3–16.

ARENDT, Hannah. 'Active Patience' in *The Jewish Writings* (Jerome Kohn and Ron H. Feldman eds.). New York: Schocken Books, 2007, pp. 139–42.

———. 'Franz Kafka, Appreciated Anew' (Martin Klebes trans.) in Susannah Young-ah Gottlieb (ed.), *Hannah Arendt: Reflections on Literature and Culture*. Stanford: Stanford University Press, 2007, pp. 94–109.

———. 'The Jew as Pariah: A Hidden Tradition' in Susannah Young-ah Gottlieb (ed.), *Hannah Arendt: Reflections on Literature and Culture.* Stanford: Stanford University Press, 2007, pp. 69–90.

ASCHHEIM, Steven E. *Brothers and Strangers: The East European Jew in German and German Jewish Consciousness 1800–1923.* Madison: University of Wisconsin Press, 1982.

BARBIER, Frédéric. 'Construction d'une capitale: Leipzig et la librairie allemande, 1750–1914' in Christophe Charle and Daniel Roche (eds), *Capitales culturelles, capitales symboliques: Paris et les expériences européennes.* Paris: Publications de la Sorbonne, 2002, pp. 335–57.

BARNARD, Frederick M. *Herder on Nationality, Humanity and History.* Montreal: McGill-Queen's University Press, 2003.

BAUMGARTEN, Jean. *Le Yiddish. Histoire d'une langue errante.* Paris: Albin Michel, 2002.

BAUSINGER, Hermann. *Volkskunde: von der Altertumsforschung zur Kulturanalyse.* Tübingen: Tübinger Vereinigung für Volkskunde, 1987.

BECHTEL, Delphine. *La Renaissance culturelle juive: Europe centrale et orientale, 1897–1930: langue, littérature et construction nationale.* Paris: Belin, 2002.

—— (ed.). *Les Villes multiculturelles en Europe central.* Paris: Belin, 2008.

BENJAMIN, Walter. 'Franz Kafka. On the Tenth Anniversary of His Death', in *Selected Writings, Volume 2: 1921–1934* (Michael W. Jennings, Howard Eiland and Gary Smith ed., Rodney Livingstone et al. trans). Cambridge and London: Belknap Press, 1999, pp. 794–818.

BERDICHEVSKY, Micha Joseph, Rahel Bin Gorion and Emanuel Bin-Gorion. *Die Sagen der Juden.* Frankfurt: Rütten and Loening, 1919.

BERGMANN, Hugo. 'Schulzeit und Studium' in Hans-Gerd Koch (ed.), *'Als Kafka mir entgegenkam.' Erinnerungen an Franz Kafka.* Berlin: Verlag Klaus Wagenbach, 1995, pp. 13–24.

BIASI, Pierre-Marc. *Gustave Flaubert: Une manière spéciale de vivre.* Paris: Grasset, 2009.

BIBÓ, István. *Misère des petits États d'Europe de l'Est* (G. Kassai trans.). Paris: Albin Michel, 1993.

BINDER, Hartmut. *Kafka: Kommentar zu sämtlichen Erzählungen.* Munich: Winkler, 1975.

——. *Kafka in neuer Sicht.* Stuttgart: Metzler, 1976.

——. 'Unvergebene Schlamperei: ein unbekannter Brief Franz Kafkas', *Jahrbuch der deutschen Schillergesellschaft* 25 (1981): 133–8.

——. 'Entlarvung einer Chimäre: die deutsche Sprachinsel Prag' in Maurice Godé, Jacques Le Rider and Françoise Mayer (eds), *Allemands, Juifs et Tchèques à Prague—Deutsche, Juden und Tschechen in Prag, 1890–1924, Actes du colloque international de Montpellier, 8–10 décembre 1994.* Montpellier: Bibliothèque d'études germaniques et centre-européennes, 1996, pp. 183–209.

—— (ed.). *Kafka-Handbuch in zwei Bänden.* Stuttgart: Alfred Kröner, 1979.

—— (ed.). *Prager Profile: Vergessene Autoren im Schatten* Kafkas. Berlin: Mann, 1991.

BOKHOVE, Niels. '"The Entrance to the More Important": Kafka's Personal Zionism' in Mark H. Gelber (ed.), *Kafka, Zionism and Beyond.* Tübingen: Max Niemeyer, 2004, pp. 23–58.

BORN, Jürgen. *Kafkas Bibliothek: Ein beschreibendes Verzeichnis.* Frankfurt: Fischer, 1990.

——, Gerhard Neumann, Malcolm Pasley and Jost Shillemeit (eds), *Franz Kafka: Kritische Ausgabe. Gesammelte Werke in der Fassung der Handschrift in 12 Bänden.* Frankfurt: Fischer, 1982.

BOURDIEU, Pierre. *The Rules of Art: Genesis and Structure of the Literary Field* (Susan Emanuel trans.). Stanford: Stanford University Press, 1992.

——. 'Le sens de l'honneur' in *Esquisse d'une théorie de la pratique: Précédé de Trois études d'ethnologie kabyle.* Paris: Seuil, 2000, pp. 19–60.

———. *Masculine Domination* (Richard Nice trans.). Stanford: Stanford University Press, 2001.

BOUVERESSE, Jacques. 'Les derniers jours de l'humanité', *Critique* 339–40 (August–September 1975): 753–805.

BRAUN, Lily. *Memoiren einer Sozialistin*, 2 VOLS. Munich: Langen, 1909–11.

BROD, Max. *Tod den Toten*. Stuttgart: Juncker, 1906.

———. *Schloß Nornepygge: Der Roman Des Indifferenten*. Berlin: Axel Juncker, 1908.

———. 'Eine Jargonbühne in Prag', *Prager Tagblatt* (27 October 1911).

———. 'Der jüdische Dichter deutscher Zunge' in *Vom Judentum: Ein Sammelbuch*. Leipzig: Kurt Wolff and Verein jüdischer Hochschüler Bar Kochba in Prague, 1913, 261–3.

———. 'Brief an eine Schülerin nach Galizien', *Der Jude* 2 (May 1916).

———. *Heidentum, Christentum, Judentum: ein bekenntnisbuch*. Leipzig: Kurt Wolff, 1922.

———. *Franz Kafkas Glauben und Lehre*. Winterthur: Mondial, 1948.

———. *Streitbares Leben: Autobiographie 1884–1968*. Frankfurt: Insel Verlag, 1979.

———. *Der Prager Kreis*. Frankfurt: Suhrkamp, 1993.

———. *Franz Kafka: A Biography* (G. Humphreys Roberts and Richard Winston trans). Cambridge, MA: De Capo Press, 1995.

———. *Tycho Brahe's Path to God* (Felix Warren Crosse trans.). Evanston: Northwestern University Press, 2007.

——— (ed.). *Franz Kafka: Gesammelte Werke*. Frankfurt: Fischer, 1966.

——— (ed.). *The Diaries of Franz Kafka 1910–1923* (Joseph Kresh and Martin Greenberg trans). Harmondsworth: Penguin Books, 1972.

——— and Felix Weltsch. *Anschauung und Begriff: Grundzuge Eines Systems Der Begriffsbildung*. Leipzig: Kurt Wolff, 1913.

BRUCE, Iris. *Kafka and Cultural Zionism: Dates in Palestine*. Madison: The University of Wisconsin Press, 2007.

BUBER, Martin. *Drei Reden über das Judentum*. Frankfurt: Rütten and Loenin, 1911.

——. *Tales of the Hasidim: The Early Masters* (Olga Marx trans.). London: Thames and Hudson, 1956.

——. *The Legend of the Baal-Shem* (Maurice Friedman trans.). Princeton: Princeton University Press, 1995.

——. *The Tales of Rabbi Nachman* (Maurice Friedman trans.). New York: Humanity Books, 2011.

CAMBON, Fernand. 'La soumission et la loi', *Europe* 923 (March 2006): 98–112.

CANETTI, Elias. *The Conscience of Words* (Joachim Neugroschel trans.). London: HarperCollins, 1979.

——. 'Kafka's Other Trial' in Franz Kafka, *Letters to Felice* (Erich Heller and Jurgen Born eds, James Stern and Elisabeth Duckworth trans). New York: Schocken Books, 1988, pp. 7–94.

CASANOVA, Pascale. *The World Republic of Letters* (M. B. DeBevoise trans.). Cambridge and London: Harvard University Press, 2004.

——. 'Le méridien de Greenwich: réflexions sur le temps de la littérature' in Lionel Ruffel (ed.), *Qu'est-ce que le contemporain?*. Nantes: Cécile Defaut, 2010, pp. 113–45.

——. 'La guerre de l'ancienneté' in Pascale Casanova (ed.), *Des littératures combatives: L'internationale des nationailismes littéraires*. Paris: Raisons d'agir, 2011, pp. 11–31.

—— (ed.). *Des littératures combatives: L'internationale des nationailismes littéraires*. Paris: Raisons d'agir, 2011.

CHARLE, Christophe. 'Les théâtres et leurs publics: paris, Berlin et vienne, 1860–1914' in Christophe Charle and Daniel Roche (eds), *Capitales culturelles, capitales symboliques: Paris et les expériences européennes*. Paris: Publications de la Sorbonne, 2002, pp. 403–20.

COHEN, Gary B. *The Politics of Ethnic Survival, 1861–1914*. Princeton: Princeton University Press, 1981.

DAMISCH, Hubert. 'L'autre *Ich* ou le désir du vide: pour un tombeau d'Adolf Loos', *Critique* 339–40 (August–September 1975): 806–18.

DANÈS, Jean-Pierre. 'Situation de la littérature allemande à l'époque de Kafka' in *Prague, Kafka, Chweïk: etudes*. Versailles: Marie-Dosée Danès, 1989, pp. 39–62.

DARNTON, Robert. *The Great Cat Massacre and Other Episodes in French Cultural History*. New York: Vintage Books, 1985.

DAVID, Claude. *Franz Kafka*. Paris: Fayard, 1989.

——. 'Préface' in Franz Kafka, *Un médecin de campagne et autres récits/Ein Landarzt und andere Erzählungen*. Paris: Gallimard, 'Folio bilingue', 1996.

—— (ed.). *Franz Kafka: Oeuvres complètes*, 4 VOLS (Jean-Pierre Danès, Claude David, Marthe Robert and Alexander Vialatte trans). Paris: Gallimard, 1980.

DAVID, Yasha and Jean-Pierre Morel (eds). *Le Siècle de Kafka*. Paris: Centre Georges Pompidou, 1984.

DELEUZE, Gilles and Félix Guattari. *Kafka: Toward a Minor Literature* (Dana Polan trans.). Minneapolis: University of Minnesota Press, 1986.

DIECKHOFF, Alain. *L'Invention d'une nation: Israël et la modernité politique*. Paris: Gallimard, 1993.

——. 'Litvakie: le terreau sioniste' in Alain Dieckhoff and Yves Plasseraud (eds), *Lituanie juive, 1918–1940. Message d'un monde englouti*. Paris: Autrement, 1996, pp. 158–66.

DITTMAR, Julius. *Im neuen China: Reiseeindrücke von J. Dittmar*. Cologne: Schaffstein, 1912.

DREYFUS, Théodore. *Martin Buber*. Paris: Le Cerf, 1981.

DUBNOW, Simon. 'Ninth Letter: A Historic Moment (The Question of Emigration)' in *Nationalism and History: Essays on Old and New*

Judaism. Philadelphia: Jewish Publication Society of America, 1958, pp. 193–4.

——. 'On National Education' in *Nationalism and History: Essays on Old and New Judaism*. Philadelphia: Jewish Publication Society of America, 1958, pp. 143–54.

——. *Lettres sur le judaïsme ancien et nouveau*. Paris: Les Cerf, 1989.

EISNER, Pavel. 'Erotische Symbiose', *Prager Presse* (23 March 1930).

——. *Franz Kafka and Prague* (Lowry Nelson and Rene Wellek trans). New York: Arts, 1950.

ELBOGEN, Ismar and Eleonore Sterling. *Die Geschichte der Juden in Deutschland*. Frankfurt: Athenäum, 1988.

ERTL, Rachel. *Le Shtetl: La bourgade juive de Pologne* Paris: Payot, 1986.

——. 'La littérature yiddish: une littérature sans frontières' in Rachel Ertl (ed.), *Royaumes juifs: Trésors de la littérature yiddish*, VOL. I. Paris: Robert Laffont, 2008, pp. *ix–lv*.

FERENCZI, Rose-Marie. *Kafka: Subjectivité, histoire et structures*. Paris: Klincksieck, 1975.

FISCHER, Ernst. *Von Grillparzer zu Kafka*. Vienna: Die Buchgemeinde, 1962.

FISHMAN, Joshua A. 'Attracting a Following to High-Culture Functions for a Language of Everyday Life: The Role of the Tshernovits Language Conference in the "Rise of Yiddish" ' in Joshua A. Fishman (ed.), *Never Say Die! A Thousand Years of Yiddish in Jewish Life and Letters (Contributions to the Sociology of Language)*. The Hague: Mouton, 1981, pp. 370–91.

——. 'Le yiddish: de la tradition à la modernisation' in Shmuel Trigano (ed.), *La société juive à travers l'histoire*, VOL. 4. Paris: Fayard, 1993, pp. 511–21.

FLETCHER, Angus. *Allegory: The Theory of a Symbolic Mode*. Ithaca, New York: Cornell University Press, 1964.

FOUCAULT, Michel. *The Order of Things: An Archaeology of the Human Sciences* (Alan Sheridan trans.). London: Tavistock Publications, 1986.

FRANKEL, Jonathan. *Prophecy and Politics: Socialism, Nationalism and the Russian Jews*. Cambridge, London and New York: Cambridge University Press, 1981.

FROBENIUS, Leo. 'The Origin of African Civilizations', *Annual Report of the Board of Regents of the Smithsonian Institution for the Year Ending June 30, 1898* (B. Hoepffner trans.) (n. d.).

——. *Der Ursprung der afrikanischen Kulturen*. Berlin: Bornträgger, 1898.

——. *Das Zeitalter des Sonnengottes*. Berlin: Georg Reimer, 1904.

——. 'Fiat Lux', *Und Afrika Sprach: Bericht über den Verlauf der dritten Reise-Periode der D. I. A. F. E. in den Jahren 1910 bis 1912*. Berlin: Vita, 1913.

——. *Atlantis: Volksmärchen und Volksdichtungen Afrikas, Volumes 1 and 2: Volksmärchen der Kabyln*. Jena: Eugen Diederichs, 1921.

——. *L'Atlantide: Mythologie et cultes* (F. Gidon trans.). Paris: Éditions du rocher, 1993.

——. 'Introduction' in *Contes kabyles*, VOL. 3. Aix-en-Provence: Édisud, 1997, pp. 7–9.

FRUG, Samuel. 'Sand and Stars' (trans. anon.) and 'As the Stars and the Sands' (Joseph Jasin trans.) in *The Standard Book of Jewish Verse* (Joseph Friedlander comp., George Alexander Kohut ed.). New York: Dodd, Mead and Company, 1917, p. 700, p. 703.

FRYE, Northrop. *Anatomy of Criticism*. Princeton: Princeton University Press, 1957.

GALMICHE, Xavier. 'Multiculturalité et uniculturalisme. Le paradoxe de Prague' in Delphine Bechtel (ed.), *Les Villes multiculturelles en Europe centrale*. Paris: Belin, 2008, pp. 41–63.

GAXIE, Jean-Pierre. *L'Égypte de Franz Kafka: Une relecture*. Paris: Maurice Nadeau, 2002.

GELBER, Mark H. 'Kafka und zionistische Deutungen' in Bettina von Jagow and Oliver Jahraus (eds), *Kafka-Handbuch: Leben-Werk-Wirkung*. Göttingen: Vanderhoeck & Ruprecht, 2008, pp. 293–303.

——— (ed.). *Kafka, Zionism and Beyond*. Tübingen: Max Niemeyer, 2004.

GILMAN, Sander L. *Jewish Self-Hatred, Antisemitism and the Hidden Language of the Jews*. Baltimore and London: The Johns Hopkins University Press, 1986.

———. *Franz Kafka: The Jewish Patient*. New York and London: Routledge, 1995.

GODÉ, Maurice. 'Un "petit roman" qui a fait du bruit: Une servante tchèque de Max Brod' (1909) in Maurice Godé, Jacques Le Rider and Françoise Mayer (eds), *Allemands, Juifs et Tchèques à Prague—Deutsche, Juden und Tschechen in Prag, 1890–1924, Actes du colloque international de Montpellier, 8–10 décembre 1994*. Montpellier: Bibliothèque d'études germaniques et centre-européennes, 1996, pp. 225–40.

——— Jacques Le Rider and Françoise Mayer (eds). *Allemands, Juifs et Tchèques à Prague—Deutsche, Juden und Tschechen in Prag, 1890–1924, Actes du colloque international de Montpellier, 8–10 décembre 1994*. Montpellier: Bibliothèque d'études germaniques et centre-européennes, 1996.

——— and Michel Vanoosthuyse (eds). *Entre critique et rire: 'Le Disparu' de Franz Kafka*. Montpellier: Université Paul-Valéry de Montpellier, 1997.

GOEBEL, Rolf J. 'Kafka's "An Old Manuscript" and the European Discourse on Ch'ing Dynasty China' in Adrian Hsia (ed.), *Kafka and China: Euro-Sinica 7*. Bern: Peter Lang, 1996, pp. 97–111.

GOLDSTEIN, Moritz. *Begriff und Programm einer jüdischen Nationalliteratur*. Berlin: Jüdischer Verlag, 1912.

GRAETZ, Heinrich. *Volkstümliche Geschichte der Juden*. Leipzig: Oskar Leiner, 1887–1889.

———. *History of the Jews*, 6 VOLS (Bella Löwy ed. and trans.). Philadelphia: The Jewish Publication Society of America, 1891.

GRAY, Richard T. *Constructive Destruction: Kafka's Aphorisms; Literary Tradition and Literary Transformation*. Tübingen: Max Niemeyer, 1987.

HAAS, Willy. *Die Literarische Welt*. Munich: Paul List, 1958.

HALL, Murray G. 'L'édition littéraire à Vienne entre 1900 et 1914' in François Latraverse and Walter Moser (eds), *Vienne au tournant du siècle*. Paris: Albin Michel, 1988, pp. 359–72.

HAVRÁNEK, Ján. 'Structure sociale des Allemands, des Tchèques, des chrétiens et des Juifs à Prague, à la lumière des statistiques des années 1890–1930' (A. Madelain trans.) in Maurice Godé, Jacques Le Rider and Françoise Mayer (eds), *Allemands, Juifs et Tchèques à Prague—Deutsche, Juden und Tschechen in Prag, 1890–1924, Actes du colloque international de Montpellier, 8–10 décembre 1994*. Montpellier: Bibliothèque d'études germaniques et centre-européennes, 1996, pp. 71–81.

HEINRICHS, Hans-Jürgen. *Die fremde Welt, das bin ich. Leo Frobenius. Ethnologe, Forschungsreisender, Abenteurer*. Wuppertal: Peter Hammer, 1998.

HERDER, Johann Gottfried. *Outlines of a Philosophy of the History of Man* (T. O. Churchill trans.) London: J. Johnson, 1808.

HERZL, Theodor. *Die entschwundenen Zeiten*. Vienna, 1897.

————. *The Jewish State* (Sylvie d'Avigdor trans.). New York: Dover, 1988.

HOBSBAWM, Eric. *Nations and Nationalism since 1780: Programme, Myth and Reality*. Cambridge: Cambridge University Press, 1992.

HOFFMANNSTHAL, Hugo von. *The Lord Chandos Letter* (Russell Stockman trans.) Vermont: Marlboro Press, 1986.

HOLITSCHER, Arthur. *Amerika heute und morgen. Reiseerlebnisse*. Berlin: Fischer, 1913.

HOWE, Irving, with the assistance of Kenneth Libo. *World of Our Fathers: The Journey of the East European Jews to America and the Life They Found and Made*. New York: Harcourt, Brace, Jovanovich, 1976.

—— and Eliezer Greenberg (eds). *A Treasury of Yiddish Stories.* New York: Schocken Books, 1973.

HSIA, Adrian. 'China as Ethical Construct and Reflector of Europe's Self-Perception: A Historical Survey up to Kafka's Time' in Adrian Hsia (ed.), *Kafka and China: Euro-Sinica 7.* Bern: Peter Lang, 1996, pp. 22–3.

JANIK, Allan and Stephen Toulmin. *Wittgenstein's Vienna.* New York: Simon and Schuster, 1973.

JANOUCH, Gustav. *Gespräche mit Kafka: Erweiterte Ausgabe.* Frankfurt: Fischer, 1968.

——. *Conversations with Kafka* (Goronwy Rees trans.). London: Quartet Books, 1985.

——. *Conversations avec Kafka.* (Bernard Lortholary trans.) Paris: Maurice Nadeau, 1998.

JOHNSTON, William M. *The Austrian Mind.* Berkeley, Los Angeles and London: University of California Press, 1983.

JOLLES, André. *Einfache Formen: Legende, Sage, Mythe, Rätsel, Spruch, Kasus, Memorabile, Märchen, Witz.* Leipzig: Halle, 1930.

KARÁDY, Viktor. 'Les Juifs, l'État et la société dans la monarchie bicéphale' in Miklós Molnár and André Reszler (eds), *Le Génie de l'Autriche-Hongrie.* Paris: PUF, 1989, pp. 83–98.

——. 'De la métropole académique à l'université de province. Note sur la place de Vienne dans le marché international des études supérieures (1880–1938)', *Revue germanique international* 1 (1994): 221–42.

——. 'Les juifs et les États-nations dans l'Europe contemporaine (XVIIIe–XIXe siècle), *Actes de la recherche en sciences sociales* 118 (June 1997): 28–54.

KIEVAL, Hillel J. *The Making of Czech Jewry: National Conflict and Jewish Society, 1870–1918.* Oxford and New York: Oxford University Press, 1988.

KILCHER, Andreas. 'Sprachendiskurse im judischen Prag um 1900' in Marek Nekula, Ingrid Fleischmann and Albrecht Greule (eds),

Franz Kafka im sprachnationalen Kontext seiner Zeit: Sprache und nationale Identität in öffentlichen Institutionen der böhmischen Länder. Cologne, Weimar and Vienna: Böhlau, 2007, pp. 61–86.

KISCH, Egon Erwin. *Gesammelte Werke in Einzelausgaben, Volume 7: Marktplatz des Sensationen.* Berlin and Weimar: Aufbau, 1974.

KLEIN, Christian. 'Introduction: Incohérences et irritations: les impasses de la critique' in Maurice Godé and Michel Vanoosthuyse (eds), *Entre critique et rire. 'Le Disparu' de Franz Kafka.* Montpellier: Université Paul-Valéry de Montpellier, 1997, pp. 9–22.

KOCH, Hans-Gerd (ed.). *'Als Kafka mir entgegenkam.' Erinnerungen an Franz Kafka.* Berlin: Verlag Klaus Wagenbach, 1995.

—— (ed.). *'Franz Kafka: Gesammelte Werke in zwölf Bänden, Volume 1: Ein Landarzt: und andere Drucke zu Lebzeiten.* Frankfurt: Fischer Taschenbuch, 2008.

KOHN, Caroline. *Karl Kraus: Le polémiste et l'écrivain, défenseur des droits de l'individu.* Paris: Didier, 1962.

KOHN, Hans. *Living in a World Revolution: My Encounters with History.* New York: Simon and Schuster, 1970.

KRAUS, Karl. *The Last Days of Mankind: A Tragedy in Five Acts* (Frederick Ungar ed., and Alexander Gode and Sue E. Wright trans). New York: Continuum, 2000.

——. *Les Derniers jours de l'humanité.* Marseille: Agone, 2007.

KREITNER, Leopold B. 'Der junge Kafka' in Hans-Gerd Koch (ed.), *'Als Kafka mir entgegenkam.' Erinnerungen an Franz Kafka.* Berlin: Wagenbach, 1995, pp. 52–8.

KUDELA, Jirí. 'Die Emigration galizischer und osteuropäischer Juden nach Böhmen und Prag zwischen 1914–1916/17' in M. P. Beukers and J. J. Cahen (eds), *The Problem of Jewish Immigration and Jewish Identity.* Amsterdam: University Library of Amsterdam,'Studia Rosenthaliana', 1989, pp. 119–34.

KUNDERA, Milan. *Testaments Betrayed* (Linda Asher trans.). London: Faber & Faber, 1995.

KUTZINSKI, Arnold. 'Freiwilliges Ghetto', *Der Jüdische Student* 15 (June 1917): 506–09.

LAHIRE, Bernard. *Franz Kafka: Éléments pour une théorie de la création littéraire*. Paris: La Découverte, 2010.

LAQUEUR, Walter. *A History of Zionism*. New York: Schocken Books, 2003.

LAUNAY, Jean. 'Introduction' in *Ce monsieur de Linz qui inventa Vienne*. Paris: Anatolia/Éditions du Rocher, 2006, pp. 7–17.

LAZARE, Bernard. *Le Fumier de Job*. Strasbourg: Circé, 1990.

LE RIDER, Jacques. 'Prague à l'époque de Kafka' in Jacques Le Rider and Fridrun Rinner (eds), *Les Littératures de langue allemande en Europe centrale des Lumières à nos jours*. Paris: PUF, 1998, pp. 93–114.

———. *Journaux intimes viennois*. Paris: PUF, 2000.

——— and Fridrun Rinner (eds). *Les Littératures de langue allemande en Europe centrale des Lumières à nos jours*. Paris: PUF, 1998.

LORTHOLARY, Bernard. 'Préface du traducteur' in Franz Kafka, *Amerika ou Le Disparu*. Paris: Flammarion 'GF', 1988, p. 5.

———. 'Preface' in Franz Kafka, *Dans la colonie pénitentiaire et autres nouvelles* (Bernard Lortholary trans.). Paris: Flammarion, 1991.

———. 'Introduction' in Franz Kafka, *Un jeûneur et autres nouvelles* (Bernard Lortholary trans.) Paris: Flammarion, 1993.

LÖWY, Michael. *Rédemption et Utopie*. Paris: PUF, 1988.

———. *Franz Kafka, rêveur insoumis*. Paris: Stock, 2004.

LÖWY, Yitzchak. 'Tsvey Prager Dikhter [Two Prague Writers]', *Literarisher Bleter* 34 (1934).

MAPU, Abraham. *Amnon, Prince and Peasant: A Romantic Idyll of Judaea* (F. Jaffe trans.). London: Simpkin, Marshall and Co., 1887.

MEMMI, Albert. *Portrait d'un juif*. Paris: Gallimard, 1962.

MENZEL, Theodor. *Der Zauberspiegel: Türkische Märchen II*. Hanover: H. Lafaire, 1924.

MEYRINK, Gustav. *The Golem* (Mike Mitchell trans.). Cambridgeshire: Dedalus European Classics, 2011.

MICHEL, Bernard. *Prague, Belle Époque*. Paris: Aubier, 2008.

MILLER, Marc. *Representing the Immigrant Experience: Morris Rosenfeld and the Emergence of Yiddish Literature in America*. New York: Syracuse University Press, 2007.

MINCZELES, Henri. *Histoire générale du Bund: Un mouvement révolutionnaire juif*. Paris: Austral, 1995.

——. *Vilna, Wilno, Vilnius: La Jérusalem de Lituanie*. Paris: La Découverte, 2000.

MOREL, Jean-Pierre. *Le Procès de Franz Kafka*. Paris: Gallimard 'Folio', 1998.

MOSSE, George L. 'The Influence of the *Völkisch* Idea on German Jewry' in *Germans and Jews: The Right, the Left and the Search for a 'Third Force' in Pre-Nazi Germany*. New York: Howard Fertig, 1970, pp. 77–115.

MUNZ, Ludwig and Gustav Kunstler. *Adolf Loos: Pioneer of Modern Architecture*. New York: Praeger, 1966.

NEMETH, André. *Kafka ou le mystère juif* (V. Hintz trans.). Paris: Jean Vigneau, 1947.

NEUMANN, Bernd. *Franz Kafka: Aporien der Assimilation; Eine Rekonstruktion seines Romanwerks*. Munich: Wilhelm Fink, 2007.

NEUMANN, Gerhard. 'Kafka ethnologue', *Europe* 923 (March 2006): 253–71.

NOVÁK, Arne. 'Prazsky román?', *Venkov* 12(86) (April 1917).

PANOFSKY, Erwin. 'Zum problem der Beschreibung und Inhaltsdeutung von Werken der bildenden Kunst' in H. Oberer and Egon Verheyen (eds), *Aufsätze zur Grundfragen der Kunstwissenschaft*. Berlin: E. Verheyen, 1974, pp. 85–97.

PASLEY, Malcolm. *'Die Schrift ist unveränderlich' . . . Essays zu Kafka*. Frankfurt: Fischer, 1995.

PAWEL, Ernst. *The Nightmare of Reason: A Life of Franz Kafka*. New York: Vintage Books, 1984.

PAZI, Margarita. 'Max Brod—von *Schloß Nornepygge* zu *Galilei in Gefangenschaft*' in Günter Grimm and Hans-Peter Bayerdörfer (eds), *Zeichen Hiobs: Jüdische Schriftsteller und Deutsche Literatur im 20. Jahrhundert*. Königstein: Athenäum, 1985, pp. 193–212.

Pépin, Jean. *Mythe et Allégorie*. Paris: Études augustiniennes, 1976.

Peretz, Yitzkhok Leybush. *Aus dieser und jener Welt: Jüdische Geschichten*. Vienna and Berlin: Löwt, 1919.

Pešek, Jirí. 'Les étudiants des pays tchèques entre Prague et Vienne: comparaison du rôle des trois universités en 1884' in Maurice Godé, Jacques Le Rider Rider and Françoise Mayer (eds), *Allemands, Juifs et Tchèques à Prague—Deutsche, Juden und Tschechen in Prag, 1890–1924, Actes du colloque international de Montpellier, 8–10 décembre 1994*. Montpellier: Bibliothèque d'études germaniques et centre-européennes, 1996, pp. 101–13.

Pinès, Méir. *L'Histoire de la littérature judéo-allemande*. Paris: Jouve et Cie, 1911.

Politzer, Heinz. *Franz Kafka: Parable and Paradox*. Ithaca, NY: Cornell University Press, 1966.

———. 'Zwei kaiserliche Botschaften: zu den texten von Hofmannsthal und Kafka', *Modern Austrian Literature* 11(3–4) (1978): 105–22.

Pollak, Michael. 'Une sociologie en acte des intellectuels: Les combats de Karl Kraus', *Actes de la recherche en sciences sociales* 36–37 (February–March 1981): 87–103.

———. *Vienne 1900: Une identité blessée*. Paris: Gallimard 'Folio', 1992[1984].

Pulver, Max. 'Spaziergang mit Franz Kafka' in Hans-Gerd Koch (ed.), *'Als Kafka mir entgegenkam.' Erinnerungen an Franz Kafka*. Berlin: Wagenbach, 2008, pp. 130–5.

Ravy, Gilbert. 'Les années de jeunesse à Prague de Fritz Mauthner' in Maurice Godé, Jacques Le Rider and Françoise Mayer (eds), *Allemands, Juifs et Tchèques à Prague—Deutsche, Juden und Tschechen in Prag, 1890–1924, Actes du colloque international de Montpellier, 8–10 décembre 1994*. Montpellier: Bibliothèque d'études germaniques et centre-européennes, 1996, pp. 439–49.

REFFET, Michel. 'Pro Werfel contra Kraus. Eine alte Polemik aus neuer Sicht' in Kurt Krolop and Klaas-Hinrich Ehlers (eds), *Brücken nach Prag: deutschsprachige Literatur im kulturellen Kontext der Donaumonarchie und der Tschechoslowakei; Festschrift für Kurt Krolop zum 70. Geburtstag.* Frankfurt: Peter Lang, 2001, pp. 201–19.

REUSS, Roland and Peter Staengle (eds). *Franz Kafka: Historisch-kritische Ausgabe sämtlicher Handschriften, Drucke und Typoskripte.* Basel and Frankfurt: Stroemfeld/Roter Stern, 1995.

RICHARD, Lionel. *D'une apocalypse à l'autre: Sur l'Allemagne et ses production intellectuelles de Guillaume II aux années 20.* Paris: UGE, collection 10/18, 1976.

RILKE, Rainer Maria (Réne). *Two Stories of Prague* (Angela Esterhammer trans.). Hanover: University Press of New England, 1994.

RIPELLINO, Angelo Maria. *Magic Prague* (David Newton Marinelli trans.). London: Picador, 1995.

ROBERT, Marthe. *As Lonely As Franz Kafka* (Ralph Manheim trans.). New York and London: Harcourt, Brace, Jovanovich, 1982.

———. 'Kafka en France' in Yasha David and Jean-Pierre Morel (eds), *Le Siècle de Kafka.* Paris: Centre Georges Pompidou, 1984, pp. 15–20.

ROBERTSON, Ritchie. *Kafka: Judaism, Politics and Literature.* Oxford: Clarendon Press, 1985.

———. 'The Creative Dialogue between Brod and Kafka' in Mark H. Gelber (ed.), *Kafka, Zionism and Beyond.* Tübingen: Max Niemeyer, 2004, pp. 283–96.

ROBIN, Régine. *L'Amour du Yiddish. Écriture juive et sentiment de la langue, 1833–1940.* Paris: Le Sorbier, 1984.

———. 'Le yiddish et l'allemand: la langue de l'autre, l'autre de la langue' in Max Kohn and Jean Baumgarten (eds), *L'Inconscient du yiddish.* Paris: Anthropos, 2003, pp. 61–77.

ROSENBAUM, Karol. 'Herder und die slowakische nationale Wiedergeburt' in Gerhard Ziegengeist, Helmut Grasshof and Ulf Lehmann (eds), *Zur Herder-Rezeption in Ost- und Südeuropa*. Berlin: Akademie-Verlag, 1978, pp. 92–106.

ROZENBLIT, Marsha L. 'The Jews of Austria and Germany: A Comparative Perspective' in Robert S. Wistrich (ed.), *Austrians and Jews in the Twentieth Century: From Franz Kafka to Waldheim*. New York: St. Martin's Press, 1992, pp. 1–18.

RUDENT, Gérard and Brigitte Vergne-Cain, 'Mai 1910-mai 1913: la percée' in Gérard Rudent and Brigitte Vergne-Cain (eds), *Franz Kafka: Récits, romans, journaux* (François Matthieu, Axel Nesme, Marthe Robert, Gérard Rudent and Brigitte Vergne-Cain trans). Paris: Livre de Poche, 2000.

——— (eds). *Franz Kafka: Récits, romans, journaux* (François Matthieu, Axel Nesme, Marthe Robert, Gérard Rudent and Brigitte Vergne-Cain trans). Paris: Le Livre de poche, 2000.

RUNFOLA, Patrizia. *Prague au temps de Kafka*. Paris: La Différence, 2002.

SARTRE, Jean-Paul. *Anti-Semite and Jew* (George J. Becker trans.). New York: Schocken Books, 1948.

SCHMIDT, Friedrich. 'Sprache, Medien, und Kritik. Kafkas Sprachskepsis im Kontext ihrer Zeit' in Marek Nekula and Ingrid Fleischmann, Albert Greule (eds), *Franz Kafka im Sprachnationalen Kontext seiner Zeit. Sprache und nationale Identität in öffentlichen Institutionen der böhmischen Länder*. Cologne, Weimar and Vienna: Böhlau, 2007, pp. 31–60.

SCHNITZLER, Arthur. *Lieutenant Gustl*. Vienna: Neue Freie Presse, 1901.

———. *None But the Brave* (Richard L. Simon). New York: Simon and Schuster, 1926.

———. *Anatol* (Frank Marcus trans.). London: Methuen, 1982.

———. *La Ronde* (Frank Marcus and Jacquelline Marcus trans). London: Methuen, 1982.

———. *Professor Bernhardi* in *Professor Bernhardi: And Other Plays* (G. J. Weinberger trans.). Riverside, CA: Ariadne Press, 1993, pp. 3–146.

——. *The Road to the Open* (Horace Samuel trans.) Evanston: Northwestern University Press, 1991[1913].

SCHOLEM, Gershom. 'Martin Buber's Interpretation of Hasidism' in *The Messianic Idea in Judaism and Other Ideas on Jewish Spirituality* (Michael A. Meyer and Hillel Halkin trans). New York: Schocken Books, 1971, pp. 228–50.

——. *The Messianic Idea in Judaism and Other Ideas on Jewish Sprituality* (Michael A. Meyer and Hillel Halkin trans). New York: Schocken Books, 1971.

——. *On Jews and Judaism in Crisis: Selected Essays* (Werner Dannhauser ed. and trans.). New York: Schocken Books, 1976.

——. 'With Gershom Scholem: An Interview' in *On Jews and Judaism in Crisis: Selected Essays* (Werner Dannhauser ed. and trans.). New York: Schocken Books, 1976, pp. 1–48.

——. *Fidélité et Utopie* (Marguerite Delmotte and Bernard Dupuy trans). Paris: Calmann-Lévy, 1978.

——. 'On the Social Psychology of German Jews between 1900 and 1930' in David Bronson (ed.), *Jews and Germans from 1860–1933: The Problematic Symbiosis*. Heidelberg: Carl Winter Universitäts Verlag, 1979, pp. 9–32.

——. *Walter Benjamin: The Story of a Friendship* (Harry Zohn trans.). Philadelphia: The Jewish Publication Society of America, 1981.

——. 'A propos de la psychologie sociale des juifs d'Allemagne entre 1900 et 1930' in Scholem, *De la Création du Monde jusqu'à Varsovie* (Maurice-Ruben Hayoun trans.). Paris: Le Cerf, 1990. pp. 223–44.

——. *De la Création du Monde jusqu'à Varsovie* (Maurice-Ruben Hayoun trans.). Paris: Le Cerf, 1990.

——. *From Berlin to Jerusalem: Memories of My Youth* (Harry Zohn trans.). Philadelphia: Paul Dry Books, 2012.

SCHOPENHAUER, Arthur. *The Wisdom of Life: The Essays of Arthur Schopenhauer* (T. Bailey Saunders trans.). Fairford: The Echo Library, 2006.

———. *Die Kunst sich Respekt zu verschaffen*. Munich: C. H. Beck, 2011.

SCHORSKE, Carl E. *Fin-de-siècle Vienna: Politics and Culture*. New York: Vintage Books, 1981.

———. 'Generational Tension and Cultural Change: Reflections on the Case of Vienna' in *Thinking with History: Explorations in the Passage to Modernism*. Princeton: Princeton University Press, 1998.

SERVIER, Jean. 'Préface' in Leo Frobenius, *L'Atlantide. Mythologie et cultes* (F. Gidon trans.). Paris: Éditions du Rocher, 1993.

SFORIM, Mendele Mocher. *Fischke der Krumer* (Warsaw: Mendele, 1910).

———. *Fishke the Lame* (Gerald Stillman trans.). New York: Thomas Yoseloff, 1960.

SHAPIRA, Abraham. 'Buber's Attachment to Herder and German 'völkism', *Studies in Zionism* 14(1) (1993): 1–30.

SHAPIRA, Anita. 'Anti-Semitism and Zionism', *Modern Judaism* 15(3) (October 1995): 215–32.

SHATZMILLER, Joseph. 'Les limites de la solidarité: antagonismes au sein de la société juive ancienne et moderner' in Shmuel Trigano (ed.), *La Société juive à travers l'histoire*, VOL. 4. Paris: Fayard, 1993, pp. 387–425.

SION, Ariel. 'Séculier et religieux: le paysage scolaire' in Alain Dieckhoff and Yves Plasseraud (eds), *Lituanie juive, 1918–1940. Message d'un monde englouti*. Paris: Autrement, 1996, pp. 122–41.

SPECTOR, Scott. *Prague Territories: National Conflict and Cultural Innovation in Franz Kafka's Fin de Siècle*. Berkeley, Los Angeles and London: University of California Press, 2000.

SPRENGEL, Peter. *Scheunenviertel-Theater. Jüdische Schauspieltruppen und jiddische Dramatik in Berlin (1900–1918)*. Berlin: Fannei & Waltz, 1995.

STACH, Reiner. *Kafka: Die Jahre der Entscheidungen*. Frankfurt: Fischer, 2002.

STIEG, Gerald. 'Wer ist Kafkas Bote Barnabas?', *Austriaca* 17 (1983): 151–6.

STÖLZL, Christoph. *Kafkas böses Böhmen: Zur Sozialgeschichte eines Prager Juden*. Munich: Text + Kritik, 1975.

TAMINE, Joëlle Gardes (ed.). *L'Allégorie corps et âme. Entre personnification et double sens*. Aix-en-Provence: Publications de l'université de Provence, 2002.

TAYLOR, Charles. 'To Follow a Rule . . .' in Craig Calhoun, Edward LiPuma and Moishe Postone (eds), *Bourdieu: Critical Perspectives*. Cambridge: Polity Press, 1993, pp. 45–60.

TEIGE, Karel. 'Guillaume Apollinaire a jeho doba' in *Svet stavby a básne: studie z dvacátych let*. Prague: Ceskoslovensky spisovatel, 1966, pp. 371–404.

THIROUIN, Marie-Odile. 'Annexe' in Philippe Zard (ed.), *Sillages de Kafka*. Paris: Le Manuscrit, 2007, pp. 82–91.

TIMMS, Edward. *Karl Kraus: Apocalyptic Satirist; The Post-War Crisis and the Rise of the Swastika*. New Haven and London: Yale University Press, 2005.

TORNTON BECK, Evelyn. *Kafka and the Yiddish Theater: Its Impact on His Work*. Madison, Milwaukee and London: The University of Wisconsin Press, 1971.

TRAUTMAN-WALLER, Céline. *Quand Berlin pensait les peuples. Anthropologie, ethnologie et psychologie (1850–1890)*. Paris: CNRS, 2004.

UNSELD, Joachim. *Franz Kafka. Ein Schriftstellerleben: Die Geschichte seiner Veröffentlichungen*. Frankfurt: Fischer Taschenbuch, 1984.

UTITZ, Emil. *Egon Erwin Kisch: Der klassische Journalist*. Berlin, 1956.

TRAVERSO, Enzo. 'Une utopie ambiguë: notes sur l'histoire du sionisme' in *Pour une critique de la barbarie moderne: Écrits sur l'histoire des Juifs et de l'antisémitisme*. Lausanne: Page Deux, 1996, pp. 117–21.

VALÉRY, Paul. *Oeuvres*, VOL. 2. Paris: Gallimard, 'Bibliothèque de la Pléiade', 1960.

VASSOGNE, Gaëlle. 'Max Brod et Prague: Identité et médiation'. Doctoral thesis, University of Paris-III-Sorbonne nouvelle, 2004.

VERMES, Pamela. *Martin Buber*. London: Halban, 1988.

VOISINE-JECHOVA, Hana. *Histoire de la littérature tchèque*. Paris: Fayard, 2001.

VON JAGOW, Bettina and Oliver Jahraus (eds). *Kafka Handbuch: Leben-Werk-Wirkung*. Göttingen: Vanderhoeck & Ruprecht, 2008.

WAGENBACH, Klaus. *Franz Kafka: Les années de jeunesse (1883–1912)* (Élisabeth Gaspar trans.). Paris: Mercure de France, 1967.

———. *Kafka* (Eweld Osers trans.). London: Haus Publishing, 2003.

———. *Franz Kafka: Biographie seiner Jugend*. Berlin: Verlag Klaus Wagenbach, 2006.

WEIGL, Joseph. *Jüdische Helden*. Frankfurt: Jüdischer Volksschriften-verlag, 1911.

WELTSCH, Robert. *Max Brod and His Age*. New York: Leo Baeck Institute, Leo Baeck Memorial Lecture 13, 1970.

WERFEL, Franz. *Der Weltfreund*. Berlin: Axel Juncker, 1911.

———. 'Die Metaphysik des Drehs: Ein offener Brief an Karl Kraus', *Die Aktion* 7(9–10) (1917): 124–8.

———. *Spiegelmensch: magische Trilogie*. Leipzig: Kurt Wolff, 1920.

WERMESTER, Cathérine. *Grosz: L'homme le plus triste de l'Europe*. Paris: Allia, 2008.

WIENER, Oskar. *Deutsche Dichter aus Prag: Ein Sammelbuch*. Vienna and Leipzig: Strache, 1919.

WOLITZ, Seth L. ' "Le paon doré s'est envolé . . ." La culture ashkénaze, 1860–1940: une trop brève renaissance' in Nathalie Hazan-Brunet (ed.), *Futur antérieur. L'avant-garde et le livre yiddish (1914–1939)*. Paris: Flammarion, 2009.

WOLLSTEIN, Georg. 'Neue Kompromisse', *Der Jüdische Student* 15 (January 1917): 353–4.

YACINE-TITOUH, Tassadit. *Chacal ou la ruse des dominés: Aux origines du malaise culturel des intellectuels algériens*. Paris: La Découverte, 2001.

ZARD, Philippe. 'Der Verschollene, un récit de l'exil occidental' in Maurice Godé and Michel Vanoosthuyse (eds), Entre critique et rire: 'Le Disparu' de Franz Kafka. Montpellier: Université Paul-Valéry de Montpellier, 1997, pp. 99–116.

———. La Fiction de l'Occident: Thomas Mann, Franz Kafka, Albert Cohen. Paris: PUF, 1999.

——— (ed.). Sillages de Kafka. Paris: Le Manuscrit, 2007.

ZIMMERMANN, Hans Dieter. 'Kafkas Prag und die kleine Literaturen' in Bettina von Jagow and Oliver Jahrhaus (eds), Kafka Handbuch: Leben-Werk-Wirkung. Göttingen: Vanderhoeck & Ruprecht, 2008, pp. 165–80.

ZWEIG, Arnold. 'Uber jüdische Legenden', Mitteilungen des Verbandes der jüdischen Jugendvereine Deutschlands (1914): 16–17.

DATE